GLOBAL STUDIES

AFRICA

Third Edition

Dr. Jo Sullivan
Outreach Program at the African Studies Center
Boston University

The Dushkin Publishing Group, Inc., Sluice Dock, Guilford, Connecticut 06437

Africa

BOOKS IN THE GLOBAL STUDIES SERIES

- Africa
- China
- Latin America
- The Soviet Union and Eastern Europe
- The Middle East
- Western Europe
  India and South Asia
  Japan and the Pacific Rim
  Southeast Asia

- Available Now

Third Edition

Manufactured by The Banta Company, Harrisonburg, Virginia 22801

Library of Congress Catalog Number: 89-050261

ISBN: 0-87967-801-1

Africa

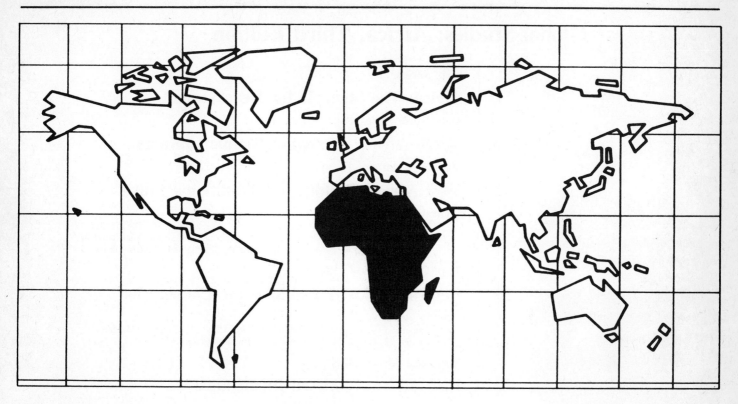

Dr. Jo Sullivan

Dr. Jo Sullivan, the author/editor of *Global Studies: Africa, Third Edition*, is the director of the Outreach Program at the African Studies Center, Boston University. Dr. Sullivan holds an M.A. and Ph.D. in African history and has taught at the university level in the United States and Nigeria, as well as at the elementary level in Liberia as a Peace Corps volunteer. She has contributed to academic journals and books on African history, specializing in the history of Liberia, and is an author and consultant in global studies and multicultural and international education.

This revised and updated edition draws on essays and country reports written by Dr. Jane Martin, the contributing editor for the first edition. She is currently executive director of the United States Educational and Cultural Foundation, Monrovia, Liberia.

Selected regional essays and country reports originally were written by:

Lisa Anderson
William Freund
Bennet Fuller
G. Michael LaRue
F. Jeffress Ramsay

SERIES CONSULTANT

H. Thomas Collins
Washington, D.C.

Contents

Global Studies: Africa, Third Edition

North Africa   Page 7

West Africa   Page 17

Central Africa   Page 63

East Africa   Page 87

South Africa   Page 125

Introduction

THE GLOBAL AGE

As we approach the end of the twentieth century, it is clear that the future we face will be considerably more international in nature than ever believed possible in the past. Each day of our lives, print and broadcast journalists make us aware that our world is becoming increasingly smaller and substantially more interdependent.

The energy crisis, world food shortages, nuclear proliferation, and the regional conflicts in Central America, the Middle East, and other areas that threaten to involve us all, all make it clear that the distinctions between domestic and foreign problems are all too often artificial—that many seemingly domestic problems no longer stop at national boundaries. As Rene Dubos, the 1969 Pulitzer Prize recipient stated: ". . . [I]t becomes obvious that each (of us) has two countries, (our) own and planet earth." As global interdependence has become a reality, it has become vital for the citizens of this world to develop literacy in global matters.

THE GLOBAL STUDIES SERIES

It is the aim of this Global Studies series to help readers acquire a basic knowledge and understanding of the regions and countries in the world. Each volume provides a foundation of information—geographic, cultural, economic, political, historical, artistic, and religous—which will allow readers to better understand the current and future problems within these countries and regions and to comprehend how events there might affect their own well-being. In short, these volumes attempt to provide the background information necessary to respond to the realities of our Global Age.

Author/Editor

Each of the volumes in the Global Studies series has been crafted under the careful direction of an author/editor—an expert in the area under study. The author/editors teach and conduct research and have traveled extensively through the regions they are writing about.

The author/editor for each volume has written the umbrella essay introducing the area. For the third edition of *Global Studies: Africa*, the author/editor has extensively revised and updated the regional essays and country reports. In addition, she has overseen the gathering of statistical information for each country and has been instrumental in the selection of the world press articles that appear at the end of the book.

Contents and Features

The Global Studies volumes are organized to provide concise information and current world press articles on the regions and countries within those areas under study.

Area and Regional Essays

Global Studies: Africa, Third Edition, covers North Africa, Central Africa, West Africa, East Africa, and Southern Africa. Each of these regions is discussed in a regional essay focusing on the geographical, cultural, sociopolitical and economic aspects of the countries and people of that area. The purpose of the regional essays is to provide the reader with an effective sense of the diversity of the area as well as an understanding of its common cultural and historical backgrounds. Accompanying each of the regional narratives is a full-page map showing the political boundaries of the countries within the region. In addition to these regional essays, the author/editor has also provided a narrative essay on the African continent as a whole. This area essay examines a number of broad themes in an attempt to define what constitutes "Africa."

A Special Note on the Regions of Africa

The countries of Africa do not fall into clear-cut regions. Many of the political divisions that exist today are the product of Africa's colonial heritage, and often they do not reflect cultural, religious, or historical connections. This has created tensions within nations, and it makes abstract divisions somewhat arbitrary. Nations that share geographical aspects with one group of countries may share a cultural history with a different group. The regional essays give rationales for the way countries have been grouped in this volume. Readers may encounter different arrangements in other sources. The regional essays should be read carefully to understand why the author/editor chose the divisions made here.

North Africa

North Africa is a special case in relation to the rest of the African continent. Culturally, geopolitically, and economically, the Muslim countries of North Africa are often major players on the Middle Eastern stage, as well as on the African scene. For this reason, we have included a regional essay for North Africa in this volume, but the individual country reports and the world press articles for that region appear as part of the expanded coverage of North Africa in *The Middle East* volume of the Global Studies series.

Country Reports

Concise reports on each of the regions with the exception of North Africa follow the regional essays. These reports are the heart of each Global Studies volume. *Global Studies: Africa, Third Edition*, contains 48 country reports.

The country reports are comprised of five standard elements. Each report contains a map which positions the country amongst its neighboring states; a detailed summary of statistical information; a current essay providing important historical, geographical, political, cultural, and economic information; a historical timeline offering a convenient visual survey of a few key historical events; and four graphic indicators, with summary statements about the country in terms of development, freedom, health/welfare, and achievements, at the end of each report.

A Note on the Statistical Summaries

The statistical information provided for each country has been drawn from a wide range of sources. The most frequently referenced are listed on page 240. Every effort has been made to provide the most current and accurate information available. However, occasionally the information cited by these sources differs significantly; and all too often, the most current information available for some countries is quite dated. Aside from these discrepancies, the statistical summary of each country is generally quite complete and reasonably current. Care should be taken, however, in using these statistics (or, for that matter, any published statistics) in making hard comparisons among countries.

World Press Articles

Within each Global Studies volume are reprinted a number of articles carefully selected by our editorial staff and the author/editor from a broad range of international periodicals and newspapers. The articles have been chosen for currency, interest, and the differing perspectives they give to a particular region. There are world press articles for each region, with the exception of North Africa. The article section is preceded by a *Topic Guide.* The purpose of this guide is to

(Oxfam photo)

We must understand the hopes, problems, and cultures of the people of other nations in order to understand our own future.

indicate the main theme(s) of the articles. Readers wishing to focus on a particular theme, say, religion, may refer to the Topic Guide to find those articles.

Spelling

In many instances, articles from foreign sources may use forms of spelling that are different from the American style. Many Third World publications reflect the European usage. In order to retain the flavor of the articles and to make the point that our system is not the only one, spellings have not been altered to conform with the U.S. system.

Glossary, Bibliography, Index

At the back of each Global Studies volume, readers will find a *Glossary of Terms and Abbreviations*, which provides a quick reference to the specialized vocabulary of the area under study and to the standard abbreviations (UN, WHO, GATT, etc.) used throughout the volume.

Following the Glossary is a *Bibliography*. The bibliography is organized into general reference volumes, national and regional histories, novels in translation, current events publications, and periodicals that provide regular coverage on Africa.

The *Index* at the end of the volume is an accurate reference to the contents of the volume. Readers seeking specific information and citations should consult this standard index.

Currency and Usefulness

This third edition of *Global Studies: Africa*, like other Global Studies volumes, is intended to provide the most current and useful information available necessary to understanding the events that are shaping the cultures of Africa today.

We plan to revise this volume on a continuing basis. The statistics will be updated, regional essays rewritten, country reports revised, and articles completely replaced as new and current information becomes available. In order to accomplish this task, we will turn to our author/editor, and—hopefully—to you, the users of this volume. Your comments are more than welcome. If you have an idea that you think will make the volume more useful, an article or bit of information that will make it more current, or a general comment on its organization, content, or features that you would like to share with us, please send it in for serious consideration for the next edition.

The maps which appear in the individual country reports use the legend key below to identify major geographical elements.

∗	Capital City
•	Major Cities
——	Major Rivers
----	Major Roads
—··—··—	Bordering Countries

United States of America

Comparing statistics on the various countries in this volume should not be done without recognizing that the figures are within the timeframe of our publishing date and may not accurately reflect today's conditions. Nevertheless, comparisons can and will be made, so to enable you to put the statistics of different countries into perspective, we have included comparable statistics on the United States. These statistics are drawn from the same sources that were consulted for developing the statistical information in each country report.

The United States is unique. It has some of the most fertile land in the world, which, coupled with a high level of technology, allows the production of an abundance of food products—an abundance that makes possible the export of enormous quantities of basic foodstuffs to many other parts of the world. The use of this technology also permits the manufacture of goods and services that exceed what is possible in a majority of the rest of the world. In the United States are some of the most important urban centers in the world focusing on trade, investment, and commerce as well as art, music, and theater.

GEOGRAPHY

Area in Square Kilometers (Miles):
9,372,614 (3,540,939)
Capital (Population): Washington, DC
(638,432)
Climate: temperate

PEOPLE

Population
Total: 247,498,000
Annual Growth Rate: 0.7%
Rural/Urban Population Ratio: 21/79
Ethnic Makeup of Population: 80%
white; 11% black; 6.2% Spanish
origin; 1.6% Asian and Pacific
Islander; 0.7% American Indian,
Eskimo, and Aleut

Health
Life Expectancy at Birth: 71.5 (male);
78.5 (female)
Infant Death Rate (Ratio): 8.9/1,000
Average Caloric Intake: 138% of FAO
minimum
Physicians Available (Ratio): 1/520

Religion(s)
55% Protestant; 36% Roman
Catholic; 4% Jewish

Education
Adult Literacy Rate: 99.5%

COMMUNICATION

Telephones: 182,558,000
Newspapers: 1,676 dailies;
approximately 63,000,000 circulation

TRANSPORTATION

Highways—Kilometers (Miles):
6,208,552 (3,866,296); 5,466,612
(3,398,810) paved
Railroads—Kilometers (Miles):
270,312 (167,974)
Usable Airfields: 15,422

GOVERNMENT

Type: federal republic
Independence Date: July 4, 1776
Head of State: President George Bush
Political Parties: Democratic Party;
Republican Party; others of minor
political significance
Suffrage: universal at 18

MILITARY

Number of Armed Forces: 2,116,800
*Military Expenditures (% of Central
Government Expenditures):* 29.1%
Current Hostilities: none

ECONOMY

Per Capita Income: $13,451
Gross National Product (GNP): 4,200
billion
Inflation Rate: 4%
Natural Resources: metallic and
nonmetallic minerals; petroleum;
arable land
Agriculture: food grains; feed crops;
oilbearing crops; cattle; dairy
products
Industry: diversified in both capital-
and consumer-goods industries

FOREIGN TRADE

Exports: $250.4 billion
Imports: $424.0 billion

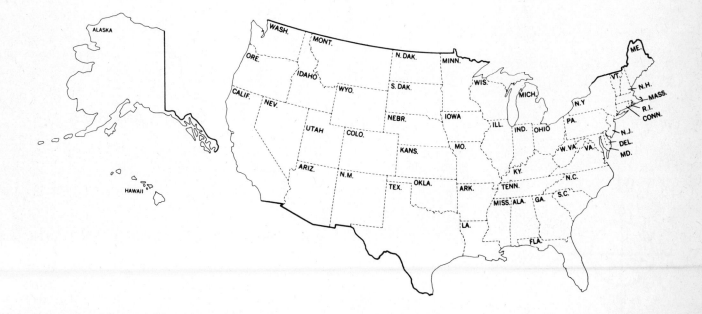

U.S.

CANADA

NORTH AMERICA

UNITED STATES

EUROPE

MEXICO

CARIBBEAN

CENTRAL AMERICA

SOUTH AMERICA

N

W   E

S

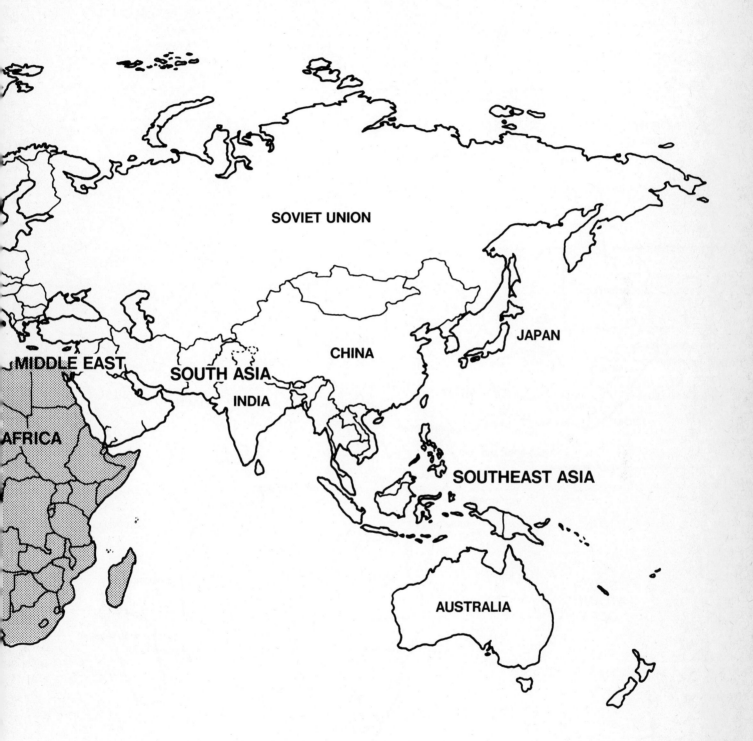

MIDDLE EAST

AFRICA

SOVIET UNION

SOUTH ASIA

INDIA

CHINA

JAPAN

SOUTHEAST ASIA

AUSTRALIA

This map of the world highlights the nations of Africa that are discussed in this volume. Regional essays and country reports are written from a cultural perspective in order to give a frame of reference to the current events in that region. All of the essays are designed to present the most current and useful information available today. Other volumes in the Global Studies series will cover different areas of the globe and examine the current state of affairs of the countries within those regions.

Africa

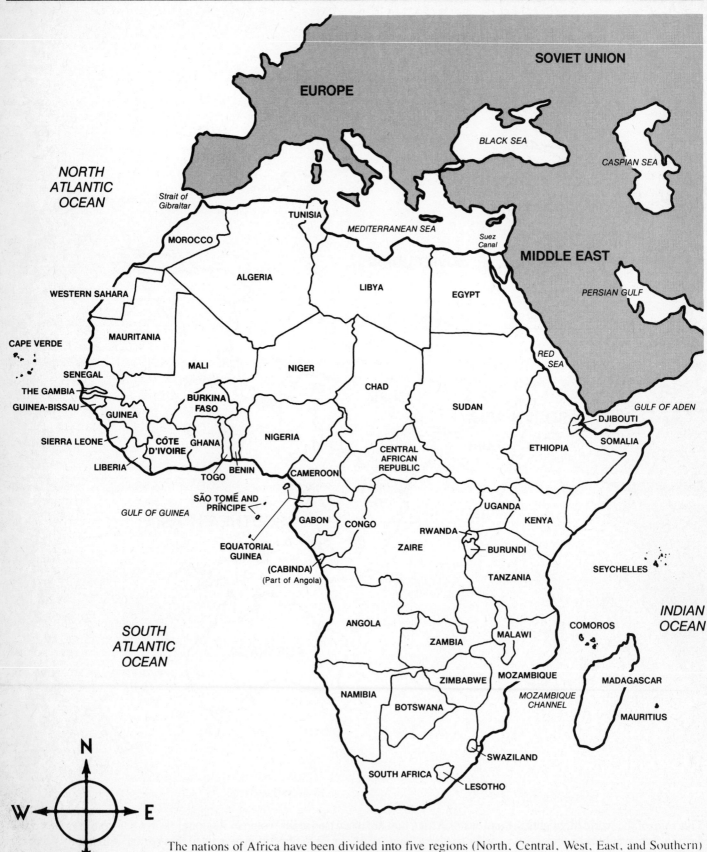

EUROPE

SOVIET UNION

BLACK SEA

CASPIAN SEA

NORTH
ATLANTIC
OCEAN

*Strait of
Gibraltar*

TUNISIA

MEDITERRANEAN SEA

*Suez
Canal*

MIDDLE EAST

MOROCCO

ALGERIA

LIBYA

EGYPT

PERSIAN GULF

WESTERN SAHARA

MAURITANIA

*RED
SEA*

CAPE VERDE

MALI

NIGER

CHAD

SUDAN

GULF OF ADEN

SENEGAL

THE GAMBIA

BURKINA
FASO

DJIBOUTI

GUINEA-BISSAU

GUINEA

NIGERIA

CENTRAL
AFRICAN
REPUBLIC

ETHIOPIA

SOMALIA

SIERRA LEONE

CÔTE
D'IVOIRE

GHANA

LIBERIA

TOGO

BENIN

CAMEROON

SÃO TOMÉ AND
PRÍNCIPE

UGANDA

KENYA

GULF OF GUINEA

GABON

CONGO

RWANDA

EQUATORIAL
GUINEA

ZAIRE

BURUNDI

SEYCHELLES

*INDIAN
OCEAN*

(CABINDA)
(Part of Angola)

TANZANIA

*SOUTH
ATLANTIC
OCEAN*

ANGOLA

ZAMBIA

MALAWI

COMOROS

NAMIBIA

ZIMBABWE

MOZAMBIQUE

MADAGASCAR

BOTSWANA

*MOZAMBIQUE
CHANNEL*

MAURITIUS

SWAZILAND

SOUTH AFRICA

LESOTHO

N

W — E

S

The nations of Africa have been divided into five regions (North, Central, West, East, and Southern)
for an easier understanding of a diverse continent. See page vi for further discussion of regions within
Africa.

Africa: The Struggle for Development

"This is Africa's 'age of glamour,' " Africans observed in 1960. The times were electric, as governments changed hands and country after country moved to independent nationhood. Leaders were acclaimed, new goals were proposed, and hopes were high. In the United States and other Western countries, some of the myths about Africa were being questioned.

Today, 3 decades after "the age of glamour," conditions in Africa are sobering rather than euphoric, and development seems a desperate struggle rather than an exhilarating challenge. Africa is described in the media as "a continent in crisis," "a region in turmoil," "on a precipice," and "suffering"—phrases that sound like those of the nineteenth-century explorers and missionaries.

Foreign governments have often become involved in African civil conflicts, while the aid that is offered imposes restraints and often aggravates the distress. Observers wonder whether a new imperialism, a new "scramble for Africa," is in the making.

Africa's circumstances today are indeed difficult. Yet the last 30 years have brought progress as well as problems. Africans have remained in control of their own futures. The following review of the African heritage and of the achievements since independence, as well as Africa's current difficulties and their origins, provides a more balanced picture of Africa today.

TRADITION AND CHANGE

The 500,000,000 contemporary Africans maintain extraordinarily diverse ways of life. More than a thousand languages and a variety of households, kinship systems, religious beliefs, and art styles—to mention only a few of the cultural areas—enrich the continent.

These ways of life have always been changing over time. As cities have grown and people have moved back and forth between village and town, new social groups, institutions, occupations, religions, and schools make their mark in the countryside as well as in the urban centers. All Africans—the elite as well as the working class—have taken on new practices and interests, yet have maintained African traditions. Thus, whether they are professional civil servants, day laborers, or students, urban dwellers (whose numbers have increased drastically in recent decades) may still have their roots in the countryside. African institutions, African values, and African histories underlie their contemporary lifestyles.

Memories of ancient kingdoms are a source of pride and community to peoples throughout Africa. The Mali kingdom of western Sudan, the Fulani caliphate of northern Nigeria, the great Zimbabwe, and the kingdoms around the Great Lakes in Uganda are all remembered. The past is connected to the present through the generations and by ties to the land. In a continent where the majority of peoples are still farmers, land remains "the mother that never dies." It is valued for its fruits and because it is the place to which the ancestors came and where they are buried.

The art of personal relationships continues to be important in Africa. Typically, people live in large families. Children are "precious like coral," and large families are still desired for social as well as economic reasons. Elders are an important part of a household; nursing homes and retirement communities do not exist. People are not supposed to be loners. "I am because we are" remains a valued precept—and the "we" may refer to an ethnic community even in this age of nation-states. Obligations to the extended family often take precedence over other loyalties.

Religious forces continue to make their presence felt. A family is built on a good relationship with the ancestors, and traditional beliefs remain important. Well-educated professionals, migrant workers, and market women as well as rural people still visit professional traditional healers who will explain an illness or suggest remedies for sterility or bad fortune. Historically, Islam has been a strong force in Africa and is today the fastest-growing religion on the continent. In some areas, Islam may accommodate traditional ways. People may also join new religious movements and churches, such as the Brotherhood of the Cross and Star in Nigeria or the Church of Simon Kimbangu in Zaire, that link Christian and traditional beliefs and practices as well as completely new ideas and rituals. Like other institutions in the towns and

(World Bank photo by Pamela Johnson)
This is an electrical transformer at the Volta Aluminum Company in Tema, Ghana. Modern technology and new sources of power are among the factors spurring economic development.

(Save the Children photo)

Good health is an important goal in Africa. Immunizations against cholera, tetanus, and other diseases have helped to reduce death rates.

cities, the churches also provide new social networks. Traditional art forms reflect these changes and interactions. An airplane is featured on a Nigerian *gelede* mask, the Apollo space mission inspired an ancient Burkina Faso form, and a Ndebele dance wand is a beaded electric pole.

THE TROUBLED PRESENT

Some of the crises in Africa today may threaten even the deepest traditions. The facts are grim: in material terms, Africans are poorer today than they were at independence, and it is predicted that poverty will increase in the future. In the 1980s widespread famine occurred in 22 African nations, with 4 countries still suffering from famine and at least 15 in need of outside aid. Drought conditions have led to abnormal food shortages in countries of every African region. The Food and Agricultural Organization (FAO) of the United Nations estimated that 70 percent of African people did not have enough to eat in the mid-1980s. The outpouring of assistance and relief efforts saved as many as 35 million lives, and although agricultural output rose in 1985 and 1986, the long-term crisis remains. In the late 1980s declining commodity prices, recurring drought, and infestations of locusts counterbalanced agricultural gains. Problems of climate irregularity, transport, seeds and tools, and storage have required continued assistance and long-range planning. Diseases that were once conquered have reappeared: rinderpest has been discovered among cattle, and cholera has been found among populations where it has not been seen for a long time. Wood, the average person's source of energy, grows scarce. The spread of acquired immune deficiency syndrome (AIDS) also threatens lives and long-term productivity.

Conflicts—including the destabilizing activities of South Africa in Namibia, Angola, and Mozambique; the civil wars in the Horn; and past crises in Uganda, Zaire, and Burundi—as well as other disasters, have caused many people to flee their homes. Almost 6 million refugees are registered with the United Nations Commissioner on Refugee Relief (UN-HCR), but it is believed that a more accurate estimate of the number of people who have sought refuge and food in countries other than their own is up to 7 million.

Almost all African governments are in debt (as is the United States). The entire debt of African countries is more than $200 billion. Although a smaller amount than that of

Latin America, the debt is rising very swiftly. The industrial output of African countries is lower than that of other nations of the world. While the majority of Africans are engaged in food production, not enough food is produced in most countries to feed their citizens. The decline of commodity prices—including oil—on the world market means less national income. The foreign exchange needed to import food and machinery is very limited. Excluding South Africa, the continent's economy in 1987 grew by only 0.8 percent, up from 1986 figures, but far below the population growth rate. Cereal production declined 8 percent, and overall agricultural production grew by only 0.5 percent.

In order to obtain money to meet debts and to pay running expenses, African governments must accept the terms of world lending agencies such as the World Bank and the International Monetary Fund (IMF). These terms have caused great hardship through austerity measures, the abandonment of price controls, and the freezing of wages—measures that can open the way to social distress and political upheaval in urban centers. African countries such as Tanzania and Mozambique have been forced to compromise socialist ideologies in order to meet the terms.

African governments and some experts are questioning these terms because of the devastating effects on the poor and on workers. The aggregate result of the loans has meant that, for example, in 1986, 16 African countries transferred 350 percent more money to the IMF than they received in 1985.

(Peace Corps photo)

Partnerships among the nations of Africa and the countries of Europe and North America may encourage Africa's development. Here a Sierra Leonean road is built with U.S. Peace Corps help.

THE EVOLUTION OF AFRICA'S ECONOMIES

Africa has seldom been rich, although it has vast potential resources and some rulers and classes have been very wealthy. In earlier centuries the slave trade as well as other internal factors limited African material expansion. During the era of European exploration and the colonial period, Africa became increasingly involved in the world economy. Policies and practices developed that still exist today and are of mixed benefit to African peoples.

During the 70 or so years of British, French, Portuguese, German, Spanish, and Italian rule in Africa, the nations' economies were shaped to the advantage of the colonizers. Cash crops such as cocoa, coffee, and rubber began to be grown for the European market. Some African farmers benefited from these crops, but the cash-crop economy also involved large foreign-run plantations. It also encouraged the trends toward use of migrant labor and the decline in food production. Many people became dependent for their livelihood on the forces of the world market, which, like the weather, were beyond their immediate control.

Mining also increased during colonial times—again for the benefit of the colonial rulers. The ores were extracted from African soil by European companies. African labor was employed, but the machinery came from abroad. The copper and gold—and later the iron ore, uranium, and oil—were shipped overseas to be processed and marketed in the Western economies. Upon independence African governments received a varying percentage of the take through taxation and consortium agreements. But mining remained an "enclave" industry, sometimes described as a "state within a state" because such industries were run by outsiders who established Western-style communities, used imported machinery and technicians, and exported the products to industrialized countries.

Inflationary conditions in other parts of the world have had adverse effects on Africa. Today the raw materials that Africans produce receive low prices on the world market, while the manufactured goods that African countries import are expensive. Local African industries lack spare parts and machinery; cash-crop farmers cannot afford to transport crops to market for such low prices. The whole economy slows down. Thus, Africa—because of the policies of former colonial powers and current independent governments—is tied into the world economy in ways that do not always serve Africa itself.

THE PROBLEMS OF GOVERNMENT

Outside forces are not the only, or even the major, cause of Africa's current crises. Governments face the major task of maintaining national unity with very diverse and sometimes divided citizenries. These problems have historical roots; they spring from the artificial nature of the states, the Western forms of their governments, and the development of class interests within the population.

Although the states of Africa may overlay and overlap historic kingdoms, they are new formations. Their boundaries were fashioned during the late nineteenth century, when colonial powers competed and (sometimes literally) raced to claim the lands. Ethnic groups were divided by arbitrary lines drawn on the African map at conferences in Europe during the 1890s and early 1900s. In the years of colonial rule, administrative systems, economic and educational structures, as well as road and rail lines linked areas that had not necessarily been joined before. Leaders of African independence movements worked within the colonial boundaries. Even when they joined together in the Organization of African Unity (OAU), member states agreed to recognize the sovereignty of these new nations, while espousing and working toward African unity.

The government systems of the individual states also have their roots in the colonial past. To citizens of the Western Hemisphere, these governments may seem familiar: there are parliaments, parties, presidents, ministers, elections, and courts. Often these systems were inherited institutions, created by colonial governors and implemented by African nationalists even before independence.

The forms of government have not necessarily fitted well with the African foundations on which they have been built, and many institutions have changed since the early 1960s. Almost all new governments had to unite peoples of many ethnic groups, whose competitions and claims could disrupt a new nation. The civil wars in Chad and Sudan illustrate the explosive power of these internal conflicts. The development of one-party states was one solution to the disruptions resulting from ethnic politics. Since 1965, in a large number of nations, military coups have brought new forces—and sometimes new forms—to prominence.

Some of the strong personalities who led countries to independence remain in power. Felix Houphouet-Boigny of Côte d'Ivoire, and Hastings Banda of Malawi gradually shaped the forms of their governments. Personalities and the ideologies centered around them became the bases of government.

Other leaders, such as Julius Nyerere of Tanzania and Leopold Senghor of Senegal, retired, handing power to successors. Western-educated elites often controlled governments to their own advantage, and accusations of corruption and mismanagement abounded.

Socialist regimes were established in many African states. Though leaders often professed a Marxist orientation, they were more concerned with building an African socialist government. It was felt that a special African socialism could be built on the communal and cooperative traditions characteristic of many African societies. In countries such as Angola, Mozambique, and Guinea-Bissau, the current governments were first established in the liberated zones during the struggles for independence and were based differently from those handed over by the more benign colonial regimes of Ghana and Senegal. Socialist governments have not been free from personality cults, nor from corruption and oppressive measures. So, too, governments that practice forms of capitalism have also developed public corporations and plans similar to those of Marxist governments for their economic

(FAO photo by W. Wisse)

Literacy has risen dramatically in many African nations as a result of universal primary education and adult-literacy campaigns, often in African languages.

development. In recent years more and more governments—partly in line with IMF and World Bank requirements, but also because of the inefficiency and losses of their public corporations—have reformed their *parastatals* (as the public corporations are called) and have encouraged private enterprise.

Liberation and self-determination are still vital issues for Africa. In the Southern African nations of Namibia and South Africa, nationalist movements are fighting white-minority governments to gain political power.

Many African governments are in transition, whether they are socialist or capitalist in their orientation. Some states discard old ways, while others seek to incorporate indigenous systems of government. Some administrations are paying more attention to village cooperatives and local associations, recognizing their needs and their potential for development. Agriculture (the livelihood of the majority of the people), rather than industry, is increasingly emphasized. As governments develop closer ties with the traditional forms of decision making in African societies, African states may be greatly strengthened.

REASON FOR OPTIMISM

Although problems facing African countries have grown since independence, so have achievements. The number of persons who can read and write traditional languages as well as English, French, or Portuguese has increased enormously—the result of universal primary-education programs and adult-literacy campaigns. People can peruse news-

"There is no wealth where there are no children" is an African saying.   (Oxfam photo)

papers, follow instructions for fertilizers, and read the labels on medicine bottles. Professionals trained in modern technology, who plan electrification schemes, organize large office staffs, and develop medical facilities, for example, are more available because of the large number of African universities that have developed in the past 3 decades. Health care has expanded and improved, and Western-educated doctors and nurses as well as traditional midwives have increased the ranks of those in the medical services. Infant care in particular has improved; infant-mortality figures have declined, and Africans today can expect to live several years longer than they could in 1960.

Especially important is the increasing attention that African governments and intra-African agencies are giving to women. The pivotal role of women in agriculture is being recognized, and their work is being supported. Prenatal care and hospital care for mothers and their babies have increased, conditions for women workers in factories have been highlighted, new cooperatives for women's activities have been developed, and ministries dealing with women's issues have been established. Women have been included in cabinets of governments and on local village councils.

The advances that have been made in Africa are important ones, but they could be undercut if declining economic conditions continue. Africa needs debt relief and outside aid to maintain these gains and to move further toward a better life for ordinary people. Yet as the African proverb observes, "someone else's legs will do you no good in traveling." Self-reliance and Africa-centered approaches are the key to

development, no matter what help others offer.

The Organization of African Unity celebrated its 25th anniversary in 1988, renewing its commitment to fulfill the primary aim of liberation for Africans under South African rule. Taking a hard look at the lack of economic development, states pledged to promote higher standards of living, longer life, and better education. The effort of African countries to develop regional economic groups and to increase their power and their economic progress through cooperation is a hopeful development. The Southern African Development Coordination Conference (SADCC) and the Economic Community of West African States (ECOWAS) are two regional organizations within which African nations are developing practical programs so they can move ahead together. The Lagos Plan of Action adopted by African heads of state in 1980 provides target goals and steps by which continent-wide aims may be reached.

CONCLUSION

Africa, as the individual country reports in this volume reveal, is a continent of many and varied resources. There are rich minerals and a vast agricultural potential. The people—the youths who make up more than half of the population, and the elders who have maintained the traditions—are sources of African strength. The continent's history provides lessons for planning the future. The rest of the world can also benefit from the resources and learn from the activities and history of Africa.

North Africa

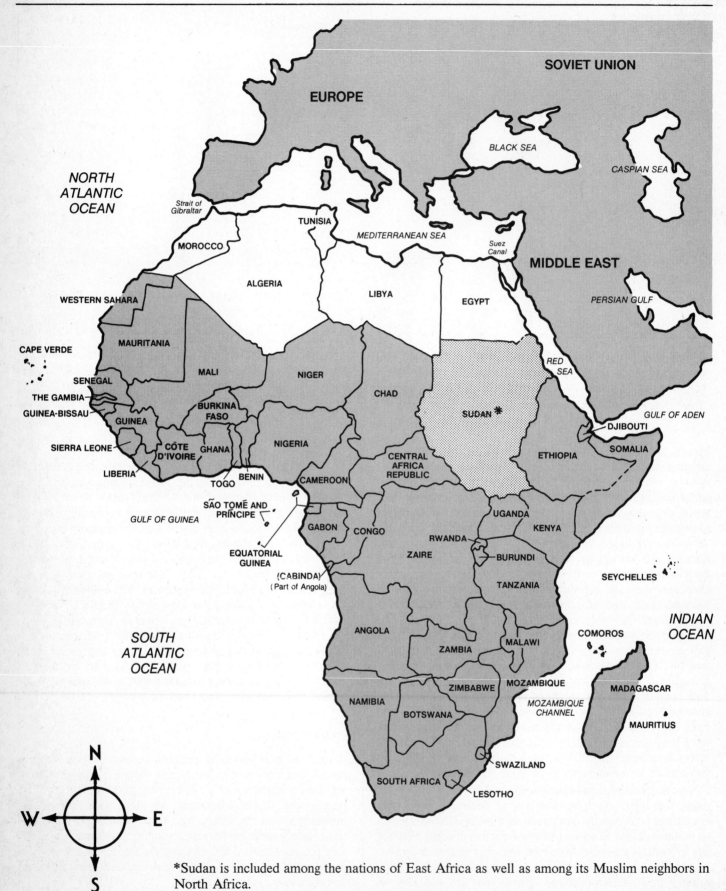

*Sudan is included among the nations of East Africa as well as among its Muslim neighbors in North Africa.

North Africa: Changing Islamic Cultures

Located at the geographical and cultural crossroads between Europe, Asia, and the rest of the African continent, the northern edge of the African continent has long been both a link and a barrier to Africa's relations with the rest of the world. Historically, the region was an early source of African products to Western civilizations. Leather goods from West African artisans were brought to the Mediterranean coast by northern traders, as were gold, salt, and slaves. North African neighbors brought European and Asian goods to sub-Saharan Africans and, perhaps more important, introduced them to one of the world's great universal religions: Islam.

North Africa's role as an African crossroads declined with the development of transoceanic navigation (and, eventually, of air transport), which fostered direct contact between Europe, Asia, and Africa. However, the countries of North Africa have continued to play an important part in the continent's history and development in recent centuries. Early supporters of African independence movements, they now participate actively in the affairs of the continent as full—indeed founding—members of the Organization of African Unity (OAU).

The countries of North Africa—Morocco, Algeria, Tunisia, Libya, and Egypt—and their millions of people differ a great deal from one another, but they share a heritage of common geography and culture that distinguishes them still more from the rest of Africa. To understand the cultures and politics of North Africa and its role in the rest of the continent, one must examine the geography of the region, which has provided the environment for social life as various as pastoral nomadism, peasant agriculture, merchant trade, and flourishing cities; the cultural and political heritage of Islam, the Middle East, and Europe; the diversity of contemporary political institutions within the region and efforts for regional integration; and, finally, the role of North Africa in African organizations designed to give the continent a greater voice in world affairs.

GEOGRAPHY AND POPULATION

Except for Tunisia, which is relatively small, the countries of North Africa are sprawling nations. Algeria, Libya, and Egypt are among the biggest countries on the continent, and Morocco is not far behind. Their size can be misleading, however, for much of the land is barren desert. The populations range from Egypt's 49 million people to Libya's 3.8 million; Morocco has 23.1 million people, Algeria has 22.1 million, and Tunisia is home to 7.3 million. Populations hug the coastlines and riverbanks, in search of the precious and scarce resource that can make the land productive: water. The great Nile River courses through the Egyptian desert, creating a narrow green ribbon of agricultural productivity

Land has been less of a barrier to regional cohesiveness in North Africa than have politics and ideology.

unrivaled in Africa. Ninety-five percent of Egypt's population live within 12 miles of the river's banks. Ninety percent of the people of Algeria, Tunisia, and Libya live in the northern third of their countries, and they depend on the moderating influences of the Mediterranean Sea coasts and low coastal mountain ranges to provide rainfall where there are no navigable rivers. Morocco, with both Atlantic and Mediterranean coastlines and with somewhat higher mountains, has a more even distribution of its population, but here as well it is determined by the availability of water.

Not only has the temperate, if often too dry, climate of North Africa influenced where people live, it has also encouraged great diversity in local economies and lifestyles.

(United Nations photo by Y. Nagata)
Oil and gas discoveries in North Africa produced wide-ranging economic effects.

There is intensive agriculture along the coasts and rivers, and Morocco and Tunisia are well known for their tree and vine crops—notably citrus fruits, olives, and wine grapes. Egypt's Nile Valley is intensively irrigated and now produces world-famous, high-quality cotton, as well as locally consumed foodstuffs. (Recent lowered levels of the Nile River have forced Egypt to practice ecological conservation.) In the oases that dot the Sahara Desert across the southern regions of these countries, date palms are irrigated, and their sweet fruit is harvested annually. Throughout the steppe lands, between the fertile coasts and the desert, nomads follow flocks of sheep and goats or herds of cattle and camels in search of pasture. Now very few in number, the nomads nonetheless enjoy a tradition of prestige as providers of meats, milk, and leathers. It was the nomads' knowledge of the landscape that permitted development of the extensive overland trans-Saharan trade. As paved roads and airports have replaced the caravan routes, long-distance nomadism has declined. But the traditions it bred, including loyalty to family and love of independence, are still critical to the cultural heritage of North Africa.

Urban life has also been a characteristic element of the North African economies and cultures. Supported by trade and by local industries—especially textiles, such as carpets, and metalworking—great cities have flourished. Cities such as Marrakesh, Fez, Rabat, Algiers, Tunis, Kairouan, and Tripoli as well as Cairo have been the administrative centers of great medieval empires. Those located by the sea have provided harbors for seafaring merchants. In the modern era these cities have been transformed into bustling industrial centers, ports, and political capitals.

Geography—or, more precisely, geology—has recently played an important role in providing resources for the national economies of North Africa. Although agriculture continues to provide employment in Algeria and Libya for as much as a third of the labor force, discoveries of oil and natural gas in the 1950s dramatically altered the nations' economic structures. For example, between 1960 and 1980, Libya's annual per capita income jumped from $50 to almost $10,000, transforming it from among the poorest to among the richest countries in the world. Algeria also benefited from discoveries of oil, although less dramatically, and Tunisia and Egypt have small oil industries that provide valuable domestic energy and foreign exchange. Morocco, while it has no oil, profits from its control of much of the world's phosphate production, earning needed income for its development efforts. However, the decline in oil prices in the 1980s reduced revenues, increased unemployment, and created unrest in many North African countries.

CULTURAL AND POLITICAL HERITAGES

The vast majority of the inhabitants of North Africa are Arabic-speaking Muslims. Islam and Arabic entered the region between the sixth and eleventh centuries. By the time of the Crusades in the eastern Mediterranean, the societies of North Africa were thoroughly incorporated into the Muslim world. Except for Egypt, where about 6 percent of the population are Christians (principally followers of the Egyptian Coptic Church), there is virtually no Christianity among North Africans. Important Jewish communities have existed in all of the North African countries, although the numbers have dwindled since the state of Israel was established in 1948. There are now very small Jewish communities in Morocco, Tunisia, and Egypt.

With Islam came Arabic, the language of the Arabian Peninsula and of the Koran. The local languages of North Africa—known collectively as Berber (from which the term "Barbary" was derived)—were almost completely supplanted in Egypt and Libya. Berber speakers, often considered the indigenous inhabitants—in contrast to the Arabs who settled in North Africa in the wake of the expansion of the Muslim empires—remain a significant proportion of the populations of Tunisia, Algeria, and Morocco. As many as a third of the Moroccans speak Berber as their first language. The mixture of Arabs and Berbers and their common adherence to Islam have left them virtually indistinguishable ethnically, although disputes have developed in Morocco and Algeria over the advisability of teaching Berber as a national language in schools. The linguistic issue has been complicated in North Africa, as well as in many sub-Saharan countries, by the legacy of European rule and the introduction of European languages—particularly French—as the language of technology and administration.

At the beginning of the nineteenth century all of the countries of North Africa except Morocco were formally provinces of the Ottoman Empire, which was based in present-day Turkey and included much of the contemporary Middle East. Morocco was an independent state; indeed, it was one of the first to recognize the independence of the United States from England after the American Revolution. Throughout the nineteenth century European expansion encroached on the independence of the Ottoman Empire; like their sub-Saharan counterparts, all of the states of North Africa eventually fell under European rule. Algeria was occupied by France in 1830, and France eventually ruled Tunisia (1881). Both France and Spain ruled Morocco (1912). The United Kingdom occupied Egypt in 1882, and Italy claimed Libya in 1911.

The different traditions of these European colonial rulers, while not weakening the underlying cultural unity of these predominantly Muslim and Arab states, did influence their political and social characters, creating great diversity. Algeria, which was incorporated into France as a province for 120 years, did not win its independence until 1962, after a protracted and violent revolution. Morocco, by contrast, was accorded independence from France in 1956 after only 44 years of French administration, during which the local monarchy continued to reign. Tunisia's 75 years of French rule also ended in 1956, as a strong nationalist party took the reins of power. Egypt, though formally independent of the United Kingdom, did not win genuine political independence until 1952, when Gamal Abdel Nasser came to power and overthrew the British-supported monarchy. Libya, which had fiercely resisted Italian rule, particularly during the

(United Nations photo)

The Egyptian president, Hosni Mubarak, continues the legacy of his predecessor, Anwar al-Sadat.

Fascist era, became a ward of the United Nations after Italy lost its colonies in World War II. The nation was granted independence by the new world body in 1951, under a monarch whose religious followers had led much of the early resistance.

POLITICAL INSTITUTIONS AND REGIONAL POLITICS

Egypt

Egypt took a position on the world stage soon after Gamal Abdel Nasser came to power. One of the major figures in the Non-Aligned Movement, Nasser gave voice to the aspirations of millions in the Arab world and Africa, championing nationalist movements throughout the region. Faced with the problems of a burgeoning population at home and his nation's limited natural resources, Nasser refused to let Egypt become dependent on a single foreign power, declaring the country nonaligned. He adopted a policy of developmental socialism at home. Because of mounting debts, which were spurred by enormous military spending, and increasing economic problems, many people had already begun to reassess Egypt's activist foreign policy by the time Nasser died in 1970. His successor, Anwar al-Sadat, reopened Egypt to foreign investment in hopes of attracting much-needed capital and technology. Eventually Sadat drew Egypt closer to the United States by signing the peace treaty that ended nearly 30 years of war with Israel in 1979. Sadat's abandonment of socialism and ties to the United States made him a target of domestic discontent, however, and in 1981 he was assassinated. Sadat was succeeded by his vice president, military officer Hosni Mubarak.

Rapid urbanization, declining revenues, debt, and unemployment have strained the economy, causing discontent among civilians, military-coup plots, and 17,000 police to riot in 1987. Reelected to a 6-year term in late 1987, Mubarak sought Egyptian reconciliation with Arab neighbors. Gradually some members of the Arab League renewed diplomatic relations with Egypt. Resentment of dependence on the United States and the increasing opposition of some Islamic religious leaders continue to compound the economic woes and to challenge the Egyptian government.

Libya

For years Libya was ruled by a pious autocratic king whose domestic legitimacy was always in question. The nation was heavily influenced by the foreign oil companies that discovered and produced the country's only substantial resource until 1969. In that year Colonel Muammar al-Qadhafi overthrew the monarchy. Believed to be about 27 at the time of the coup, Qadhafi was an ardent admirer of Nasser; he saw Libya as heir to Egypt's activist nonaligned foreign policy. He spent billions of dollars in ambitious domestic development, successfully ensuring universal health care, housing, and education by the end of the 1970s. He also spent billions more on military equipment and support of what he deemed nationalist movements throughout the world. Considered a maverick, he quarreled with many of the leaders of Africa and the Arab world. In spite of efforts at regional alliances, political differences and the expulsion of workers due to declining oil revenues increased tensions between Libya and its neighbors and within the military and middle class in Libya.

Strained relations between Libya and the United States

(United Nations photo by B. P. Wolff)

Population pressures continue to mount in Egypt, straining available resources and shaping domestic policy.

over Middle Eastern policies led to military hostilities in the Gulf of Sidra and a U.S. air raid on Tripoli in 1986. The United States required American businesses and citizens to leave Libya, and sought ways to undermine Qadhafi. Qadhafi made overtures to some neighbors, but Libya's war with Chad escalated in 1986 and 1987. OAU members pressed the parties for peace talks in 1988, and, surprising many, Qadhafi agreed to recognize the Hissein Habré government of Chad.

Tunisia

Tunisia, with the fewest natural resources of the North African countries, enjoyed the most stable and successful postindependence development experience of the region. Habib Bourguiba, leader of the nationalist party known as the neo-Destour, led the country to independence while retaining close economic and political ties with Europe. Bourguiba's government was a model of pragmatic approaches to both economic growth and foreign policy, developing the nation's Mediterranean coast as a vacation spot for European tourists and emphasizing education and the private sector's contribution to development.

However, in the 1980s, after a quarter-century of single-party rule and rising debt, many Tunisians grew uneasy with the aging leader's refusal to recognize opposition political parties. Strikes, demonstrations, and opposition from Muslim fundamentalists and the left led to a successful bloodless coup by P. M. Zine al-Abidine ben Ali in 1987. His efforts in 1988 to release jailed Muslim activists and to open political dialogue led to a period of optimism and widespread support. By the middle of that year he had replaced most of the Cabinet ministers who had served under Bourguiba.

Algeria

Algeria, wracked by the long and destructive revolution that preceded independence in 1962, was ruled by a coalition of military and civilian leaders who had made their names as revolutionary partisans during the war. (Algeria became a republic in 1976.) Although these leaders differed over what policies and programs to emphasize, they nonetheless agreed on the need for a foreign policy of nonalignment and for rapid industrialization at home—policies that came to be known in Algeria as "Islamic socialism." The country's substantial oil and gas revenues were invested in large-scale industrial projects. But by the end of the 1970s serious declines in agricultural productivity and major growth in urban unemployment had sent hundreds of thousands of Algerian workers to France in search of jobs, and the leaders were taking steps to rectify these problems. The Algerian leadership, although it has enforced a policy of domestic austerity, has enjoyed a reputation both at home and abroad of commitment to equity and development.

Recent moves for closer ties to the United States and plans to encourage the private sector at home brought criticism from dissidents within Algeria and exiles abroad; and led to bloody riots protesting food-price rises in 1988; 100 people were killed. A referendum on political reform may give more power to the Parliament. But internationally, Algeria is known for its role in difficult diplomatic negotiations, mediating in such international crises as air hijackings. Algeria also reached out to its neighbors and, seeking a solution to the war in Western Sahara, resumed diplomatic relations with Morocco in 1988.

Morocco

Morocco is ruled by King Hassan II, who came to power in 1961 when his highly respected father, King Muhammad V, died. The political parties that developed during the struggle against French rule have continued to contest elections. However, Hassan has rarely permitted them genuine influence in policymaking, preferring to reserve the role for himself and his advisers. As in Tunisia, Moroccan agricultural development has been based on technological innovations rather than on land reform. The latter, while it would raise productivity, would likely anger the propertied supporters of the king. Elites also oppose business-tax reforms, yet the government needs revenues to repay its $14-billion debt. Much of the country's economic development has been left to the private sector. High birth rates and unemployment have led many Moroccans to join the Algerians and Tunisians seeking employment in Europe.

(United Nations photo by M. Jimenex)

Morocco's King Hassan II is a leader whose influence is often pivotal in North African regional planning.

Ben Balla

(World Bank photo by Ray Witlin)

Geography has produced unique advantages as well as problems for North African nations.

The war to retain control of phosphate-rich Western Sahara, formerly a colony of Spain and now claimed by Morocco (a claim opposed by the nationalist movement Polisario), causes discontent among Moroccans and drains the treasury. (It costs $1 billion per year.) Despite military and economic assistance from the United States, France, and Saudi Arabia, Morocco is unable to crush the Polisario resistance. United Nations (UN) and OAU missions to both Morocco and Western Sahara in 1987, as well as Saudi Arabian pressure in 1988, led to meetings with Algeria (a Polisario supporter) to seek an end to the war, raising hopes for a settlement of the dispute.

REGIONAL UNITY

During the 1950s and 1960s regional integration was widely discussed in North Africa. Egypt was a leader of the pan-Arab movement and briefly joined Syria in a union from 1958 to 1961. The three former French colonies—Morocco, Algeria, and Tunisia, sometimes known as the Maghrib (Arabic for "land of the setting sun")—considered proposals for economic integration, which might eventually lead to political unity. Libya picked up the theme of integration in the 1970s, when Qadhafi called for Arab and Islamic unions.

None of these efforts has borne fruit. Indeed, many of the governments in the region have had serious disputes with one another. Qadhafi has been accused of subverting all of his neighbors' governments; Algeria and Morocco have disagreed over the disposition of the Western Sahara; and each

country has, at one point or another, closed its borders to the citizens of its neighbors. Yet after 10 years of strained relations, Egypt and many of its neighbors renewed relations (as did Algeria and Morocco) in 1988. The idea of regional cooperation clearly has retained much of its original attractiveness, reflecting as it does the common cultural and social foundations of the region.

NORTH AFRICA AND THE REST OF THE CONTINENT

North Africa's relations with the rest of the continent have reflected both its cultural and geographical roots in Africa and the national interests and aspirations of each country. Both as members of the Organization of African Unity and as active supporters of anticolonial movements, the North African countries have had strong diplomatic and political ties with the rest of Africa. They are, however, also deeply involved in regional affairs outside Africa—particularly those of the Arab and Islamic world—and there have been tensions because of these various commitments during the postindependence period. Requests by the northern nations that African countries break diplomatic relations with Israel were met promptly after the oil price rises of the early 1970s; many African countries hoped in return for Arab development aid. Although such aid was eventually offered (mostly from the Gulf countries, not the North African oil producers), it was less generous than expected and came only after some other conditions had been met. Many sub-

12

(United Nations photo by John Isaac)

Nomatic traditions including loyalty to family and love of independence are still important to the cultural inheritance of North Africa.

Saharan African leaders were disappointed. Under U.S. pressure, some, such as Liberia, Zaire, and Cameroon, resumed diplomatic relations with Israel.

Border disputes, ideological differences, and internal conflicts have caused tension among African states. Algerian support for Polisario in Western Sahara and Tunisian support for Eritrean rebels against Ethiopia, for example, have badly divided the OAU. When the Organization of African Unity recognized the Polisario movement in 1984, Morocco with-

drew its membership in the OAU. Thus, the North African role in continental affairs has not been without its problems. Nonetheless, North African participation has been mutually beneficial. OAU mediation led to the resolution of a Morocco-Algeria border dispute in 1974 and the countries' resumption of diplomatic relations in 1988. As evidenced by the amicable 1988 celebration of the OAU's 25th anniversary, the organization continues to play an important role in airing and resolving disputes as well as in presenting the African perspective on world affairs.

West Africa

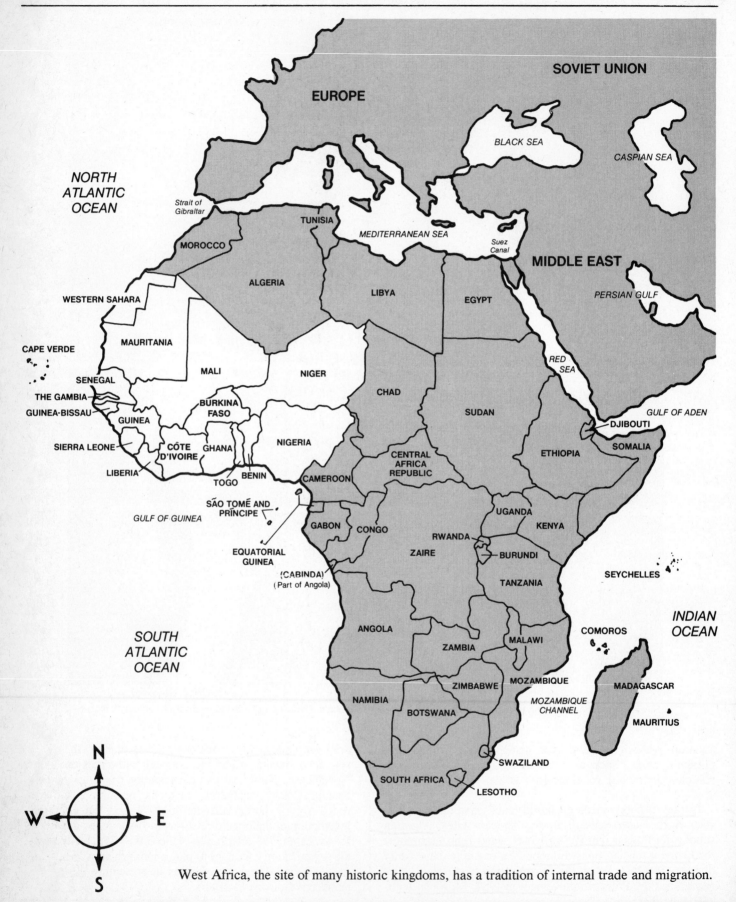

SOVIET UNION

EUROPE

BLACK SEA

CASPIAN SEA

NORTH
ATLANTIC
OCEAN

Strait of
Gibraltar

TUNISIA

MEDITERRANEAN SEA

Suez
Canal

MIDDLE EAST

MOROCCO

ALGERIA

LIBYA

EGYPT

PERSIAN GULF

WESTERN SAHARA

MAURITANIA

MALI

NIGER

CHAD

RED
SEA

CAPE VERDE

SENEGAL

THE GAMBIA

GUINEA-BISSAU

GUINEA

BURKINA
FASO

NIGERIA

SUDAN

GULF OF ADEN

DJIBOUTI

SOMALIA

SIERRA LEONE

CÔTE
D'IVOIRE

GHANA

ETHIOPIA

LIBERIA

TOGO

BENIN

CAMEROON

CENTRAL
AFRICA
REPUBLIC

SÃO TOMÉ AND
PRÍNCIPE

GULF OF GUINEA

GABON

CONGO

UGANDA

KENYA

EQUATORIAL
GUINEA

RWANDA

ZAIRE

BURUNDI

SEYCHELLES

(CABINDA)
(Part of Angola)

TANZANIA

SOUTH
ATLANTIC
OCEAN

ANGOLA

ZAMBIA

MALAWI

COMOROS

INDIAN
OCEAN

ZIMBABWE

MOZAMBIQUE

MADAGASCAR

NAMIBIA

BOTSWANA

MOZAMBIQUE
CHANNEL

MAURITIUS

SWAZILAND

SOUTH AFRICA

LESOTHO

N

W   E

S

West Africa, the site of many historic kingdoms, has a tradition of internal trade and migration.

West Africa: Building on Traditional Links

Anyone looking at a map of Africa will identify West Africa as the great bulge on the western coast of the continent. It is a region bound by the Sahara Desert to the north, the Atlantic Ocean to the south and west, and in part by the Cameroonian Mountains and the highlands to the east. Every boundary has, at one time or another, been a bridge to the rest of the world.

At first glance, the great variety of the region is more striking than any of its unifying features. It contains the extremes of desert and rain forest. The people who live there are predominantly agriculturalists, yet every type of occupation can be found, from herders to factory workers. Hundreds of different languages are spoken; some are as different from one another as English is from Arabic or Japanese. The cultural traditions and the societies that practice them are myriad.

Yet the more one examines West Africa, the more one is impressed with the developments that give the region a certain coherence and unity and that cross the boundaries of the states within the region. These states were the artificial creations of the competing colonial powers of the United Kingdom, France, Germany, and Portugal when Africa was partitioned by the imperialists at the end of the nineteenth century.

Some of the common characteristics and cross-cutting features of the area known as West Africa include the vegetation belts that stretch across the region from west to east, creating somewhat similar environments in all the states; the common history and characteristics that distinguish many of the peoples of the West African region—especially the influence of the great kingdoms of the savanna and forest regions, the early development of urban centers, and the linking patterns of trade; the movement of peoples throughout the regions, providing a kind of social "glue"; and efforts being made by West African governments to work for integration in the region, primarily through economic organizations.

WEST AFRICAN VEGETATION AND CLIMATE ZONES

Traveling north from the coast in Nigeria, Ghana, or Côte d'Ivoire, one first encounters tropical rain forests, then moves into woodland savanna areas, and later crosses more open and drier plains. In Mali, Niger, and other countries to the north, the trip would take one from savanna into the Sahel areas close to the Sahara Desert, and finally into the desert itself. These vegetation zones stretching across West Africa are bands across the land, "citizens" of many countries.

The peoples of these countries share the benefits and the problems of similar environments. Cocoa, coffee, yams, and cassava are among the cash and food crops planted in the cleared forest and woodland zones in Liberia or Nigeria, for instance. Groundnuts, sorghum, and millet are among the crops harvested in the savannas of Senegal, The Gambia, Mali, and northern Nigeria. Niger herders who cannot go too far south with their cattle because of the presence of the tsetse fly in the forest (and the accompanying danger of diseases that kill cattle) easily cross the borders into the savannas of Mali and Nigeria.

People in each country in the West African region have felt the effects of the droughts of recent years, and population pressures on the land have contributed to changing conditions. The border lands between savanna and desert, known as the Sahel, have deteriorated, leading to large-scale migrations. The woodland savannas farther south have given way to grasslands as forests have been cut to grow food and cash crops. Drought and widespread brush fires in Ghana, Côte d'Ivoire, Togo, and Benin have caused forests to become savannas and savannas to become deserts. The harmattan, the dry wind that blows from the Sahara in January and February, now reaches to many parts of the coast. The dust and haze have become a sign of the new year—and of agricultural problems throughout West Africa.

The rivers of West Africa, including the Senegal, the Gambia, the Niger, and their tributaries, have become more and more important, not only because they are used for travel and trade but also because of the water they provide. Countries have united to harness the waters for irrigation and for hydroelectric power through joint organizations. Eight countries—Cape Verde, The Gambia, Burkina Faso, Mali, Senegal, Niger, Chad (in Central Africa), and Mauritania—have united in the Committee for Struggle Against Drought in the Sahel (CILSS) to counter the effects of the drought.

(United Nations photo)

Weaving long narrow strips of cloth is men's work throughout West Africa. The cloth is highly valued for blankets and robes.

THE LINKS OF HISTORY AND TRADE

The peoples of West Africa have never been members of one political unit, and their diversity is far more noticeable than the features they share. Yet some of the ancient kingdoms that overarched different regions are still remembered, providing bases for current and future cooperation. The Mali empire of the thirteenth to fifteenth centuries, the Songhai empire of the sixteenth century, and the northern Nigerian Fulani caliphate of the nineteenth century were widely known and influential. They represent only a few, if the largest, of the expanding state systems and kingdoms that overlapped the savanna zones in earlier centuries. The kingdoms of the southern forests, such as the Asante Confederation of Ghana, the Dahomey kingdom, and the Yoruba states, were smaller than the Sudanese empires to the north. Although later in origin and quite different in character from the Sudanese systems, the forest kingdoms were well known and influential throughout the regions where they developed.

One of the distinctive features of these kingdoms and of the history of the region was the presence of cities and traditional systems of trade. The remains of Kumbi Saleh,

the capital of ancient Ghana, have been uncovered in Mauritania. Other cities that pre-date any Western influence include present-day Timbuctu and Gao in Mali; Ouagadougou in Burkina Faso; as well as Ibadan, Benin, and Kumasi in the forest zones nearer the coast. Traditional systems of trade linked many of these cities, and trade routes crisscrossed the area. Gold, kola, leather goods, cloth, and slaves were carried from the south to the north. Salt and other goods were transported to the south. The population density of some of the West African regions and the early agricultural surpluses of the predominantly agricultural areas may have encouraged the trade. These traditional marketing activities have long contributed to the vitality of the region's towns. Trading, land-holding, and social systems in West Africa did change over time, but they were not radically disrupted by intruding groups of European settlers as in Southern and East Africa, where white settlers radically altered the pattern of development.

The trading cities of the savannas became the links to North Africa and were especially influenced by Islam, which early gained a following among the ruling groups of the

(IFC/World Bank photo by Ray Witkin)

A worker cuts cloth at a textile mill in Côte d'Ivoire. The patterns are similar to traditional patterns. Most of the cloth will be exported.

savanna and later spread through trade and conquest. The more southern areas were also influenced by that religion, and today there are many converts to Islam in the south. However, these southern areas were much more strongly influenced by other factors, including the mixed heritage of a disastrous slave trade; another faith (Christianity); and direct contacts with European explorers, officials, and others. New cities such as Dakar, Freetown, and Lagos developed rapidly in the southern areas because of the increased activities of European powers on the shorelines. The impact from the north and south on West Africa is still evident. For example, from the north, Libya has offered military and other assistance to governments and their opponents, and the Western trading system has pulled cash crops and minerals to the south and out through the Atlantic ports.

THE MOVEMENT OF PEOPLES

Today, as in the past, one characteristic of the West African region has been the never-ending migration of people. Although Africa is sometimes viewed as a continent of isolated groups, it is subject to constant ebbs and flows. Herders have moved east and west across the savanna zones and south into the forests; traders and laborers have moved north and south. Professionals have moved to new coastal centers or to interior towns in other countries to service bureaucracies and schools.

Some peoples of West Africa have been especially mobile, including the Malinke, Fulani, Hausa, and Mossi. In the past the Malinke journeyed from Mali, the center of Malinke habitation, to the coastal areas in Senegal and The Gambia. Over time, Malinke traders called Dyoula made their way to Burkina Faso, establishing towns such as Bobo Dioulasso and Ouagadougou, and took up residence in the interior towns of Sierra Leone and Liberia, where they are known as Mandingoes. And they are still on the move.

The Fulani have developed their own patterns of transition and seasonal movement. They herd their cattle south across the savanna areas in the dry season, move them north in the rainy season, and then return to where they started. Town-oriented groups of Fulani historically made journeys west to east, introducing people to Islam and Islamic learning as well as to the possibilities of trade. Today Fulani move south in large numbers as a result of the deterioration of their grazing lands. Although the residents of Monrovia, Abidjan, or Lagos may be startled to see Fulani herders with their canes and hide bags on the city streets, the Fulani presence there is not surprising, in light of their past ventures.

The Hausa, the traders of northern Nigeria and Niger, are also found throughout many areas of West Africa. They are known less for their large numbers than for their trading activities. Their presence is so widespread that Hausa has been suggested as a possible future common language for West Africa. Mossi migrations from Burkina Faso are regular and extensive. The Mossi and other Burkinabe laborers as well as laborers from Niger and Mali have gone regularly to Côte d'Ivoire and Ghana, for instance, establish-

(United Nations photo)

Vegetable stalls at an outdoor market in the delta region of St. Louis, Senegal.

ing an interdependence between these northern and southern regions.

These migrations have been duplicated by the movements of other groups in West Africa. The drastic expulsion of aliens by the Nigerian government in the 1980s was startling to the outside world in part because few realized that so many Ghanaians, Nigeriens, Togolese, Beninois, and Cameroonians had recently taken up residence in Nigeria. Such immigration is not new, even though in this case it was stimulated by Nigeria's oil boom. Peoples along the West African coast, such as the Yoruba, the Ewe, and the Vai, who are divided by the boundaries that colonialism arbitrarily imposed, have silently defied such boundaries and maintained close links across borders with their own peoples. Other migrations have roots in the past: Sierra Leonians worked all along the coast as craftsmen; Dahomeyans became the assistants of French administrators in other parts of French West Africa; and Yoruba traded in markets in a number of cities.

(Malcolm Harper, Oxfam)

The balafon, a distinctive zylophone with gourd resonators, is popular throughout West Africa, and probably spread with the movement of peoples.

THE PROGRESS OF
WEST AFRICAN INTEGRATION

The governments of the countries in the West African region have recognized the weaknesses inherent in the proliferation of states. Most agree that the peoples of the region would benefit from political cooperation and economic integration. Yet there are many obstacles blocking the efforts at regional development. National identity is valued as much today as it was in the days when Kwame Nkrumah, the charismatic Ghanaian leader, spoke of African unity and met with reluctance from other states. The wealthier states, such as Nigeria and Côte d'Ivoire, are reluctant to share their wealth with smaller countries, which feel threatened by Nigerian and Ivoirian strengths.

Political and economic systems in West Africa include the military regime of Nigeria, the one-party state of Togo, the multiparty government of Senegal, and states such as Niger that are struggling toward varied constitutional systems. Constructing any type of umbrella organization that can encompass these diverse systems still challenges even the most skilled political tactician. Because the countries were under the rule of different colonial powers, French, English, and Portuguese all serve as official languages in different nations, and a variety of administrative traditions still hang on. Moreover, during colonial times independent infrastructures were developed in each country; these continue to orient economic activities toward the coast and Europe rather than encouraging links between West African countries.

Political changes also affect regional cooperation and domestic development. The confederation of Senegal and The Gambia (Senegambia) is dominated by Senegal and resented by many Gambians. Nigeria experienced military coups in 1983 and 1985, its new leaders challenged by debt and a faltering economy, while Liberia, after questionable elections in 1985, put down attempted coups with bloody repression and restrictions on opponents.

Multinational Organizations

Despite these problems, multinational organizations have developed in West Africa, stimulated both by the common problems that the countries face and by the obvious benefits of cooperation. There are only a few political confederations, such as Senegambia and the Mali Guinea Union, although there are many other organizations with limited and specific goals. Countries cooperated to settle border disputes or to alleviate drought conditions, and river-basin commissions were created to manage the area's river systems. Of these, the Organization for the Development of the Senegal River (OMVS) has shown the most practical progress. Five groundnut-producing countries work together in the Groundnut Council; seven countries of the Volta River Basin cooperate with the World Heath Organization and other programs to eradicate river blindness; the West African Examinations Council standardizes secondary-school examinations in several countries.

The most important and encompassing organization in the region is the Economic Organization of West African States (ECOWAS), which includes all states except Western Sahara. Established in 1975 by the Treaty of Lagos, ECOWAS aims to promote trade, cooperation, and self-reliance. The progress of the organization thus far has been limited. Its major accomplishment, say some people, is that it exists and is recognized.

ECOWAS can point to valuable achievements. Several joint ventures have been developed; steps toward tariff reduction are being taken; and the competition between ECOWAS and the Economic Community of West Africa (CEAO), the economic organization of French-speaking states, has been lessened by limiting CEAO; and states have agreed in principle to establish a common currency by 1992. At the 11th annual summit in 1988, a record 15 heads of state discussed debt, trade liberalization, and sources of funding for the organization. The issue of toxic-waste dumping in West Africa brought a unified response from member states. (Many countries have been approached as sites, and dumping has already occurred in Benin, Guinea-Bissau, Nigeria, and Senegal.) The leaders condemned such dumping prac- tices by industrialized countries and sought ways to clean up current waste and to prevent future occurrences. It is hoped that ECOWAS can become more effective at a grass-roots level, eventually developing an African solution to regional development. The cross-cutting geographic zones, the over- linking histories, and the long tradition of African migrations provide a base on which practical moves for unity such as ECOWAS can be built.

(FAO photo by F. Mattioli)

The nations of West Africa seek unity and cooperation in solving regional problems.

Benin (People's Republic of Benin)

GEOGRAPHY

Area in Square Kilometers (Miles):
112,620 (43,483) (slightly smaller than Pennsylvania)
Capital (Population): Porto-Novo (330,000)
Climate: tropical

PEOPLE

Population
Total: 4,150,000
Annual Growth Rate: 3.1%
Rural/Urban Population Ratio: 80/20
Languages: official: French; others spoken: Fon; Yoruba; Adja; Bariba; others

Health
Life Expectancy at Birth: 47 years
Infant Death Rate (Ratio): 143/1,000
Average Caloric Intake: 100% of FAO minimum
Physicians Available (Ratio): 1/20,343

Religion(s)
80% traditional indigenous; 12% Muslim; 8% Christian

Education
Adult Literacy Rate: 28%

COMMUNICATION

Telephones: 8,650
Newspapers: 1

THE DAHOMEY KINGDOM

The Dahomey kingdom, established in the early eighteenth century by the Fon people, was a highly organized state. The kings had a standing army, which included women; a centralized administration, whose officers kept census and tax records and organized the slave and, later, the oil trade; and a sophisticated artistic tradition. Benin, like Togo, has important links with Brazil which date back to the time of the Dahomeyan kingdom. Current Beninois families—such as the da Souzas, the da Silvas, and the Rodriguezes—are descendants of Brazilians who settled on the coast in the mid-nineteenth century. Some were descended from former slaves, who may have been taken from Dahomey long before. They became the first teachers in Western-oriented public schools and continued in higher education themselves. In Brazil, Yoruba religious cults, which developed from those of the Yoruba in Benin and Nigeria, have become increasingly popular in recent years.

TRANSPORTATION

Highways—Kilometers (Miles): 8,400 (5,208)
Railroads—Kilometers (Miles): 579 (360)
Commercial Airports: 1 international

GOVERNMENT

Type: Marxist-Leninist
Independence Date: August 1, 1960
Head of State: President (General) Ahmed Mathieu Kérékou
Political Parties: People's Revolutionary Party of Benin
Suffrage: universal for adults

MILITARY

Number of Armed Forces: 6,100 (estimate)
Military Expenditures (% of Central Government Expenditures): 17.2%
Current Hostilities: none

ECONOMY

Currency ($ U.S. Equivalent): 288 CFA francs = $1
Per Capita Income/GNP: $250/$1.1 billion
Inflation Rate: n/a
Natural Resources: none known in commercial quantities
Agriculture: palm products; cotton; corn; yams; cassava; cocoa; coffee; groundnuts
Industry: shoes; beer; textiles; cement; processed palm oil

FOREIGN TRADE

Exports: $304 million
Imports: $590 million

	The French conquer the Dahomey kingdom and declare a French protectorate **1892**		Dahomey becomes independent **1960**	Kérékou comes to power in the sixth attempted military coup since independence **1972**	The name of Dahomey is changed to Benin **1975**	An attempted coup involves exiles, mercenaries, and implicates Gabon, Morocco, and France **1977**
The kingdom of Dahomey is established **1625**						

1980s

President Kérékou is reelected	International loans are sought for rural development	The government acknowledges that the Soviet Union dumped radioactive waste in Benin

BENIN

"I want the young people to stay and not slip away to Nigeria," M. Armand, the district chief of Za-kpota in southern Benin, told a visitor. As a result, Armand has encouraged his people to build a cultural center with a dance hall and a cinema. Such attractions may offer short-term appeal, but it is doubtful that they will keep Benin citizens at home. Some will go to the larger cities; others will travel to Nigeria, Niger, or Togo.

A COUNTRY OF MIGRANTS

For decades emigration has been a way of life for many Beninois. Young men were educated in schools established by the French who ruled Dahomey (as Benin was called until 1975), and Beninois worked in the administration throughout French West Africa. After 1960 each independent country of French-speaking Africa developed its independent civil service, and Benin citizens lost their jobs. They returned home, where the competition for upper-level jobs intensified. This competition heightened the rivalry of different groups and regions in the political system.

Benin citizens continue to migrate today. Professionals may go to teach or practice in other West African countries. Other Beninois go to Nigeria carrying goods to sell—especially food crops, which are in great demand across the border. The movement from Benin to Nigeria is a natural one, for Yoruba peoples in both countries are linked by strong family and cultural ties.

The area of transport and trade is one of the most vital sectors of Benin's economy,

and many people find legal as well as illegal employment in carrying goods. This is partly due to Benin's special geographical characteristics. The state is long and thin, encompassing several ecological zones and reaching inland to the landlocked countries. Traditionally it provided good routes to the coast, because the savanna reaches the coast and there is little rain forest to impede travel. The roads are comparatively well developed, and the railroad carries goods from the port at Cotonou to northern areas of the country. An extension of the railroad will reach Niamey, the capital of Niger.

LIMITED DEVELOPMENT

There has been little development of the productive capacities of the country, and many citizens seek a living in other countries or through illicit trading across the borders. Benin remains among the least developed countries of the world. Production of cash crops such as palm oil, cocoa, coffee, and groundnuts has declined because of the declining official prices of such products. Many farmers sell their cash crops on the black market, smuggling them across the borders. Some have switched to yams, cassava, and other food crops, but the economy is deteriorating. Although crops are in demand in other regions of Benin, they are actually sold in Nigeria, where the prices are better. There are very few industries, but sugar, cement, and palm-oil factories are proposed, and a joint Libyan-Benin Company, Belimes, has been established for mineral development.

Some Beninois attribute the lack of

progress to the government under which they live. For a dozen years after independence there was little stability of government. In 1972 General Mathieu Kérékou came to power; he has maintained control of the country ever since. A 1977 coup attempt which involved European mercenaries and implicated Morocco, Gabon, and France provoked a long-lasting fear of opposition and criticism. However, the government seems less dictatorial and arbitrary than some would imply. The leaders declare themselves to be Marxist-Leninists. This orientation has resulted in a one-party state (the People's Revolutionary Party of Benin); the nationalization of industries, banks, and insurance companies; the nationalization of schools; and a special court system. (Other developments, such as the encouragement of private investment, are not in line with Marxist-Leninism.)

Benin is still controlled by the military, but a constitution was developed in 1979. Ties with France were reinstituted. In 1987 Kérékou resigned from the army and reshuffled the Cabinet in order to emphasize civilian rule.

Kérékou conducted a purge of the armed forces after an alleged coup plot in 1988, jailing political opponents. As the economy stagnates and smuggling escalates, stability may continue to elude the government of Benin.

DEVELOPMENT

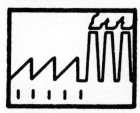

Palm-oil plantations were established in Benin in the mid-nineteenth century by Africans. They have continued to be African-owned and capitalist-oriented in a society that is proclaimed socialist. Today there are some 30 million trees, and palm-oil products are a major export used for cooking, lighting, soap, margarine, and lubricants.

FREEDOM

The People's Revolutionary Party of Benin does not allow for much internal competition, and the media is also controlled. Student strikes at the University of Benin in 1987 were met with repression. Prisoners of conscience are detained without trial.

HEALTH/WELFARE

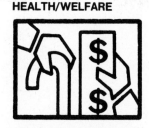

One-third of the national budget of Benin goes to education, and the number of students receiving primary education has risen to 50% of the school-age population. College graduates serve as temporary teachers through the National Service System, but more teachers and higher salaries are needed.

ACHIEVEMENTS

Fon appliqued cloths have been described as "one of the gayest and liveliest of the contemporary African art forms." Formerly these cloths were made and used by the Dahomeyan kings. Now they are sold to tourists, but they still portray the motifs and symbols of past rulers and the society they ruled.

Burkina Faso

GEOGRAPHY

Area in Square Kilometers (Miles):
274,500 (106,000) (about the size of Colorado)
Capital (Population): Ouagadougou (442,000)
Climate: tropical to arid

PEOPLE

Population
Total: 8,335,000
Annual Growth Rate: 1.7%
Rural/Urban Population Ratio: 90/10
Languages: official: French; others spoken: Mossi, Senufo, Fula, Bobo, Mande, Gurunsi, Lobi, others

Health
Life Expectancy at Birth: 42 years
Infant Death Rate (Ratio): 176/1,000
Average Caloric Intake: 95% of FAO minimum
Physicians Available (Ratio): 1/70,033

Religion(s)
45% traditional indigenous; 43% Muslim; 12% Christian

Education
Adult Literacy Rate: 8%

COMMUNICATION

Telephones: 10,625
Newspapers: 4

CROSS-NATIONAL TIES

Burkina Faso has many ties with Côte d'Ivoire. Côte d'Ivoire is a major customer for Burkina Faso exports, oil comes from an Abidjan refinery, and thousands of workers migrate to Côte d'Ivoire every year. It is not surprising, then, that Felix Houphouët-Boigny, the president of Côte d'Ivoire, has been described as "the godfather of Voltaic [Burkinabe] political life." Hence, it is in Burkina Faso's best interest to consolidate the traditional friendship and cooperation between the two nations.

Relations between Burkina Faso and Côte d'Ivoire have been strained because their domestic and foreign policies are so different. Yet in spite of tensions between Burkina Faso and Côte d'Ivoire and other neighbors, both Thomas Sankara and his successor as head of state, Blaise Compaore, have tried to reconcile with other West African leaders.

TRANSPORTATION

Highways—Kilometers (Miles): 13,134 (8,143)
Railroads—Kilometers (Miles): 517 (320)
Commercial Airports: 2 international

GOVERNMENT

Type: republic under control of a military council
Independence Date: August 5, 1960
Head of State: Blaise Compaore
Political Parties: banned following the 1980 coup
Suffrage: universal for adults

MILITARY

Number of Armed Forces: 8,750
Military Expenditures (% of Central Government Expenditures): 20%
Current Hostilities: none

ECONOMY

Currency ($ U.S. Equivalent): 286 CFA francs = $1
Per Capita Income/GNP: $150/$1.2 billion
Inflation Rate: 8.4%
Natural Resources: manganese; limestone; marble; gold; uranium; bauxite; copper
Agriculture: millet; sorghum; corn; rice; livestock; peanuts; shea nuts; sugar cane; cotton; sesame
Industry: agricultural processing; brewing; light industry

FOREIGN TRADE

Exports: $55 million
Imports: $279 million

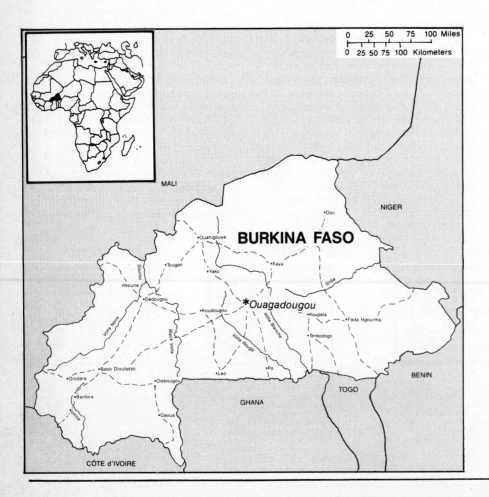

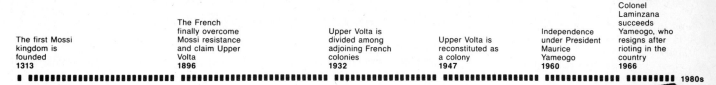

The first Mossi kingdom is founded
1313

The French finally overcome Mossi resistance and claim Upper Volta
1896

Upper Volta is divided among adjoining French colonies
1932

Upper Volta is reconstituted as a colony
1947

Independence under President Maurice Yameogo
1960

Lieutenant Colonel Laminzana succeeds Yameogo, who resigns after rioting in the country
1966

1980s

After several military coups, Captain Thomas Sankara comes to power

The country's name is changed to Burkina (Mossi for "land of honest men") Faso (Dioula for "democratic republic")

Sankara is assassinated; Compaore succeeds as head of state

BURKINA FASO

"Speed it up PM" *(Accelerez la Vitesse)* read one of the banners displayed at a rally in Ouagadougou, the capital of Burkina Faso (formerly called Upper Volta), on April 16, 1983. The slogan illustrated the popular feeling that the government of Jean-Baptiste Ouedraogo had neither established a course of national regeneration nor begun to implement it. In response to popular pressure, Prime Minister Thomas Sankara, to whom the opening statement was directed, took power on August 5, 1983 in a military coup.

The government of Burkina Faso has changed several times since independence in 1960. Yet neither military nor civilian regimes have been able to cope fully with the challenges of meeting the people's needs.

DEBILITATING DROUGHTS

Burkina Faso, one of the poorest countries in the world, has been held back by successive droughts during the past 2 decades. In the countryside, traditional patterns of life have been disrupted by years of drought. Some farmers' needs have been served by the many aid missions that came to Burkina Faso within the course of a year, and by the 5-year UN World Food Program that in the 1980s distributed 35,000 tons of food to people in development work. Most important has been the work of farmers themselves and their families, working through the traditional cooperatives, or *naam*, to make the best use of new pumps, grinding mills, hoes, and medical supplies through community action.

Most Burkinabe are agriculturalists and herders, but many are wage workers, members of a strong trade-union movement, and residents of the cities of Bobo-Dioulasso and Ouagadougou, both with substantial populations. Many people combine farming and wage labor. At least a million work as migrant laborers in other parts of West Africa, a pattern that dates back to the early twentieth century. Approximately 700,000 of these workers migrate to Côte d'Ivoire. Returning workers, a large number of them Mossi, infuse the country with a working-class and cosmopolitan perspective.

UNIONS FORCE CHANGES

Trade-union leaders representing these workers have been instrumental in forcing changes in government. They have spoken out vigorously against government efforts to ban strikes and restrain unions and have demanded that something be done to change the declining standards of living. They are a force to be reckoned with for any Burkinabe government. After coming to office, Sankara had some clashes with the unions, especially the teacher's union. Some suggested that the government-instituted Revolutionary Committees were designed to replace the unions, which are difficult to control.

Sankara promoted radical policies and anti-imperialism, which gained him popularity at home and a cautious reception from more conservative neighbors. His government abolished individual ownership of land, created a Ministry of Peasant Affairs, and established links with Libya. Sankara also recognized the importance of good relations with France and Côte

d'Ivoire. France is Burkina Faso's major trading partner, a source of corporate investment and financial aid. French investment in the development of a massive manganese mine and a railroad from Ouagadougou may contribute to economic growth.

CHANGE AND UNCERTAINTY

In 1987, in the fifth coup since independence, soldiers under Sankara's colleagues in government—Captain Blaise Compaore, Major Bonkary Lingani, and Captain Henri Zorgo—killed Sankara and overthrew his government. The killing shocked Burkina Faso citizens and African neighbors alike.

The new leaders, with Compaore as head of state, claimed that Sankara's rule was too arbitrary, that he had resisted forming a party with a set of rules. Although many Burkinabe shared these criticisms, people mourned Sankara's death in large numbers, and the new government has had an uneasy leadership. While Compaore seeks meetings of reconciliation with other African heads of state, uncertainty and unrest simmer. Admiration for the popular Sankara lives on, as evidenced by the widespread use of a new cloth pattern, known locally as "homage to Sankara."

DEVELOPMENT

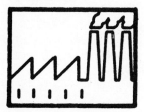

The traditional association, the naam, has been the basis of education about agricultural techniques and new crops that can stimulate production. One problem during drought has been the need to assure that available foods are priced low enough for ordinary people and yet are not bought up by rich merchants.

FREEDOM

There is a strong tradition of respect for individual rights in Burkina Faso. Under Sankara, people were able to organize meetings and to speak out critically. Journalists report arrests and police torture of former officials and politicians since the Compaore coup.

HEALTH/WELFARE

Burkina Faso has an integrated, country-wide health plan, which includes health education, improvement of water supplies, and immunization. All citizens are now being vaccinated against measles, polio, whooping cough, tetanus, and tuberculosis as part of the immunization program.

ACHIEVEMENTS

The biannual Pan-African Film Festival is held in Ouagadougou. This festival has contributed significantly to the development of the film industry in Africa. Burkina Faso has nationalized its movie houses, and the government has encouraged the showing of films by African filmmakers.

Cape Verde (Republic of Cape Verde)

GEOGRAPHY

Area in Square Kilometers (Miles):
4,033 (1,557) (a bit larger than Rhode Island)
Capital (Population): Praia (40,000)
Climate: temperate

PEOPLE

Population
Total: 350,000
Annual Growth Rate: 1.4%
Rural/Urban Population Ratio: 74/26
Languages: official: Portuguese; others spoken: Kriolu, others

Health
Life Expectancy at Birth: 60 years male; 64 years female
Infant Death Rate (Ratio): 89/1,000
Average Caloric Intake: 133% of FAO minimum
Physicians Available (Ratio): 1/6,862

Religion(s)
80% Catholic; 20% traditional indigenous

Education
Adult Literacy Rate: 37%

CAPE VERDEANS IN THE UNITED STATES

Large-scale immigration of Cape Verdeans to the United States began in the nineteenth century. Today the Cape Verdean-American community is larger than the population of Cape Verde itself; it is concentrated in southern New England. Most early immigrants arrived in the region aboard whaling and packet ships. The 1980 United States census was the first to try to count Cape Verdeans as a separate ethnic group.

The community has, on the whole, prospered, and is currently better educated than the U.S. national norm. Cape Verdeans in the United States maintain close ties with their homeland, assisting in local development projects. Evidence of these ties is the recent addition of Cape Verde Airlines—Cape Verde to Boston, Massachusetts route.

COMMUNICATION

Telephones: 1,739
Newspapers: 7 weeklies

TRANSPORTATION

Highways—Kilometers (Miles): 2,250 (1,395)
Railroads—Kilometers (Miles): none
Commercial Airports: 1 international

GOVERNMENT

Type: republic
Independence Date: July 5, 1975
Head of State: President Aristides Maria Pereira; Prime Minister (General) Pedro Verona Rodrigues Pires
Political Parties: African Party for the Independence of Cape Verde
Suffrage: universal over 18

MILITARY

Number of Armed Forces: 1,000
Military Expenditures (% of Central Government Expenditures): n/a
Current Hostilities: none

ECONOMY

Currency ($ U.S. Equivalent): 73 escudos = $1
Per Capita Income/GNP: $350/$121 million
Inflation Rate: 12%
Natural Resources: fish; agricultural land; salt desposits
Agriculture: corn; beans; manioc; sweet potatoes; bananas
Industry: fishing; flour mills; salt

FOREIGN TRADE

Exports: $2 million
Imports: $68 million

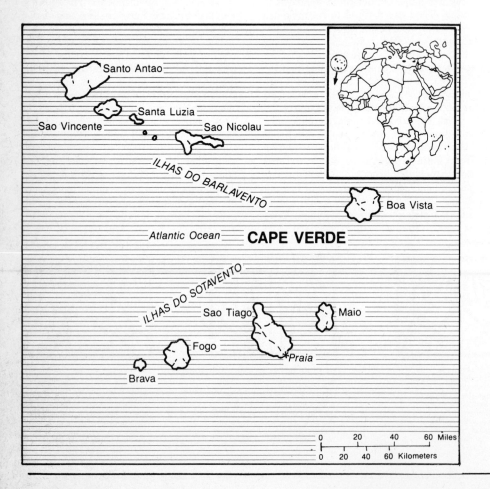

24

| Cape Verdean settlement begins 1462 | Slavery is abolished 1869 | Thousands of Cape Verdeans die of starvation during World War II 1940s | The PAIGC is founded 1956 | Warfare begins in Guinea-Bissau; Amilcar Cabral is assassinated 1973 | A coup in Lisbon initiates the Portuguese decolonization process 1974 | Independence 1975 | 1980s |

| Pereira visits the UN and the United States | Pereira is reelected to a third 5-year term by Parliament | Cape Verde signs cultural and technical accords with Morocco and Mauritania |

THE REPUBLIC OF CAPE VERDE

The Republic of Cape Verde is an archipelago located about 400 miles west of the Senegalese Cape Verde, or "Green Cape," after which it is named. Unfortunately, green is a color that today is all too rarely seen by the islands' citizens, who for 2 decades have suffered from drought. As a result, the young republic—independent since 1975—has had to rely on foreign aid and remittances from Cape Verdeans living abroad for its survival. Despite this desperate situation, most Cape Verdeans are proud to finally be their own masters after nearly 500 years of Portuguese colonial rule.

Most Cape Verdeans are the descendants of Portuguese colonists (who were often convicts) and African slaves. Both groups began to settle on the islands during the mid-fifteenth century, and their early interaction led to the development of the Cape Verdean Kriolu language. This language today serves as a common language not only in Cape Verde but in Guinea-Bissau as well. Under Portuguese rule, Cape Verdeans were generally treated as second-class citizens, although a few rose to positions of prominence. Economic stagnation, exacerbated by cycles of severe drought, drove many islanders to emigrate elsewhere in Africa, Western Europe, and the Americas. The largest of these overseas Cape Verdean communities today can be found in the United States.

LIBERATION STRUGGLE

In 1956 the African Party for the Independence of Guinea-Bissau and Cape Verde (PAIGC) was formed under the dynamic leadership of Amilcar Cabral, who was assassinated in 1973. Between 1963 and 1974 PAIGC organized a successful liberation struggle against the Portuguese in Guinea-Bissau, which was ultimately instrumental in bringing about the independence of both territories. For a period in the late 1970s Cape Verde and Guinea-Bissau were ruled separately by a united PAIGC, but after a 1980 coup in Guinea-Bissau, the party divided along national lines. In 1981 the Cape Verdean PAIGC formally renounced its Guinea links and became the PAICV.

The greatest challenge for the PAIGC/CV since independence has been coping with the effects of the drought. Lack of rainfall in the past has occasionally resulted in the deaths of up to 50 percent of the islands' population. Although the availability of international food aid—which accounts for about 90 percent of the caloric consumption—has warded off famine in recent years, malnutrition remains a serious problem. The government has undertaken a number of initiatives in order to strengthen local food production as well as to create employment opportunities for the nearly 80 percent of the workforce who are agrarian. These steps include drilling for underground water, terracing, irrigating, and building a wa-

ter-desalinization plant with United States assistance. Along with other Sahelian leaders, President Aristides Pereira has called for stronger efforts to control the spread of the Sahara and to foster self-sufficiency in food. Nevertheless, the islands are likely to remain dependent on imported food for the foreseeable future.

LITTLE INDUSTRY

Although a few factories have been built recently, there are few industries and virtually no known exploitable mineral reserves on the islands. Exports pay for a very small percentage of the nation's imports. Trade deficits are partially offset, however, by the external earnings of the local service sector—most particularly the international airport on Sal Island, which conducts lucrative business with South African Airways and provides 50 percent of Cape Verde's foreign exchange. Because of this dependence, President Pereira reiterated in 1988 his country's inability to participate in economic sanctions against South Africa. It appears that Cape Verde's overall economic picture is likely to remain bleak for quite some time.

DEVELOPMENT

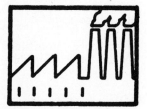

Since independence, the greatest progress has taken place in social services, particularly education. Approximately 95 percent of primary school-age children attend school.

FREEDOM

Dissent is limited, but tolerated, in Cape Verde's one-party system. Government decision makers are answerable to elected bodies.

HEALTH/WELFARE

Greater access to health facilities has resulted in a sharp drop in infant mortality and a rise in life expectancy. Clinics have begun to encourage family planning.

ACHIEVEMENTS

Cape Verdean culture is renowned for its artistic creativity, particularly in music and poetry. Popular Cape Verdean music groups, such as Balinundo, have enjoyed an increasing international audience.

Côte d'Ivoire (Republic of Côte d'Ivoire)

GEOGRAPHY

Area in Square Kilometers (Miles):
323,750 (124,503) (slightly larger than New Mexico)
Capital (Population): Abidjan (economic) (1,686,100); Yamoussoukro (political) (n/a)
Climate: tropical

PEOPLE

Population
Total: 10,545,000
Annual Growth Rate: 5%
Rural/Urban Population Ratio: 58/42
Languages: official: French; others spoken: Dioula, Agni, Baoulé, Kru, Senufo, Mandinka, others

Health
Life Expectancy at Birth: 47 years male; 50 years female
Infant Death Rate (Ratio): 93/1,000
Average Caloric Intake: 112% of FAO minimum
Physicians Available (Ratio): 1/24,696

THE ARTS OF CÔTE d'IVOIRE

The arts of Côte d'Ivoire, including music, weaving, dance, and sculpture, have flourished. The wood carvings of the Senufo, Dan, and Baoulé peoples are famous the world over for their beauty and intricate design. Masks are particularly valued and admired by outsiders, but many collectors have never met the Ivoirian people for whom the art has social and religious significance. The Dan mask, for example, is not only beautiful—it also performs a spiritual function. When worn as part of a masquerade performance, it represents religious authority, settling of disputes, enforcing the laws of the community, and respect for tradition.

Religion(s)
66% traditional indigenous; 22% Muslim; 12% Christian

Education
Adult Literacy Rate: 41%

COMMUNICATION

Telephones: 87,700
Newspapers: 3

TRANSPORTATION

Highways—Kilometers (Miles): 53,736 (33,316)
Railroads—Kilometers (Miles): 657 (408)
Commercial Airports: 1 international

GOVERNMENT

Type: republic
Independence Date: August 7, 1960
Head of State: President Félix Houphouët-Boigny
Political Parties: Democratic Party of Côte d'Ivoire
Suffrage: universal over 21

MILITARY

Number of Armed Forces: 7,140
Military Expenditures (% of Central Government Expenditures): n/a
Current Hostilities: none

ECONOMY

Currency ($ U.S. Equivalent): 286 CFA francs = $1
Per Capita Income/GNP: $1,100/$6 billion
Inflation Rate: 4.3%
Natural Resources: agricultural lands; timber
Agriculture: coffee; cocoa; bananas; pineapples; palm oil; corn; millet; cotton; rubber
Industry: food and lumber processing; oil refinery; textiles; soap; automobile assembly

FOREIGN TRADE

Exports: $1.7 billion
Imports: $2.9 billion

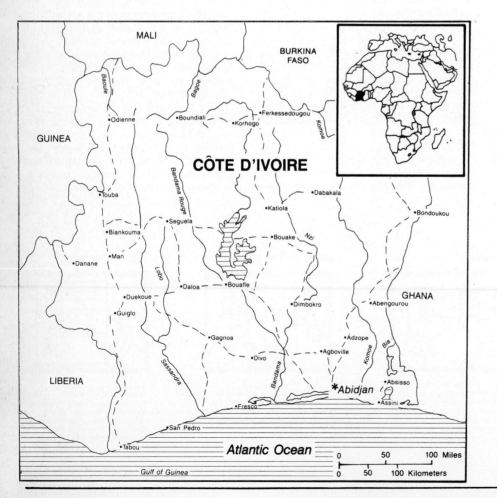

CÔTE d'IVOIRE

Côte d'Ivoire is one of the most productive countries in West Africa. From 1960 to 1970 Côte d'Ivoire had one of the highest growth rates in sub-Saharan Africa. Statistics indicate that Ivoirians have a longer, healthier life than the residents of many other countries of the region. The average per capita income is higher than that of Côte d'Ivoire's interior neighbors (but much less than in the early 1980s). Côte d'Ivoire is a country of great diversity, and it has a capitalist economy, but its prosperity is not shared equally by its people. Moreover, recent conditions have led to a slowdown in economic progress.

PROSPERITY FOR WHOM?

The large European (primarily French) expatriate community is thousands strong. Many are quasi-permanent residents, managing plantations on which they have long leases. They are also advisors to Cabinet ministers and manage many sectors of the economy. Their salaries are well above the average figure.

The Ivoirian planter class is extremely large. These farmers grow cocoa, coffee, and sometimes bananas and pineapples as well as other cash crops for export. Côte d'Ivoire is the world's largest producer of cocoa and the third largest producer of coffee. Coffee is one of the principal sources of income for the 2.5 million Ivoirians who farm and provide services for the industry. Some of the Ivoirian farmers are wealthy. Prices for cash crops like coffee and cocoa have fluctuated on the world market in recent years, causing overproduction when prices rise, resulting in low income later. As prices declined in 1988, President Houphouët-Boigny held cocoa in storage to force prices to rise. Moreover, the *caisse de stabilization*, or marketing board, through which farmers must sell their harvest, pays lower prices for these crops than farmers might receive on their own. The government is encouraging farmers to replace cocoa with food crops such as yams, corn, and plantain, for which there is a broad West African as well as Ivoirian market. However, the cash crops still provide most of the foreign exchange.

Ivoirian planters often hire low-paid laborers who come from other West African countries. The average per capita income does not necessarily apply to them. There are about 2 million migrant laborers in Côte d'Ivoire, employed in many sectors of the economy. Their employment is not a new phenomenon but goes back to colonial times. Burkina Faso, where many laborers come from, was actually a part of Côte d'Ivoire at one time. Other areas were also associated with Côte d'Ivoire because the French colonialists established an administration over all of their West African territories. The countries from which the laborers come need the foreign exchange that is gained from the wages that laborers send home. A good road system and the Ivoirian railroad, which extends as far as Ouagadougou in Burkina Faso, help migrant workers and Ivoirians to travel to Abidjan and other cities, as well as to the cash-crop areas.

Other factors may determine how much an Ivoirian benefits from the country's development. Residents of Abidjan, the capital, and its environs near the coast receive more services than the citizens of interior areas. Professionals in the cities make better salaries than laborers on farms or in small industries. Yet inflation and world recession have made daily life difficult for the middle class as well as for peasants and workers. In 1983 teachers went on strike to protest the discontinuance of their housing subsidies. The government refused to yield and banned

(United Nations photo)

The prosperity of the Ivoirian economy is not shared equally by all the people.

Agni and Baoulé peoples migrate to Ivory Coast from the East **1700s**	Ivory Coast officially becomes a French colony **1893**	Samori Touré, a Malinke Muslim leader and empire builder, is defeated by the French **1898**	The final French pacification of the country **1915**	Ivory Coast becomes independent under Felix Houphouët-Boigny's leadership **1960**

1980s

The PDCI approves a plan to move the capital from Abidjan to Yamoussoukro, the president's birthplace	The country's name is officially changed from Ivory Coast to Côte d'Ivoire	Côte d'Ivoire renews diplomatic ties with Israel and the Soviet Union

the teacher's union; the teachers went back to work. The ban has been lifted, but the causes of discontent remain, for no teacher can afford the high rents in the cities. Moreover, teachers deeply resent the fact that other civil servants, ministers, and French *cooperants* (helpers on the Peace Corps model) did not have their subsidies cut back, and they demand a more even "distribution of sacrifices." And in 1987 teachers' leaders were detained by the government.

Conditions are likely to become more difficult for Ivoirians before they become better. State industries have been making low profits, and they are being cut back if they are in debt. Serious brush fires, mismanagement in the timber industry, and the clearing of forests for cash-crop plantations have all endangered one of the rich natural resources of the country. Plans for expansion of oil production have not been implemented, because the billions of dollars needed for investment have not been raised. Côte d'Ivoire has heavy debts to international banks and has been forced to borrow to pay interest on these debts. After Côte d'Ivoire requested rescheduling of some debts, Canada forgave millions of dollars in debt in 1987. The debt situation has led to austerity measures that affect all citizens, but long-term prospects for the economy are good, because of increased and diversified agricultural production.

POLITICAL STABILITY

The government of Côte d'Ivoire has changed little in the years since indepen-dence in 1960. Felix Houphouët-Boigny, now in his 80s, was the leader of the independence struggle and the founder of the Democratic Party of the Côte d'Ivoire (PDCI), the only legal party. Houphouët-Boigny developed a system of councils, committees, and advisors through which he governs. He is a consummate politician who has portrayed himself as the nation's grandfather and the citizens as his brothers, sons, and grandchildren. He prevented ethnic tension by incorporating representatives of most ethnic groups in his Cabinet. He brought dissenters over to his side by persuasive discussion (and perhaps through using financial incentives as well). It is a matter of concern to many Ivoirians that Houphouët-Boigny has kept such a tight hold on power and has not indicated a successor, although a constitutional amendment now provides for an interim leader after the death or resignation of the head of state.

Houphouët-Boigny's skills have not been able to prevent disturbances. Students as well as teachers have demonstrated against the government. In 1982 students demonstrated over the cancellation of a lecture to be given at the university by one of the president's critics, as well as over larger issues of political freedom and the slowness of Ivoirianization. Then, as in the teachers' strike, the government responded quickly, broke the strike, and banned political activity at the university. The problem was not solved.

Although Houphouët-Boigny has taken a conservative line in foreign policy, in recent years he has broadened his interna-tional connections. Hostile to Libya and receptive both to Israel and to dialogue with South Africa, Côte d'Ivoire remains one of France's best friends, receiving aid and military assistance and encouraging French investment in the country. In the late 1980s Côte d'Ivoire resumed diplomatic relations with the Soviet Union. President Houphouët-Boigny also broke a 15-year tradition by attending a meeting in Burkina Faso, and he spoke with Flight Lieutenant Jerry Rawlings of Ghana at the 1988 ECOWAS meeting.

TRADITIONAL STRENGTHS

A teacher in a school in Bouaké, a worker in a service industry in Abidjan, and a laborer on a cocoa farm in the south are examples of the many Ivoirians who have left their homes but who keep attachments to rural communities and return at holidays. Many different peoples live in Côte d'Ivoire, with different traditions, histories, and languages. These peoples and their rich cultures have become well known in other parts of the world, because of the tourist ventures encouraged by the Ivoirian government. It remains to be seen whether diverse cash-crop production, industry, and tourism will bring prosperity to this diverse population.

DEVELOPMENT

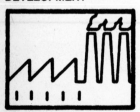

It has been said that Côte d'Ivoire is "power hungry." The Soubre Dam, being developed on the Sassandra River, is the sixth and largest hydroelectric project in Côte d'Ivoire. It will serve the eastern area of the country. Another dam is already planned on the Cavalla River between Côte d'Ivoire and Liberia.

FREEDOM

Houphouët-Boigny keeps a tight control over political processes. In 1980 elections were made more open and competitive at all levels, and this has led to changes of leadership locally as well as nationally. Amnesty International reports that the detention of teachers and trade unionists in 1987 was for political reasons.

HEALTH/WELFARE

Education absorbs about 40 percent of the Ivoirian budget, and experiments in television courses have been tried out for more than a decade in Côte d'Ivoire. Training of Ivoirians has drastically reduced the reliance on French technicians.

ACHIEVEMENTS

Côte d'Ivoire textiles are varied and prized. Block printing and the dyeing produce brilliant designs; woven cloths made strip by strip and sewn together include the white Korhogo tapestries, covered with Ivoirian figures, birds, and symbols drawn in black. Manufactured cloths often copy handmade prints.

The Gambia (Republic of The Gambia)

GEOGRAPHY

Area in Square Kilometers (Miles): 11,295 (4,361) (smaller than Connecticut)
Capital (Population): Banjul (49,200)
Climate: subtropical

PEOPLE

Population
Total: 699,000
Annual Growth Rate: 3.2%
Rural/Urban Population Ratio: 79/21
Languages: official: English; others spoken: Mandinka, Wolof, Fula, Sarakola, Diula, others

Health
Life Expectancy at Birth: 41 years male; 44 years female
Infant Death Rate (Ratio): 217/1,000
Average Caloric Intake: 97% of FAO minimum
Physicians Available (Ratio): 1/10,588

Religion(s)
85% Muslim; 14% Christian; 1% traditional indigenous

Education
Adult Literacy Rate: 12%

HALEY'S *ROOTS*

"Kambay Bolong" and "Kunte Kinte" were two of the unfamiliar terms that Alex Haley's grandmother repeated as she told him of their "furthest back" ancestor, the African. When Haley started the search for his roots, he consulted linguists as well as Africans about these words. "Kambay Bolong" was identified as the Gambia River and "Kinte" as one of the major Mandinka lineages or large families. Thus began Haley's association with The Gambia, which culminated in his visit to the town of Juffure in Gambia's interior. There Haley heard the history of the Kinte clan from a *griot*, or bard, and identified his past ancestor. Today many Americans and others who have read or heard of Haley's story are among the tourists who visit The Gambia.

COMMUNICATION

Telephones: 3,476
Newspapers: 6

TRANSPORTATION

Highways—Kilometers (Miles): 2,990 (1,853)
Railroads—Kilometers (Miles): none
Commercial Airports: 1 international

GOVERNMENT

Type: republic
Independence Date: February 18, 1965
Head of State: President (Sir) Alhaji Dawda Kairaba Jawara
Political Parties: Progressive People's Party; National Convention Party; Gambia People's Party
Suffrage: universal for adults

MILITARY

Number of Armed Forces: 550
Military Expenditures (% of Central Government Expenditures): n/a
Current Hostilities: internal conflicts

ECONOMY

Currency ($ U.S. Equivalent): 7.27 dalasis = $1
Per Capita Income/GNP: $275/$179 million
Inflation Rate: 22.1%
Natural Resources: fish; ilmenite; zircon; rutile
Agriculture: peanuts; rice; cotton; millet; sorghum; fish; palm kernels; livestock; rutile
Industry: peanuts; brewing; soft drinks; agricultural-machinery assembly; wood and metal working; clothing; tourism

FOREIGN TRADE

Exports: $32 million
Imports: $104 million

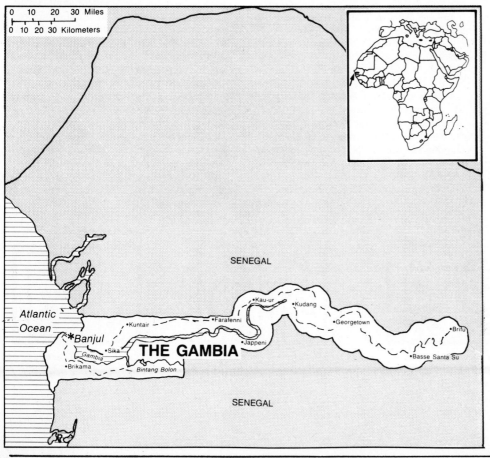

British build Fort
James at
current site of
Banjul on the
Gambia River
1618

The Gambia is
ruled by the
United Kingdom
through Sierra
Leone
1807

Independence
1965

1980s

Attempted coup
against the
government of
Jawara while he
is out of the
country

Jawara is
reelected
president

Treason trials of
government
opponents

THE GAMBIA

"The Gambia is a banana in the teeth of Senegal," goes an African saying, and some believe that Senegal is preparing to enjoy a good meal. An agreement establishing the confederation of Senegambia was signed in 1981, and the new alliance was inaugurated in 1982. A Cabinet of five Senegalese and four Gambians was instituted to administer the evolving confederation.

Senegalese and Gambians could benefit from such an arrangement. Mandinka, Wolof, and Fulani peoples make up a substantial percentage of both countries' populations, and these peoples commute regularly across the borders. They share Islamic beliefs and practices as well as economic patterns based on herding and agriculture, including the cultivation of groundnuts as a cash crop.

SENEGAMBIAN PROSPECTS

Yet the confederation has not been the result of popular feeling, and the two countries have different colonial traditions and are divided in their orientations today. In the seventeenth and eighteenth centuries British merchants on the Gambia River competed against the French in present-day Senegal, and the rivalry continued during the colonial period. The peoples were influenced by different types of administration and education, and they learned different European languages. In the 1870s the two colonial powers discussed exchanges of territory that would have made The Gambia a French territory, but no exchange occurred. In the years before and after independence the possibility of union was raised but never followed through.

The Gambians—whose state is one of the smallest in Africa—have been resistant to the confederation. There was no popular referendum on the union, and opposition members of Parliament walked out when the agreement was presented for a vote. It is not only that Gambians fear being swallowed up by Senegal, whose economic and monetary policies would not be to their advantage; many also believe the movement toward union was designed to keep President Dawda Jawara in power in The Gambia. The first public announcement about the confederacy followed on the heels of a coup attempt against Jawara's government in 1981, during which 400 to 500 persons were killed. A group of the Gambian Paramilitary Field Force attempted to set up a socialist state in the capital, Banjul, during Jawara's absence in England. Jawara called on Senegal for help, and President Abdul Diouf sent troops. Military integration of the two forces was the first step toward eventual union, and Senegalese troops remain in the country.

Jawara has been able to maintain his position. More than 1,000 people were jailed at the time of the coup, and trials resulted in some executions. Other Gambians went into exile. In the 1982 elections Jawara received 72 percent of the ballots cast. His opponent, Sheriff Dibba, who was in prison at the time and who opposed the confederation, received one-fourth of the vote. In 1986 opponents formed the Gambian People's Party (GPP) in preparation for the 1987 elections, which Jawara won. Treason trials in 1988 accused both Gambians and Senegalese of training in Libya to overthrow the government, from 1984 to 1988.

ECONOMIC DIFFICULTIES

Economic and social conditions cause Gambians to question their government even further. Uneven harvests of groundnuts, the major cash crop, have had adverse effects on farmers, with prices lower than ever before. The tourist trade from the United States and Scandinavian countries was once a major source of foreign exchange, but economic conditions in Europe and the coup in The Gambia cut the number of tourists. The continuing effects of drought have caused crowded grazing conditions as well as food scarcity and have increased the migration of young people to Banjul.

The government hopes to alleviate the economic problems facing Gambians by emphasizing rural development, encouraging rice and cotton production, and expanding tourist facilities. Structural adjustment programs, including the removal of subsidies and privatization, may create hardships for ordinary Gambians. Yet it is hoped that the development of a bridge and dam on the Gambia River and the irrigation programs planned through AMVG—the Gambia River Organization, consisting of Senegal, The Gambia, Mali, and Guinea—may make life better for Gambians and also reconcile them to a future within Senegambia.

DEVELOPMENT

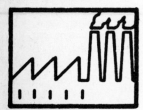

Groundnuts were Gambia's main economic support at the time of independence. The harvests have been reduced one-third during recent dry seasons. Now there are efforts to modernize groundnut production and to develop alternate cash crops such as cotton and rice.

FREEDOM

Although the death sentences of coup plotters were commuted and the state of emergency lifted, new treason laws make conviction much easier. Plots to overthrow the government can be prosecuted with only a single witness.

HEALTH/WELFARE

The Community and Rural Development Training Center at Mansakonko provides a 2-year course with field work for community-development workers, who are then stationed in villages.

ACHIEVEMENTS

Gambian *griots*—hereditary bards and musicians such as Banna and Dembo Kanute—have maintained a traditional art. Formerly, griots were attached to ruling families; now they perform over Radio Gambia and are popular throughout West Africa.

Ghana (Republic of Ghana)

GEOGRAPHY

Area in Square Kilometers (Miles):
238,538 (92,100) (slightly smaller than Oregon)
Capital (Population): Accra (965,000)
Climate: tropical to semiarid

PEOPLE

Population
Total: 13,552,000
Annual Growth Rate: 3.1%
Rural/Urban Population Ratio: 63/37
Languages: official: English; others spoken: Akan (including Fanti, Asante, Twi), Ewe, Ga, Hausa, others

Health
Life Expectancy at Birth: 50 years male; 54 years female
Infant Death Rate (Ratio): 98/1,000
Average Caloric Intake: 85% of FAO minimum
Physicians Available (Ratio): 1/9,422

Religion(s)
45% traditional indigenous; 43% Christian; 12% Muslim

Education
Adult Literacy Rate: 30%

COMMUNICATION

Telephones: 72,000
Newspapers: 3

NKRUMAH

Kwame Nkrumah is a name that is remembered by peoples all over the world. Nkrumah developed ideas and institutions for peacefully but actively resisting British domination of Ghana, and he founded the Convention People's Party (CCP), which involved peoples of all walks of life in that struggle. Nkrumah believed that none of Africa was free until all of Africa was free. His efforts to develop a united Africa and his exploration of and warnings about neo-colonialism in Africa remain influential. Although his government was overthrown by a military coup, later regimes that criticized him nevertheless recognized his greatness and importance.

TRANSPORTATION

Highways—Kilometers (Miles):
32,200 (20,009)
Railroads—Kilometers (Miles): 953 (592)
Commercial Airports: 2 international

GOVERNMENT

Type: military; governed by Provisional National Defense Council
Independence Date: March 6, 1957
Head of State: Flight Lieutenant Jerry Rawlings (chairman of Provisional National Defense Council)
Political Parties: banned after 1981 coup
Suffrage: universal over 18

MILITARY

Number of Armed Forces: 11,000
Military Expenditures (% of Central Government Expenditures): n/a
Current Hostilities: internal conflicts

ECONOMY

Currency ($ U.S. Equivalent): 183 cedis = $1
Per Capita Income/GNP: $390/$4.7 billion
Inflation Rate: 43.6%
Natural Resources: gold; diamonds; bauxite; manganese; fish; timber; oil
Agriculture: cocoa; coconuts; coffee; subsistence crops; rubber
Industry: mining, lumber; light manufacturing; fishing; aluminum

FOREIGN TRADE

Exports: $617 million
Imports: $731 million

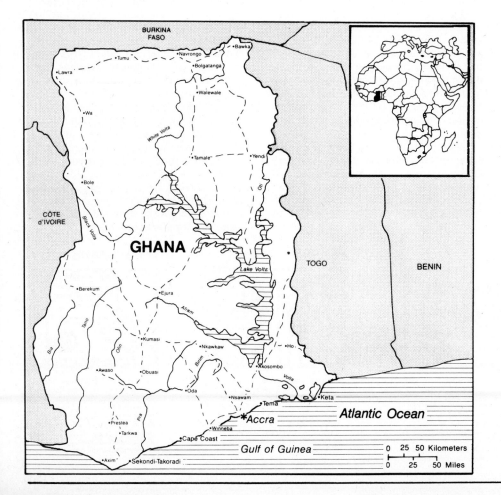

Portuguese fort is built at Elmina 1482	Establishment of the Asante Confederation under Osei Tutu 1690s	The "Bonds" of 1844 signed by British officials and Fante chiefs as equals 1844	British finally conquer the Asante; a final step in British control of the region 1901	Ghana is the first of the colonial territories in sub-Saharan Africa to become independent 1957	Nkrumah is overthrown by a military coup 1966	First coup of Flight Lieutenant Rawlings 1979

1980s

GHANA'S POLITICAL HERITAGE

Ghana became independent in 1957 and was a leader in the continental struggle for independence. People were optimistic about the country's future. In hindsight, it seems that Ghana went backward instead of forward.

Many explanations have been given for the backward turn. There were no consistent government policies to meet the country's needs. During President Kwame Nkrumah's time, political controls increased the power of the government but did not lead to economic development or the fulfillment of socialist aims. Corruption increased. Mismanagement, limited technical resources, and lack of skilled personnel were responsible for some failures. The decline in the price of Ghana's major export, cocoa, and the rise in the costs of imports contributed to worsening conditions. In 1966 Nkrumah was overthrown by a group of military officers, followed by successive civilian and military governments.

A PEOPLE'S REVOLUTION?

Not long after the December 31, 1981 coup that brought him to power in Ghana for the second time in 3 years, Flight Lieutenant Jerry Rawlings said, "What we would like to do is to set up conditions to make sure that the people will not be taken for granted anymore." People must, he continued, "take their destiny into their own hands."

Right after the coup and the establishment of the Provisional National Defense Council (PNDC) of civilians and soldiers, People's Defense Committees, made up of ordinary citizens, began to operate throughout the country as watchdogs and overseers. Students marshalled forces in a volunteer emergency effort to move 100,000 tons of cocoa from interior farms to the ports. People's Courts were formed later in 1982, and laymen acted as judges. New district assemblies were formed in 1988 amid plans for elections to those bodies later that year.

After a slow start, the government made steady economic gains. It moved slowly in dealing with the economic problems that brought the military to power. In the early 1980s food costs doubled and tripled, Ghana had almost no foreign exchange, and the PNDC banned all imports, including the fertilizer needed to nourish the country's "Green Revolution." Nearly a million Ghanaians expelled from Nigeria strained the country's food resources and expanded the number of the unemployed.

A campaign to encourage agricultural production led to increased cultivation, with special efforts to address the loss of cocoa revenue and to develop forestry preservation. Successive devaluations of the cedi and austerity measures approved by the World Bank and the International Monetary Fund (IMF) led to Western aid—as well as criticism from some leftists.

Under IMF pressure, commodity subsidies were reduced, with ordinary Ghanaians bearing the burden of the austerity measures. After an international conference on the social costs of IMF reforms, Ghana has concentrated on assisting citizens. The World Bank provides

Second coup by Rawlings; PNDC is formed	Ghana is accused of supporting an invasion of Togo	Rawlings accepts World Bank and IMF austerity measures

credit for small-scale enterprise; food aid supports gold miners in order to stabilize the workforce and increase gold production. By 1988 these efforts had increased production and reduced Ghana's foreign debt.

GHANA'S STRENGTHS

Ghana has many strengths on which to build. The Ghanaians themselves are the country's most important resource. They belong to nearly 75 different ethnic groups.

Traditional leaders have maintained their positions and influence, if not their power, in Ghana. They and the citizens around them are proud of the historically important state systems that they inherited, such as the Asante Confederation that was centered around the interior city of Kumasi. Modern Ghanaian governments cannot interfere with a chief's jurisdiction in traditional matters. As Rawlings himself has said, "the chief is the embodiment of his people."

Under Rawlings, Ghana takes an anti-imperialist stance in its foreign policy. Ghana has good relations with Libya and close ties with its neighbor Burkina Faso. Conversely, there has been tension with more conservative governments, such as that of Côte d'Ivoire. In 1986 Togo accused Rawlings of supporting an invasion of that country. The year 1988, however, brought efforts at reconciliation.

DEVELOPMENT

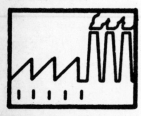

To reduce dependence on oil imports, Ghana aims to expand the use of solar energy for telecommunications and for water pumps and irrigation projects.

FREEDOM

Curfews, closed borders, pressure on the press, and courts that do not allow for appeal are measures imposed by the government. Executions take place. Students, union leaders, and others protested these restrictions, but many were imprisoned or exiled. Authorities closed universities in 1987 and 1988.

HEALTH/WELFARE

To lessen the austerity measures and to counteract years of decline, Ghana plans to support food programs for workers, give credit to small-scale farmers and market sellers, promote self-help projects, and finance water supply, sanitation, health care, and housing.

ACHIEVEMENTS

In 1988 Ghana celebrated the 25th anniversary of the School of the Performing Arts at the University of Legon. Integrating the world of dance, drama, and music, the school has trained a generation of artists committed to Ghanaian, African, and international traditions in the arts.

Guinea (Republic of Guinea)

GEOGRAPHY

Area in Square Kilometers (Miles):
246,048 (95,000) (slightly larger than
Oregon)
Capital (Population): Conakry
(705,000)
Climate: tropical

PEOPLE

Population
Total: 6,339,000
Annual Growth Rate: 2.8%
Rural/Urban Population Ratio: 75/25
Languages: official: French; others
spoken: Fula, Mandinka, Susu,
Malinke, others

Health
Life Expectancy at Birth: 39 years
male; 42 years female
Infant Death Rate (Ratio): 159/1,000
Average Caloric Intake: 78% of FAO
minimum
Physicians Available (Ratio): 1/22,884

Religion(s)
85% Muslim; 10% Christian; 5%
indigenous

Education
Adult Literacy Rate: 35%

COMMUNICATION

Telephones: 10,000
Newspapers: 1

SAMORI TOURÉ

In the late nineteenth century Malinke leader Samori Touré established a
powerful state in the interior of Guinea and Côte d'Ivoire. Samori,
called "the Napoleon of the Sudan," was a Muslim, and he converted
many of the areas that he conquered, but he was not a jihadist. His state
was based on modern military organization and tactics; this enabled him
to resist the European conquest longer and more effectively than any
other West African leader. Through alliances, sieges, control of arms
trade, and, ultimately, manufacture of guns and ammunition, Samori
fought the French and resisted conquest throughout the 1890s. Manipulating African competition and people's fear of Samori, the French allied
with African leaders and prevented a unified resistance to their rule.

TRANSPORTATION

Highways—Kilometers (Miles):
28,400 (13,608)
Railroads—Kilometers (Miles): 940
(582)
Commercial Airports: 2 international

GOVERNMENT

Type: republic, under military regime
Independence Date: October 2, 1958
Head of State: President (General)
Lansana Conté
Political Parties: none
Suffrage: universal over 18

MILITARY

Number of Armed Forces: 9,900
*Military Expenditures (% of Central
Government Expenditures):* n/a
Current Hostilities: none

ECONOMY

Currency ($ U.S. Equivalent): 440
francs = $1
Per Capita Income/GNP: $305/$1.9
billion
Inflation Rate: 5.6%
Natural Resources: bauxite; iron ore;
diamonds; gold; water power
Agriculture: rice; cassava; millet;
corn; coffee; bananas; palm products;
pineapples
Industry: bauxite; alumina; light
manufacturing and processing

FOREIGN TRADE

Exports: $537 million
Imports: $403 million

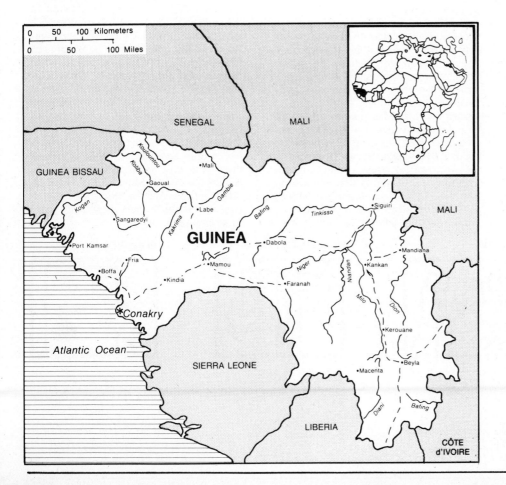

33

A major Islamic kingdom is established in the Futa Djalon
1700s

Samori Touré, the leader of a state in the Guinea and Ivory Coast interior, is defeated by the French
1898

Led by Sekou Touré, Guineans reject continued membership in the French Community; an independent republic is formed
1958

French President d'Estaing visits Guinea; the beginning of a reconciliation between France and Guinea
1978

1980s

The death of Sekou Touré is followed by a military coup

The World Court finds in favor of Guinea in a dispute with Guinea-Bissau over offshore oil reserves

Rioters in Conakry protest rising prices

GUINEA

Nineteen eighty-eight marked the 30th anniversary of Guinea's independence from France, the colonial power that established dominance over the area and people in the late nineteenth century and determined their government for 60 years. In a 1958 referendum, Guineans voted to leave the community of self-governing West African states, which France had established. They were the only people in the community to opt for freedom. The French reacted harshly, withdrawing all aid, personnel, and equipment—even removing telephones and geranium plants. This event had a major influence on the contemporary history of this formerly socialist one-party state. Guinea was isolated from Western countries, which did not come to its aid, and close ties were developed with countries of the Eastern bloc.

SEKOU TOURÉ AND HIS SUCCESSORS

The 1980s also marked the end of an era, with the sudden death of President Ahmed Sekou Touré in 1984. It was Touré who urged people to vote for independence in 1958 and who was reelected to the presidency in 1982 by an overwhelming majority. Touré was descended from Samori Touré, the revolutionary Malinke warrior.

On April 3, 1984, a week after President Touré's death, the army stepped in, fearing a power struggle among his successors. The coup was accomplished without a shot and was well received by Guineans. The powerful Democratic Party of Guinea was disbanded, a new government was formed under the leadership of Colonel Lansana Conté, and a 10-point program for national recovery was set forth, including the restoration of human rights and the renovation of the economy.

Over the years Sekou Touré jailed all those whom he perceived as opponents to his rule and philosophy. Guinean exiles in France and other places as well as a 1982 Amnesty International campaign publicized human-rights violations in Guinea.

The new government of President Lansana Conté freed all political prisoners. Two months after releasing former officials from custody in 1985, the Conté government itself faced a coup attempt, led by Colonel Diara Traoré, whose position as prime minister had been abolished in December 1984. The coup involved some of those recently released, and 20 plotters were executed. In 1987 the government announced that nearly 60 people, including 9 former ministers and 30 military officers, had been sentenced to death. Amnesty International notes that these people were actually killed after the 1985 coup attempt. Sentenced to prison terms were 133 others; 140 people were acquitted.

For 2 decades Guinea maintained its socialist ideology despite the lack of progress in the economy. In the late 1970s popular resistance included demonstrations by women's groups—usually Touré's strong supporters—over the scarcity of necessary commodities. Touré himself, in his last few years, began to modify socialist policies and seek new friends abroad. He encouraged private traders within the country. He sought ties with countries of the Arab world, stressing the unity that they shared in Islam. A renewed association with France was highlighted by the visit of President Giscard d'Estaing to Guinea in 1978 and by the later contacts between Touré and his personal friend, socialist French President François Mitterand. Conté has continued Toure's efforts to improve relations with neighboring countries such as Mali, Sierra Leone, Liberia, and Côte d'Ivoire. It seems certain that Guinea's longstanding commitment to African unity will not change.

The new government, faced with an empty treasury, is dismantling the socialist economy, encouraging private enterprise, and seeking help from abroad. Public corporations have been disbanded and private traders encouraged. Acceptance of International Monetary Fund reforms in 1987 and 1988 meant the devaluation of the currency, reduction of civil-service jobs, and removal of food and fuel subsidies. While the World Bank praised these reforms, trebled food prices led to campus and urban riots in 1988. This challenge to Conté's rule and discontent among the military led Conté to postpone some price increases and to reshuffle his Cabinet.

Conté's government has maintained a low profile and indicates that it intends that its role will be a transitional one. The leaders have declared that they will stay in office until the evils of "racism, regionalism, sectarianism, and nepotism" have been abolished.

DEVELOPMENT

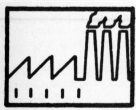

Guinea has a wide variety of minerals, and mining has been described as the "linchpin" of its economy. Foreign-capital investment has been encouraged for the exploitation of the 1.8 billion tons of iron ore found in the interior Nimba Mountain range. The mine will supplement the bauxite and alumina mines and plants that provide the bulk of Guinea's exports.

FREEDOM

The Conté government released all political prisoners in 1984, after the detention and disappearance of 2,900 people during the Touré years. Touré officials and associates were released from custody in 1985, and some were later executed for their part in a failed coup. Touré supporters were sentenced to death or to prison in a 1987 trial.

HEALTH/WELFARE

With foreign aid, hospitals in Conakry were refurbished, a rural primary-school project funded, and roads improved.

ACHIEVEMENTS

The sensitive and poetic writings of novelist Camara Laye (1924–1983) have introduced many African, European, and American readers to African ways of life and beliefs. The autobiographical The African Child illustrates the varied experiences faced by students in Africa in contemporary times.

Guinea-Bissau (Republic of Guinea-Bissau)

GEOGRAPHY

Area in Square Kilometers (Miles):
36,125 (13,948) (about the size of Indiana)
Capital (Population): Bissau (110,000)
Climate: tropical

PEOPLE

Population
Total: 935,000
Annual Growth Rate: 2.2%
Rural/Urban Population Ratio: n/a
Languages: official: Portuguese; others spoken: Kriolo, Fula, Mandinka, Manjara, Balante, others

Health
Life Expectancy at Birth: 42 years
Infant Death Rate (Ratio): 137/1,000
Average Caloric Intake: 74% of FAO minimum
Physicians Available (Ratio): 1/8,657

Religion(s)
65% traditional indigenous; 32% Muslim; 3% Christian

Education
Adult Literacy Rate: 15%

AMILCAR CABRAL

Amilcar Cabral (1924–1973), born in Cape Verde and raised in Guinea-Bissau, was an idealist who developed plans for his country's liberation and an activist who worked to put these plans into action. He was a friend of Agostinho Neto of Angola, a founding member of Angola's present ruling party MPLA, and he worked in Angola. Cabral worked for an African system of government, a change in structures that would mean "a reorganization of the country on new lines." He believed that a revolution could not result from leadership alone; everyone must fight a mental battle and know their goals before taking arms. Cabral's work with peasants from 1952 to 1954, while carrying out an agricultural census, helped him to understand and reach rural peoples who were to be the crucial force in the development of Guinea-Bissau's independence from Portugal.

COMMUNICATION

Telephones: 3,000
Newspapers: 1

TRANSPORTATION

Highways—Kilometers (Miles): 5,058 (3,135)
Railroads—Kilometers (Miles): none
Commercial Airports: 1 international

GOVERNMENT

Type: republic; overseen by Revolutionary Council
Independence Date: September 24, 1973
Head of State: President (Major) João Bernardo Vieira
Political Parties: African Party for the Independence of Guinea-Bissau and Cape Verde (PAIGC)
Suffrage: universal over 15

MILITARY

Number of Armed Forces: 7,125
Military Expenditures (% of Central Government Expenditures): n/a
Current Hostilities: none

ECONOMY

Currency ($ U.S. Equivalent): 650 pesos = $1
Per Capita Income/GNP: $165/$190 million
Inflation Rate: 30%
Natural Resources: bauxite; timber; shrimp; fish
Agriculture: peanuts; rice; palm kernels; groundnuts
Industry: agricultural processing; hides and skins; beer; soft drinks

FOREIGN TRADE

Exports: $9 million
Imports: $57 million

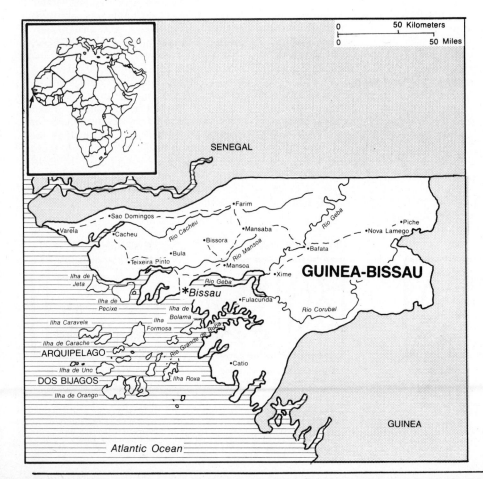

The Portuguese ships arrive; claimed as Portuguese Guinea; slave trading develops
1446

Portugal gains effective control over most of the region
1915

The African Party for the Independence of Guinea-Bissau and Cape Verde (PAIGC) is formed
1956

Liberation struggle in Guinea-Bissau under the leadership of the PAIGC and Amilcar Cabral
1963–1973

Cabral is assassinated; PAIGC declares Guinea-Bissau independent
1973

Revolution in Portugal leads to Portugal's recognition of Guinea-Bissau's independence and the end of war
1974

1980s

A coup in Guinea-Bissau brings Vieira to power and leads to separation of Cape Verde and Guinea-Bissau

Alleged coup plot, led by former Vice President Paulo Correia

Tensions with Portuguese over their fishing vessels in Guinea-Bissau waters

GUINEA-BISSAU

Guinea-Bissau, a small country with an archipelago of islands, is wedged between Senegal and Guinea on the west coast of Africa. It is best known for the liberation struggle waged by its people against the Portuguese colonial government in the years 1962 to 1974. This movement—similar to those in Angola and Mozambique but broader and deeper—was to become a model of resistance to colonialism that others around the world have followed.

Portuguese control of Guinea-Bissau reached back to the fifteenth century and was characterized first by the slave trade and later by policies of forced labor. Portugal claimed to offer equal rights to Africans who became assimilated to Western ways, but only 0.3% of the population could gain the education and other criteria necessary for "assimilado" status.

INDEPENDENCE MOVEMENT

In 1956 six such educated men, led by Amilcar Cabral, founded the African Party for the Independence of Guinea-Bissau and Cape Verde (PAIGC). The movement had many Cape Verdean leaders, but it developed its largest following and most numerous activities on the mainland. By 1963, when armed resistance began, villagers were committed to its ideas and participated in its decision making. By the late 1960s two-thirds of the territory of Guinea-Bissau was in the hands of the PAIGC.

The liberated communities, under the party's guidance, built new institutions—new administrations, people's stores, peo-

ple's courts, and schools, as well as new opportunities for women and new fighting forces. A National Assembly was elected in 1973. Portugal recognized Guinea-Bissau's independence in 1974.

CHALLENGES OF INDEPENDENCE

Since 1974 the leaders of Guinea-Bissau have tried to confront the problems of independence while maintaining the goals of the revolutionary movement. Their efforts have had limited success. The new government inherited a poor national economy, which had remained undeveloped during centuries of Portuguese domination and which was damaged during droughts in 1977 and 1980. There were massive imports of rice.

Guinea-Bissau has little manufacturing, and although explorations have revealed major sources of oil, bauxite, and phosphates, these minerals have not yet been exploited. The lack of roads and rails and a limited communications network challenged the PAIGC forces during the liberation struggle, and visitors were impressed with the way members of the PAIGC confronted these difficulties and went on to victory. Now the limited infrastructure must be built up.

Initially the democratic grass-roots system of government found in the liberated zones was the base for the new government institutions. Elections for a National Assembly were carried out in 1976. Difficulties increased the authoritarian nature of the government, and the former revolutionary zest waned. Frequent coup attempts since 1980 have marred political and economic progress.

MILITARY COUP AND A NEW CONSTITUTION

Amilcar Cabral, the charismatic leader of the PAIGC, was assassinated in 1973 and his brother, Luis Cabral, who became president of the new state, was overthrown in a military coup in 1980. João Vieira, military commander during the liberation war and later prime minister, took over and ruled without elected bodies. Relations between Cape Verde and Guinea-Bissau worsened during this time, and Cape Verde finally left the union.

Elections took place in 1984, and the new National Assembly was presided over by Carmen Periera, a well-known woman leader. A new Constitution was approved, and President Vieira was unanimously elected chairman of the Council of State.

In an effort to revive the economy and turn around a debt that took 90 percent of export earnings, in 1987 Guinea-Bissau imposed reforms in order to obtain World Bank and International Monetary Fund (IMF) assistance. They devalued the peso, dismissed civil servants, and in 1988 reduced fuel subsidies. The effects of these reforms on urban workers are to be cushioned with foreign aid, but the people of Guinea-Bissau will have to struggle for economic independence for some time to come.

DEVELOPMENT

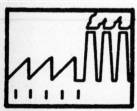

Two joint-venture fishing companies, the Soviet-Guinean Estrela do Mar and the Franco-Guinean SEMPESCA, have exploited Guinea-Bissau's rich fishing reserves, and local fishermen are supported by international funding. Fishing is a top priority, but production and consumption is still far behind that of other West African countries.

FREEDOM

PAIGC leadership controls all organizations as well as the government. PAIGC nominated one-third of the candidates for elections to regional councils. Vieira commuted the death sentences of 6 of 12 coup plotters. Forty-four others received jail terms; 5 of the accused died in police custody.

HEALTH/WELFARE

The development of schools and new texts was emphasized during the liberation struggle, but the illiteracy rate remains high. To accommodate demand for primary-school space, the International Development Association assisted in refurbishing 300 schools and training 3,000 teachers.

ACHIEVEMENTS

A major agricultural-industrial complex at Cumeré was completed in 1981 through the support of Saudi Arabia, Italy, and the Islamic Development Bank. Groundnuts and cereals produced by farmers or rural-development projects are processed by Cumeré.

Liberia (Republic of Liberia)

GEOGRAPHY

Area in Square Kilometers (Miles):
111,370 (43,000) (somewhat larger
than Pennsylvania)
Capital (Population): Monrovia
(425,000)
Climate: tropical

PEOPLE

Population
Total: 2,500,000
Annual Growth Rate: 3.3%
Rural/Urban Population Ratio: 60/40
Languages: official: English; others
spoken: Kpelle, Bassa, Dan, Vai,
Wee, Loma, Kru, Glebo, Mano,
Gola, Mandinka

Health
Life Expectancy at Birth: 54 years
Infant Death Rate (Ratio): 127/1,000
Average Caloric Intake: 114% of FAO
minimum
Physicians Available (Ratio): 1/10,593

Religion(s)
60% Christian; 25% traditional
indigenous; 15% Muslim

KRU MARINERS

For 400 years Kru-speaking peoples from the southeast of Liberia have
worked on European ships as sailors, navigators, and stevedores. They
have guided ships to shore, unloaded cargo, and provided food supplies
to passing traders. Many have sold goods from their canoes on their
return trips to the Liberian coast, while others have established Kru
communities in port cities such as Freetown, Accra, and Calabar. Their
trading activities, acquaintance with European culture, and mobility
enabled them to resist Liberian settler control throughout the nineteenth
century. In 1915 their revolt against the Liberian government ended when
United States troops bombarded the Kru Coast.

Education
Adult Literacy Rate: 35%

COMMUNICATION

Telephones: 8,510
Newspapers: 4

TRANSPORTATION

Highways—Kilometers (Miles): 7,732
(4,794)
Railroads—Kilometers (Miles): 226
(140)
Commercial Airports: 1 international

GOVERNMENT

Type: republic
Independence Date: July 26, 1847
Head of State: President Samuel
Kanyon Doe
Political Parties: National
Democratic Party of Liberia;
Liberian Action Party; Liberian
People's Party (banned); Liberian
Unification Party; Unity Party;
United People's Party
Suffrage: universal over 18

MILITARY

Number of Armed Forces: 5,990
*Military Expenditures (% of Central
Government Expenditures):* n/a
Current Hostilities: none

ECONOMY

Currency ($ U.S. Equivalent): 1
Liberian dollar = $1
Per Capita Income/GNP: $520/$990
million
Inflation Rate: 1.2%
Natural Resources: iro ore; rubber;
timber; diamonds
Agriculture: rubber; rice; palm oil;
cassava; coffee; cocoa; sugar
Industry: iron and diamond mining;
rubber processing; food processing;
lumber milling

FOREIGN TRADE

Exports: $424 million
Imports: $429 million

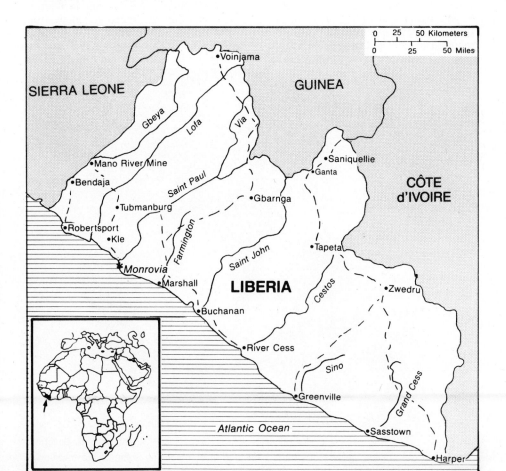

LIBERIA

"Cassava can only grow in the shade of its own leaves." The military coup that occurred in Liberia in 1980 is like the cassava that grows there. Just as the cassava's roots and branches cannot exist apart, so the origins of the coup lie deep in the society that it affects, and recent changes—even when dramatic—live in the shade of traditional life.

THE COUP AND ITS ORIGINS

In August 1980 Master Sergeant Samuel Kanyon Doe and a group of 17 noncommissioned officers and enlisted men entered the Executive Mansion and assassinated President William R. Tolbert, Jr. A ruling body, the People's Redemption Council (PRC), was formed of civilian and military ministers. It was a profound change.

For nearly a century and a half the independent country of Liberia had been governed by an elite primarily descended from one group of Liberia's inhabitants. The ruling group were descendants of black Americans and West Indians who returned to Africa under the auspices of the American Colonization Society. They made up a small percentage, perhaps 5 percent, of the Liberian population.

Most Liberians are descendants of peoples who came to Liberia from the interior several centuries ago. There are about 16 ethnic groups in Liberia, speaking languages as different as English is from Russian, and following different ways of life. Traditional village democracies and loose confederations resisted the dominance of the state, but Liberia won the struggles, often with the support of the United States Navy.

Gradually people from groups such as the Vai, the Kru, and the Kpelle gained important positions in the state by accepting the standards and practices of the elite. Yet Western education, Christian affiliation, and use of English helped a person to rise to power only if he or she accepted the status quo and developed a personal client relationship with an important Liberian. On the other hand, important chiefs could gain advantages from such relationships without taking on Western ways.

In the mid-twentieth century the system began to change as new forces such as Firestone rubber plantations (established in 1927), new iron-ore mines, and urbanization occurred. President William V. S. Tubman (1944–1971) proclaimed a Unification Policy and an Open-Door Policy to encourage national integration and outside private investors. The conditions of investment benefited outsiders, and most of the profits left the country. The wealth that remained went into the hands of the old

elite. Tubman's government controlled the change, and the "powers that be" were not weakened.

In the decade after Tubman's death, during William Tolbert's administration, Liberians became more conscious of the inequities of society and the ineffectiveness of government, as well as the possibilities for change. An increasing number of professionals and students educated in Liberia or abroad refused to join the ranks of the regime. New groups such as the Movement for African Justice (MOJA) and the Progressive Alliance of Liberia (PAL) criticized the government and organized for elections.

Meanwhile, economic conditions worsened. Only 4 percent of the population controlled 60 percent of the wealth, while ordinary people lived a modest—indeed, a spare—existence. The well-to-do secured large farms in the interior and many people moved to Monrovia in a search for jobs. Inflation affected everyone. In a country where "if you haven't eaten rice you haven't eaten," it was not surprising that the government decision to increase the price of rice by 50 percent led to riots in 1979. As many as 140 persons were killed, and hundreds were injured when police fired into the demonstrating crowds. Chaos and rioting resulted, and the government appealed to Guinea for troops. The feeling that the old regime must, and could, be changed grew during

the following months. When the coup occurred just a year later, it had widespread support.

MAJOR CHANGES

Liberian history books talk of the revolution of 1871, when one settler government lost power to another. Nothing else changed. The 1980 coup, however, did bring change. Many of the new military leaders have become rich, causing many Liberians to comment: "Same taxi, different driver." But this "car" may be a new model—even though, perhaps, a paste job. The soldiers who came to power were primarily people of northeastern Liberia, representative of traditional groups.

The new government ended some formerly dominant institutions. The True Whig Party, through which the elite kept their political dominance, no longer exists. The Masonic Temple was destroyed at the time of the coup. Government institutions such as the House and Senate were suspended. The hated hut tax was abolished, although it was later reinstituted. Offices have changed hands, but the old administrative system persisted in the countryside.

The military government promised to return Liberia to civilian rule in 1986. A new constitution, reflecting input from citizens, was approved in a countrywide referendum. This Constitution, like the old one, is based on the United States

(FAO photo by G. Tortoli)

Changes in the political system of Liberia have had little impact on some of the traditional methods of subsistence.

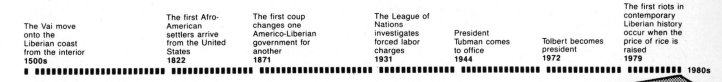

The Vai move onto the Liberian coast from the interior
1500s

The first Afro-American settlers arrive from the United States
1822

The first coup changes one Americo-Liberian government for another
1871

The League of Nations investigates forced labor charges
1931

President Tubman comes to office
1944

Tolbert becomes president
1972

The first riots in contemporary Liberian history occur when the price of rice is raised
1979

1980s

The assassination of Tolbert; a military coup brings Doe to power

Doe is elected president amidst accusations of election fraud

Doe puts down successive coup attempts with bloody repression and detentions

model, and was designed to put curbs on power without drastically changing the economic system. The 4-year ban on politics was lifted in 1984, but the Doe government prevented 2 parties from organizing and banned several opposition leaders. Doe himself ran for president.

In spite of harassment, thousands of Liberians went to the polls in October 1985. Samuel K. Doe was declared the winner, after much evidence of ballot tampering. One month later, exiled General Thomas Quiwonkpa led an abortive coup against Doe. Hundreds of military and civilians were killed for alleged participation, and opposition leaders were jailed.

In January 1986 Doe was inaugurated as a civilian under the new Constitution, but several opposition-party members refused to take their seats in the National Assembly. With their lives in jeopardy, many opposition leaders fled to Europe and the United States.

Opponents, sympathizers, and human-rights activists called on the U.S. government to withhold aid until detainees were freed and new elections held. The U.S. Congress criticized the Doe government, but American financial and moral support continued. Since 1986 Doe has claimed three coup attempts, accusing opposition leaders such as Gabriel Bacchus Mathews, jailing United Peoples Party leader Gabriel Kpolleh, and killing former vice head of state Nicholas Podier during an alleged invasion in July 1988. Political and financial instability are evident in the constant Cabinet reshuffling amid accusations of corruption.

Criticism and dissent are rarely toler-ated. Newspapers have been banned, presses burned, and newsprint withheld. In 1988 Doe banned broadcasting of Voice of America and BBC Africa programs.

THE PERSISTENT PATTERNS

The majority of Liberia's people continue to live in the countryside in small towns where electricity, health care, and good water are scarce or nonexistent and where traditional slash-and-burn agriculture continues to produce food crops. Many farmers grow a little coffee, cocoa, or rubber. The citizens of these towns travel widely, often stopping in Monrovia to visit relatives; to sell cane juice, kola, or cloth; to look for health care or schooling; or to seek wage employment.

The interlinking of immigrant and indigenous families continues. Thirteen former government leaders lost their lives in a public execution at the time of the coup, and houses and farms of leading government officials were stripped. But the former elite, as a group, were not destroyed or forced out of the country, and many former True Whig party members hold positions in the current government. Sometimes patron and client have changed places, but personal relationships remain the gateway to securing a government position.

So, too, continues the association that Liberia has had with the United States for more than a century and a half. United States aid, much of it military, totaled $500 million from 1980 to 1988. The military connections, Voice of America installations, and independent United States Christian missions remain. Doe—

after some exploration of more radical friendships with Libya, Ethiopia, and North Korea—returned to Liberia's "special friend," the United States. Diplomatic relations with Israel were reestablished.

Financial conditions have deteriorated. When the military came to power, they claimed to have inherited an empty treasury and many debts—several resulting from the vast expenses of the Organization of African Unity (OAU) meetings in Liberia in 1979. The rise in the cost of oil, the decline in world prices for rubber and iron ore, and the closing of the sugar plant as well as one of Firestone's plantations are not the result of the coup, but they may determine the future of the government. Civil servants wait months for slim paychecks, and protests and strikes have increased. Nonpayment of debts and political instability have kept investors wary.

Liberia currently owes more than $400 million to the International Monetary Fund (IMF), and its currency has lost value. Because of the debt and allegations of corruption, in 1988 a number of American financial experts arrived to take up key positions in Liberian ministries (10 in Finance). Their impact on Liberia's economy remains to be seen, but without political stability, ordinary Liberians have little hope of economic progress.

DEVELOPMENT

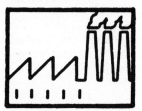

Liberia is the third largest exporter of iron ore in the world, and iron ore has been the main source of government revenue—superceding rubber—since the 1960s. The first iron-ore mine at Bomi Hills has mined out the profitable ore, and its decline is an ominous illustration of the limited value of mineral exploitation.

FREEDOM

The 1980s have been marked by press restrictions, detention of political opponents, deaths in detention, and executions of opponents, all in violation of the newly approved Constitution.

HEALTH/WELFARE

Among the important educational institutions in Liberia are the University of Liberia and Cuttington College, one of the only private higher educational institutions in Africa, funded by the Protestant Episcopal Church and the government. But education has suffered greatly under the economic strains of the 1980s.

ACHIEVEMENTS

Through a shrewd policy of diplomacy, Liberia managed to maintain its independence when the United Kingdom and France conquered neighboring areas during the late nineteenth century. It espoused African causes during the colonial period; for instance, Liberia brought the case of Namibia to the World Court in the 1950s.

Mali (Republic of Mali)

GEOGRAPHY

Area in Square Kilometers (Miles):
1,240,142 (478,819) (about the size of
Texas and California combined)
Capital (Population): Bamako
(862,000)
Climate: tropical to arid

PEOPLE

Population
Total: 8,730,000
Annual Growth Rate: 2.7%
Rural/Urban Population Ratio: 79/21
Languages: official: French; others
spoken: Bamanankan, Mandinka,
Voltaic, Tamacheg (Tuareg), Dogon,
Fulde, Songhai, Malinké

Health
Life Expectancy at Birth: 41 years
male; 44 years female
Infant Death Rate (Ratio): 178/1,000
Average Caloric Intake: 83% of FAO
minimum
Physicians Available (Ratio): 1/12,652

DOGON COSMOLOGY

The Dogon, a people numbering about one-quarter million, share religious beliefs that govern their daily lives and their art and that are based on careful astronomical observances. A most significant aspect is the Grand Mask, which represents the creation myth and divine order. About every 60 years a new mask is carved to represent the ancestor of the Dogon who first knew Death. The rituals surrounding the carving and creation of a new mask recall Dogon origins and unite all the Dogon people. The dance performances of this mask determine planting seasons, celebrate new generations of Dogon men, and commemorate at the funerals of initiates. The Grand Mask brings together myth, ritual, and the community; it is "the soul of the Dogon."

Religion(s)
90% Muslim; 9% traditional
indigenous; 1% Christian

Education
Adult Literacy Rate: 10%

COMMUNICATION

Telephones: 9,537
Newspapers: 2

TRANSPORTATION

Highways—Kilometers (Miles): 15,700
(9,756)
Railroads—Kilometers (Miles): 642
(400)
Commercial Airports: 3 international

GOVERNMENT

Type: military republic
Independence Date: June 20, 1960
Head of State: President (General)
Moussa Traoré
Political Parties: Democratic Union
of Malian People
Suffrage: universal over 21

MILITARY

Number of Armed Forces: 7,300
*Military Expenditures (% of Central
Government Expenditures):* 17%
Current Hostilities: none

ECONOMY

Currency ($ U.S. Equivalent): 300
CFA francs = $1
Per Capita Income/GNP: $190/$1.1
billion
Inflation Rate: 9%
Natural Resources: bauxite; iron ore;
manganese; lithium; phosphate;
kaolin; salt; limestone; gold
Agriculture: millet; sorghum; corn;
rice; sugar; cotton; peanuts; livestock
Industry: food processing; textiles;
cigarettes; fishing

FOREIGN TRADE

Exports: $146 million
Imports: $233 million

The Mali empire extends over much of the upper regions of West Africa
1250–1400s

The Songhai empire controls the region
late 1400s–late 1500s

The French establish control over Mali
1890

Mali gains independence as part of Mali Confederation; Senegal secedes from the confederation months later
1960

A military coup brings Traoré and Military Committee for National Liberation to power
1968

The Democratic Union of the Malian People (UDPM) is the single ruling party; Traoré is secretary general
1979

School strikes and demonstrations; teachers and students are detained
1979–1980

1980s

Traoré is reelected president, receiving 99% of the vote

Locust infestations threaten crops

Canadian-financed gold mining begins

MALI

The epic of Sundiata Keita, the thirteenth-century founder of the great Mali Empire, is well known among the peoples of Mali and the other countries that once shared in the empire. *Griots*, or traditional bards, sing of Sundiata's deeds at special gatherings and on radio programs. The story of this Malinké hero is a source of unity and pride for Mali's people.

A HERITAGE OF CONFEDERATION

Although Sundiata was a conqueror, the kingdom he founded was based on a confederation of rulers who accepted his leadership. In modern times Mali has worked for cooperation or closer union with the other countries of the area that also share in the heritage of the Mali Empire. Under the French, in the period from the 1890s to 1960, Mali (then called French Sudan) was part of the territory called French West Africa and was linked to Dakar. When the territories became independent within the French Community, Senegal and Mali formed the Mali Confederation. This union lasted only a few months. Mali and Senegal broke their political ties, but today they cooperate in the Organization for the Development of the Senegal River (OMVS) and other organizations, as well as in planning the exploitation of their joint iron-ore resources.

Meanwhile, Mali has strengthened its ties with nearby Guinea. In 1983 the two countries signed an agreement to unify their countries and established a permanent organization to harmonize policies and structures. Mali's President Moussa Traoré said that this is the integration of "two lungs in the same body." President Sekou Touré of Guinea spoke of "the reconstitution on the basis of an egalitarian and democratic state, of the ancient Mali Empire," a political entity that will embrace all the states in the region. These goals of regional unity were marred by border clashes with Burkina Faso in 1985, but the problems were settled by dividing the disputed territory in 1986.

TRADITIONAL VALUES

Christianity has gained a small following in Mali, but most Malians are followers of Islam and of traditional religions. Some peoples, such as the Dogon of the Bandiagara Cliffs, have little interest in Islam and maintain the rituals that grow from their complex cosmological beliefs. Other groups, such as the Bamanan, have increasingly accepted Islam while still practicing traditional ceremonies and belonging to secret associations. Even the Malinké, who are most likely to identify themselves as Muslims, continue to hold some religious beliefs of their non-Muslim ancestors.

ENVIRONMENTAL CHALLENGES

The people of Mali are very poor. There are few resources, and those that exist, such as manganese and iron ore, have not yet been exploited. The land on which people make their living is semiarid, made drier by years of drought. The Niger River is the lifeline of the Fulani pastoralists who depend on the water for their herds; Malinke and Bamanan farmers also use it for their fields. In earlier centuries the country sustained great trading cities such as Timbuctu and Djenne. Today the most important city in Mali is Bamako.

Successive governments have sought to better the conditions of the people. The first president, Modibo Keita, from the clan of Sundiata, established radical socialist policies and practices, but efforts to "go it alone" outside the French Franc Zone were not very successful. General (now President) Traoré led a coup against Keita in 1968 and gradually modified, though did not eliminate, Keita's policies. Agreements with the International Monetary Fund (IMF) ended some government monopolies, but it is not certain whether their functions can be carried out by private bodies. The reentry of Mali into the Monetary Union of West Africa should limit smuggling and encourage economic growth. However, because of the costs of imported food and fertilizers and because a huge proportion of the budget goes toward civil-servant salaries, there is little money to spend on development. Drought and continued expansion of the Sahara limit food production and have meant that herders must change their centuries-old lifestyle to practice settled agriculture.

Other natural disasters, such as locusts, plague Mali. These obstacles to a better life challenge all Malians and their government.

DEVELOPMENT

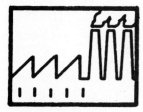

Water has always been one of Mali's major needs. It is estimated that only 9% of Malians, mostly in the urban areas, have access to pure water. Financed by the UN Development Fund and China, an antidesertification program began in 1988.

FREEDOM

There are few political prisoners confined in Mali, but 9 people were given death sentences for embezzlement in 1987. It is not known whether any were carried out.

HEALTH/WELFARE

About a third of Mali's budget is devoted to education. A special literacy program in Mali teaches rural people how to read and write and helps them with the practical problems of daily life by using booklets that concern fertilizers, measles, and measuring fields.

ACHIEVEMENTS

A carefully planned agricultural project, Isle de Paix (Island of Peace), along the Niger River has produced substantial harvests in spite of severe drought. Rice yields were almost 3 times as productive as other, more expensive projects.

Mauritania (Islamic Republic of Mauritania)

GEOGRAPHY

Area in Square Kilometers (Miles):
1,030,700 (398,000) (about the size
of Texas and California combined)
Capital (Population): Nouakchott
(500,000)
Climate: arid to semiarid

PEOPLE

Population
Total: 2,015,000
Annual Growth Rate: 2%
Rural/Urban Population Ratio: 75/25
Languages: official: Arabic, French;
others: Hasanya, Bamanankan, Fulde,
Sarakole, Wolof, Berber languages

Health
Life Expectancy at Birth: 45 years
Infant Death Rate (Ratio): 138/1,000
Average Caloric Intake: 94% of FAO
minimum
Physicians Available (Ratio): 1/19,563

Religion(s)
More than 99% Sunni Muslim

Education
Adult Literacy Rate: 17%

WHO ARE THE MOORS?

The term "Moors" has been popularly used through history to refer to
Arabic- and Berber-speaking Muslims who live in North Africa and
across the Sahara. However, it is more accurate to refer to them by the
names of the groups of which they are members. In Mauritania, Moors
are peoples such as the Tuareg and the Sanhaja Berbers. They are
probably descendants of the Almoravids, who spread Islam through the
Western Sahara during their conquests in the eleventh century. Traditionally nomadic, they maintain complex social systems. Aristocrats,
including religious leaders and former warriors, are the "bones" (*adma*)
of the society. Commoners are the "flesh" (*ahma*). Other groups in
society are more subservient. Today, these people's lives are changing
as—willingly or unwillingly—they move to cities and take up a settled
lifestyle.

COMMUNICATION

Telephones: 3,161
Newspapers: 1

TRANSPORTATION

Highways—Kilometers (Miles): 8,900
(5,530)
Railroads—Kilometers (Miles): 650
(404)
Commercial Airports: 3 international

GOVERNMENT

Type: military republic
Independence Date: November 28,
1960
Head of State: Colonel Moauia Ould
Sidi Mohamed Taya, prime minister
and chairman of the Military
Committee for National Recovery
Political Parties: none
Suffrage: none

MILITARY

Number of Armed Forces: 14,870
*Military Expenditures (% of Central
Government Expenditures):* n/a
Current Hostilities: internal conflicts

ECONOMY

Currency ($ U.S. Equivalent): 72
ouguiyas = $1
Per Capita Income/GNP: $466/$614
million
Inflation Rate: 10%
Natural Resources: iron ore; gypsum;
fish; copper
Agriculture: livestock; millet; corn;
wheat; dates; rice; peanuts
Industry: iron-ore mining; fish
processing

FOREIGN TRADE

Exports: $275 million
Imports: $215 million

The Almoravids
spread Islam in
the Western
Sahara areas
through
conquest
1035–1055

The Mauritanian
area becomes a
French colony
1920

Mauritania
becomes
independent
under President
Moktar Ould
Daddah
1960

A military coup
brings Khouma
Ould Haidalla
and the Military
Committee for
National
Recovery to
power
1978

The Algiers
Agreement:
Mauritania
makes peace
with Polisario
and abandons
claims to
Western Sahara
1979

1980s

Mauritania
recognizes the
Polisario State
in Western
Sahara (SADR)
as a sovereign
nation

Taya takes over
as prime
minister through
a coup

Taya makes a
state visit to
China, which
has given aid to
Mauritania since
1965

THE REPUBLIC OF MAURITANIA

Mauritania,, most of which is desert, grows ever drier as unpredictable droughts continue. Grass cover has disappeared; vast herds of cattle, camels, sheep, and goats are threatened; and sand has drifted over homes and highways. In the south, arable land for growing grains and rice has been greatly reduced. In 1982 a plague of grasshoppers destroyed 15 percent of the already-diminished harvest, and locusts threatened the entire region in 1987–1988. Ninety percent of Mauritania's food is imported.

In the face of such natural disasters, people have moved. In 1962 only 8 percent of the citizens lived in the country's few cities and towns. Now 25 percent of the population are urban dwellers. The pastoralists come from a nomadic world in which Arab culture and aristocratic Moorish-Berber values have been maintained. They have moved to places such as the capital, Nouakchott, and pitched tents in shantytowns on the outskirts of town. Many have gone south to settle in Mali.

LIMITED OPPORTUNITIES

As the cities have grown, poverty has become more obvious. People seek new ways to make a living away from the land, but there are few jobs. About 30,000 Mauritanians are employed; most work in the Tazadit iron-ore mine in the northern desert. Although this mine will soon be depleted, a nearby iron-ore complex is now operating. Iron ore provides 70 to 85 percent of the exports and foreign exchange of the country and gives Mauritania a figure for average per capita income that understates the basic needs of the people.

DIVISION AND UNITY

Mohammed Khouna Ould Haidalla and the Military Committee for National Recovery came to power in a military coup in 1978. Steps toward constitutional rule were halted after a coup attempt in 1981, and new forms of political and social organization were discussed, but not implemented. Colonel Ould Taya overthrew Haidalla (who was out of the country at the time) in a bloodless coup in December 1985, citing mismanagement of the economy.

Like its neighbor Chad, Mauritania is a nation of many different peoples, and there are long-existing hostilities between northerners and southerners. The Arab-oriented northerners claim to be in the majority, but ethnic black southerners contest that claim, and the census figures of 1977 have never been revealed. Southerners have objected to the exclusive use of Arabic in schools. In an attempt to "paper over the cracks in national unity," the government stresses the unity of Islam. The Sharia, or Islamic law, has been made an alternative to the regular legal system. However, a common faith has not always been able to harmonize the differences between the ethnic groups, and sometimes the differences have grown more obvious as peoples have lived closer together in the cities.

After an alleged coup attempt against Taya in late 1987, 50 people (mostly blacks) were arrested. The government is fragile, contending with unrest and protests, resulting in repression of black Mauritanians. And many believe that the real power in the government is Djibril Ould Abdallahi, the minister of interior and telecommunications.

THE STRUGGLE IN WESTERN SAHARA

Fighting in the Western Sahara, on Mauritania's northern border, made life uncertain for Mauritanian citizens and eroded limited finances. Mauritania claimed portions of the Western Sahara in the 1970s and its army expanded tenfold, to 17,000 men, during this time. (The number of troops has since declined.) In 1979 the government renounced sovereignty over any part of the region and later recognized the Polisario Front, the liberation movement of the Western Sahara.

Recent Saudi Arabian and Organization of African Unity (OAU) diplomatic efforts may bring a settlement, but the war of the Polisario with Morocco continues. Morocco's sixth "wall of sand" to keep out Polisario fighters comes very close to Mauritanian rail lines. On a positive note, Mauritanian village councils have established connections with villages in Morocco and Algeria. But Mauritania's relationships with Morocco, the Polisario, and other African states with an interest in Western Sahara continue to kick up controversy for Mauritianians.

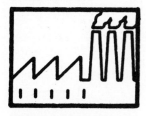

DEVELOPMENT

Dams being built on the Senegal River will increase the land available for farming by preventing the inland flow of salt water and irrigating thousands of acres in Mauritania, Senegal, and Mali. Sixty scientists, funded by the Dutch government, will study the coastal waters off Mauritania to develop fisheries.

FREEDOM

While arresting Haidalla and other government officials, Taya released political detainees held under Haidalla and urged opposition groups to return to Mauritania. After the alleged 1987 coup attempt, 3 leaders were executed and 18 were given life sentences. Southern blacks protest inequities.

HEALTH/WELFARE

Former nomads now living in Rosso have built an innovative housing development in cooperation with the Association for the Development of Traditional African Urbanism and Architecture (ADAUA). Women, who head the majority of the households, took the initiative in the work.

ACHIEVEMENTS

There is a current project to restore ancient Mauritanian cities, such as Chinguette, which are located on traditional routes from North Africa to Sudan. These centers of trade and Islamic learning were points of origin for the pilgrimage to Mecca and were well known in the Middle East.

Niger (Republic of Niger)

GEOGRAPHY

Area in Square Kilometers (Miles):
1,267,000 (489,191) (almost 3 times
the size of California)
Capital (Population): Niamey
(300,000)
Climate: arid to semiarid

PEOPLE

Population
Total: 6,608,000
Annual Growth Rate: 3%
Rural/Urban Population Ratio: 84/16
Languages: official: French; others
spoken: Hausa, Zarma/Songhai, Kanuri,
Fulde, Tamacheg (Tuareg), others

Health
Life Expectancy at Birth: 43 years
Infant Death Rate (Ratio): 135/1,000
Average Caloric Intake: 91% of FAO
minimum
Physicians Available (Ratio): 1/38,500

Religion(s)
97% Muslim; 3% traditional
indigenous

MATERNAL-LANGUAGE SCHOOLS

In Niger, more and more primary-school pupils are attending classes
conducted in their native languages. These maternal-language schools,
as they are called, have been developed over a number of years through
careful planning and experimentation, and are based on the idea that the
mastery of basic concepts is most successfully achieved in one's first
language. These schools also work to foster and reinforce values of the
community through a curriculum that reflects the cultural heritage of the
pupils. Niger's maternal-language schools are dedicated to providing
students with strong foundations in reading, writing, and arithmetic as
well as to the formation of individuals with a strong sense of their own
cultural identity.

Education
Adult Literacy Rate: 8%

COMMUNICATION

Telephones: 9,320
Newspapers: 1

TRANSPORTATION

Highways—Kilometers (Miles): 8,547
(5,299)
Railroads—Kilometers (Miles): none
Commercial Airports: 2 international

GOVERNMENT

Type: republic, administered by
Supreme Military Council
Independence Date: August 3, 1960
Head of State: President (Brigadier
General) Ali Saibou
Political Parties: banned
Suffrage: universal over 16

MILITARY

Number of Armed Forces: 5,928
*Military Expenditures (% of Central
Government Expenditures):* n/a
Current Hostilities: none

ECONOMY

Currency ($ U.S. Equivalent): 300
CFA francs = $1
Per Capita Income/GNP: $200/$1.1
billion
Inflation Rate: 22%
Natural Resources: uranium; coal;
iron; tin; phosphates
Agriculture: millet; sorghum; peanuts;
beans; cotton
Industry: mining; textiles; cement;
agricultrual products; construction

FOREIGN TRADE

Exports: $362 million
Imports: $438 million

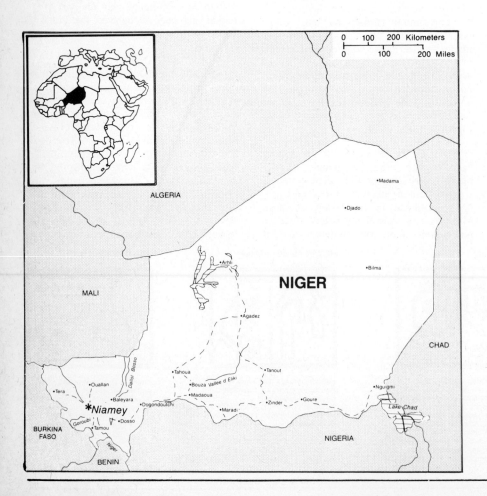

| Mali empire includes territories and peoples of current Niger areas **1200s–1400s** | Hausa states develop in the south of present-day Niger **1400s** | The area is influenced by the Fulani empire centered at Sokoto, now in Nigeria **1800s** | France consolidates rule over Niger **1906** | Niger becomes independent **1960** | A military coup brings Colonel Seyni Kountché and a Supreme Military Council to power **1974** |

1980s

President Kountché dies

Peaceful transition to military ruler Saibou

Completion of national census

NIGER

"Before we cultivated much larger areas and sometimes got nothing. Now, with the project, even on smaller plots we can produce enough millet," said Hassan Moussa, a Hausa farmer who participates in one of the programs of the Maradi Rural Development Project in Niger. The project is introducing new agricultural techniques and fertilizers, pesticides and seeds to more than 65,000 Nigerien farmers to help them expand and improve their harvests.

THE HERITAGE OF THE DROUGHT

Nigerien farmers need this help badly. The droughts of the late 1960s and early 1970s had a catastrophic effect, disrupting the delicate balance of desert and savanna in this large but very poor country located deep in the interior of West Africa. Only 5 percent of the land has been farmed; while another 50 percent can be used for grazing. Herders have also suffered during the droughts, losing 60 percent of their cattle. However, those losses have now been partly recovered.

The recovery in food production in recent years has been promising, yet optimism must be tempered with caution. Projects like the one in which Hassan Moussa is involved are of limited value because the costs of bureaucracy and accompanying expenses have been great. Individual farmers could never afford these irrigation resources without outside assistance. The project manager himself has admitted that farmers would be better

served by simple wells or other, more modest and integrated aids.

NIGER'S RESOURCES

Projects such as the Maradi Rural Development Project are funded by Niger as well as by outside agencies. This has been possible because Niger's deserts contain uranium ore. Two mines are now in operation; Niger is the fifth largest producer of uranium in the world. Thirteen other deposits are being investigated. Mining provides 90 percent of Niger's foreign exchange and has been of great value to the country. Yet such developments have limitations. All of the materials for uranium exploitation come from abroad, and the ore itself is exported and may someday be mined out. The mining communities are places where no one really belongs nor intends to stay. Niger is able to show a budget surplus, but the decline in uranium demand and prices since 1980 shows the dangers of depending on one resource.

A NEW POLITICAL ORGANIZATION

It has been said that the development made possible through uranium exploitation may have diverted popular attention from the limits on political activity in Niger. A constitutional government under President Hamani Diori existed from 1960, the year of independence, to 1974, when Lieutenant Colonel (later Major General) Seyni Kountché, a leader described as austere and upright, took power in a bloodless coup. Kountché proposed that a constitution be developed, he

had no military representatives in his Cabinet, and National Development Councils were planned at all levels.

French influence remained important to Niger. There is still a French military garrison as well as continued military assistance to defend against foreign intervention. Libya, which has disputed its border with Niger, is suspected of having backed an assassination attempt against Kountché and an attempted coup in 1983 and of backing Tuareg raids against Nigerien targets.

In 1987 Kountché died of natural causes and was succeeded by Colonel (now Brigadier General) Ali Saibou. When Saibou took over he retained the same structural arrangement for his government but made sweeping personnel changes. These were not complete until July 1988, when his new Cabinet was officially made public. The former head of Kountché's National Development Council, Meimane Oumarou, became prime minister. Development efforts continue to struggle against drought, to develop private enterprise in the economy, and to achieve educational reform.

DEVELOPMENT

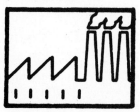

Village cooperatives, especially marketing cooperatives, pre-date independence and have grown in size and importance in recent years. They have successfully competed with private well-to-do traders for control of the grain market.

FREEDOM

Although political parties remain suspended, the Development Society gives opportunities for political activity to Nigerien citizens. Upon coming to power, Saibou released political prisoners, including former President Diori.

HEALTH/WELFARE

A national conference on educational reform in Zinder stimulated a program to use Nigerien languages in primary education and integrated the adult-literacy program into the whole rural development efforts. The National Training Center for Literacy Agents is crucial to literacy efforts.

ACHIEVEMENTS

The government has made efforts to maintain harmony and unity among the different ethnic groups in Niger and to avoid ethnic tensions by equally distributing economic benefits.

Nigeria (Federal Republic of Nigeria)

GEOGRAPHY

Area in Square Kilometers (Miles):
923,768 (356,669) (about the size of
California, Arizona, and Nevada
combined)
Capital (Population): Lagos
(5,000,000) (Abuja will be the new
capital after 1990)
Climate: tropical to arid

PEOPLE

Population
Total: 105,000,000
Annual Growth Rate: 3.3%
Rural/Urban Population Ratio: 77/23
Languages: official: English; others
spoken: Hausa, Yoruba, Igbo, Efik,
Idoma, Ibibio, others (250 languages
are recognized by the Nigerian
government)

Health
Life Expectancy at Birth: 48 years
male; 52 years female
Infant Death Rate (Ratio): 127/1,000
Average Caloric Intake: 91% of FAO
minimum
Physicians Available (Ratio): 1/11,347

AFRICA'S NOBEL LAUREATE

Nigerian writer Wole Soyinka received the Nobel Prize for Literature in
1986. Soyinka is noted for his many works, ranging from plays such as
The Trials of Brother Jero to novels such as *The Interpretors*, many
poems, and nonfiction writings. The son of a Yoruba pastor and an
active Christian mother, Soyinka grew up in the western Nigerian town
of Abeokuta. Warm and vivid scenes of his childhood are recalled in
detail in his autobiography, *Ake: The Years of Childhood*. An outspoken
critic of the federal government during the Nigerian Civil War, Soyinka
was jailed from 1967 to 1969. His plays are produced all over the world,
and he continues to speak out on the arts and politics.

Religion(s)
47% Muslim; 34% Christian; 19%
traditional indigenous

Education
Adult Literacy Rate: 42%

COMMUNICATION

Telephones: 708,390
Newspapers: 48

TRANSPORTATION

Highways—Kilometers (Miles):
107,990 (67,104)
Railroads—Kilometers (Miles): 3,505
(2,178)
Commercial Airports: 4 international

GOVERNMENT

Type: federal republic; under control
of military government
Independence Date: October 1, 1960
Head of State: President Ibrahim
Babangida
Political Parties: banned since 1983
coup
Suffrage: universal for adults

MILITARY

Number of Armed Forces: 94,500
*Military Expenditures (% of Central
Government Expenditures):* 9.3%
Current Hostilities: none

ECONOMY

Currency ($ U.S. Equivalent): 4.23
naira = $1
Per Capita Income/GNP: $790/$74
billion
Inflation Rate: 39%
Natural Resources: oil; minerals;
timber
Agriculture: cotton; cocoa; rubber;
yams; cassava; sorghum; palm
kernels; millet; corn; rice; livestock
Industry: mining; crude oil; natural
gas; coal; tin; columbite; processing:
oil, palm, cotton, rubber, petroleum;
manufacturing: textiles, cement,
building materials, chemicals, beer
brewing

FOREIGN TRADE

Exports: $12.5 billion
Imports: $8.8 billion

NIGERIA

Nigeria is a land of extremes that for many has typified both the hopes and frustrations of contemporary Africa. It is Africa's most populous country; at least two West Africans in three live there. A national census in 1989 will be the first in Nigeria since independence, but it is estimated that there are approximately 105 million Nigerians. Thanks to its oil fields, Nigeria is also the wealthiest African nation. Yet its 3 decades of independence have already witnessed a bloody civil war, terrible interethnic violence, 16 years of military rule, restoration of Western-style representative politics, and—following a military coup in 1983—a return to military government.

The river Niger, which flows to the sea through a great delta in Nigeria, links savanna and forest. For centuries it was the route through which population groups and cultures interrelated. Nigeria is remarkable for its great cultural and historic variety. Archaeologists and historians have revealed ancient states and cultures with a rich and complex artistic and political heritage.

More than 250 languages are spoken in Nigeria. Pidgin English, which is based on African grammar, is widely used in the towns. Roughly two-thirds of Nigerians speak Hausa, Yoruba, or Igbo. During and after the colonial era the leaders of these cultural groups clashed politically from their separate regional bases.

Before the colonial conquest Nigerians established powerful states such as the Sokoto caliphate (which helped to Islamize much of the country), Oyo, and Benin. Meanwhile, thousands of smaller independent villages and family commonwealths held sway elsewhere. Precolonial Nigerians produced a wide range of craft goods, including leather, glass, and metalware; they grew such agricultural surplus products as cotton and indigo. The southern part of the country was a major source of slaves, particularly those destined for the United States, during the Atlantic slave trade era.

BRITISH RULE

The British, who conquered most of the country in the late nineteenth and early twentieth centuries, ruled Nigeria through a federal structure. The predominantly Muslim north became something of a world unto itself because it was governed under "indirect rule." The British virtually excluded Christian missionaries from much of the north.

During the relatively brief colonial era Nigerians were able to show a dynamism unusual in Africa. The old ruling classes, especially in the north, remained very important. Commercial networks, while subordinated to British business, expanded and intensified, to the benefit of some African traders. In the south, Christianity and Western education spread rapidly. Yoruba farmers cultivated cocoa on a scale rivaling Ghana; the Igbo, who lacked an equivalent lucrative crop, spread throughout the federation in their roles as artisans, wage workers, and traders.

REGIONAL CONFLICTS

Following independence in 1960 Nigerian politics deteriorated into intensive conflict between the different regions, each of which threatened to secede at one time or another. Civilian government collapsed and two massacres led to the flight of Igbo from the north in 1966. The east then broke away and proclaimed itself to be the Republic of Biafra. It took 3 hard years of war to reunite the country. Even before the war had begun the military had determined to break up the regions into smaller states that would not be able to counterpose themselves against one another.

NATIONAL OUTLOOK

Not surprisingly, until recently most literature on Nigerian politics focused on the problem of national unity and contended that ethnic tensions were Nigeria's main problem. This ethnically based conflict is now waning. For all its failings, the military government of Yakubu Gowon (1966–1975) succeeded in healing the worst wounds of the ethnic politics of the First Republic, through a policy of national reconciliation and the creation of new states. The oil boom helped this effort by concentrating vast resources in the hands of the federal government in Lagos. Today the Nigerian elite, who once thought almost exclusively in terms of ethnicity, religion, or region, are increasingly national in outlook.

Thirteen years of military rule (never once producing a one-person dictatorship) ended in 1979. A new Constitution was implemented, which abandoned the British parliamentary model and instead followed the complex balance-of-powers system of the United States. There was a bicameral legislature, and to be elected, the president had to receive one-fourth of the vote in two-thirds of the states.

CIVILIAN POLITICS

Five political parties ran in 1979. All promised social welfare for the masses, support for Nigerian business, and a nominal international stance of nonalignment. Radicals, who talked in terms of class conflict, were found in several parties, especially in the People's Redemption Party (PRP), which initially took the governorship in two northern states.

The most successful party in 1979 was the National Party of Nigeria (NPN), whose candidate, Shehu Shagari, won the presidency. Most observers classified the NPN as the most rightwing of the parties, with virtually no radical members. It emphasized policies that were consistent with previous Nigerian administrations in order to assist in the development of a strong and affluent Nigerian class of capitalists.

New national elections took place in August and September 1983. Shagari received just over 12 million of 25.5 million votes. However, the newly elected government did not survive long. On December 31, 1983, there was a military coup, led by Major General Muhammed Buhari, former petroleum commissioner in the military government of General Gowan. The 1979 Constitution was suspended; Shagari and others were arrested; and a federal military government was established. The change was welcomed by many.

FORMER REPUBLIC OF THE PRIVILEGED

Superficially, the political picture seemed very bright in the early 1980s. A commitment to national unity was well established and effective. Two elections had successfully taken place, although marred by incidents of violence. Due process of law, judicial independence, and press freedom—never eliminated under military rule—were extended and were well entrenched.

Many Nigerian intellectuals, however, were beginning to write about the new republic as "the republic of the privileged and rich," in which the poor masses held little stake. The whole electoral system, while balancing the interests of the power elites in different sections of the country, did not empower ordinary people. Corrupt officials and some businesspeople became millionaires overnight. Moreover, economic circumstances were creating burdens almost too difficult for ordinary people to bear. The outlook was far different from that of the 1970s.

OIL BOOM

Nigeria, a member of the Organization of Petroleum Exporting Countries (OPEC), saw a period of very rapid social and economic change during the 1970s. The recovery of oil production after the Civil War and the subsequent hike in prices attracted Western business to the country

Flourishing of ancient life 1100–1400	The beginning of Usuman dan Fodio's Islamic jihad (struggle) 1804	First British protectorate established at Lagos 1851	Protectorate proclaimed over the north 1900

on a large scale and made a few Nigerians very rich. At first, as a result of this wealth, there was a rapid expansion of social services. Universal primary education was introduced, and the number of universities grew from 5 in 1970 to 21 in 1983. A great deal of money was spent on importing such commodities as automobiles, motorcycles, and phonograph equipment for private consumption. This fueled inflation, which ultimately undercut the economics of internal production.

The NPN government, however, promised to create many new states and was constructing, at vast expense, a new federal capitol at Abuja in the center of the country. Such forms of expenditure seemed prestigious and provided many opportunities for Nigerian businesspeople and politicians, but they extended nonproductive sectors of the economy while intensifying import dependence.

AGRICULTURE

Nigerian agriculture, unable to afford the higher wages spawned by inflation, entered a period of crisis, and the rapidly growing cities imported foreign food products to feed the urban populations. Lagos now contains several million inhabitants; Ibadan, Kano, Kaduna, and Port Harcourt have more than 1 million. Nigeria imported more than 2 million tons

of rice and wheat. The nonpetroleum exports that were once so important have either entirely disappeared (as is the case with peanuts, once the staple of the colonial north) or declined drastically (as have cocoa, tin, rubber, and palm oil).

While at first glance gross indicators appeared to report impressive industrial growth in Nigeria, most of the new industry depended heavily on foreign inputs and was geared toward direct consumption rather than the production of machines or spare parts. Selective import bans merely served to feed the immense smuggling business.

ADJUSTMENTS NECESSARY

The "golden years" of the middle and late 1970s were also banner years for inappropriate expenditure, corruption, and waste. At the time, given the scale of revenues coming in, it looked as if these were manageable problems. However, with world trade recession and the decline of oil revenues, it became apparent that Nigeria would be forced to make painful and unprecedented adjustments. The gross national product (GNP) fell drastically in the 1980s with the collapse of oil prices, reducing foreign exchange and the availability of imports.

The entire social and political system owed its stability to the effective distribu-

tion of the oil wealth to many groups of Nigerians. However, Nigeria's new wealthy class was increasingly resented by the masses. At the end of 1980 an Islamic movement condemning corruption, wealth, and private property defied authorities in the northern metropolis of Kano. The army was called in and killed nearly 4,000 poor Hausa-speaking peasant migrants. Similar riots subsequently occurred in Maiduguri, Yola, and Gombe. Attempts by the government to control organized labor through reorganizing the union movement into one legal centralized federation met with unofficial strikes (including a general strike in 1981) and illicit breakaways. In an attempt to give jobs to Nigerians, more than 1 million West Africans, particularly Ghanians, were expelled from Nigeria.

ECONOMIC AND POLITICAL REFORM

The main aim of the Buhari government was to solve some of the economic problems of the nation. The government apprehended and tried political leaders whose economic crimes reached vast proportions. The discovery of private caches of millions of naira caused public outrage and added to the treasury. Tribunals sentenced former politicians to long jail terms.

In its zeal, the government jailed jour-

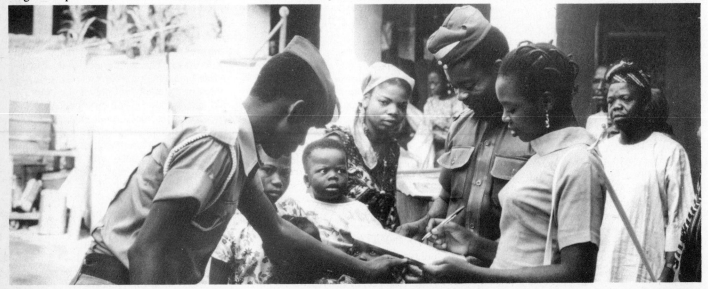

(United Nations photo)

Nigeria has the largest population of any African state, but the controversial nature of the 1963 and 1973 censuses have caused governments to postpone the process.

Nigeria becomes independent as a unified federal state **1960**	Military seizure of power; proclamation of Biafra; the Civil War **1966–1970**	An oil-price hike inaugurates the oil boom **1973**	Elections restore civilian government **1979**

1980s

Buhari's military coup ends the second republic; later Buhari is toppled by Babangida	Wole Soyinka is awarded the Nobel Prize for Literature	Austerity measures provoke protests and strikes

nalists and threatened those who spoke out on national issues. In 1985 Major General Ibrahim Babangida led a successful military coup, charging Buhari with abuse of human rights, keeping power within a small group in the military, and mis-management of the economy.

Babangida released detained journalists and former politicians who were not yet charged with crimes, and he encouraged all Nigerians to participate in national debates on the benefits of an International Monetary Fund loan and future political structures. The government turned down the IMF loan but implemented many of the austerity measures recommended. The 1986 budget was severe, yet was promising in the areas of education, health, and a commitment to infrastructure. Much of that austere budget has not been implemented, because of the continued sharp drop in oil prices, still 80 percent of Nigeria's foreign-exchange revenues.

To comply with IMF guidelines and to encourage foreign loans and investment, the government initiated a structural adjustment program (SAP) in 1986. The naira was devalued, budgets restricted, and plans made for privatizing state-run industries. Because salaries remained the same while prices rose, the cost of basic goods rose dramatically, with painful consequences for poor working-class and middle-class Nigerians.

Although the price of oil on the world market stabilized somewhat in 1988, after a huge drop (to $13 per barrel) in 1986, the government began a gradual reduction in fuel subsidies in 1988. To counteract

divisions within the Nigerian Labour Congress (NLC) and to preempt strikes over fuel prices, the government appointed an administrator over the NLC. When some transport owners raised fares 50 to 100 percent, students and workers protested and bank staff and other workers went on strike. When students and others protested in Jos, police killed demonstrators.

The Babangida government has faced internal challenges while seeking to project an image of stability to foreign investors. A coup attempt was foiled in 1985; and university unrest was put down with force in both 1986 and 1988, closing campuses for months at a time. Religious riots between Christians and Muslims in northern cities in 1987 led to many deaths. Several people implicated in those disturbances were sentenced to jail, but religious tensions continue to simmer.

Despite statements supporting press freedom, restrictions on the media resurfaced under Babangida. Dele Giwa, the outspoken editor of *Newswatch* magazine, was killed by a parcel bomb in 1986. His killers have yet to be found. The remaining editors were arrested in 1986, and the magazine was banned for several months in 1987. In 1988 the government banned satellite monitoring of foreign broadcasts.

While struggling with the economy, the government is gradually moving toward civilian rule after national study groups made recommendations. In 1988 local elections were held and a Constituent Assembly, elected to enact a new constitution, was sworn in. Local and state elections are to be completed by 1990,

with a legislature and the president to be elected in 1992. Nevertheless, many Nigerians remain pressimistic about prospects for democracy.

FOREIGN POLICY

The oil boom encouraged Nigerian regimes of the 1970s to take an aggressive foreign-policy stance supporting a radical nationalist view of the continent of Africa. In 1976 Murtala Muhammad, whose brief administration ended with his assassination, was quick to recognize the MPLA as the sole government of Angola, a decision that remains a source of pride to Nigerian nationalists. Nigeria also took a lead in supporting the new Mugabe government in Zimbabwe in 1980.

Making a strong commitment to liberation in Southern Africa, Nigeria announced in 1987 that African National Congress (ANC) fighters would be trained in Nigeria, and Babangida continued to pressure British Prime Minister Margaret Thatcher to impose comprehensive sanctions against South Africa.

Within the region, Nigeria was a founding member of the Economic Community of West African States (ECOWAS) and still plays a leading role in promoting West African unity and tackling regional issues such as the dumping of toxic wastes in Africa.

DEVELOPMENT

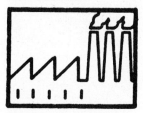

Nigeria hopes to mobilize its human and natural resources to encourage labor-intensive production and self-sufficient agriculture. Recent bans on food imports such as rice and maize will increase local production, and restrictions on imported raw materials should encourage research and local input for industry.

FREEDOM

Although the Babangida government freed journalists and critics jailed by Buhari, student protests have been dealt with harshly, and journalists and trade-union officials have been arrested. Convicted criminals and drug dealers are executed.

HEALTH/WELFARE

Despite plans for 4 new diagnostic hospitals, health care for the poor is often appalling, with rural infant mortality rates of 150 per 1,000 and up. Strains in the economy have left hospitals without drugs and new equipment.

ACHIEVEMENTS

Nigeria has a long tradition of an outspoken and lively press, under both civilian and military governments. Private and state-sponsored newspapers abound in all the large cities and are eagerly read by Nigerian citizens. Recently, national and international magazines specializing in investigative journalism have expanded their readership.

Senegal (Republic of Senegal)

GEOGRAPHY

Area in Square Kilometers (Miles):
196,840 (76,000) (about the size of
South Dakota)
Capital (Population): Dakar
(978,000)
Climate: tropical

PEOPLE

Population
Total: 6,800,000
Annual Growth Rate: 2.6%
Rural/Urban Population Ratio: 70/30
Languages: official: French; others
spoken: Wolof, Fulde, Oyola,
Mandinka, Sarakole, Serer

Health
Life Expectancy at Birth: 45 years
male; 48 years female
Infant Death Rate (Ratio): 102/1,000
Average Caloric Intake: 100% of FAO
minimum
Physicians Available (Ratio): 1/10,441

Religion(s)
75% Muslim; 20% traditional
indigenous; 5% Chistian

Education
Adult Literacy Rate: 11%

COMMUNICATION

Telephones: 45,000
Newspapers: 3

TRANSPORTATION

Highways—Kilometers (Miles): 14,700
(9,114)
Railroads—Kilometers (Miles): 905
(561)
Commercial Airports: 4 international

GOREE ISLAND

The tiny, rocky island of Gorée, opposite Dakar on the mainland, has a
tragic history. Beginning in the seventeenth century Gorée was occupied
by European traders as an easily defensible slave entrepôt. For more
than 200 years the French, Dutch, and English used Gorée as a
collection and distribution center for the Atlantic slave trade. Slaves
from the Senegalese interior and many other parts of West Africa were
housed and examined in cramped slave quarters before walking the
narrow passageway to the sea and transport to the Americas.

GOVERNMENT

Type: republic
Independence Date: April 4, 1960
Head of State: President Abdou Diouf
Political Parties: Socialist Party;
Democratic Party; African
Independence Party; Republican
Movement; National Democratic
Alliance; others
Suffrage: universal for adults

MILITARY

Number of Armed Forces: 7,750
*Military Expenditures (% of Central
Government Expenditures):* 2.3%
Current Hostilities: none

ECONOMY

Currency ($ U.S. Equivalent): 258
CFA francs = $1
Per Capita Income/GNP: $380/$2.4
billion
Inflation Rate: 11.8%
Natural Resources: fish; phosphates
Agriculture: millet; sorghum; manioc;
rice; cotton; groundnuts
Industry: fishing; food processing;
light manufacturing

FOREIGN TRADE

Exports: $498 million
Imports: $820 million

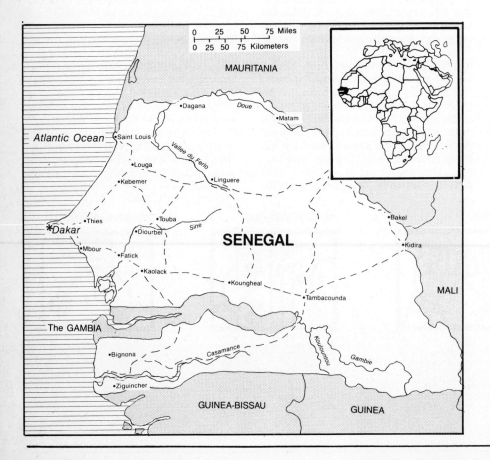

				Senegal becomes independent as part of the Mali Confederation; shortly afterwards, it breaks from the confederation.
The French occupy present-day St. Louis and, later, Gorée Island **1659**	The Jolof kingdom controls much of the region **1700s**	All Africans in 4 towns of the coast vote for a representative to the French Parliament **1848**	Interior areas are added to the French colonial territory **1889**	**1960**

1980s

Senghor hands over power to Diouf	Diouf is reelected as president and as secretary general of the ruling Socialist Party	The University of Dakar is renamed after Cheikh Anta Diop, a world-renowned scholar

SENEGAL

Ibrahima Dieng, an ordinary citizen of Senegal, is a Muslim who lives with his two wives in a traditional compound in the capital city, Dakar. When Dieng receives a money order from his nephew in Paris, he cannot cash it, because he lacks the connections and skills to overcome the bureaucratic obstacles that stand in his way. The lawyer he enlists to help him steals the money. "In a country like ours only the scoundrels live well," says Dieng.

The story is fictional, the plot of an amusing and thought-provoking film, *Mandabi*, by the Senegalese filmmaker Ousmane Sembene. Yet it illustrates a reality: the uneasy meeting of traditional African customs, Islamic practices, and Western influences in an important African city and, to a certain extent, in the interior beyond Dakar.

THE IMPACT OF ISLAM

The majority of Senegalese are Muslims. Islam was introduced into the region as early as the eleventh century and spread through trade, holy men, and the practices of theocratic Islamic states during the seventeenth, eighteenth, and nineteenth centuries.

Most Muslims are associated with one of the Brotherhoods or "ways" of Islam, similar to Western Protestant denominations or Catholic orders. The leaders of the Brotherhoods, often called *marabouts*, have been identified as "spokesmen for the rural areas" as well as "spiritual directors." Abdou Diouf, the current president of Senegal, had the support of the marabouts in his campaigns for the presidency.

The Brotherhoods have also been important economically. Members of the Mouride Brotherhood, who number about 700,000, grow groundnuts on the dry, flat Senegalese plains. This cash crop, the primary export of Senegal's predominantly agricultural economy, has made members of the Brotherhood prosperous.

THE INFLUENCE OF FRANCE

While Islamic influences have come into Senegal from the north and east, Western ways were introduced from the coast. French merchants developed bases for slave and gum trades and claimed the territory as French. Many Senegalese along the coast have had French connections for generations.

The French language is the common language of the country, and the educational system maintains a French character. Many Senegalese, like the fictional Dieng's nephew, go to France, either to attend school or (more often) to work as ill-paid laborers. The French maintain a military force near Dakar and are major investors in the Senegalese economy. The Constitution and government of Senegal are modeled after Western forms, and the bureaucracy that plagued Dieng has its roots in the old colonial system.

Diouf, after succeeding the renowned first president, Leopold Senghor, liberalized the government, welcomed the participation of other political parties, changed his Cabinet to make government more efficient and responsive, and fought corruption.

In national elections in 1988, Diouf won 77 percent of the vote, and his Socialist Party won a majority. Opponents protesting fraud clashed with police. Diouf declared a state of emergency and arrested his main opponent, Abdoulaye Wade, and others of the Senegalese Democratic Party. In an attempt at reconciliation, Diouf met with Wade after his release. They announced a plan for nonpartisan discussions of Senegal's ills, but many opposition politicians remain wary of the government's intentions.

THE STATE OF THE ECONOMY

Only one-third of Senegalese citizens live in cities; most are rural dwellers. Drought and locusts have made life difficult for Senegalese farmers and herders. Groundnuts have been affected by disease as well as by lack of water, and consequently groundnut exports have declined. The decline of prices on the world market has also affected the growers, and the government has become increasingly indebted to outside financial institutions. Although Canada forgave millions of dollars of debt in 1987, austerity measures imposed by the International Monetary Fund (IMF), while reducing the external debt, caused hardship for many Senegalese.

The Senegambia Confederation—inaugurated on February 1, 1982—was long sought by Senegal. The Senegalese government is the more powerful partner, and many Gambians resent the confederation.

DEVELOPMENT

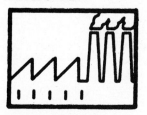

Diouf's administration is developing a water-supply program for the entire country. With Kuwaiti assistance, 212 water centers and 10 ponds will provide water for millions.

FREEDOM

There are 14 political parties in Senegal, 7 of which claim to be Marxist-Leninist. Four call themselves socialist. A ban on opposition-party coalitions and arrests of leaders contradict government claims to openness and diversity. A student strike at the university in 1988 was put down with violence.

HEALTH/WELFARE

When honoring President Diouf with its 1987 Africa Prize for Leadership for the Sustainable End of Hunger, the Hunger Project praised Senegalese policy reforms, programs to combat desertification, and efforts to boost cereal production.

ACHIEVEMENTS

As part of a broader campaign to improve health conditions, the government increased child immunizations from 20% to 75% of the population in only 1 year.

Sierra Leone (Republic of Sierra Leone)

GEOGRAPHY

Area in Square Kilometers (Miles):
72,325 (27,925) (slightly smaller than
South Carolina)
Capital (Population): Freetown
(470,000)
Climate: tropical

PEOPLE

Population
Total: 3,666,000
Annual Growth Rate: 2.3%
Rural/Urban Population Ratio: 78/22
Languages: official: English; others
spoken: Krio, Temne, Mende, Vai, Kru,
Fulde, Mandinka, others

Health
Life Expectancy at Birth: 46 years
Infant Death Rate (Ratio): 195/1,000
Average Caloric Intake: 85% of FAO
minimum
Physicians Available (Ratio): 1/18,609

Religion(s)
52% traditional indigenous; 36%
Muslim; 12% Christian

Education
Adult Literacy Rate: 15%

COMMUNICATION

Telephones: 220,000
Newspapers: 1

TRANSPORTATION

Highways—Kilometers (Miles): 7,460
(4,635)
Railroads—Kilometers (Miles): 84
(54)
Commercial Airports: 1 international

FOURAH BAY COLLEGE

Fourah Bay College, a significant educational institution for all of West
Africa, was founded in Sierra Leone in 1814 as a Christian school. By
1827 it was a training institution for teachers and missionaries, and in
1876 it was affiliated with the University of Durham in the United
Kingdom. As the only option for higher education for Africans on the
continent before 1918, Fourah Bay College trained many early nationalists and coastal elites during the colonial period. These graduates formed
a network of Western-educated African leaders throughout West Africa.

GOVERNMENT

Type: republic
Independence Date: April 27, 1961
Head of State: President Joseph Saidu
Momoh
Political Parties: All People's
Congress; others in exile
Suffrage: universal over 21

MILITARY

Number of Armed Forces: 3,280
*Military Expenditures (% of Central
Government Expenditures):* 7.4%
Current Hostilities: none

ECONOMY

Currency ($ U.S. Equivalent): 30.6
leones = $1
Per Capita Income/GNP: $232/$1
billion
Inflation Rate: 77%
Natural Resources: diamonds;
bauxite; rutile; chromite; iron ore
Agriculture: coffee; cocoa; ginger;
rice; piassava
Industry: mining; beverages;
cigarettes; construction materials

FOREIGN TRADE

Exports: $111 million
Imports: $135 million

| Early inhabitants arrive from Africa's interior **1400–1750** | Settlement by people from the New World and recaptured slave ships **1787** | Sierra Leone is a Crown colony **1801** | Mende peoples unsuccessfully resist the British in the Hut Tax War **1898** | Independence **1961** | The new Constitution makes Sierra Leone a one-party state **1978** |

1980s

Stevens steps down; Momoh, as sole candidate, is elected in first nationwide presidential election

Following countrywide unrest, a coup attempt by police fails

Retired President Stevens dies

A DISTINCTIVE POPULATION

One can find a distinctive blend of cultures in this small country. Sierra Leoneans are of ethnic groups such as the Temne or Mende that migrated into the region from the interior several centuries ago. Some came from down the coast, like the Kru. Other residents arrived from overseas. "The Black Poor," a group of about four hundred, arrived in Sierra Leone from England in 1787; freed slaves from Nova Scotia and Jamaica soon joined them. (The 200th anniversary of the founding of Freetown was celebrated in 1987.) About 40,000 recaptured Africans who were released from slave ships captured on the West African coast were settled in Freetown and the surrounding areas in the first half of the nineteenth century. The British became the governors of the colony and encouraged mission efforts, including the establishment of mission villages and schools such as Fourah Bay College.

The descendants of the settlers blended African and British ways and were called Creoles because of their mixed heritage. They traveled and lived in other places along the West African coast. Some found their original homes in Nigeria, from where they had been taken as slaves, and went back. When the British gained control over the interior, Creole people sometimes served as their administrators. Creoles in the interior were attacked during the Hut Tax Rebellion of 1898, and fear of Creole domination existed among traditional leaders during the twentieth century.

In the 1950s, as more and more people were given the vote, interior peoples— rather than Creoles—dominated the political system. The Sierra Leone People's Party (SLPP), under Sir Milton Margai, became powerful through the support of traditional chiefs and remained the leading party when Sierra Leone gained independence in 1961. After 1967 the All People's Congress (APC), representing a broader spectrum of the population, won control. The APC became the only recognized party in 1978. Siaka Stevens, the leader of the APC, was president of Sierra Leone for 17 years until stepping down in 1985 for his chosen successor, Major General Joseph Momoh.

POLITICAL AND ECONOMIC COMPETITION

Although competition between ethnic groups is minor, there are other sources of controversy and conflict in Sierra Leone. In 1981 a general strike—the first ever— occurred as a result of worsening economic conditions, and student protests in 1984 led to the closing of Fourah Bay College. People protested rising prices throughout 1986 and 1987. A 1987 coup attempt by police was put down, and 16 plotters, including Sierra Leone's first vice president, were sentenced to death. As difficult economic conditions continue, there is more struggle over the national wealth.

That wealth is small. Sierra Leone is a poor country and was recently added to the list of Least Developed Countries by the United Nations. Its resources are limited. Deposits of diamonds, once central to the economy and the basis for the prosperity of the 1950s, are almost depleted.

The rural population suffers the most. Falling prices for cocoa and coffee have cut into the income of farmers, a majority of the population. Those who grow rice cannot compete with the imported rice, which the government subsidizes. Financial problems have resulted in the cutting back of development programs. Health care in the countryside is poor, educational facilities have become more limited, and clean water and electricity are scarce.

Although the government agreed to International Monetary Fund (IMF) austerity measures in 1987, these reforms have not been carried out, since devaluing the currency and reducing food subsidies will be politically unpopular. In November 1987 Momoh declared an economic state of emergency, promoting a recovery policy which included restrictions on diamond- and gold-mining licenses and tough penalties for smugglers. Critics have challenged his authority, under the current Constitution, to declare such a state of emergency.

Balancing the demands of his people and the pressures from international lenders for debt repayment, while keeping political control, are the major challenges facing both Momoh and Sierra Leone.

DEVELOPMENT

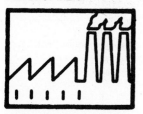

In 1988 Sierra Leone signed an agreement with neighboring Gambia to cooperate in the areas of commerce, education, transportation, fisheries, tourism, and the law.

FREEDOM

Human rights are guaranteed in the Sierra Leone Constitution, and there have not been major violations. One hundred and eighty persons, including 80 trade union leaders, were arrested after a general strike in 1982; they were later released. Those opposed to one-party APC rule are among Sierra Leone exiles. Coup plotters were sentenced to death in 1987.

HEALTH/WELFARE

Medical care now reaches only 30% of the people, and the infant mortality rate is one of the highest in the world. Worker grievances have included hospital conditions. Sixteen patients died during a 2-week strike by hospital workers in 1987.

ACHIEVEMENTS

The Sande Society, a women's organization that trains Mende young women for adult responsibilities and regulates women's behavior, has contributed positively to life in Sierra Leone. Beautifully carved wooden helmet masks are worn by women leaders in the society's rituals. Ninety-five percent of Mende women of all classes and education join the society.

Togo (Republic of Togo)

GEOGRAPHY

Area in Square Kilometers (Miles):
56,600 (21,853) (slightly smaller than West Virginia)
Capital (Population): Lomé (366,000)
Climate: tropical

PEOPLE

Population

Total: 3,158,000
Annual Growth Rate: 2.9%
Rural/Urban Population Ratio: 85/15
Languages: official: French; others spoken: Ewe, Mina, Dagomba, Kabye, others

Health

Life Expectancy at Birth: 47 years
Infant Death Rate (Ratio): 107/1,000
Average Caloric Intake: 92% of FAO minimum
Physicians Available (Ratio): 1/22,727

Religion(s)

58% traditional indigenous; 22% Christian; 20% Muslim

TOURISM IN TOGO

Often described as the Switzerland of Africa (a description frequently used for Lesotho and Malawi as well), Togo has encouraged the development of numerous fashionable hotels in Lomé, the capital on the coast, and inland. Two national game parks have been publicized, as have dance and music groups. There are quite a few foreign tourists. Africans from Ghana, Benin, and Nigeria, and Europeans and North Americans vacation in Togo. The government employed a public-relations firm from the United States to help in the development of its tourist industry and in making contacts with various corporations that might do business in Togo.

Education

Adult Literacy Rate: 45% male; 20% female

COMMUNICATION

Telephones: 11,105
Newspapers: 1

TRANSPORTATION

Highways—Kilometers (Miles): 7,850 (4,867)
Railroads—Kilometers (Miles): 525 (326)
Commercial Airports: 2 international

GOVERNMENT

Type: republic; under military rule
Independence Date: April 27, 1960
Head of State: President (General) Gnassingbé Eyadéma
Political Parties: Togolese People's Union
Suffrage: universal for adults

MILITARY

Number of Armed Forces: 5,910
Military Expenditures (% of Central Government Expenditures): n/a
Current Hostilities: none

ECONOMY

Currency ($ U.S. Equivalent): 285 CFA francs = $1
Per Capita Income/GNP: $240/$696 million
Inflation Rate: 8.3%
Natural Resources: phosphates; limestone
Agriculture: yams; manioc; millet; sorghum; cocoa; coffee; rice
Industry: phosphates; textiles; agricultural products; tourism

FOREIGN TRADE

Exports: $246 million
Imports: $266 million

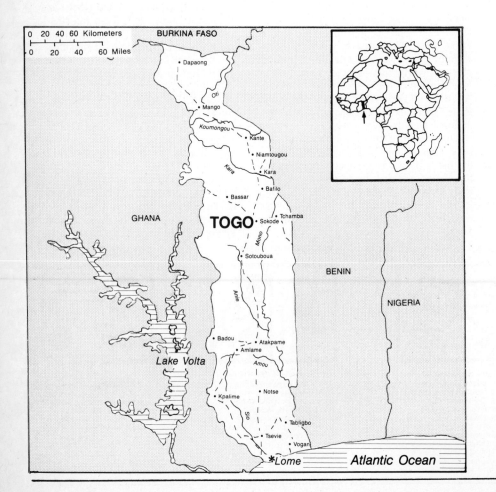

	Togo is mandated to the United Kingdom and France by the League of Nations following Germany's defeat in World War I	UN plebicites result in the independence of French Togo and incorporation of British Togo into Ghana	Independence is achieved	Murder of President Sylvanus Olympio; new civilian government organized after coup	Coup of Colonel Etienne Eyadéma, now President Gnassingbé Eyadéma	RPT becomes the only legal party in Togo
Germany occupies Togo 1884	1919	1956–1957	1960	1963	1967	1969

1980s

The first national multiparty elections take place; constitutional changes broaden electoral participation

A coup attempt is thwarted

Togo hosts ECOWAS summit of 15 heads of state

TOGO

The problem of developing national unity in a country where people speak many different languages and have very different lifestyles can be found in many African nations, including Togo. There are more than 40 ethnic groups in this long, narrow country. A government commission of 1968 declared that unity was very difficult to achieve because the northern and southern groups differed so much economically, socially, and culturally.

NATIONAL UNITY IS ENCOURAGED

Togo, like other African states, was an artificial creation of the colonial powers, yet there are age-old links between the regions. The cattle trade has operated in the north and south for generations. However, there was no unifying African kingdom. Now Togolese are all part of one nation, and the government of President (and General) Gnassingbé Eyadéma is making efforts to encourage national unity. Following the example of Mobutu of Zaire, Eyadéma has encouraged the use of indigenous names and of national languages in the schools, and he has proposed "an authentic model of national development," which would respect the culture of the country.

The Rassemblement du People Togolais (Rally of the Togolese People, or RPT), formed in 1969, is the only recognized political party. All regional groups are represented in the party, which is about 1 million strong.

EWE SEEK REUNIFICATION

These efforts have limits, and ethnic problems remain. The Ewe people, one of the largest and most powerful groups, have a high proportion of educated persons and have monopolized many of the varied positions in the government and the economy, causing some animosity. Ewe live in Ghana as well as in southern Togo. They are very conscious of the fact that Ewe were all part of one German colony before World War I. With the defeat of the Germans, the territory was divided between the British and the French. In the mid-1950s Ewe in the French zones decided to join Togo, while those in the British-governed area chose to become part of the new Ghana. Now many Ewe people would like to reunite, a movement not favored by either government.

Other forms of conflict exist. Relatives and supporters of Togo's murdered President Sylvanus Olympio maintain a government in exile, and several coup attempts, the most recent in 1986, have been thwarted. Eyadéma accused Ghana of supporting coup plotters, and borders were closed. These issues, as well as large-scale smuggling, created tension between the governments of Ghana and Togo.

ECONOMIC PROBLEMS

Economic problems also disrupt the state. Togo is poor, with few resources. The government is concentrating on diversifying the economy, creating small- and medium-size industries, and encouraging rural agriculture. Falling prices for phosphates, Togo's major export, led to cutbacks in development programs. Cocoa production, which first began on African plantations established before 1914, is declining because of the continuing low prices for this product. Instead of working at home, Togolese migrate to Ghana and other countries where they can earn more money. Many northerners worked in Ghana in colonial times and continue that tradition. Both countries have cooperated in recent times to reduce illegal traffic.

Eyadéma has worked for peace among the peoples of Togo and among African states, including the border conflicts between Burkina Faso and Mali and between Nigeria and Cameroon. He helped to bring Houphouët-Boigny of Côte d'Ivoire and Sekou Touré of Guinea together. At the 1988 summit of the Economic Community of West African States (ECOWAS), Eyadéma greeted Ghana's Jerry Rawlings, easing 2 years of tension. Togo was one of the first countries to join ECOWAS, and Eyadéma has a strong commitment to the success of the organization (Togo is one of only two countries whose payments are up to date).

DEVELOPMENT

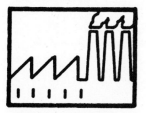

Phosphate mining has been the major source of exports and development funds. The mines were nationalized in 1974. However, the fluctuating and unpredictable price of phosphates on the world market have made it an unreliable source of prosperity. Loans to rehabilitate transportation are expected to assist agricultural and tourist development.

FREEDOM

Togo seeks to improve its human-rights record. Although there are reports of arbitrary arrests, detentions, and torture, recently Togo inaugurated a 13-member National Commission for Human Rights, has been retraining police, and has been receptive to the International Commission of Jurists.

HEALTH/WELFARE

Togo plans to build the first windmill factory in Africa to promote energy-efficient irrigation and water resources.

ACHIEVEMENTS

Hosting the 1988 ECOWAS summit in Lomé, Eyadéma spoke out against the dumping of toxic wastes in Africa, noting: "Our efforts for the economic development of our states and for the progress of our peoples will be in vain if we do not . . . preserve the lives of our peoples and our environment."

Western Sahara (Saharawi Arab Democratic Republic)

GEOGRAPHY

Area in Square Kilometers (Miles):
266,770 (102,703)
Capital (Population): El Ayoun
(20,010)
Climate: temperate coast; arid to
semiarid inland

PEOPLE

Population
Total: 142,000
Annual Growth Rate: 2.8%
Rural/Urban Population Ratio: n/a
Languages: official: Arabic; others
spoken: Spanish, Berber languages

Health
Life Expectancy at Birth: n/a
Infant Death Rate (Ratio): n/a
Average Caloric Intake: n/a
Physicians Available (Ratio): n/a

Religion(s)
primarily Muslim

Education
Adult Literacy Rate: 20%

THE REGUIBAT

The Reguibat is the largest group, or *qabila*, in Western Sahara. Like the other peoples of the country, its members claim descent from a holy father of Islam. This group, often known as "people of the gun," were once warriors but now have a settled lifestyle. Like other Saharawi people, they speak Arabic and are of mixed Arab, Berber, and black African descent. The Reguibat people make up 52 percent of the population of Western Sahara and live in Mauritania, Mali, and Morocco as well. They are a majority within Polisario. However, as it has been said, Polisario is made up of many different ethnic groups, but they are all one people. In this way, the liberation struggle has forged the nation.

COMMUNICATION

Telephones: 1,000
Newspapers: n/a

TRANSPORTATION

Highways—Kilometers (Miles): 6,100
(3,660)
Railroads—Kilometers (Miles): none
Commercial Airports: 2 international

GOVERNMENT

Type: legal status of territory and
question of sovereignty unresolved.
Morocco controls the major
northwestern area.
Independence Date: none
Head of State: —
Political Parties: —
Suffrage: —

MILITARY

Number of Armed Forces: n/a
*Military Expenditures (% of Central
Government Expenditures):* n/a
Current Hostilities: conflict between
Polisario Liberation Movement and
Morocco for administrative control of
the territory

ECONOMY

Currency ($ U.S. Equivalent): n/a
Per Capita Income/GNP: n/a
Inflation Rate: n/a
Natural Resources: phosphate; iron
ore; fish
Agriculture: camels; sheep; goats
Industry: phosphate and iron mining;
fishing; handicrafts

FOREIGN TRADE

Exports: n/a
Imports: n/a

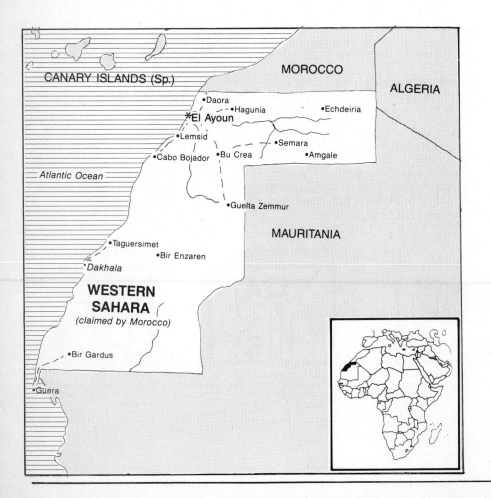

The Saharawi fight against Spanish colonialists
1934

The Polisario movement fights against the Spanish
1973–1974

S.A.D.R. is formed
1976

Mauritania signs the Algiers Agreement, recognizes Polisario, and withdraws from Western Sahara
1979

1980s

Mauritania recognizes S.A.D.R. as a sovereign state

S.A.D.R. takes a seat at OAU meetings, recognized by a majority of members

Algeria-Morocco rapprochement and international pressures for a settlement

WESTERN SAHARA

"The baptism of a child before its conception," is how Sekou Touré of Guinea described the admission of the Saharawi Arab Democratic Republic (S.A.D.R.) to the Organization of African Unity before a referendum had been carried out among the people. A majority of the states in the OAU have recognized S.A.D.R. as the 51st member of the organization, but its existence as a sovereign state is still a matter of dispute.

DOES S.A.D.R. EXIST?

Does S.A.D.R. exist? A strong case can be made in its favor.

The country is situated on the Atlantic edge of the Sahara Desert. Spain claimed this desert land, and it was administered as a Spanish colony from the 1930s to 1975. In 1975–1976 Spain determined to withdraw from the territory. Despite moves that had been made toward self-government in the region, Spain secretly negotiated to give the area to Morocco and Mauritania.

The peoples of Western Sahara did not agree with this new colonialism. The liberation movement, the Polisario Front, which had fought against the Spanish from 1973 to 1975, continued to struggle against the Moroccans and Mauritanians. In 1979 Mauritania signed an agreement with the Polisario and withdrew from Western Sahara. Morocco still claims the territory and is at war with the Polisario.

Today a majority of this arid land is controlled by the Polisario Front, which founded S.A.D.R. in 1976. Morocco controls significant territories, including two important coastal enclaves. The main enclave, called "the useful triangle," is located in the extreme northwest of the country and contains the major settlements, including El Ayoun, and the valuable phosphate mines, which were reopened in 1982 after 6 years of inactivity. This area is protected by a 1,000-mile wall of sand, behind which the Moroccans have established minefields, sensors, artillery, and troops (funded by the United States, France, and Saudi Arabia). Between 120,000 and 150,000 soldiers are estimated to be stationed in this tiny area. Meanwhile, Polisario forces number about 10,000. However, unlike the Moroccans, the Polisario are Saharawi who know the desert intimately. Extension and fortification of the wall have given Morocco the advantage on the ground and led Polisario to adopt tactics of smaller, more frequent raids.

PLANS FOR A REFERENDUM

Everyone has agreed that the Saharawi have a right to take part in a referendum to determine their future. More than half of the people live in the area now occupied by Morocco. Traditional citizens are "sons of the clouds," nomadic people who seek water and food for their herds, but the people of the settlements have often developed a different lifestyle. There are also Western Saharans living in refugee camps in Algeria. It will be difficult to organize a referendum.

However, the greatest obstacle to discovering the people's view is the attitude of Morocco's King Hassan. Hassan has declared that Morocco will not give up its "amputated Saharan provinces," especially not to S.A.D.R., which Hassan views as an ally of Algeria. Division over the issue caused tensions in the OAU in the 1980s.

A majority of the OAU now recognize S.A.D.R.. Both the OAU and the United Nations support S.A.D.R. demands for direct talks with Morocco, withdrawal of troops, and neutral supervision of a referendum. Despite visits by the outgoing OAU Chairman Kenneth Kaunda and UN Secretary-General Javier Pérez de Cuellar in 1988, Morocco's Hassan has refused.

While Libya withdrew military support for Polisario, Algeria continues its support (and housing of thousands of refugees) in spite of its recent renewal of diplomatic relations with Morocco. Visitors to Western Sahara note that in spite of the long war and the military power of Morocco, the Saharawi are not demoralized and continue to struggle on the ground and in diplomatic circles. S.A.D.R. celebrated its 12th anniversary in February 1988 and is now recognized by 69 countries.

DEVELOPMENT

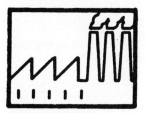

Phosphate deposits were discovered in 1943. There are reserves of 1.7 billion tons. Polisario has attacked the Fosbucraa conveyer belt used for transmission of the ore, but the operations continue. Western Sahara is the sixth major phosphate exporter in the world, with the returns going to Morocco.

FREEDOM

The United States has played a role in obstructing the freedom of S.A.D.R. by tripling military aid to Morocco, selling tanks when the UN was seeking a settlement, and failing to challenge Morocco for use of U.S. military personnel in its war in Western Sahara.

HEALTH/WELFARE

There is little evidence of increased health and well-being for Saharawi peoples in the midst of the liberation war.

ACHIEVEMENTS

Traditionally, Saharawi peoples had no central government administration. Decisions were made at local levels by assemblies of free men. Polisario has been a focus for unity, governed by a president, a 9-member Executive Council and a 21-member Politburo.

Central Africa

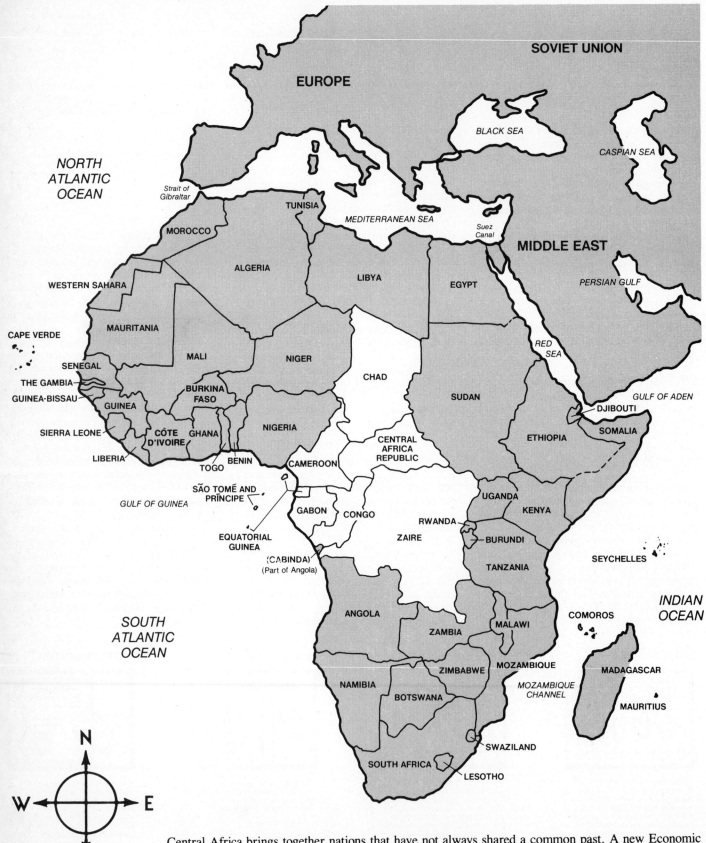

Central Africa brings together nations that have not always shared a common past. A new Economic Community of those states may stimulate their cooperation.

Central Africa: Possibilities for Cooperation

(United Nations photo)

In Africa, cooperative work groups often take on jobs that would be done by machinery in industrialized countries.

The Central African region, as defined in this book, brings together countries that have not always shared a common past, nor do they necessarily seem destined for a common future. Cameroon, Chad, Central African Republic, Congo, Gabon, Zaire, Equatorial Guinea (which includes the island of Fernando Po, now called Bioko), and the island nation of São Tomé and Príncipe have not historically been grouped together as one region. Indeed, users of this volume who are familiar with the continent will associate the label "Central Africa" with states such as Angola and Zambia as well as the states mentioned here. The peoples of southern Zaire have historic links with peoples of Angola and Zambia, but today these states seem more deeply involved with Southern African issues. Thus, there is an arbitrary and shifting nature to the Central African label.

THE DIVERSITY OF THE REGION

The countries of Central Africa incorporate a vast variety of peoples and cultures, resources, environments, systems of government, and national goals. Most of the modern nations overlay both societies that are village-based and localized and others that were once part of famous and extensive kingdoms. Islam has had little influence in the region, except in Chad and northern Cameroon, and there is no unanimity of religious belief and practice; many Christian churches as well as traditional rituals and faiths are found throughout the area.

Wooden sculptures are one of the great achievements of African societies. They are thought to have spiritual potential and are associated with beliefs in the ancestors or are valued as prestige objects. However, the art forms are myriad and distinctive, and their diversity is more striking than the common features they possess.

Present-day governments range from the conservative regime of President Bongo of Gabon, the self-designated Marxist-Leninist government of the People's Republic of the Congo, the military regime of Kolingba (who replaced Emperor Bokassa's successor in Central African Republic), and the "Mobutuism" practiced by Mobutu in Zaire. A long-lasting war devastated Chad, with Central African states taking opposing sides in that war.

Yet there is much that the Central African states share. These include some of the geographic features that characterize the area and influence the lives of its peoples; the colonial backgrounds (primarily French and Belgian) that established political and economic patterns that have lasted until the present day; and the limited recent efforts to build a community of Central African states.

GEOGRAPHIC DISTINCTIVENESS

All of the states of the Central African region except Chad encompass equatorial rain forests. Citizens who live in these regions must cope with a climate that is both hot and moist and must face the challenges of clearing and using the great equatorial forests. The problems of living in these heavily

(Peace Corps photo)

The manufacture and sale of traditional crafts are important to many Central African economies. The Traditional Handicrafts Cooperative Society in Cameroon facilitates trade in these local items.

forested areas account in part for the very low population densities of the Central African states. The difficulty of creating roads and railroads impedes communication and development.

The peoples of the rain-forest areas tend to cluster along river banks and rail lines. In modern times, because of the extensive development of minerals, many inhabitants have moved to the cities, accounting for a comparatively high urban population. The rivers are lifelines, perhaps more important than in other regions. The watershed in Cameroon between the Niger and Zaire rivers provides a natural divide between the West and Central African regions. The Zaire is the largest of the rivers, but the Oubangi, Chari, and Ogooue, as well as other rivers, are also important for the communication and trading opportunities they offer. The rivers flow to the Atlantic Ocean and encourage the orientation of the Central African states toward the West.

Many of the countries of the region share similar sources of wealth, including the hydroelectric potential of the rivers and the rain forests. Every country except Chad and São Tomé and Príncipe exports lumber. Other forest products such as rubber and palm oil traditionally have been widely marketed. Lumbering and clearing activities for agriculture have led to the disappearance of many of the rain forests in West and Central Africa, and there are now movements to halt this destruction. Poor countries have not financed the reforestation efforts recommended by environmentalists, leading to boycotts of endangered hardwoods. These boy-

cotts are gaining recognition throughout Europe and will affect the efforts of Central African countries to raise their incomes.

As one might expect, Central Africa is one of the areas least affected by the conditions of drought that currently characterize much of Africa. Yet not all of these countries are drought-free. People in Chad and Central African Republic are suffering from food shortages. Savanna lands are found to the north and the south of the forests. Whereas rain forests have inhibited travel, the savannas have been transitional areas, great lanes of migration linking East and West Africa and providing opportunities for cattle herding as well as agriculture. Such regions characterize Chad, Central African Republic, northern Cameroon, and southern Zaire.

Besides the products of the forest, there are many other resources that the countries of the Central African region have in common. Especially important are the oil resources of Cameroon, Chad, Congo, and Gabon (although Chad does not exploit its petroleum reserves). Uranium, formerly exported by Zaire, is now mined in Gabon and Central African Republic, and uranium deposits are also found in Chad. Other mineral resources abound, and the process of their exploitation as well as the demand for them among the developed nations of the world are issues of common concern in the region. Many of the states also grow coffee, cocoa, and cotton for export and are affected by the fluctuation of prices for these crops on the world market. The similarity of their environments and products provides a

(WFP photo by F. Mattioli)

Women in Chad winnow sesame seed. Cash crops such as sesame seed and cotton can encourage an economy, but they also can divert labor from food production.

foundation on which these states can build cooperative institutions and policies.

THE LINKS TO FRANCE

Many of the different ethnic groups in Central Africa overlap national boundaries. The Fang are found in Gabon and Equatorial Guinea; the Bateke in Congo and Gabon; and the Kongo in Zaire, Angola, and Congo. However, the widespread ethnic groupings seem less important for building regional unity than the European colonial systems that the countries inherited. Equatorial Guinea was controlled by Spain, São Tomé and Príncipe by Portugal, and Zaire by Belgium. However, the predominant power in the region was France. Central African Republic, Chad, Congo, and Gabon were all members of French Equatorial Africa. This administrative federation established by the French rulers provided links among the four territories.

The early economic impact of the colonists was similar.

All of the Central African states were affected by European companies, which were given concessions (often 99-year leases with economic and political rights) to exploit such products of the forest zones as ivory and rubber. At the beginning of the twentieth century, 41 companies controlled 70 percent of the territory of present-day Congo, Gabon, and Central African Republic. Large plantations were established to increase palm-oil production, for example, while companies exploited mineral resources. Individual production by Africans was encouraged, and forced labor was common. Meanwhile, colonial companies encouraged production and trade but did little to aid the growth of infrastructure or long-term development. Only in Zaire was industry more extensively promoted.

Neither the colonial policies of the Belgians and French nor the companies themselves offered many opportunities for Africans to gain training and education, and there was little encouragement of independent entrepreneurs. Felix Eboué, the governor of French Equatorial Africa in the early

1940s, increased opportunities for the urban elite in Congo, Gabon, and Central African Republic. The Brazzaville Conference of 1944, recognizing the important role that the people of the French colonies had played in World War II, abolished forced labor and granted citizenship to all. Yet political progress toward self-government was limited in the Central African region. Only in Cameroon did political activity start early, and this was due to the fact that Cameroon was held by France as a trust territory of the United Nations (UN). When the countries gained independence during the 1960s few people could shoulder the bureaucratic and administrative tasks of the regimes that took power. This was especially true in Zaire. People who could handle the economic institutions for the countries' benefit were scarce, and, in any case, the nations' economies remained (for the most part) securely in outside hands.

The Spanish of Equatorial Guinea and the Portuguese of São Tomé and Príncipe also benefited from plantation agriculture while depending on forced labor. Here, too, political opportunities were limited. Neither country gained independence until fairly recently: Equatorial Guinea in 1968, and São Tomé and Príncipe in 1975.

In the years since independence most of the countries of Central Africa have been influenced, pressured, and supported by the former colonial powers, especially France. French firms in Congo, Central African Republic, and Gabon are exploiting new products as well as old resources. All are only slightly encumbered by the regulations of independent governments, and all are geared toward European markets and needs. Financial institutions are branches of French institutions, and all of the countries are members of the Franc Zone. French expatriates serve in government as well as with companies, and French troops are stationed in these countries. France is not only the major trading partner of these states but also contributes significantly to their budgets. Zaire, although less influenced by the French, did call on French troops during civil disturbances in eastern Zaire in 1977, and it hosted the annual meetings of French-speaking African nations in 1982. France played a role in a coup in Equatorial Guinea in 1979 and has increased its aid and investment to the government there.

EFFORTS AT COOPERATION

Although many Africans in Central Africa recognize that links among their countries would be beneficial, there have been fewer initiatives toward political unity or economic integration in this region—either at the time of independence or after that time—than in East, West, or Southern Africa. In the years before independence, Barthelemy Boganda of what is now Central African Republic espoused and publicized the idea of a "United States of Latin Africa," which was to include French and Portuguese territories as well as Zaire, but he was not supported by others in the region.

When France offered independence to the countries of French Equatorial Africa in 1960, soon after Boganda's death, the possibility of forming a federation was discussed;

(World Bank/CIRC photo by Alain Prott)

Timber from the rain forests is one of the major resources of Central Africa. Environmentalists are very concerned about ecological effects of the exploitation of this resource.

but Gabon, which was much wealthier than the other countries, declined to participate. Chad, Central African Republic, and Congo almost signed an agreement that would have created a federal legislature and executive branch governing all three countries, but there was concern over their separate diplomatic and United Nations status, and all of the countries became independent separately.

There have been some formal efforts at economic integration among the former French states. A Customs and Economic Union of the Central African States (UDEAC) was established in 1964, but membership did not remain stable. Chad and Central African Republic withdrew to join Zaire in an alternate organization. (Central African Republic later returned, bringing the number of members to six.) The East and Central African states together planned an economic community in 1967, but this did not materialize.

Only recently have there been new and hopeful signs of progress toward economic cooperation. Urged on by the UN Economic Commission on Africa (ECA) and with the stimulus of the Lagos Plan of Action, signed in 1980, the Central African states met in 1982 to prepare for a new economic grouping. In 1983, all of the Central African states, as well as Rwanda and Burundi in East Africa, signed a treaty estab-

(World Bank photo by Ivan Albert Andrews)

This palm oil processing mill was financed by the World Bank as part of a development project in Cameroon.

lishing the Economic Community of Central African States (ECCA, also known as CEEAC) to promote economic and industrial cooperation.

Some have criticized the ECCA as a duplicate of UDEAC, but its goals are broader than a customs union (though it does urge cooperation in that area also). Members hoped that the union would stimulate industrial activity—already very promising—increase markets, and reduce the dependence on France and other countries for trade and capital. But with dues often unpaid and meetings postponed, the ECCA faces many obstacles. Only 4 out of 10 members attended the 1987 meeting. Mobutu Sese Seko of Zaire took over as chairman for 1988-1989 and addressed the 9 heads of state who attended the 1988 meeting. The closing statement of the group committed to paying up dues and to a strong effort to

boost interregional trade, customs, finance, commerce, and transportation, urging that national roads be extended to aid interstate transportation.

Central African states, while sharing a difficult but rich environment, have suffered more than other regions in Africa from the neglect and exploitation of their former colonial powers. They have not found common ways to develop mineral and forest resources and to deal with outside companies. Little implementation has resulted from former unions. As the Swahili proverb goes, "The toughness of the hoe is tested in the garden." It is hoped that ECCA will lead to a pragmatic Central African market and fulfill the need for a harmonization of trade and industrial policies. Eventually, it may become one of the building blocks of a continent-wide union.

Cameroon (United Republic of Cameroon)

GEOGRAPHY

Area in Square Kilometers (Miles): 475,400 (183,568) (somewhat larger than California)
Capital (Population): Yaoundé (852,000)
Climate: tropical to semiarid

PEOPLE

Population

Total: 9,880,000
Annual Growth Rate: 2.4%
Rural/Urban Population Ratio: 69/31
Languages: official: English, French; others spoken: Fulde, Ewondo, Duala, Bamilike, Bassa, Bali, others

Health

Life Expectancy at Birth: 43 years male; 46 years female
Infant Death Rate (Ratio): 113/1,000
Average Caloric Intake: 106% of FAO minimum
Physicians Available (Ratio): 1/16,357

Religion(s)

35% Roman Catholic; 25% traditional indigenous; 22% Muslim; 18% Protestant

Education

Adult Literacy Rate: 65%

COMMUNICATION

Telephones: 47,200
Newspapers: 1

THE KORUP FOREST

"Do not call the forest that shelters you a jungle" is an African proverb. The primary rain forests in Cameroon and other parts of Central Africa are the homes of plants and animals that have developed in this environment over thousands of years and that serve humanity. Korup is one Cameroon rain forest that is to be designated a national park. A recent survey discovered more than 42,000 trees and climbers in Korup, including 17 tree species never described before. An international campaign has been launched to preserve such rain forests, under the auspices of the World Wildlife Fund (WWF) and the International Union for the Conservation of Nature and Natural Resources (IUCN). Korup is the subject of a film that is being shown to raise funds for its preservation and that of other rain forests.

TRANSPORTATION

Highways—Kilometers (Miles): 66,910 (41,484)
Railroads—Kilometers (Miles): 1,115 (691)
Commercial Airports: 4 international

GOVERNMENT

Type: republic
Independence Date: January 1, 1960
Head of State: President Paul Biya
Political Parties: Cameroon People's Democratic Movement
Suffrage: universal over 21

MILITARY

Number of Armed Forces: 10,600
Military Expenditures (% of Central Government Expenditures): $21 million (15%)
Current Hostilities: none

ECONOMY

Currency ($ U.S. Equivalent): 286 CFA francs = $1
Per Capita Income/GNP: $802/$7.3 billion
Inflation Rate: 15%
Natural Resources: timber; oil; bauxite; iron ore; rubber
Agriculture: coffee; cocoa; food crops; cotton; bananas; peanuts; tobacco; tea
Industry: small manufacturing; consumer goods; aluminum

FOREIGN TRADE

Exports: $1.9 billion
Imports: $1.1 billion

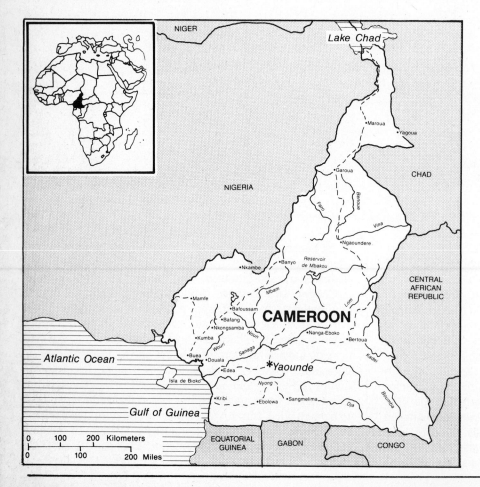

| The establishment of the German Kamerun Protectorate **1884** | Partition of Cameroon; separate British and French mandates are established under the League of Nations **1916** | The UPC is formed **1948** | The UPC is outlawed for launching revolts in the cities **1955** | Independent Cameroon Republic is established with Ahidjo as the first president **1960** | Cameroon Federal Republic reunites French Cameroon with British Cameroon after a UN-supervised referendum **1961** | The new Constitution creates a unitary state **1972** |

1980s

| Ahidjo resigns after 22 years in office; Biya assumes the presidency | Lake Nyos releases lethal volcanic gases, killing an estimated 2,000 people | Biya is reelected in the first multiple-candidate election since independence |

CAMEROON

Cameroon is frequently called the "hinge" of Africa. Its mountains divide the West African "peninsula" from the central lands, and it is thought that the Bantu-speaking peoples who now inhabit most of Central and Southern Africa originated from the area near the Nigeria and Cameroon border.

The colonial heritage has been diverse. The Germans were the first to claim the territory. After World War I the area was divided between the British and the French. Now these areas have been united (except for the northwest region, whose people joined Nigeria).

THE QUEST FOR UNITY

At the time of independence in 1960 the new government was a federation. President Ahmadou Ahidjo spearheaded a move toward a unified form of government. By 1966 regional parties were incorporated into a single party, the Cameroon National Union (CNU), and by 1971 a single trade union had absorbed other trade unions. In 1972 Ahidjo proposed the abolition of the federation, and a Constitution for a unified Cameroon was approved by an overwhelming vote. Such measures increased and extended executive power and the possibilities of its use. Ahidjo exercised this power, creating what has been called a police state.

THE TRANSFER OF POWER

In 1982 Ahidjo suddenly resigned after 22 years in office. In line with the constitutional amendment passed in 1979, Paul Biya, the prime minister, became the new president.

During his first year in office Biya made gradual changes. He took over control of the party from Ahidjo. He brought young technocrats into the ministries and called for a more open and democratic society, proposing that the presidency, for instance, be opened to candidates from outside the party.

POLITICAL AND ECONOMIC CHALLENGES

After a coup attempt in 1984 Biya tightened his control. Some members of the Presidential Guard led the revolt, and many suspect that they acted with the encouragement of Ahidjo, who was living in France. The revolt was put down, but 500 to 1,000 people died, mostly in the vicinity of the capital, Yaoundé. More than 1,000 persons were arrested, questioned, and tried by a secret military tribunal.

The press was restricted. Drastic changes occurred in the leadership of the party; it was given a new role in mobilizing the people of the provinces, and in 1985 the name of the CNU was changed to Cameroon People's Democratic Movement. Ahidjo, a northerner, had sought regional and ethnic balance in his ministry and appointments. However, southerners now dominate in the government, perhaps because of continuing fears of Ahidjo's northern base, and Anglophone citizens of the west as well as northerners express their fears of the increasing centralization of the system.

Within the new structure, elections took place in 1987 and 1988. For the first time since independence multiple candidates stood for some offices. Biya was reelected by 98 percent of the 4 million voters who turned out. When many National Assembly members were not returned to their seats, Biya reshuffled his Cabinet, appointing younger ministers, many in ministries in their fields of expertise. Because of high debt and low commodity prices, Biya faces an economic and banking crisis and a rising crime rate. Political tension continues, and Biya increasingly relies on Israeli security forces.

RELATIONS WITH OTHER COUNTRIES

Cameroon has had uneasy relations with Nigeria, Chad, and Gabon over border disputes and Cameroon nationals living in these countries. France remains Cameroon's most important trading partner and source of development assistance. U.S. ties are also close, and Cameroon renewed diplomatic relations with Israel in 1986. Cameroon, nevertheless, maintains an independent foreign policy, cooperating with Eastern-Bloc countries and supporting the liberation of Southern Africa.

DEVELOPMENT

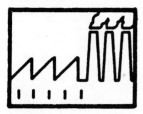

The Cameroon Development Corporation (CDC) coordinates more than half of the agricultural exports and, after the government, employs the most people. Cocoa and coffee comprise more than 50% of Cameroon's exports. Lower prices for these commodities have reduced the country's income.

FREEDOM

Cameroon's press is restricted by a new controversial press law, and foreign publications are restricted. International human-rights groups charge that prisoners of conscience were tortured and secretly executed along with coup plotters. Ministers in the former government were still in prison in 1987.

HEALTH/WELFARE

Women are equal by law and are active in the party and in the state labor union. Social and educational programs have been developed for Cameroonian women.

ACHIEVEMENTS

The art of Cameroon societies is unusual and rich. Two interesting forms are the skin-covered helmet or top-of-head masks that are found only in this area of Africa, and the highly decorated brass pipes made by the "lost wax" process. Wax is formed around a mold in the shape desired, and another mold encloses it. When heated, the wax is "lost" (runs out), and molten metal replaces it.

Central African Republic

GEOGRAPHY

Area in Square Kilometers (Miles): 622,436 (240,324) (slightly smaller than Texas)
Capital (Population): Bangui (473,000)
Climate: tropical to semiarid

PEOPLE

Population
Total: 2,800,000
Annual Growth Rate: 2.8%
Rural/Urban Population Ratio: 71/29
Languages: official: French; others spoken: Sangho, Banda, Baya, Mangia, M'Baka

Health
Life Expectancy at Birth: 44 years
Infant Death Rate (Ratio): 134/1,000
Average Caloric Intake: 92% of FAO minimum
Physicians Available (Ratio): 1/25,925

Religion(s)
35% traditional indigenous; 25% Protestant; 25% Roman Catholic; 15% Muslim

Education
Adult Literacy Rate: 33%

BARTHELEMY BOGANDA

Barthelemy Boganda, the father of his country, wanted to see a vast united Central Africa. A contemporary of Leopold Senghor of Senegal, Boganda, like Senghor, was influenced by his own culture and that of France as well. Boganda was brought up in Catholic missions in Congo Brazzaville and Yaoundé. In 1946 he ran for the French National Assembly and won. In 1949 he created the Popular Movement for the Social Evolution of Black Africa (MESAN), and he sought to associate the new organization with the traditional age grades in his country. Boganda declared that "colonialism is slavery's eldest daughter," and he fought for equal rights for all the people of Central Africa. He was especially opposed to the division of the region into many states, and he spoke out for a vast nation of former French, Belgian, and Portuguese territories in the 1950s. He even wrote a Central African constitution. Boganda was considered an agitator by French residents in the area, and he suffered imprisonment and condemnation during the independence struggle. He never saw his country achieve independence, for he died in a mysterious plan crash in 1959. Some of his followers still live. One such follower is Abel Goumba, a leader of government opposition.

COMMUNICATION

Telephones: 5,000
Newspapers: 1

TRANSPORTATION

Highways—Kilometers (Miles): 22,560 (13,987)
Railroads—Kilometers (Miles): none
Commercial Airports: 1 international

GOVERNMENT

Type: republic; under military rule
Independence Date: August 13, 1960
Head of State: General André-Dieudonné Kolingba (chief of state)
Political Parties: C.A.R. Democratic Rally
Suffrage: suspended

MILITARY

Number of Armed Forces: 10,000 paramilitary personnel
Military Expenditures (% of Central Government Expenditures): $13,500,000 (10.8%)
Current Hostilities: none

ECONOMY

Currency ($ U.S. Equivalent): 286 CFA francs = $1
Per Capita Income/GNP: $310/$680 million
Inflation Rate: 4%
Natural Resources: diamonds; uranium; timber
Agriculture: coffee; cotton; peanuts; food crops; livestock
Industry: timber; textiles; soap; cigarettes; processed food; diamond mining

FOREIGN TRADE

Exports: $145 million
Imports: $140 million

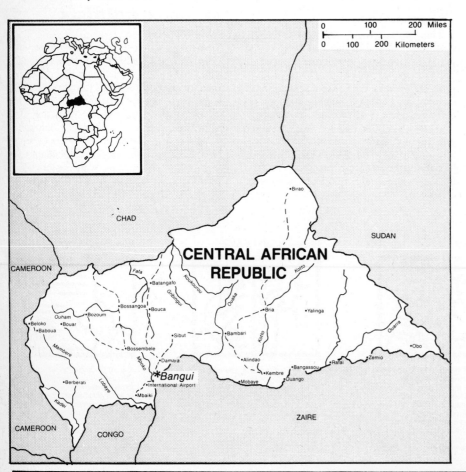

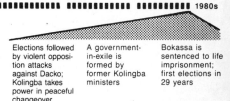

Separate French administration of the Oubangui-Chàri colony is established
1904

Gold and diamonds are discovered
1912–1913

Boganda sets up MESAN, which gains wide support
1949

Boganda dies; Dacko, his successor, becomes president at the time of independence
1960

Bokassa takes power after the first general strike
1966

Bokassa becomes emperor
1976

Bokassa is involved in the massacre of students; Dacko returns as head of state
1979

1980s

Elections followed by violent opposition attacks against Dacko; Kolingba takes power in peaceful changeover

A government-in-exile is formed by former Kolingba ministers

Bokassa is sentenced to life imprisonment; first elections in 29 years

CENTRAL AFRICAN REPUBLIC

"We aim to make a nation out of a colonial territory and a united people out of all the ethnic groups," said David Dacko, the Central African Republic's first president, at the Party Congress in 1962. The goal has been a difficult one to achieve in this landlocked country with its predominantly rural population. The country's isolated geographic location and its history of conquest and destruction underlie today's problems. The continued influence of the French, the gap between the rich and poor, and conflicts among those at the top are among the factors that have shaped the country since independence.

FRENCH CONQUEST

In the late nineteenth and early twentieth centuries the French conquered the region and claimed sovereignty over it. French pacification campaigns were destructive; even more destructive were the exploitations of the 39 French companies that sought rubber and other raw materials—causing such havoc that many peoples are yet to recover. The colony became part of French Equatorial Africa in 1910.

In 1960 C.A.R.'s population was just over 1 million. Up to 50,000 people were employed on projects managed by Europeans. The movement for independence was led by Barthelemy Boganda, a former priest who developed the Popular Movement for the Social Evolution of Black Africa (MESAN), which he hoped would build on traditional age groups. The movement did gain popularity among the peasantry. Boganda recognized the weaknesses of the nation, the probability of continued French interest, and the need for regional unity.

Boganda's death in a mysterious plane crash just before independence put the mantle of the "father of the nation" on the shoulders of David Dacko. Despite Dacko's stated goal of building a nation, the differences between the lives of the peasants and elite continued to grow.

BOKASSA DECLARES HIMSELF EMPEROR

The country suffered greatly during the rule of Jean-Bedel Bokassa, who became head of state in a coup in 1966, and who made himself emperor in 1976 in a lavish ceremony. He did away with democratic institutions, monopolized and dissipated the wealth of the country, and sparked international outcries after sanctioning the massacre of 100 young people jailed after a demonstration over school uniforms.

In 1979, following this incident, former President Dacko, with French support, came back to power in a bloodless coup while Bokassa was out of the country. He was superceded by General André Kolingba in 1981. After Bokassa's 1986 return to C.A.R. he was sentenced to death, with that sentence commuted to life imprisonment with hard labor.

Politics both before and after Bokassa have reflected competition among politicians, several of whom have been especially concerned about the gap between rich and poor. Opposition groups led by noted figures such as Abel Goumba and Ange Patasse continue to seek openings in the political system, and have been re-pressed. In 1985 the military committee was dissolved to form a new government which includes civilians. Voters endorsed a new Constitution and renewed Kolingba's rule.

PERVASIVE FRENCH INFLUENCE

The French have continued to play an important role in the country. French troops have supplemented the national force since independence. The French government provides 70 percent of official aid (it provided 40 percent of the 1987 budget). Fifty percent of the exports of the Central African Republic go to France, and the French supply more than half of the country's imports.

France has also influenced the course of recent political events. The French government contributed to the expenses of Bokassa's coronation, and—following the murder of the young students—French troops were involved in Bokassa's overthrow. The French have stated their support for Kolingba.

Export revenues have fallen in recent years, and C.A.R. is deeply in debt. Agreements with the World Bank, debt rescheduling, and France's write-off of debt may ease the long-term strains, but President Kolingba said recently that development is "an uphill task that needs the participation of all Centrafricans."

DEVELOPMENT

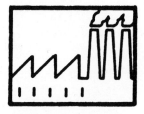

Food production rose in 1987, and Central African Republic was able to sustain self-sufficiency. Commodity prices fluctuate, with cotton prices down and coffee prices up. To increase production and transport of crops, France plans assistance in repairing a hydroelectric plant and improvements in river and road transportation.

FREEDOM

Human rights have improved since Bokassa's era. Few political prisoners are in jail, and Bokassa's death sentence was commuted to life with hard labor.

HEALTH/WELFARE

The literacy rate is very low in the Central African Republic, and teacher training is currently being emphasized, especially for primary-school teachers.

ACHIEVEMENTS

Production of cotton, one of the country's most important exports, fell seriously in the 1970s, and the nation had one of the lowest yields per growing unit of all African producers. In the 1980s increases in cotton production have been accompanied by lower prices, thus hindering economic recovery.

Chad (Republic of Chad)

GEOGRAPHY

Area in Square Kilometers (Miles):
1,284,634 (496,000) (four-fifths the
size of Alaska)
Capital (Population): N'Djamena
(511,700)
Climate: arid to semiarid

PEOPLE

Population
Total: 5,240,000
Annual Growth Rate: 2.5%
Rural/Urban Population Ratio: 80/20
Languages: official: French; others
spoken: Chadian Arabic, Fulde,
Hausa, Kotoko, Kanembou, Sara
Maba, others

Health
Life Expectancy at Birth: 43 years
male; 45 years female
Infant Death Rate (Ratio): 140/1,000
Average Caloric Intake: 72% of FAO
minimum
Physicians Available (Ratio): 1/55,744

Religion(s)
44% Muslim; 33% Christian; 23%
traditional indigenous

Education
Adult Literacy Rate: 17%

COMMUNICATION

Telephones: 3,850
Newspapers: 4

TRANSPORTATION

Highways—Kilometers (Miles):
30,725 (19,049)
Railroads—Kilometers (Miles): none
Commercial Airports: 2 international

DROUGHT AND WAR

Nature determines the cycle of drought and rain, but man-made crises
can aggravate natural conditions and produce famine. Years of war have
decimated Chad's population, disrupted pastoral and agricultural cycles,
and changed the lifestyles of a generation of Chadians. After the rains in
1985 crops were planted, and for the first time in many years Chadians
could feed themselves; however, these successes were threatened by
renewed fighting. Efforts to resettle refugees and assist herders to
cultivate millet and sorghum were supplemented by reforestation and
irrigation efforts. Even in peacetime, poor transportation hampers relief
efforts and the marketing of food and cash crops; but unless peace can be
achieved, real development and a productive life for its citizens will
elude Chad.

GOVERNMENT

Type: republic
Independence Date: August 11, 1960
Head of State: President Hissène
Habré
Political Parties: National Union for
Independence and Revolution
Suffrage: universal over 18

MILITARY

Number of Armed Forces: 22,500
*Military Expenditures (% of Central
Government Expenditures):* n/a
Current Hostilities: peace moves
between Habré and Libya may end
warfare

ECONOMY

Currency ($ U.S. Equivalent): 286
CFA francs = $1
Per Capita Income/GNP: $88/$360
million
Inflation Rate: 8.3%
Natural Resources: petroleum;
uranium; natron; kaolin
Agriculture: subsistence crops;
cotton; cattle; fish; sugar
Industry: livestock products; beer;
bicycle and radio assembly; textiles;
cigarettes

FOREIGN TRADE

Exports: $113 million
Imports: $114 million

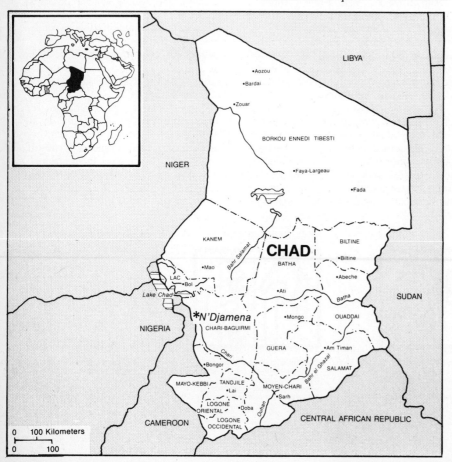

Independence is
achieved under
President
Tombalbaye
1960

Revolt breaks
out among
peasant groups;
FROLINAT is
formed
1965–1966

Establishment of
a Transitional
Government of
National Unity
(GUNT) includes
both Habré and
Goukouni
1978

1980s

Habré comes to
power through
conquest;
Goukouni and
others continue
the war

Habré
consolidates
power; war
focuses on
Libya

Qadhafi
recognizes
Habré's
government

CHAD

The vast land of Chad is one of the poorest countries in the world. Until recently it was unfamiliar to most of the world's citizens. However, Chad made headlines around the world in 1983 as a result of the internationalization of a civil war. The government of Hissène Habré called for aid from outside forces during the battle at the oasis town of Faya Largeau against Libyan-backed troops of Oueddi Goukouni and his supporters.

The United States, concerned about Libya and viewing events as an East-West conflict, sent military advisors and two AWACS radar planes to nearby Sudan in what *U.S. News & World Report* called a "high-technology version of gunboat diplomacy" in support of Habré. Habré's government received air cover and troops from the French, and relied on troops sent by President Mobutu of Zaire. Although fighting subsided in late 1984, new attacks and international assistance escalated from 1986 to 1987. Lebanese mercenaries joined Libyans, and the United States gave $15 million in military aid, including Stinger missiles.

CIVIL WAR

The dramatic international encounters between Goukouni and Libya on one side, and Habré, the United States, and France on the other obscure the reality of the situation in Chad. These military actions are just the latest events in the civil war that began 2 decades ago. It started as a peasant uprising against the increased financial demands of the first independent government of President Tombalbaye. It continued as a national liberation movement organized under the National Liberation Front of Chad (FROLINAT). The number of groups involved in the fighting grew to at least 11 factions, each with its own base of support, its own army, and a determination not to compromise. N'Djamena, the capital, changed hands regularly as a result of factional struggles.

After 1986 Habré gained more recognition and tighter control, with a weakened Goukouni stating in 1987 that Habré should be recognized as head of Chad. The conflict continued, however, with both Libya and Chad claiming the border area known as the Aouzou Strip. And another opposition leader, Achiekh Ibn Oumar, still has troops in Sudan. In 1988 Libya's leader Qadhafi announced that he would recognize the Habré government and pay compensation to Chad. The announcement was welcomed—with some skepticism—by Chadian and other African leaders, though no mention was made of the conflicting claims to the Aouzou Strip.

NORTH-SOUTH DIVISION

Behind this series of events lie longstanding differences between the northerners and southerners who became part of Chad as a result of the artificial boundaries established by European imperialists. Northerners, most of whom live in the grassland savanna belt of central Chad, engage in mixed farming and herding or are pastoralists. They are followers of Islam who speak Arabic and value Arabic traditions, and they maintain a proud independence. The southerners, on the other hand, are agriculturalists, many involved in growing cotton for export. Some southerners are urban dwellers who are French-educated and Christian. Southerners landed good government jobs during the years of French administration and became leaders in government and the army at independence in 1960. Goukouni and Habré represent northern areas, and many southerners remain suspicious of both of them.

Life for ordinary Chadians was never easy; now it has been disrupted further. During the 1980s thousands of refugees moved in and out across Chad's borders. Crops were not planted, herds were not tended, and schools were closed for several years. Food shortages were common and locust plagues posed a serious threat to crops in 1988–1989.

DEVELOPMENT

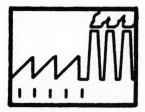

The cotton crop, one of the mainstays of the economy, suffered during the war. The problems of the war have been compounded by the recurring droughts of the 1970s and 1980s. Rains in the mid-1980s brought some relief but also fostered locust infestation.

FREEDOM

The civil war led to a breakdown in law and order. Not only were there battle casualties, but disappearances and arbitrary killings of civilians can be documented. Former refugees and families of opponents have been detained without trial.

HEALTH/WELFARE

The Medecins Sans Frontieres (composed of French, Belgian, and Swiss medical personnel) began a $5-million project to build and reorganize Chad's health-care system. Chinese medical aid was planned for 1988.

ACHIEVEMENTS

Achievements are difficult to ascertain in a time of such dislocation. There have been some signs of recovery in textile, sugar, and other enterprises, and state salaries are paid more regularly (although they have been cut). Food production increased after rains in 1985, but aid is needed to fight locusts.

Congo (People's Republic of the Congo)

GEOGRAPHY

Area in Square Kilometers (Miles):
349,650 (132,000) (slightly smaller
than Montana)
Capital (Population): Brazzaville
(595,100)
Climate: tropical

PEOPLE

Population
Total: 2,180,000
Annual Growth Rate: 3%
Rural/Urban Population Ratio: 55/45
Languages: official: French; others
spoken: Lingala, Kikongo, Teke,
Sangha, M'Bochi, others

Health
Life Expectancy at Birth: 45 years
male; 48 years female
Infant Death Rate (Ratio): 110/1,000
Average Caloric Intake: 99% of FAO
minimum
Physicians Available (Ratio): 1/7,840

Religion(s)
49% traditional indigenous; 50%
Christian; 1% Muslim

RELIGIOUS LIFE

Many different religions have gained followings among peoples of
Congo in recent times. There is even a Tenrikyo Shinto center from
Japan in the country. Many people claim affiliation with Christian faiths,
and one-third are Roman Catholic. Swedish evangelical missionaries
came to Congo in the early twentieth century, and the Salvation Army
and the Jehovah's Witnesses gained followers in the pre-independence
period. Many new religious movements developed after World War I,
often centered around figures who were considered messiahs, such as
Simon Kimbangu, who founded a Christian church that is now a member
of the World Council of Churches, and André Matsoua, an early
nationalist. Until the 1950s the only secondary schools in the country
were the two seminaries preparing priests for the Roman Catholic
Church. The current government banned nearly 30 religious bodies in
1978 and has limited the legal groups to 7—none of which is allowed to
teach religion to young people.

Education
Adult Literacy Rate: 56%

COMMUNICATION

Telephones: 9,000
Newspapers: 3

TRANSPORTATION

Highways—Kilometers (Miles): 8,246
(5,124)
Railroads—Kilometers (Miles): 517
(354)
Commercial Airports: 2 international

GOVERNMENT

Type: people's republic
Independence Date: August 15, 1960
Head of State: President (Colonel)
Denis Sassou Nguesso
Political Parties: Congolese Workers'
Party
Suffrage: universal over 18

MILITARY

Number of Armed Forces: 8,000
*Military Expenditures (% of Central
Government Expenditures):* 4.7%
Current Hostilities: none

ECONOMY

Currency ($ U.S. Equivalent): 286
CFA francs = $1
Per Capita Income/GNP: $500/$2
billion
Inflation Rate: 12.6%
Natural Resources: wood; potash;
petroleum; natural gas
Agriculture: cocoa; coffee; tobacco;
palm kernels; sugarcane; rice;
peanuts
Industry: processed agricultural and
forestry goods; cement; textiles

FOREIGN TRADE

Exports: $1.2 billion
Imports: $603 million

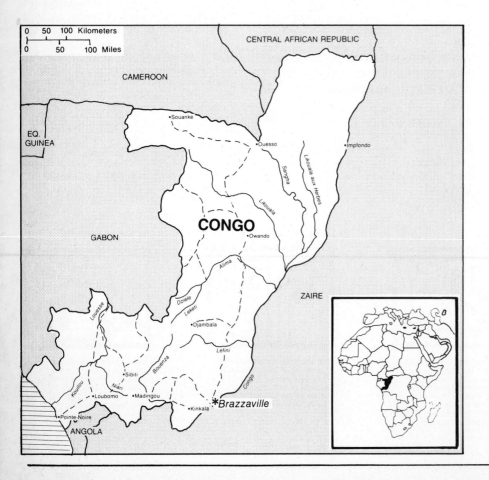

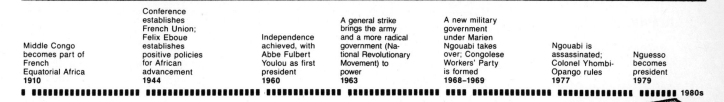

| Middle Congo becomes part of French Equatorial Africa **1910** | Conference establishes French Union; Felix Eboue establishes positive policies for African advancement **1944** | Independence achieved, with Abbe Fulbert Youlou as first president **1960** | A general strike brings the army and a more radical government (National Revolutionary Movement) to power **1963** | A new military government under Marien Ngouabi takes over; Congolese Workers' Party is formed **1968–1969** | Ngouabi is assassinated; Colonel Yhombi-Opango rules **1977** | Nguesso becomes president **1979** |

1980s

The Party Congress reelects Nguesso as president

Pierre Anga, the leader of an unsuccessful uprising in 1987, was killed in 1988

Former President Yhombi-Opango is arrested; a crisis budget is adopted to cope with the debt

CONGO

The People's Republic of the Congo is a country that is little known in the United States. North Americans are likely to confuse the awkwardly shaped former French colony with its southern neighbor, Zaire (once also called Congo), or to be completely unaware of its existence.

HISTORICAL CROSSROADS

Complex states such as the Kongo and Loango kingdoms were established over small chieftaincies in the region during the early centuries of this millennium. When the French claimed the area during the imperial competition of the late nineteenth century, they made Brazzaville, an interior town on the Congo River, the headquarters of French Equatorial Africa (which included Chad, Central African Republic, and Gabon as well as Congo). As a result, the city expanded, and the area around the administrative center developed along with it. The Congo-Ocean Railroad was built from Brazzaville to Pointe Noire on the coast after World War I and was later extended north. During the colonial period foreign concessions exploited the area brutally.

ECONOMIC AND SOCIAL DEVELOPMENT

As the economies of most African states declined Congo's economy, which depends to a large extent on oil revenues, continued to grow. Manufacturing, including cement and textiles, has a longer history and is more fully developed than in most African countries. There is a large

urban population (45 percent) and a large working class. The per capita income was drastically reduced in the 1980s. Government statistics indicate that all primary-school-age children are in school. The figures, however, are deceiving, for there are deep inequities. Urban peoples of Brazzaville and Pointe Noire, for instance, benefit more than do the rural populations, and figures of earnings and life expectancy are higher for city dwellers.

POLITICAL INSTABILITIES

Congo has had many governments, mainly military. Leaders have professed degrees of socialist philosophy, but most have also depended on a mixed economy. The resulting political instability has created problems. Politics in the republic since independence have been characterized by violent changes or attempted changes in leadership through coups, raids, and assassinations. Political figures have heightened tensions between ethnic groups, as each politician has used a base among one group as the lever for power in competitive situations. The government of Denis Sassou Nguesso, in power since 1979, is socialist, with power concentrated in the small membership of the Congolese Workers' Party.

Economic difficulties have caused unrest. An uprising in the north in 1987 was led by Pierre Anga, an aide to former President Yhombi-Opango, who was arrested at that time. In 1988 Anga, who had

fled, was found and killed in his hometown.

ECONOMIC STRENGTHS AND WEAKNESSES

One of the country's great strengths is its location at a commercial crossroads. Its rails and rivers make it a center of trade for the Central African states. Its port, Pointe Noire, is the key to international trade for the region. Although reserves are small, oil became Congo's most important resource, accounting for two-thirds of its revenues, and superceding timber, which until 1973 was the major export. French, Italian, and U.S. companies are involved in oil exploitation.

After an economic-restructuring agreement with the International Monetary Fund in 1985, Congo revised its 1982–1986 development plan, halving the budget within 2 years. Because of heavy borrowing during the oil-boom years, however, debt servicing takes about 50 percent of Congo's earnings. Nguesso announced a "crisis budget" in 1988, reducing expenditures, rescheduling loan payments, asking for sacrifices from citizens, and urging diversification away from oil toward more reliance on rural development and self-sufficiency in food.

DEVELOPMENT

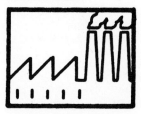

The Five-Year Plan of 1982–1986 emphasized the development of infrastructure, but many of its provisions were delayed under austerity measures imposed by the International Monetary Fund.

FREEDOM

A series of regional and local congresses as well as a National Assembly have existed since 1972. Members of these organizations are elected from party-approved lists. They regularly debate public issues. Amnesty International accused the government of detaining and torturing former officials who are currently out of favor. The press is censored, and opposition opinions are restricted.

HEALTH/WELFARE

Formerly mission schools were important; now students age 6 to 16 must attend state schools. In the first decade after independence, the number of secondary students increased seven-fold, and a major adult-literacy program was planned for the 1980s. The majority of students in higher education are studying in the Soviet Union.

ACHIEVEMENTS

There are a number of Congolese poets and novelists who combine their creative efforts with teaching and public service. Tchicaya U'Tam'si, who died in 1988, wrote poetry and novels and worked for many years for UNESCO in Geneva.

Equatorial Guinea (Republic of Equatorial Guinea)

GEOGRAPHY

Area in Square Kilometers (Miles):
28,023 (10,820) (about the size of
Maryland)
Capital (Population): Malabo
(35,000)
Climate: equatorial

PEOPLE

Population
Total: 384,000
Annual Growth Rate: 2.5%
Rural/Urban Population Ratio: n/a
Languages: official: Spanish; others
spoken: Fang, Benge, Combe,
Bujeba, Balengue, Fernandino, Bubi

Health
Life Expectancy at Birth: 44 years
male; 48 years female
Infant Death Rate (Ratio): 142/1,000
Average Caloric Intake: n/a
Physicians Available (Ratio): 1/76,800

Religion(s)
60% Catholic; 40% Protestant or
traditional indigenous

Education
Adult Literacy Rate: 55%

COMMUNICATION

Telephones: 2,000
Newspapers: 2

RELATIONS WITH SOUTH AFRICA

Equatorial Guinea has a controversial relationship with South Africa.
This erupted in 1988, when Equatorial Guinea signed an agreement with
South Africa and a conservative West German institute to allow South
Africa to build a satellite-tracking station in Equatorial Guinea and to
rebuild the airport for South African flights. Neighboring Nigeria,
fearing a nearby South African military base, protested loudly. Equatorial Guinea agreed to expel five South Africans. An unsuccessful
invasion of São Tomé and Príncipe in March 1988 is believed to have
been backed by South Africa and launched from bases in Equatorial
Guinea. Therefore, amid reports that South Africans were still there in
mid-1988, relations between Nigeria and Equatorial Guinea remained
strained.

TRANSPORTATION

Highways—Kilometers (Miles): 2,760
(1,715)
Railroads—Kilometers (Miles): none
Commercial Airports: 2 international

GOVERNMENT

Type: unitary republic; governed by
Supreme Military Council
Independence Date: October 12, 1968
Head of State: Lieutenant Colonel
Teodoro Obiang Ngeuma Mbasogo
Political Parties: Democratic Party of
Equatorial Guinea
Suffrage: universal for adults

MILITARY

Number of Armed Forces: 1,550
*Military Expenditures (% of Central
Government Expenditures):* n/a
Current Hostilities: internal conflicts

ECONOMY

Currency ($ U.S. Equivalent): 350
CFA francs = $1
Per Capita Income/GNP: $250/$95
million
Inflation Rate: 33%
Natural Resources: wood
Agriculture: cocoa; coffee; timber;
rice; yams; bananas
Industry: fishing; sawmilling; palm-
oil processing

FOREIGN TRADE

Exports: $25 million
Imports: $34 million

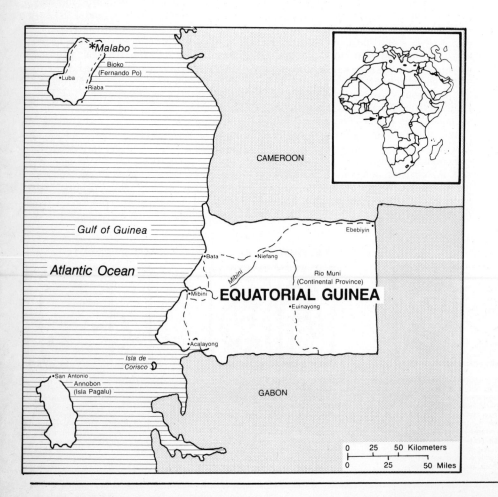

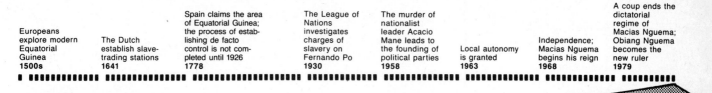

Europeans explore modern Equatorial Guinea
1500s

The Dutch establish slave-trading stations
1641

Spain claims the area of Equatorial Guinea; the process of establishing de facto control is not completed until 1926
1778

The League of Nations investigates charges of slavery on Fernando Po
1930

The murder of nationalist leader Acacio Mane leads to the founding of political parties
1958

Local autonomy is granted
1963

Independence; Macias Nguema begins his reign
1968

A coup ends the dictatorial regime of Macias Nguema; Obiang Nguema becomes the new ruler
1979

Obiang elected to his seventh term as president; the first parliamentary elections in a decade

The PDGE is formed

Regional tensions over South African presence in Equatorial Guinea

EQUATORIAL GUINEA

In recent years Equatorial Guinea has been gradually recovering from the nightmare of its first decade of independence. Under the misrule of Macias Nguema (1968–1979), virtually all public and private enterprise collapsed. During this period at least one-third of the nation's population went into exile, while an unknown (but certainly large) number of others were either murdered or allowed to die of disease and starvation. Many of those who remained were put to forced labor, and the rest were left to subsist off the land. This reign of terror and decay finally ended when Macias was overthrown in a coup, which installed his nephew and chief aide, Obiang Nguema, as the new ruler. Most members of the new government had previously worked under Macias.

The modern decline of Equatorial Guinea contrasts sharply with the mood of optimism that characterized the country when it gained its independence from Spain in 1968. At that time the new republic was buoyed by the prospects of a growing gross domestic product, potential mineral riches, and exceptionally good soils. Although the major responsibility for the decline must lie with Macias Nguema's dictatorial behavior, the uneven pattern of development among the nation's diverse regions contributed to its internal weakness. The republic is comprised of two small islands, Fernando Po (now known as Bioko) and Annobon, and the relatively larger and more populous coastal enclave of Rio Muni. Before the two islands and the enclave were united during the nineteenth century as Spain's only colony in sub-Saharan Africa, all three areas were victimized by the slave trade. Under colonial rule, however, they suffered along separate paths.

CHARGES OF SLAVERY

Spain's major colonial concern was the prosperity of the large cocoa and coffee plantations that were established on the islands, particularly on Fernando Po. Because of local resistance, labor for these estates was imported from elsewhere in West Africa. Coercive recruitment and poor working conditions led to frequent charges of slavery. About 80 percent of the island's population at independence were classified as "resident aliens," including about 7,000 Spanish settlers and nearly 45,000 laborers, mostly Nigerian.

Despite early evidence of its potential riches, Rio Muni was largely neglected by the Spanish, who only occupied its interior in 1926. During the 1930s and 1940s much of the enclave was under the political control of the *Elar-ayong*, a nationalist movement that sought to unite the Fang, Rio Muni's principal ethnic group, against both Spanish and French rule. The territory has remained one of the world's least developed areas, with poor communications and few schools, hospitals, or other basic infrastructure.

Although no community was left unscarred by Macias Nguema's tyranny, the greatest disruption occurred on the islands. By 1976 the entire resident alien population had left, along with most surviving members of the educated class. On Annobon, the government blocked all international efforts to stem a severe cholera epidemic in 1973. The near total depopulation of the island was completed in 1976, when all able-bodied men on Annobon, along with another 20,000 from Rio Muni, were drafted for forced labor on Fernando Po. Annobon subsequently became a supply base for the Soviet navy.

OPPOSITION

Army unrest led to a failed coup in 1986, and despite the improved economic and human-rights situations in Equatorial Guinea, most exile groups have remained in opposition. A ruling party, the Democratic Party of Equatorial Guinea, was formed in 1987. Obiang indicated that others may be recognized later, but exiles continue to press for democratization.

DEVELOPMENT

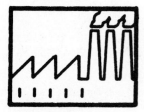

The cocoa, coffee, and plywood industries are reviving. Prospecting for a number of minerals is underway in Rio Muni. Trade with France increased during the 1980s.

FREEDOM

The new Constitution contains a Bill of Rights, which guarantees basic freedoms. While the human-rights situation has improved, there are still allegations of abuses. Exile groups in Western Europe are pressing for the repeal of laws limiting political activity.

HEALTH/WELFARE

At the time of Macias Nguema's overthrow, a handful of Chinese medics were the nation's sole health providers. Hospitals have since re-opened.

ACHIEVEMENTS

Primary education has revived and expanded since 1979, and now incorporates most of the school-age population. UNESCO is helping to train teachers.

Gabon (Gabonese Republic)

GEOGRAPHY

Area in Square Kilometers (Miles): 264,180 (102,317) (about the size of Colorado)
Capital (Population): Libreville (350,000)
Climate: tropical

PEOPLE

Population
Total: 1,220,000
Annual Growth Rate: 3.1%
Rural/Urban Population Ratio: 65/35
Languages: official: French; others spoken: Fang, Eshira, Bopounou, Bateke, Okande, others

Health
Life Expectancy at Birth: 48 years male; 51 years female
Infant Death Rate (Ratio): 162/1,000
Average Caloric Intake: 102% of FAO minimum
Physicians Available (Ratio): 1/4,603

Religion(s)
55%–75% Christian; less than 1% Muslim; remainder traditional indigenous

Education
Adult Literacy Rate: 65%

COMMUNICATION

Telephones: 11,700
Newspapers: 2

ALBERT SCHWEITZER AT LAMBARENE

Lambarene, a town of about 7,000 on the Ogooue River in Gabon's interior, is the site of the mission hospital that Albert Schweitzer built and in which he practiced medicine. Schweitzer, born in Alsace-Lorraine, then a part of Germany, was a philosopher, theologian, organist, and specialist on Bach as well as a medical missionary. At the age of 38 he came to Lambarene, where he lived and worked for 52 years. The hospital that he built was like an African village, consisting of many simple dwellings. It accommodated many patients and their relatives and operated without all the necessities of hospitals in Europe. In later times innovative changes were not always accepted by the authoritarian Schweitzer or his staff. The work at Lambarene saved lives and cured thousands. Schweitzer was awarded the Nobel Peace Prize for his efforts for "the Brotherhood of Nations." Yet he shared the distorted images of Africans so deeply ingrained among Westerners, and he did not believe that Africans could advance in Western ways.

TRANSPORTATION

Highways—Kilometers (Miles): 7,513 (4,658)
Railroads—Kilometers (Miles): 1,435 (889)
Commercial Airports: 3 international

GOVERNMENT

Type: republic; one-party presidential regime
Independence Date: August 17, 1960
Head of State: President Omar Bongo
Political Parties: Gabonese Democratic Party
Suffrage: universal over 18

MILITARY

Number of Armed Forces: 1,900
Military Expenditures (% of Central Government Expenditures): 7.2%
Current Hostilities: none

ECONOMY

Currency ($ U.S. Equivalent): 286 CFA francs = $1
Per Capita Income/GNP: $3,450/$2.8 billion
Inflation Rate: 15%
Natural Resources: timber; petroleum; iron ore; manganese; uranium; gold; zinc
Agriculture: cocoa; coffee; palm oil
Industry: petroleum; lumber; minerals

FOREIGN TRADE

Exports: $1.9 billion
Imports: $949 million

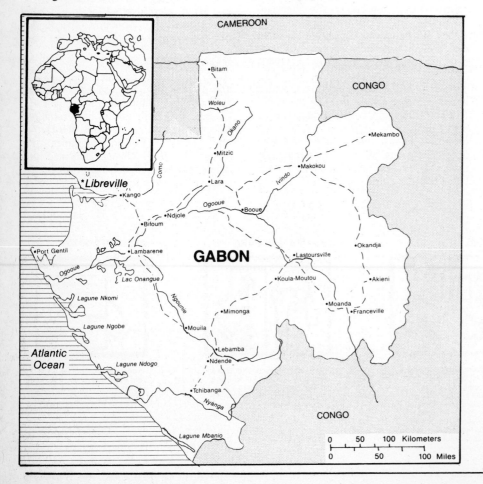

74

GABON

"The small antelope is not the child of the elephant" is a proverb of the Fang people of Gabon. Often the elephant symbolizes the European: powerful but slow. The antelope is clever though small. The proverb reminds us that the Gabonese are not entirely dependent on nor committed to the Western interests that predominate in Gabon today, as during colonial times.

In the countryside, traditional values, while changing, remain strong. The Fang peoples who migrated to Gabon in the eighteenth and nineteenth centuries absorbed earlier populations. Village and lineage links form the basis of a single homogeneous culture characteristic of much of Gabon. The values of this culture—the concern for wealth, the importance of land, and the significance of ancestors—are often symbolized by the sophisticated and unusual art forms such as the abstract figures that, like tombstones, guard ancestral remains and that have influenced many modern Western artists.

Meanwhile there is a strong urban and mining sector in Gabon. Libreville, Port Gentil, and Franceville/Moanda are the centers of modern mining developments. The major industry is oil. Oil fields began to be developed in 1957, and Gabon is now the second largest crude oil producer in sub-Saharan Africa. Gabon is also the world's largest exporter of manganese. Very rich uranium deposits are also being mined, and other untapped minerals include rich resources of iron ore.

FOREIGN DEVELOPERS

These ores are being mined by foreign corporations, which keep most of the profits from these operations. ELF-Gabon, a French-owned corporation, and AMOCO, of Indiana in the United States, play major roles in the oil industry. Gabon has a limited share in these industries: 30 percent in the oil companies, 12 percent in manganese, and 25 percent in the exploitation of uranium. In a 1988 agreement with a consortium led by the United States' Tenneco, Gabon will reimburse the consortium for exploration costs, with interest, and Tenneco will supply local refineries and finance training in hydrocarbon technology at Gabon's universities and technical institutes.

RELATIONS WITH FRANCE

France has a long history of relations with Gabon. The French established a colony of freed slaves in Libreville as early as 1849, and French forces used Libreville as a base for the conquest of other parts of Central Africa. Gabon was part of France's colonial empire and, even after independence, France maintained a powerful role in the country.

The first president, Leon M'Ba, and his chosen successor Albert Bernard (now Omar) Bongo, have been able to maintain control of their government and of the only legal party, the Gabonese Democratic Party (GDP), with French support. The presidents have included representation from different ethnic groups in their Cabinets. Demonstrations for a multiparty system have been condemned for "resurrecting tribalism" and have resulted in arrests, trials, and long prison sentences. The banned Gabonese movement for National Recovery (MORENA) formed a government-in-exile in Paris in 1985. In 1986 Bongo pardoned 27 persons accused of plotting a coup and granted amnesty to members of MORENA.

UNEVEN DISTRIBUTION OF WEALTH

The exploitation of its rich resources has made Gabon appear to be a relatively wealthy country, even though its percentage of the returns are small. However, people of the urban areas and a small elite have gained the most benefit from the sale of Gabon's mineral wealth.

The decline in oil prices caused an economic slump. International Monetary Fund-initiated reforms have reduced inflation and loans have been rescheduled, but when negotiations with the World Bank are completed there will be wide-ranging wage cuts.

FOREIGN POLICY

Gabon's policies have strained relations with its African colleagues. Reasons cited are the conservative attitudes of its government, its receptivity toward trade with South Africa, evidence of its participation in a coup planned against Benin in 1977, and the expulsion in 1988 of 3,500 immigrants in a police swoop in Gabon's cities. Nevertheless, Omar Bongo is a founder and active proponent of regional integration through the Economic Community of Central African States.

DEVELOPMENT

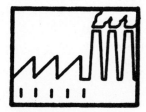

Gabon's search for hydrocarbons and minerals has revealed vast and varied sources of wealth. Oil, uranium, manganese, and iron ore are already being exploited. Other deposits of these resources have been found and barytes (used in the oil industry), talc, lead, gold, and diamonds are also available. Although some oil fields are near depletion, a new one was discovered in 1988.

FREEDOM

Gabon is a one-party state. In 1982 university demonstrations for a multiparty system led to arrests, including that of the university rector. After accusations of torture and executions, political prisoners were released in 1985; more were freed in 1986, and opponents were given amnesty.

HEALTH/WELFARE

Education is compulsory for children ages 6 to 16, and nearly all children are in school, according to government figures. The building of rural schools is a high priority. The University of Libreville began in 1970. New oil agreements plan to train Gabonese in hydrocarbon technology.

ACHIEVEMENTS

Gabon will soon have a second private television station, funded by a French cable station. Profits will be used to fund African films which will be shown on other African stations. Gabon's first private station is funded by Swiss and Gabonese capital.

São Tomé and Príncipe (Democratic Republic of São Tomé and Príncipe)

GEOGRAPHY

Area in Square Kilometers (Miles):
1,001 (387) (slightly larger than New York City)
Capital (Population): São Tomé (35,000)
Climate: tropical

PEOPLE

Population
Total: 113,000
Annual Growth Rate: 2%
Languages: official: Portuguese; other spoken: Kriolu

Health
Life Expectancy at Birth: n/a
Infant Death Rate (Ratio): 65/1,000
Average Caloric Intake: 78% of FAO minimum
Physicians Available (Ratio): 1/2,973

Religion(s)
80% Christian; 20% traditional indigenous

Education
Adult Literacy Rate: 50%

THE PEOPLE OF THE ISLANDS

The current inhabitants of São Tomé and Príncipe are mostly of mixed African and European descent. During the colonial period the society was stratified along racial lines. At the top were the Europeans—mostly Portuguese. Just below them were the *mesticos* or *filhos da terra*, the mixed-blood descendants of slaves. Descendants of slaves who arrived later were known as *forros*. Contract workers were labeled as *servicais*, while their children became known as *tongas*. Still another category was the *angolares*, who reportedly were the descendants of shipwrecked slaves. All of these colonial categories were used to divide and rule the local population; the distinctions have begun to diminish as an important sociological factor on the islands.

COMMUNICATION

Telephones: 6,100
Newspapers: 2 weeklies

TRANSPORTATION

Highways—Kilometers (Miles): 287 (178)
Railroads—Kilometers (Miles): none
Commercial Airports: 1 international

GOVERNMENT

Type: republic
Independence Date: July 12, 1975
Head of State: President Manuel Pinto da Costa
Political Parties: Movement for the Liberation of São Tomé and Príncipe
Suffrage: universal over 18

MILITARY

Number of Armed Forces: 700 Angolan troops; 200 Cuban and Soviet forces
Military Expenditures (% of Central Government Expenditures): n/a
Current Hostilities: none

ECONOMY

Currency ($ U.S. Equivalent): 37 dobras = $1
Per Capita Income/GNP: $330/$34 million
Inflation Rate: 8.8%
Natural Resources: fish
Agriculture: cacao; coconut palms; coffee; bananas; palm kernels
Industry: beer; soft drinks; palm oil; copra; tourism; manufacturing; construction

FOREIGN TRADE

Exports: $9 million
Imports: $20 million

The Portuguese settle São Tomé and Príncipe
1500s

Slavery is abolished, but forced labor continues
1876

The Portuguese massacre hundreds of islanders
1953

Factions within the liberation movement unite to form the MLSTP in Gabon
1972

Independence
1975

Pinto da Costa deposes and exiles Miguel Trovoada, the premier and former number-two man in the MLSTP
1979

1980s

São Tomé and Príncipe nationals seek aid from South Africa and UNITA; exile groups deny any affiliation

The Constitution is broadened to allow direct election

A failed coup attempt

SÃO TOMÉ AND PRÍNCIPE

On July 12, 1975, after a half-millennium of Portuguese rule, the islands of São Tomé and Príncipe took their place as one of Africa's smallest and poorest nations. Before 1975 the islands' economic life centered around the interests of a few thousand white settlers—particularly a handful of large-plantation owners who together controlled more than 80 percent of the land. After independence most of the whites fled, taking their skills and capital and leaving the economy in disarray. Under government management, however, production on the plantations has been revived for the benefit of all segments of the society.

LONG HISTORY OF FORCED LABOR

The Portuguese began the first permanent settlement of São Tomé and Príncipe in the late fifteenth century. Through the intensive use of slave labor, the islands developed rapidly as one of the world's leading exporters of sugar. Only a small fraction of the profits from this boom were consumed locally, and high mortality rates, caused by brutal working conditions, led to an almost insatiable demand for more slaves. After the mid-sixteenth century profits from sugar declined (as rapidly as they had risen) due to competition from Brazil and the Caribbean, and a period of prolonged depression set in.

In the early nineteenth century a second economic boom swept the islands, when they became leading exporters of coffee and, more importantly, cocoa. São Tomé and Príncipe's position in the world market has since declined, yet both cash crops continued to be economic mainstays. Although slavery was officially abolished during the nineteenth century, forced labor was maintained by the Portuguese into modern times. Involuntary contract workers, *servicais*, were imported to labor on the island's plantations; many died before long. Sporadic labor unrest and occasional incidents of international outrage led to some improvement in working conditions, but fundamental reforms came about only after independence. A historical turning point for the islands was the Batepa Massacre in 1953, when several hundred African laborers were killed following local resistance to labor conditions.

POLITICS

São Tomé and Príncipe is ruled as a one-party state by the Movement for the Liberation of São Tomé and Príncipe (MLSTP), which emerged in exile as the islands' anticolonial movement. Although all political processes are carried out through the party, the party itself is answerable to internal elections, which incorporate all citizens. Power seems to have become increasingly concentrated, however, in the hands of Manuel Pinto da Costa, who has led both the party and the nation since independence. After his reelection in 1985 Pinto da Costa formed a new government and began to improve relations with the West, a move praised by some of his opponents in exile.

Opposition groups—the National Resistance Front and the Democratic and Independence Union—merged in 1986 to form the Democratic Coalition of Opposition. In 1987 the Constitution was changed to allow direct elections. But in 1988 the government accused the National Resistance Front (which denied the allegation) of a failed coup attempt.

ECONOMIC DEVELOPMENT

A top economic priority for the MLSTP leadership has been the encouragement of local food production. At present only about 10 percent of the nation's food consumption is locally grown; this has contributed to a large and growing balance-of-payments deficit.

Another priority area for development planners is fishing. In 1978 a 200-mile maritime zone was declared, but the local fleet is badly in need of improvement. Manufacturing and construction make up about 7 percent of gross domestic product; their short-term prospects appear to be limited. Given its small size, the best hope for São Tomé and Príncipe's future prosperity may lie in regional economic initiatives such as the newly constituted Economic Community of Central Africa, of which the country is a member.

DEVELOPMENT

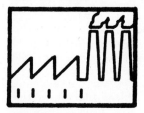

At present the country lacks a deep-water port. The government is hoping to find financial backing to build one.

FREEDOM

Individual freedoms are curbed, but there have been no reports of torture, disappearances, or state assassinations. A number of Pinto da Coasta's political rivals have been exiled.

HEALTH/WELFARE

Health care is free but limited. The government has established pre- and postnatal-care clinics as well as a malaria-eradication program.

ACHIEVEMENTS

São Tomé and Príncipe shares in a rich Luso-African artistic tradition. The country is particularly renowned for poets such as Jose de Almeida and Francisco Tenriero, who were among the first to express the experiences and pride of Africans in the Portuguese language.

Zaire (Republic of Zaire)

GEOGRAPHY

Area in Square Kilometers (Miles):
2,300,000 (905,063) (one-quarter the
size of the United States)
Capital (Population): Kinshasa
(3,000,000)
Climate: equatorial

PEOPLE

Population
Total: 30,400,000
Annual Growth Rate: 3%
Rural/Urban Population Ratio: 56/44
Languages: official: French; others
spoken: Kiswahili, Lingala, Azande,
Luba, Chokwe, Songye, Kongo,
Kuba, Lunda, Bemba, Alur, many
others

Health
Life Expectancy at Birth: 48 years
male; 52 years female
Infant Death Rate (Ratio): 106/1,000
Average Caloric Intake: 94% of FAO
minimum
Physicians Available (Ratio): 1/15,890

Religion(s)
70% Christian; 20% traditional
indigenous; 10% Muslim

Education
Adult Literacy Rate: 78% male; 44%
female

COMMUNICATION

Telephones: 31,200
Newspapers: 4

HUMAN RIGHTS IN ZAIRE

Zaire has one of the worst human-rights records on the African
continent. Detention and torture are so common and long term that the
world press no longer takes note of abuses. Amnesty International
claims that *all* political prisoners are tortured and many are held
incommunicado, and that peasants, workers, teachers, and the spouses
of opponents have been tortured. Thousands of Zairians have fled to
Zambia because of beatings and killings by soldiers. Even moderate
opponents have been jailed; 13 legislators have been in and out of prison
since 1980 for publicly criticizing President Mobutu. In 1986 two of the
legislators, Tshisekedi wa Mulumba and Kanana Ishongo wa Mwango,
were convicted of "slander against Mobutu" (reporting human-rights
abuses). Although Mobutu has tried to improve his image in the West,
detention and beatings continue. Tshisekedi has been in and out of
detention since 1986.

TRANSPORTATION

Highways—Kilometers (Miles):
160,000 (99,200)
Railroads—Kilometers (Miles): 5,116
(3,172)
Commercial Airports: 4 international

GOVERNMENT

Type: republic; strong presidential
authority
Independence Date: June 30, 1960
Head of State: President Marshal
Mobutu Sese Seko
Political Parties: Popular Movement
of the Revolutionary Party
Suffrage: universal over 18

MILITARY

Number of Armed Forces: 51,000
*Military Expenditures (% of Central
Government Expenditures):* n/a
Current Hostilities: low-intensity
insurgency

ECONOMY

Currency ($ U.S. Equivalent): 143
Zaires = $1
Per Capita Income/GNP: $160/$4.2
billion
Inflation Rate: 52%
Natural Resources: copper; cobalt;
zinc; diamonds; manganese; tin; gold;
rare metals; bauxite; iron; coal;
hydroelectric potential; timber
Agriculture: coffee; palm oil; rubber;
tea; cotton; cocoa; manioc; bananas;
plantains; corn; rice; sugar
Industry: mineral mining; consumer
products; food processing; cement

FOREIGN TRADE

Exports: $872 million
Imports: $1 billion

ZAIRE

"Together, my brothers, we are going to start a new struggle which will lead our country to peace, prosperity and greatness. . . . [W]e are going to make the Congo the hub of all Africa." So spoke Patrice Lumumba, the country's first prime minister, on June 30, 1960—the day when Zaire (then the Republic of the Congo) became an independent nation. Zaire had then, and still has, the potential to become the hub of all Africa, and yet the "peace, prosperity and greatness" of which Lumumba spoke are far from being achieved.

THE HUB OF AFRICA

In geographic terms, Zaire is certainly the hub of Africa. Located at Africa's center, it encompasses the entire Zaire River Basin and is a fourth the size of the United States. Although the tropical climate has impeded people's development of their environment, the country encompasses a great variety of land forms and has good agricultural possibilities. It contains a vast range of rich resources, some of which (such as copper) have been intensively exploited for several decades. The river itself is the potential source of 13 percent of the world's hydroelectric power.

Zaire links Africa from west to east. The country faces the Atlantic, with a very narrow coast on that ocean. At the same time eastern Zaire has been influenced by forces from the East African coast. In the mid-nineteenth century Swahili, Nyamwezi, and other traders from Tanzania established control over areas in the present-day Shaba Province of eastern Zaire, and traded for ivory and slaves. These events had deep cultural consequences. The Swahili language continues to be spoken in these regions, and Islam has also influenced peoples of the area.

THE PEOPLES AND THEIR HERITAGE

Zaire's 30,400,000 people are members of about 250 different ethnic groups, speak nearly 700 different languages and dialects, and have varied lifestyles. Boundaries established in the late nineteenth century hemmed in portions of the Azande, the Kongo, the Chokwe, and the Songye peoples within present-day Zaire. However, they maintain contacts with their kin in other countries, an indication of Zaire's hub-like character.

Many important precolonial kingdoms were centered in Zaire, including the Luba, the Kuba, and the Lunda kingdoms—the latter of which in earlier centuries exploited the salt and copper of southeast Zaire, in present-day Shaba Province. The kingdom of Kongo, located at the mouth of the Congo River since at least the year 1400, established diplomatic relations with Portugal in the sixteenth century. The elaborate political systems of these kingdoms are an important heritage for Zaire.

A TROUBLED PAST

The European impact, like the Swahili and Arab influence from the east, was to have disruptive results for Zaire's peoples. The Congo Basin was explored and exploited by private individuals before it came under Belgian domination. King Leopold of Belgium, in his capacity as a private citizen, sponsored H. M. Stanley's expeditions to explore the great river. In 1879 Leopold set up a so-called Congo Independent State over the whole region. This state was actually his private kingdom, and the companies and employees whom he admitted into the region took ivory and sought the rubber that could be used by an industrializing Europe. Armed militias used force to collect quotas of rubber from the people, and the atrocities they committed gained worldwide attention. Ten million people were killed during his rule. Finally, in 1908, the territories were transferred to Belgium.

During the years of Belgian administration control was more benign than during Leopold's regime, but the tradition of abuse was established. The colonial authorities used armed forces for "pacification" campaigns, tax collection, and labor recruitment. New men were made chiefs and given power that they would not have had under the traditional systems. Concessionary companies used force to recruit steady labor to work on plantations and in the mines. The most famous companies were Lever Brothers and the Union Minière, which exploited the minerals of Shaba Province.

The Belgian colonial regime encouraged the presence and work of Catholic missions. Health facilities as well as a paternalistic system of education were developed. A strong elementary-school system was part of the colonial program, but the Belgians never instituted a major secondary-school system, and there was no institution of higher learning. The small group of Western-educated Congolese, known as évolués, served the needs of an administration that never intended nor planned for Zaire's independence.

THE COMING OF INDEPENDENCE

In the 1950s independence movements developed in the countries surrounding Congo and throughout the African continent. The Congolese—especially those in the towns—were affected by these forces of change. The Belgians themselves began to recognize the need to prepare for a different future. Small initiatives began to be allowed; nationalist associations were first permitted in 1955. In the same year a publication proposed independence in 30 years' time and sparked discussion. Some évolués as well as Belgians agreed with its proposals. Other Congolese, including the members of the Alliance of the Ba-Kongo (ABAKO), an ethnic association in Kinshasa, and the National Congolese Movement (MNC), led by Patrice Lumumba, reacted against it.

A serious clash at an ABAKO demonstration in 1959 resulted in 50 deaths and sparked plans for immediate independence. A constitutional conference in January 1960 established a federal-government system for the future independent state. There was, however, no real preparation for such a drastic political change. Belgian colonial civil servants expected that they would stay on to work with each new Congolese government minister or administrator; they were to be disappointed.

A DIFFICULT BEGINNING

The Democratic Republic of the Congo became independent on June 30, 1960 under the leadership of President Joseph Kasavubu and Prime Minister Patrice Lumumba. Before a week had passed an army mutiny had stimulated widespread disorder. The majority of the extensive Belgian community fled the country. The wealthy Katanga Province (now Shaba) and South Kasai seceded. Lumumba called upon the United Nations for assistance, and troops came from a variety of countries to serve in the UN force. Later, as a result of a dispute between President Kasavubu and himself, Lumumba called for Soviet aid. Congo could have become a Cold War battlefield, but the army, under Joseph Desiré Mobutu, intervened, and the Soviets were expelled. By the end of the year Lumumba had been assassinated under suspicious circumstances in which the U.S. Central Intelligence Agency (CIA) was implicated. Rebellion, supported by foreign mercenaries, continued through 1967, especially in Katanga Province, and reappeared in 1977. Tensions in that area continue today.

MOBUTU'S GOVERNMENT

On November 24, 1965 Army Chief of Staff Joseph Desiré Mobutu led a coup that established a new government. He broke the deadlock between competing politicians and eliminated rebels in

Leopold sets up
the Congo
Independent
State as his
private kingdom
1879

Congo becomes
a Belgian colony
1909

Congo gains
independence;
civil war begins;
a UN force is
involved;
Lumumba is
murdered
1960

Congo. Mobutu declared a 5-year moratorium on party politics; this is still in effect. A single-party state has been developed, in which power has been centralized around the figure of Mobutu, the "Founding President." He runs the party, the Popular Revolutionary Movement (MPR), and the Central Committee (which has superceded the Political Bureau, the decision-making body of the party and government). Almost all of the country's institutions come under the party's and Mobutu's jurisdiction.

Mobutuism is the ideology of the state, and "authenticity" (*authenticité*) is its slogan. This has meant the recovery of old symbols, the use of traditional rather than European names, and an emphasis on ancient rituals. Mobutu has changed his own name to Mobutu Sese Seko, and in 1971 Congo became Zaire. The policy has been followed by many other African leaders, but it has not involved deep changes. To promote nationalism, Mobutu put Union Minière and other corporations under government control. In 1973–1974 plantations, commercial institutions, and other businesses were also taken over, in a "radicalizing of the Zairian Revolution."

However, the expropriated industries and businesses have personally enriched a small elite, rather than benefiting the nation. Consequently, the economy has suffered. Industries and businesses have been mismanaged or ravaged. Some individuals have become extraordinarily wealthy, while the population as a whole has suffered. Mobutu is said to be the wealthiest person in Africa, with a fortune estimated at $5 billion, most of it invested and spent outside of Africa. He and his relatives own mansions all over the world.

Mobutu has allowed no opposition. Those who are critical of his government face imprisonment or, at the least, beating. Those who suggest that other political parties should be allowed can be jailed for sedition. Student demonstrations have resulted in the closure of the university and forced conscription into the army for students. Workers' strikes are not allowed. Secessionist movements in Shaba Province in 1977 and 1978 were suppressed with Moroccan and French assistance. The Roman Catholic Church and the Kimbanguist Church of Jesus Christ Upon This Earth are the only institutions that have been able to speak out without fear of reprisal.

ECONOMIC DISASTER

Zaire's economic potential was developed by and for the Belgians, but by 1960 that development had gone further than in many other African colonial territories. Zaire started as an independent nation with a good economic base. The chaos of the early 1960s brought development to a standstill, and little advancement has been made in Mobutu's time. Outside investment has been encouraged, but projects have not been carefully planned. World economic conditions, including the low prices of copper and other minerals on the world market, have contributed to Zaire's economic difficulties.

However, "the corruption of the team

(Photo by Joseph Cornet. Courtesy of the Peabody Museum, Harvard University)

The African cup that is used for drinking often satisfies the eye as well as sustaining the body. Ordinary and sacred wooden objects reveal the artistry of African sculptors.

Mobutu takes
command in a
bloodless coup
1965

The name of the
state is changed
to Zaire
1971

1980s

Mobutu is
elected
president for a
third 7-year
term; all citizens
above 18 years
are required to
vote

Mobutu woos
former critics in
exile with
government
posts, while
detaining others

Economic
decline raises
political tensions

in power" has been recognized as the main obstacle to economic progress. An organized system of exploitation transfers wealth from peasants to officials to the elite. Sometimes called a "kleptocracy," Zaire is rife with corruption. With its elite stealing millions, the entire society operates on an "invisible" tax system, whereby citizens must, for example, bribe nurses for medical care, bureaucrats for documents, and principals for school admission.

Ordinary people suffer. Real wages of urban workers are only 2 percent of what they were in 1960. Rural conditions have deteriorated.

Although Zaire's agriculture has great economic potential, the returns from this sector continue to shrink. Zaire must now import 60 percent of the food for its population. Rural people move to the city or, for lack of employment, move back to the country and take up subsistence agriculture, rather than cash-crop farming, in order to ensure their own survival. The deterioration of roads and bridges has led to the decline of all trade. Since 1983 the government has implemented International Monetary Fund (IMF) austerity measures, but this has only cut public expenditures. It has had no effect on the endemic corruption, nor increased taxes on the rich. More than 30 percent of Zaire's budget goes for debt servicing.

U.S. SUPPORT FOR MOBUTU

The Mobutu regime has been able to sidestep its financial crises and repress political opposition that could lead to its downfall because the U.S. government underwrites its survival. The United States has viewed Mobutu as the symbol of stability in Central Africa and as a firm opponent of the Soviet Union and communism.

Mobutu has been a friend of the West since 1960. He supported the United States-backed National Front for the Liberation of Angola (FLNA) against the Marxist-oriented Popular Movement for the Liberation of Angola (MPLA) in the 1960s, and he has stood behind unpopular U.S. resolutions in the United Nations. Millions of American dollars are being used to refurbish roads and airstrips at Kamina in Shaba Province, away from population centers and internal transport needs. Evidence suggests that these are used by the CIA to supply the National Union for the Total Independence of Angola (UNITA) rebels fighting the Angolan government; they could also be used for military action in any part of the continent. Zaire sent 2,000 troops to Chad to support the U.S.-backed government of Hissené Habré. France, too, under President Mitterrand, has continued to recognize and support Zaire.

The United States has clear evidence of Mobutu's human-rights violations and of the oppression and corruption that characterize the Zaire government. Defectors from the highest levels of government in Zaire have revealed many of the evils of the regime. Public-relations efforts by Mobutu in 1987 and 1988 to defuse criticism have muted some U.S. congressional critics, but detentions and abuse continue. In 1988 58 members of Congress signed a letter protesting the house arrest of critic Tshisekedi wa Mulumba, and legislation has been introduced to stop U.S. aid to Zaire until the human-rights situation improves. The continued U.S. support of Mobutu, however, reflects the West's perception that there is no satisfactory alternative to his rule nor any pro-Western successor who could replace Mobutu in this strategic area of Africa.

Mobutu has also allied himself with conservative forces in Africa. Moroccan troops came to his aid during the revolts in Shaba Province in 1977. He has maintained ties with South Africa, selling Zaire's diamonds through the DeBeers-owned Central Selling Organization, using South Africa's rails and ports, and importing almost half its food from the apartheid state. In 1982 Zaire was the first African country to renew diplomatic ties with Israel after the break following the takeover of the Sinai in 1973. About 50,000 refugees from conflicts in Zaire are in neighboring countries, and Zaire hosts more than 300,000, many of whom are Angolans fleeing warfare there. In 1985 the governments of Zaire and Angola reached an agreement to stop attacks launched from within their borders on each other's territories, but in 1988 Zaire still allowed U.S. aid to UNITA through Zaire's territory. Any claim that Zaire might be "the hub of Africa" is weakened by the positions that have been taken in African and world affairs today.

DEVELOPMENT

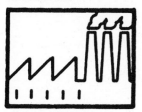

The United States and Western European countries continue to aid development projects for transportation, health, and education. However, mismanagement, corruption, and lack of maintenance have resulted in little improvement for Zaire's citizens.

FREEDOM

Zaire has shown little respect for human rights. Thirteen parliamentarians were recently sentenced to 15 years each for proposing an alternative political party. Some were released, but others have been rearrested numerous times.

HEALTH/WELFARE

In 1978 more than 5 million students were registered for primary schools and 35,000 for college. However, the level of education is declining. Many teachers were laid off in the 1980s, though nonexistent "ghost teachers" remained on the payroll. The few innovative educational programs are outside the state system.

ACHIEVEMENTS

Kinshasa is a musical center, the home of creative popular styles of vocal music and new dance bands. Souskous is one style, and Pablo Lubadika of the group Le Peuple is one of the most popular singers. Rochereau and Franco are vocalists with longstanding reputations. Zaire music is popular and sets styles throughout Africa as well as in Europe and America.

East Africa

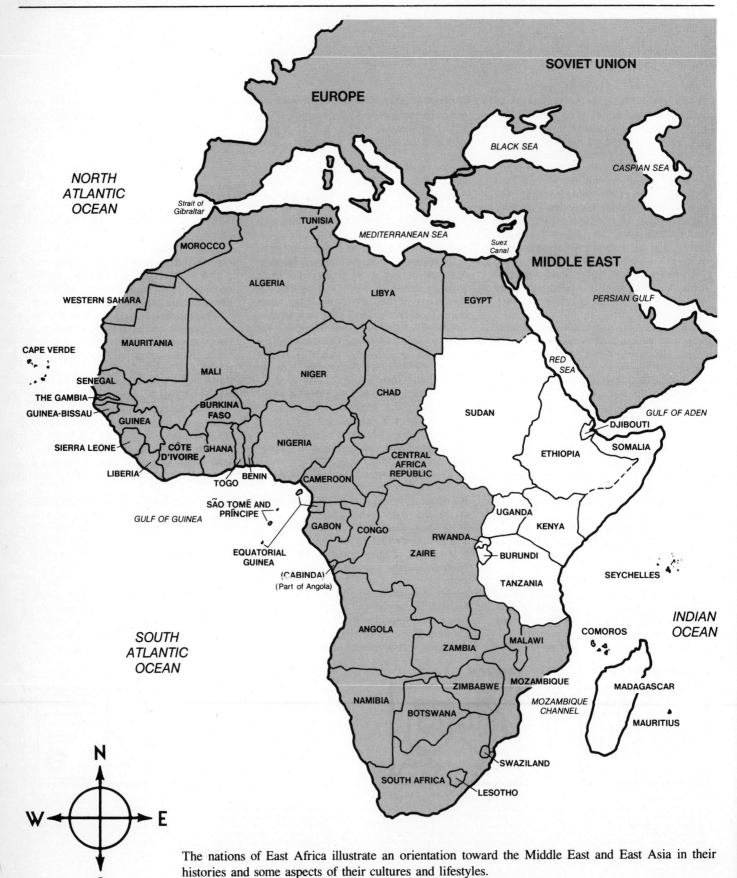

The nations of East Africa illustrate an orientation toward the Middle East and East Asia in their histories and some aspects of their cultures and lifestyles.

East Africa: A Mixed Inheritance

The vast East African region, ranging from Sudan with its North African ties to Tanzania in the south, is an area of great diversity and complexity. Although the Indian Ocean islands have a distinctive civilization because of their Asian and Pacific ties, their interactions with the mainland give their inclusion here validity. Ecological features such as the Great Rift Valley, the prevalence of cattle-herding lifestyles, and historical Arab and Asian influences are aspects associated with the whole area.

CATTLE-HERDING SOCIETIES

A long-horned cow seems an appropriate symbol for the East African region—more so than the use of a similar symbol for the American West. The increasing populations of the cities come from different backgrounds, but most rural inhabitants, who make up the majority of people from the Horn to Lake Malawi, value cattle for their social as well as their economic importance. The Nuer of the Sudan, the Somali near the Red Sea (who, like many other peoples of the Horn, herd camels as well as cattle, goats, and sheep), and the Maasai of Tanzania and Kenya are among the pastoral peoples whose herds are their livelihood and their companions. The Kikuyu and the Baganda, whose communities are built on farming as

(World Bank photo by Kay Muldoon)

Lively and extensive trade and migration patterns have characterized East Africa throughout much of its history.

well as herding, also prize cattle. Even Malagasy devote more than half of their lands to grazing, and their attitudes toward cattle are similar to those of mainland East Africans. The other Indian Ocean islands do not maintain cattle.

The land is well suited for herding. In the rain forests of West and Central Africa, the presence of tsetse flies limits cattle holding. Tropical rain forests are almost nonexistent in East Africa; they are found only on the east coast of Madagascar and scattered on the East African rim of the Indian Ocean. Belts of tropical and temperate savannas have provided grazing lands for animals and people who have migrated north and south as well as east and west throughout history. Pastoralists predominate in the savanna zones of West Africa, as well as East Africa, and this region below the desert has historically been a trans-African highway.

People have been moving into and through the East African region throughout its history. The Great Rift Valley, which continues from the Red Sea as far south as Malawi and Zambia, is characterized by mountains as well as valleys and features the Great Lakes such as Lake Albert, Lake Tanganyika, and Lake Malawi. According to linguistic and archaeological evidence as well as oral tradition, over the centuries agricultural peoples speaking Bantu languages, iron workers, pottery makers, local traders, Nilotic speakers, warriors, and others have moved into the area and settled or moved beyond. Inhabitants of the region—then and now—have had to confront insufficient and unreliable rainfall. Drought and famine in the Horn and in areas of Kenya and Tanzania have caused suffering, changed lifestyles, and prompted refugee movements.

ISLAMIC INFLUENCE

Many of the areas of East Africa have been influenced and continue to be influenced by the Middle East and, to an extent, by Asia. Even Christian Ethiopia and the inland states of Rwanda and Burundi were familiar with the followers of Islam, the Arab traders of the Swahili Coast or Sudan. Somalia, Djibouti, and Sudan, which border the Red Sea and are in close range of the Arabian Peninsula, have been most influenced by the travelers who came across the straits. Mogadishu, the capital of Somalia, began as an Islamic trading post in the tenth century. The Islamic faith, its various sects or brotherhoods, the Koran, and the Sharia (the Islamic law code) have influenced the people and the governments in the Horn. Today many Somali and others migrate to the oil-rich states of Arabia to work.

Farther south, in the communities and cultures on the perimeters of the east coast, Arab newcomers and African people mixed as early as the ninth century but especially during the 1200s to 1400s. The result of this intermingling is the culture and the language that we now call Swahili.

Much later, in the first half of the nineteenth century, the sultan of Oman, Seyyid Said, transferred his capital to Zanzibar, thereby recognizing the important positions that Omani Arabs held in the East African lands. Arab traders settled in towns in the interior and developed contacts (not always as peacefully or as positively as residents would have liked), leading some interior peoples to accept Islam or, at the least, to take part in—and sometimes to take over—the trading systems that the Arabs operated.

The whole region from the Horn to Tanzania was affected by the slave trade through much of the nineteenth century. Slaves went from Uganda and southern Sudan north to Egypt and the Middle East or from Ethiopia across the Red Sea. Many were taken to the coast by Arab, Swahili, or African traders to work on the plantations in Zanzibar or were shipped to the Persian Gulf or the Indian Ocean islands.

In the late nineteenth and early twentieth centuries Indian laborers were brought in by the British to build the East African railroad. Indian traders already resided in Zanzibar; others now came and settled in Kenya and Tanzania, becoming shopkeepers and bankers in inland centers such as Kampala and Nairobi, as well as on the coast in Mombasa and Dar es Salaam or in smaller stops along the railroad.

The subregions of East Africa include the following: the countries of the Horn, Ethiopia, Somalia, and Djibouti as well as Sudan, farther north, which have a common identity not because of a common heritage or because of the compatibility of their governments (for, indeed, they are often hostile to one another) but because of the movements of peoples across borders in recent times; the East African states of Kenya, Tanzania, and Uganda, which have underlying cultural ties and a history of economic relations in which Rwanda and Burundi have also shared; and the Indian Ocean islands of Madagascar, Comoros, Mauritius, and the Seychelles, which—despite the expanses of ocean that separate them—have cultural aspects and current interests in common.

ETHIOPIA, SUDAN, AND THE HORN

Traditionally, Ethiopia has had a distinct and isolated history which has separated the nation from its neighbors. This early Christian empire was centered in the dissected highlands of the interior, surrounded by peoples whom the nation was later to dominate. Only infrequently was it reached by outside envoys. In the latter part of the nineteenth century Ethiopian rulers made major conquests of Somali and other peoples who today resist Ethiopian rule. Although Islam influenced some of the peoples, the empire was not as affected by Islamic forces as was the rest of the Horn.

Great Power Interference

Yet peoples of Ethiopia, like those of present-day Somalia, Djibouti, and Sudan, were to be influenced by the great world powers that have historically been involved in the area because of its strategic location. In the nineteenth century the United Kingdom and France became interested in the Horn, because the Red Sea was the link between their countries and the territories they had acquired in Asia. When the Suez Canal was completed in 1869 the importance of the region to these countries increased. In the 1880s France and England both acquired ports on the Red Sea. The issue of

who would control the Nile also absorbed the attention of France and England during the imperialist decades. In the 1890s French forces, led by Captain Marchand, literally raced from the present-day area of the People's Republic of the Congo to reach the upper Nile before the British. England won at the diplomat's table and claimed Sudan as a British territory.

The Italian interest in the Horn was first encouraged by the British to keep out the French. Italy's defeat by the Ethiopians at the battle of Adowa in 1896 did not deter its efforts to dominate the coastal areas, and parts of present-day Somalia soon fell into the hands of the very young Italian

(United Nations photo by Ray Witlin)

In the drought-affected areas of East Africa, people must devote considerable time and energy to the search for water.

84

state. Later Italy, under Mussolini, was to conquer and hold Ethiopia for the years between 1936 and 1941.

Today great-power competition for control of the Red Sea and the Gulf of Aden—the gateways to the Middle East—continues as the United States and the Soviet Union vie for power. Events in Africa have led to shifts in the power plays. Before 1977, for instance, the United States was allied with Ethiopia—first during the empire and then when the new socialist state of the Dergue took control. In 1977–1978 Ethiopia allied with the Soviet Union, receiving in return billions of dollars of military aid, on loan, for use in the civil war in the southern province of Ogaden where Somali peoples live, as well as for use in Eritrea. The United States soon established relations with President Siad Barre of Somalia, formerly the ally of the Soviet Union, who agreed to terms whereby the U.S. military would support the Somali regime. Cuban as well as Soviet presence in Ethiopia is now matched by United States access to port facilities in Somalia, and increased military aid to Sudan is seen as a "buffer to U.S. interests in the Middle East."

The countries of the Horn, unlike the East African states farther south or the island states, have been alienated from one another, and no regional community appears to have been contemplated. The introduction of world-power conflicts in the region has only widened the distances among these countries. An African proverb seems relevant: "When two elephants fight, it is the ground that gets trampled."

Drought and Disorder

Meanwhile problems of drought and disorder have created population movements that affect all the countries. Today the Horn is bound together—or torn apart—by its millions of refugees. The movement of peoples is so great that they are certain to unsettle traditional ways of life and bring about changes that go deep into the fabric of societies. Only half of the refugees of the Horn and Sudan (perhaps more than 1 million) are directly supported by international relief agencies, indicating that their hosts—sometimes, but not always, of their own ethnic group—have taken them in temporarily or helped them to recreate their lives in a new society.

Ethiopians leave their homes for Somalia, Djibouti, and Sudan for relief from drought, famine, and civil war. Every country harbors not only refugees but also dissidents from neighboring lands, or has a citizenry related to those who live in adjoining countries. Peoples such as the Affars, a minority in Djibouti, seek support from their kin in Ethiopia during trouble. Somali liberation fighters who have left Somalia mobilize from Ethiopia against the Somalian government. Somali soldiers help other Somalis in the Ogaden as they fight against Ethiopia and claim their right to Somalian citizenship. The situation grows more complex. Ethiopia assists southern rebels against the government of Sudan, and Sudan in turn supports the Tigray and Eritrean movements against Ethiopia. Famine and movement of refugees escalate with increasing warfare in the region; and millions of people were at risk for starvation in the late 1980s.

(WHO photo)
East African peoples, especially along the coast, blend heritages from Asia, the Middle East, and Africa.

(United Nations photo by M. Grant)

President Daniel arap Moi of Kenya, a statesman of East Africa, has worked with neighboring nations to improve relations.

EAST AFRICA

The peoples of Kenya, Tanzania, and Uganda, as well as Burundi and Rwanda, have underlying connections from the past, despite the great variety of lifestyles that characterize them today. Kingdoms around the Great Lakes in Uganda, Rwanda, and Burundi, though they have been overridden in modern times, are remembered. Myths about a heroic dynasty of rulers, the Chwezi, who ruled over an early Ugandan kingdom, are widespread. Archaeological evidence attests to their existence, probably in the sixteenth century. Peoples in western Kenya and Tanzania, who live under less centralized systems, have rituals similar to those of the Ugandan kingdoms. The Chwezi dynasty became associated with a spirit cult, which has been spread by mediums through many areas.

The Swahili culture and language of the coast, like the specialized kinship and social relationships of the Great Lakes area, was spread west and north—along with iron, salt, pottery, and grain—through regional trading networks as well as by warrior groups, changing as it developed new forms.

Rwanda and Burundi both became Belgian colonies in the late nineteenth century and have a different colonial heritage from Tanzania, Uganda, and Kenya. The latter two nations were taken over by the British in the late nineteenth century; Tanzania, originally conquered by Germany, became a British colony after World War I.

The British colonials first affected Kenya, which became distinguished by a large settler community. These settlers took over the land, had access to political power, and demanded exactions from the African populations, while whites in neighboring nations did not. Development was fostered there by a colonial government that expected whites to stay. As a result, Kenya had more investment and infrastructure at the time of independence, which made integration with its poorer neighbors difficult.

Perhaps the most important British policies for the integration of the areas under their control were those connected with the East African Common Services Organization (comprised of Kenya, Tanzania, and Uganda), which was transformed into the East African Community (EAC) in 1967. The EAC collectively managed the railway system, a harbor program, an international airway, posts, and telecommunication facilities. It also maintained a common currency and a common market, a development bank, and other economic, cultural, and scientific services. Peoples moved freely across the borders of the three states in the EAC. The links between the three countries were so important in the early 1960s that President Julius Nyerere of Tanzania proposed that Tanzania wait to become independent until Kenya was given freedom, in hopes that the two countries would then join together.

This did not occur. Gradually, the East African Community itself began to unravel, as conflicts over its operations grew. It fell apart in 1977. The countries disputed the benefits of the association, which seemed to be garnered primarily by Kenya. The ideologies and personalities of Nyerere, Jomo Kenyatta, and Idi Amin differed so much that there was little to encourage the three leaders to solve the problems of the EAC. Relations between Kenya and Tanzania deteriorated so drastically that the border between them was closed when EAC ended.

In 1983 Kenya, Tanzania, and Uganda agreed on the division of the assets of the old Community; Kenya experienced the largest losses. Tanzania and Kenya opened their borders and began rebuilding their relationship. The economic strains that all three countries face in their dealings with the world economy make the EAC's importance clear. Changes in leadership, however, affect regional unity. Daniel arap Moi, Kenyatta's vice president, succeeded as president in Kenya, but Uganda still suffers from years of warfare and instability. Although Milton Obote took over from the ousted Amin, Obote himself was overthrown in a 1985 coup. The new president, Yoweri Museveni, maintains an uneasy control over a Uganda still plagued by violence from rebels and criminals. Although the governments of Rwanda, Kenya, Sudan, Tanzania, and Zaire pledged in 1986 to prevent exiles from using asylum to destabilize their homelands, tensions in the region continue. Relations between Uganda and Kenya have been strained over harboring dissidents in each other's country. However, those governments met to ease tension after trade and transport disagreements in 1987 and 1988 led to violence at the border. And in a peaceful succession following the retirement of Nyerere, Ali Hassan Mwinyi was elected to lead Tanzania, though Nyerere remains chairman of the ruling party.

A number of joint projects in East Africa may help set a mood or an example for a new community. Tanzania and Rwanda as well as Burundi and Uganda have reached agreement on a massive hydroelectric project on the Kagera River, and other projects will improve the lake traffic and the lake ports, which are especially important for Rwanda and Burundi. Plans have been made for Ugandan commanders to go to Kenya for training, and for Tanzanian military personnel to train Ugandan soldiers in their country. In addition, the governments of Burundi, Rwanda, Tanzania, and Zaire have met to discuss security, trade, and cultural exchange in the region.

Rwanda and Burundi are members of the Economic Community of Central African States (ECCA), which links them with their western neighbor, Zaire. However, their economic ties with East African states have led the UN Economic Commission on Africa as well as others to include them in the East African regional groupings. The Preferential Trade Area of 19 East and Southern African nations, established in 1981, is one regional group that can increase the economic integration of the area.

There has been much talk of improving relations. "Think East Africa," the *Standard* of Kenya wrote, commenting on the cultural links that existed in the area before colonialism.

Salim Salim, a Tanzanian statesman, noted, "You can choose a friend, but you cannot choose a brother . . . In this case Kenyans and Ugandans are our brothers." On the other hand, the ideological differences that contributed to the split remain, and the economic worries the countries share can lead just as easily to further barriers and increased competition.

THE ISLANDS

The Seychelles, Mauritius, and the Comoros are like satellites surrounding Madagascar, but each island polity holds its own in this relationship. There is much which all four share. They have populations which derive from early East Asian contacts, either with India or Indonesia, and some have Arab and French as well as African ancestors. Madagascar and the Comoros have populations that originated in the Pacific Melanesian Islands as well as in Africa. The citizens of Mauritius and the Seychelles are European as well as African and Asian.

All four island groups have been influenced by France. Mauritius and the Seychelles were not permanently inhabited until the 1770s. French settlers came with African slaves and were joined later by Asians and other Africans. The British took control of these two island groups after the 1830s, but a French-based Creole remains the major language today.

In 1978 the islands, along with Réunion, formed the Indian Ocean Commission. Originally a body with a socialist orientation, the commission campaigned for independence for Réunion and the return of the island of Diego Garcia to Mauritius as well as the dismantling of the U.S. naval base located there. The aims of an alternate body made up of Madagascar, Mauritius, and Seychelles are to work for economic cooperation, police the fishing grounds, and encourage the search for oil and stimulate trade among the islands. President Albert René of the Seychelles appealed for cooperation among the islands for conservation of their common Indian Ocean environment.

(UN photo)

Refugees at camp in Jijiga, Ethiopia waiting for their daily supply of water.

Burundi (Republic of Burundi)

GEOGRAPHY

Area in Square Kilometers (Miles): 27,834 (10,759) (about the size of Maryland)
Capital (Population): Bujumbura (272,000)
Climate: tropical to temperate

PEOPLE

Population
Total: 4,920,000
Annual Growth Rate: 2.6%
Rural/Urban Population Ratio: 98/2
Languages: official: Kirundi, French; others spoken: Kiswahili, others

Health
Life Expectancy at Birth: 43 years male; 46 years female
Infant Death Rate (Ratio): 137/1,000
Average Caloric Intake: 99% of FAO minimum
Physicians Available (Ratio): 1/22,778

Religion(s)
60% Roman Catholic; 38% traditional indigenous; 2% Muslim

Education
Adult Literacy Rate: 30%

COMMUNICATION

Telephones: 6,000
Newspapers: 1 daily

ETHNIC RIVALRIES

The long-standing domination of the Hutu majority by the Tutsi aristocracy has left a bitter legacy. Following the Hutu uprising of 1972 more than 100,000 Hutu were massacred (some estimates are as high as 300,000). Those killed were the educated and the skilled, chosen for death because they might compete with the ruling class. Subsequent governments, all Tutsi, have not eased the hatreds of the 1970s. President Jean-Baptiste Bagaza led a campaign against the Roman Catholic Church from 1985–1987, expelling missionaries, banning Catholic newspapers, radio stations, a youth movement, and closing schools. Outspoken about human-rights abuses, the Catholics were accused of pro-Hutu statements. Although the new leader, Pierre Buyoya, stated support for religious freedom, Tutsi domination was guaranteed. Tensions exploded again in 1988, with Hutu bearing the brunt of the thousands of casualties.

TRANSPORTATION

Highways—Kilometers (Miles): 7,800 (4,846)
Railroads—Kilometers (Miles): none
Commercial Airports: 1 international

GOVERNMENT

Type: republic
Independence Date: July 1, 1962
Head of State: President (Major) Pierre Buyoya
Political Parties: Union for National Progress
Suffrage: universal over 19

MILITARY

Number of Armed Forces: 7,500
Military Expenditures (% of Central Government Expenditures): $312,500 (3.2%)
Current Hostilities: internal ethnic violence

ECONOMY

Currency ($ U.S. Equivalent): 119 Burundi francs = $1
Per Capita Income/GNP: $273/$1 billion
Inflation Rate: 14.3%
Natural Resources: nickel; uranium; cobalt; copper; platinum
Agriculture: coffee; tea; cotton; food crops
Industry: light consumer goods; beer brewing

FOREIGN TRADE

Exports: $99 million
Imports: $183 million

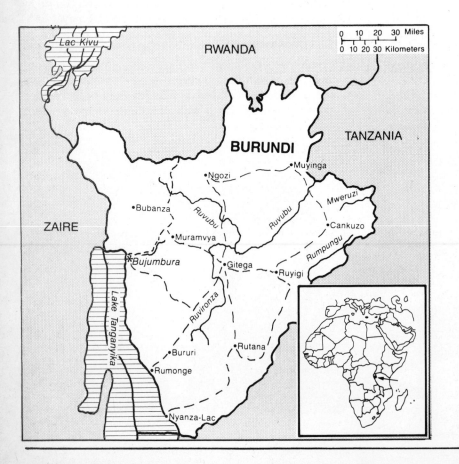

| Mwami Ntare Rugaamba expands the boundaries of the Nkoma kingdom **1795** | The area is mandated to Belgium by the League of Nations after the Germans lose World War I **1919** | Rwagasore leads a nationalist movement and founds UPRONA **1958–1961** | Rwagasore is assassinated; independence is achieved **1961** | A failed coup results in purges of Hutu in government and army; Micombero seizes power **1965–1966** | A Hutu uprising is followed by the massacre of nearly 100,000 Hutu **1972** | Bagaza comes to power in a military coup **1976** |

1980s

| Voters participate in elections for the National Assembly, choosing 52 deputies from 104 candidates | Bagaza is overthrown in a military coup led by Buyoya | Ethnic violence leaves 5,000 dead and 100,000 homeless |

BURUNDI

Burundi is a small, beautiful, and crowded country where contemporary changes have increased historical internal divisions. Those in power have been successful in maintaining traditional systems of status and obligation. Efforts to change historic practices and values have not only been ineffective but, in the 1970s and 1980s, led to the deaths of more than 100,000 people, and accompanying terror and flight.

ETHNIC GROUPS

Three distinctive groups of people live in Burundi: the Twa, the first inhabitants, are a pygmy people and make up less than 1 percent of the population. Most Burundi are Hutu (85 percent); they are usually farmers. The dominant group has been the cattle-holding Tutsi; members of Tutsi clans have been rulers and made up the aristocratic class in the society. The long-horned cattle of the Tutsi have prestige value as well as economic importance.

The Hutu and the Tutsi differ in appearance, but historians do not believe that the Tutsi first came as conquerors. It is possible that the two peoples lived in adjoining regions, gradually developing the relations that have become characteristic of the Hutu and the Tutsi in the nineteenth and twentieth centuries. Hutu became clients of Tutsi aristocrats, receiving cattle and protection in return for services.

The elaborate social and political system in Burundi was continued under the Germans, the first colonialists, and later by the Belgians, to whom the region was mandated by the League of Nations in 1919.

NATIONALIST MOVEMENT

In the late 1950s Prince Louis Rwagazore tried to unite all the Burundi people in a movement for nationalist goals, and he established the Union for National Progess (UPRONA) for this purpose. He was assassinated before independence, but the king remained a symbol of unity and established governing Cabinets, where Hutu and Tutsi were equally represented. This effort, never very successful, was abandoned in the mid-1960s, when Hutu leaders attempted a coup. Colonel Michel Micombero took over the government after abolishing the monarchy, and his "Government of Public Safety" purged Hutu members from the government and the army.

CHALLENGES TO THE GOVERNMENT

In 1972 a second Hutu uprising killed 1,000 Tutsi and resulted in a government massacre of more than 100,000 Hutu. Another 100,000 Hutu fled to Uganda, Rwanda, Zaire, and Tanzania; most still reside in these countries.

The then President (Colonel) Jean-Baptiste Bagaza sought to heal past divisions, but his Five-Year Plan (1973–1983), which emphasized rural agricultural development, did not have positive results. The new Constitution allows citizens the right to elect deputies and a president for the first time in 19 years, but the control of UPRONA—the only legal party—by upper-class elements limited Hutu (and Tutsi who are not of the favored clan) efforts to gain power. Tutsi still dominated all institutions, and in 1985 Bagaza began a

campaign against the Catholic Church, Seventh Day Adventists, and Jehovah's Witnesses, alleging Hutu sympathies. In a 1987 military coup, Major Pierre Buyoyo expressed concern over this repression and the accusations of fraud and corruption.

Ethnic violence erupted again in 1988. Apparently some Hutu killed Tutsi in northern Burundi, in response to rumors of another massacre of Hutu. In retaliation, the army massacred more than 5,000 Hutu. About 40,000 Hutu fled to Rwanda, and 100,000 were left homeless.

LAND REFORMS

Burundi remains one of the poorest countries in the world, despite its rich volcanic soils and its dense population, one of the highest in Africa. Most Burundi are peasants who live on separate farms rather than in villages. Peasants were released from certain taxes (enforced savings has been substituted) and from former services and obligations to landlords. However, patron-client relationships still exist, and a land-reform program is being implemented very slowly. Increasing pressure on the land means that the farmers cannot grow enough for survival, let alone for sale, and efforts at villagization have not succeeded.

DEVELOPMENT

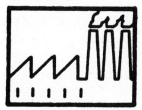

The sources of wealth are limited. There is no active development of mineral resources, although sources of nickel have been located and may be mined soon. There is little industry, and the coffee crop, which contributes 75% to 90% of export earnings, has declined.

FREEDOM

The government is Tutsi, with few Hutu representatives, and ethnic bitterness is an obstacle to equal rights for all. Roman Catholic schools were closed, priests were detained, and the press was restricted in recent years because of alleged Hutu sympathies. Thousands were killed by the army in 1988.

HEALTH/WELFARE

Much of the educational system has been in private hands, especially the Roman Catholic Church. Burundi lost many educated and trained personnel because of the Hutu massacres in the 1970s and 1980s.

ACHIEVEMENTS

Burundi's plans for future economic development show consideration of regional possibilities. Sugar, cheese, cooking oil, and soft-drink and beer factories are expected to benefit from demand throughout this area. Transportation will be improved through regional cooperation with East African rail networks.

Comoros (Comoros Federal Islamic Republic)

GEOGRAPHY

Area in Square Kilometers (Miles): 2,171 (838) (about the size of Delaware)
Capital (Population): Moroni (26,000)
Climate: tropical; marine

PEOPLE

Population
Total: 422,500
Annual Growth Rate: 3.3%
Rural/Urban Population Ratio: n/a
Languages: official: Shaafi-Islam; others spoken: French, Arabic, Kiswahili, English, Malagasy

Health
Life Expectancy at Birth: 47 years male; 50 years female
Infant Death Rate (Ratio): 93/1,000
Average Caloric Intake: 102% of FAO minimum
Physicians Available (Ratio): 1/21,125

Religion(s)
86% Shirazi Muslim; 14% Roman Catholic

MAYOTTE ISLAND

In 1974, when the other Comoran islands voted overwhelmingly for independence, Mayotte opted to remain French by a two-to-one margin. Since then the French have continued to administer the island with the support of the local population—more than 95 percent of whom have, in recent years, voted in favor of becoming an overseas department of France. Unlike the other islands, Mayotte is predominantly Christian. Historically, it has been greatly influenced by Malagasy and French culture. Comoran claims to the island are supported by the Organization of African Unity, and in the United Nations only France voted against a resolution calling for their inclusion in the Comoros. Despite the location of its naval base on the island, France may be eager to withdraw from Mayotte, but is reluctant to do so against the wishes of Mayotte and domestic opinion.

Education
Adult Literacy Rate: 15%

COMMUNICATION

Telephones: 3,000
Newspapers: n/a

TRANSPORTATION

Highways—Kilometers (Miles): 750 (465)
Railroads—Kilometers (Miles): none
Commercial Airports: 1 international

GOVERNMENT

Type: Islamic republic
Independence Date: July 6, 1975
Head of State: President Ahmed Abdullah Abderemane
Political Parties: Comoran Union for Progress
Suffrage: universal for adults

MILITARY

Number of Armed Forces: 700
Military Expenditures (% of Central Government Expenditures): $2,900,000 (16%)
Current Hostilities: none

ECONOMY

Currency ($ U.S. Equivalent): 286 Comoran francs = $1
Per Capita Income/GNP: $339/$106 million
Inflation Rate: n/a
Natural Resources: agricultural land
Agriculture: perfume essences; copra; coconuts; cloves; vanilla; cinnamon; yams; rice
Industry: perfume distillation; tourism

FOREIGN TRADE

Exports: $15 million
Imports: $24 million

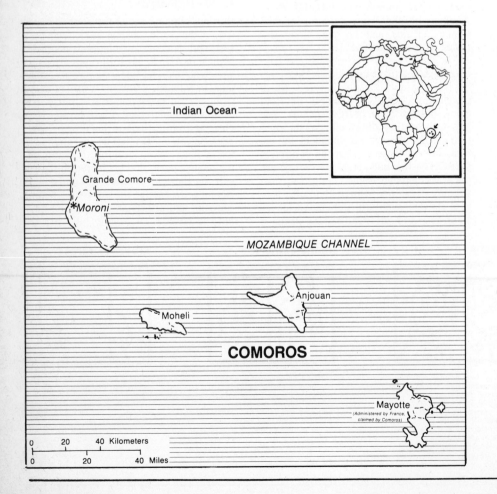

Various groups
settle in the
islands, which
become part of
a Swahili trading
network
1500s

French rule over
Mayotte is
established
1843

French
protectorate
over the
remaining
Comoro islands
is proclaimed
1886

The islands are
ruled as part of
the French
colony of
Madagascar
1914–1946

Independence is
followed by a
mercenary c_up,
which installs Ali
Soilih
1975

Ali Soilih is
overthrown by
mercenaries;
Abdullah is
restored
1978

1980s

Union Com-
orienne pour le
Progress is made
the sole political
party; unop-
posed, Abdullah
is reelected presi-
dent

Attempted coups
by members of
the presidential
guard

Economic crisis
and austerity
plans

REPUBLIC OF COMOROS

At the time of its unilateral declaration of independence from France in 1975 the Comoros was listed by the United Nations as one of the world's least developed nations. The years since have not been especially kind to the Comorans; their lives have been made even more difficult by natural disaster, eccentric leadership, and external intervention.

HISTORY AND POLITICS

The Comoros archipelago was populated by a number of Indian Ocean peoples, who—by the time of the arrival of the first Europeans during the early sixteenth century—had already combined to form the predominantly Muslim, Swahili-speaking society found on the islands today. In 1886 the French, who had already colonized the neighboring island of Mayotte, proclaimed a protectorate over the three main islands that currently constitute the Islamic republic. Throughout the colonial period the Comoros were especially valued by the French for strategic reasons. A local elite of large landholders prospered from the production of cash crops, while life for most Comorans remained one of extreme poverty.

A month after independence in 1975 the first Comoran government, led by the wealthy Ahmed Abdullah Abderemane (known as Ahmed Abdullah), was overthrown by mercenaries, who installed Ali Soilih in power. The new leader promised a socialist transformation of the nation

and began to implement land reform. This program was never completed, however, because Soilih rapidly lost support both at home and abroad. Under his leadership, gangs of undisciplined youths terrorized society, while the basic institutions and services of government all but disappeared. The situation was made even worse by a major volcanic eruption, which left 20,000 people homeless, and by the arrival of 16,000 Comoran refugees after a massacre of Comorans in Madagascar.

In 1978 another band of mercenaries—this time led by the notorious Bob Denard, whose exploits in Zaire during the 1960s had made his name infamous throughout Africa—overthrew Soilih and eventually restored Abdullah to power under the republic's first functioning Constitution. Although most of the mercenaries left by the end of 1978, Denard remained as an officer in the presidential guard. He made frequent trips to South Africa and is believed to have encouraged closer ties between Comoros and Pretoria. The government attracted much-needed outside aid, principally from France, Saudi Arabia, and international donor agencies. In 1982 the country legally became a one-party state. Attempted coups in 1985 and 1987 aggravated political tensions. Many Comorans resent the influence of European mercenaries.

ECONOMY AND DEVELOPMENT

After experiencing a 23-percent decline

during the 2 years of Ali Soilih's rule, the economy recovered somewhat. Up to 90 percent of the population are supported by farming, which contributes about 40 percent of the national gross domestic product. Comoros is the world's leading exporter of ylang-ylang, an essence used to make perfume, and is the second leading producer of vanilla. (Competition with Madagascar for the vanilla market aggravated an economic crisis because of the rising costs of imports, including petroleum and food.) Rice is the islands' staple, but only 20 percent of the country's consumption is produced locally. The government has tried to encourage agricultural diversification by promoting alternative crops such as maize. Yet setbacks were suffered in 1983 and 1987, when crops were destroyed by cyclones, a common occurrence.

What little industry exists on the island consists almost entirely of agricultural processing, including perfume distillation. The one sector of the economy with potential for growth is tourism, but many believe that Comoros would have to reduce the close ties to South Africa before that industry could be promoted.

DEVELOPMENT

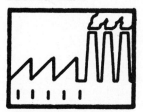

One of the important projects undertaken since independence has been the ongoing expansion of the port at Mutsamudu, which will allow the country to dock large cargo ships for the first time. However, it has yet to be completed.

FREEDOM

President Abdullah pardoned many of the prisoners sentenced to long jail terms after the 1985 coup attempt, but critics note that others have died in detention.

HEALTH/WELFARE

The hospitals and clinics now operating are totally inadequate to meet the nation's needs. Life expectancy is low, and the infant mortality rate is among the world's highest.

ACHIEVEMENTS

The Comoros has been known as a center of the world's finest perfumes since very early in its history.

Djibouti (Republic of Djibouti)

GEOGRAPHY

Area in Square Kilometers (Miles):
23,200 (8,960) (about the size of
New Hampshire)
Capital (Population): Djibouti
(250,000)
Climate: arid to semiarid

PEOPLE

Population
Total: 470,000
Annual Growth Rate: 6.4%
Rural/Urban Population Ratio: n/a
Languages: official: French, Arabic;
others spoken: Somali, Saho-Afar

Health
Life Expectancy at Birth: 50 years
Infant Death Rate (Ratio): 132/1,000
Average Caloric Intake: n/a
Physicians Available (Ratio): 1/1,021

Religion(s)
92% Muslim; 6% Christian; 2%
other

Education
Adult Literacy Rate: 17%

COMMUNICATION

Telephones: 6,400
Newspapers: 3 weeklies

TERRITORY OF THE AFARS AND ISSAS

Djibouti, with its critical port on the Red Sea, was the subject of great dispute during the early 1960s. As France granted independence to its colonies in other regions of Africa, Djibouti was largely ignored.

A referendum was held in 1967, which resulted in a vote by the residents of the colony to remain under French control. This became the focus of struggle between the Ethiopian-backed Afar peoples and the Issa, who were supported by Somalia as part of an effort to annex the territory and ensure itself a port on the Red Sea. The result of this struggle was a resolution renaming the colony the "Territory of the Afars," a title later expanded under French pressure to "Territory of the Afars and Issas." Independence was officially declared on June 27, 1977, following another referendum.

TRANSPORTATION

Highways—Kilometers (Miles): 2,906
(1,801)
Railroads—Kilometers (Miles): 106
(66)
Commercial Airports: 1 international

GOVERNMENT

Type: republic
Independence Date: June 27, 1977
Head of State: President Hassan
Gouled Aptidon
Political Parties: People's Progress
Assembly
Suffrage: universal for adults

MILITARY

Number of Armed Forces: 3,000
*Military Expenditures (% of Central
Government Expenditures):*
$2,900,000 (3.4%)
Current Hostilities: none

ECONOMY

Currency ($ U.S. Equivalent): 177
Djibouti francs = $1
Per Capita Income/GNP: $400/$307
million
Inflation Rate: 1.7%
Natural Resources: none
Agriculture: goats; sheep; camels;
cattle; coffee
Industry: port and maritime support;
construction

FOREIGN TRADE

Exports: $66 million
Imports: $152 million

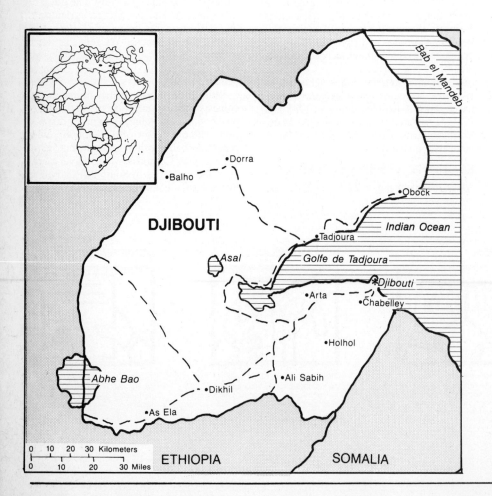

France buys the port of Obock 1862	France acquires the port of Djibouti 1888	The Addis Ababa-Djibouti railroad is completed 1917	Djibouti votes to remain part of Overseas France 1958	Independence; the Ogaden War 1977

1980s

Drought and warfare increase the flow of refugees	President Gouled is reelected for a third term, with 90% of the vote	Gouled appoints a new Cabinet; political jockeying for succession to Gouled

DJIBOUTI

Tiny Djibouti, situated between Ethiopia and Somalia, guards the southern mouth of the Red Sea. Because the historic domains of the two main ethnic groups (the Somali-speaking Issas in the south and the Afars near Ethiopia and Eritrea) are cut by international boundaries, external conflicts often have internal ramifications.

Much of Djibouti's territory is a barren desert, with harsh volcanic outcroppings, shifting sands, high temperatures, and minimal rainfall. Despite this, humidity can be very high during the monsoon seasons of May and September.

HISTORY

Djibouti's modern history is closely linked with international competition over the Red Sea routes. France responded to the United Kingdom's earlier moves in Aden by first exploring and then negotiating to open up trade with the kingdom of Shoa in what is now Ethiopia. In 1862 France bought the port of Obock and its hinterland, later part of Djibouti.

With the opening of the Suez Canal in 1869, the Red Sea was the major route from Europe to India and the Far East. Italy began its expansion in Eritrea that same year. In the 1880s France began developing Obock as a port, and in 1888 the French acquired the town of Djibouti, later the capital of French Somaliland. A treaty with the emperor of Ethiopia permitted the construction of the Addis Ababa-Djibouti railroad, which ensured the prosperity of the port of Djibouti. Franco-Italian rivalries in the region were heightened by Italy's occupation of Ethiopia during World War II.

Following World War II Djibouti became an overseas territory of France, and all residents became French citizens. By 1960 other French colonies had gained independence. The Somali Republic had been created next door, and interest in independence grew in Djibouti. To counter the effects of Somali nationalism, the French favored the Afars in local politics and hired them for jobs in the civil service and the port. In 1967 an electrified barbed-wire fence was built around the capital to prevent Issas from entering the town illegally.

After the 1967 Arab-Israeli War the Suez Canal was closed until 1975, and Djibouti's port suffered. The new supertankers were too large to use the canal even when it reopened. This crisis made Djibouti rely on French economic aid. In 1974 Ethiopia's revolution and the Somali drought transformed the situation in Djibouti. Ethiopia's new government sought new outlets for its trade. The Somali drought forced ethnic Somali refugees into Djibouti, tipping the electoral and ethnic balance away from the Afars and toward independence from France.

On June 27, 1977 the Republic of Djibouti became independent. An ethnically balanced Cabinet was formed, with an Issa, Hassan Gouled Aptidon, as president, and an Afar, Ahmed Dini, as prime minister. Later in 1977 war broke out in Ogaden between Ethiopia and Somalia. Djibouti remained neutral, but ethnic tensions mounted as more Somali refugees arrived. In 1978 the Afars withdrew from the government. Gouled was reelected for a third 6-year term in 1987. Possible successors from within his fam-

ily and from both the Afar and Issa groups are now competing for political support.

By 1981 the Eritrean and Ogaden conflicts had caused nearly 50,000 refugees to flee to Djibouti, where many were settled in camps set up by the United Nations High Commission for Refugees (UNHCR). Many were repatriated in 1986, but thousands remain, with little hope for resettlement or incorporation. As wars in Somalia and Ethiopia escalate, the number of refugees is likely to rise.

ECONOMY

Djibouti is unable to feed its own people. The agricultural sector consists of little more than small-scale market gardening and date cultivation. More than half of the population are nomadic pastoralists.

Aside from the port, there is little industry in Djibouti. The port, unable to handle supertankers, now faces competition from Ethiopian and Arab ports.

Because of its strategic location, Djibouti has received foreign aid from many countries, including France, Saudi Arabia, Iraq, Libya, Gulf states, and West Germany, as well as from multilateral agencies. The continued French military presence has helped to support the economy and to prevent Djibouti from being swallowed up by either of its larger neighbors. To secure their interests, the French are making contacts with all candidates aspiring to succeed Gouled.

DEVELOPMENT

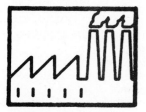

Construction of an international container terminal valued at $23 million was begun in 1981. In 1983 Djibouti's new radio transmitter was dedicated. The radio station was built with French and West German aid.

FREEDOM

Djibouti's first Constitution is still incomplete, although the first parts of it were introduced in 1981. For topics not yet covered by local laws, the courts draw on the Napoleonic code, a relic of the nation's French colonial past, or the Muslim Sharia, which is based on the Koran.

HEALTH/WELFARE

Life expectancy is only 50 years, caused partly by a high level of infant mortality. The government has responded to the lack of agricultural potential that lies at the base of the country's nutritional and health problems by encouraging Djiboutians to supplement their diets with fish caught locally.

ACHIEVEMENTS

In spite of its small size, Djibouti has hosted thousands of refugees from neighboring countries. Many Ethiopians were resettled in 1983, but thousands have been forced by famine, drought, and warfare to return to Djibouti. Somali refugees from the Ogaden have added to the crush of refugees.

Ethiopia (People's Democratic Republic of Ethiopia)

GEOGRAPHY

Area in Square Kilometers (Miles): 1,221,900 (471,800) (about four-fifths the size of Alaska)
Capital (Population): Addis Ababa (1,412,000)
Climate: temperate in highlands; arid to semiarid in lowlands

PEOPLE
Population
Total: 43,882,000
Annual Growth Rate: 2.6%
Rural/Urban Population Ratio: 89/11
Languages: official: Amharic; others spoken: Tigrinya, Oromo, Somali, Arabic, Italian, English, others

Health
Life Expectancy at Birth: 41 years male; 44 years female
Infant Death Rate (Ratio): 168/1,000
Average Caloric Intake: 78% of FAO minimum in areas not severely affected by drought
Physicians Available (Ratio): 1/87,067

Religion(s)
40%–45% Muslim; 35%–40% Ethiopian Orthodox Christian; 15%–25% traditional indigenous and others

Education
Adult Literacy Rate: 55%

COMMUNICATION
Telephones: 100,000
Newspapers: 3

FAMINE AND RELIEF EFFORTS

In Ethiopia, severe drought, years of warfare, regional rivalries, and logistics have combined to produce terrible famine, resulting in deaths, malnutrition, disease, and hundreds of thousands of refugees. Beginning in 1984 private and governmental responses from the international community have brought massive food aid and have begun to assist Ethiopians in solving the long-range problems of infrastructure, tools, seeds, and retraining of famine victims. Lack of rainfall and escalating warfare led to recurring famine in 1987 and 1988, with 6 million to 7 million people at risk of starvation.

Critics accuse the Ethiopian government of politicizing the relief efforts, thereby exacerbating the famine. Another problem is rebels who attack food convoys. The government allegedly prevented food from reaching the Tigray, Oromo, and Eritrean regions, and resettling of victims led to accusations of politically motivated forced removals. Critics and supporters alike agree, however, that the Ethiopian administration of relief is generally efficient and free from corruption.

TRANSPORTATION
Highways—Kilometers (Miles): 30,000 (18,600)
Railroads—Kilometers (Miles): 782 (485)
Commercial Airports: 4 international

GOVERNMENT
Type: provisional military government
Independence Date: none
Head of State: President Mengistu Haile Mariam
Political Parties: Workers' Party of Ethiopia
Suffrage: universal over 21

MILITARY
Number of Armed Forces: 336,500
Military Expenditures (% of Central Government Expenditures): 9.8%
Current Hostilities: internal conflicts with liberation groups in several provinces; border disputes with Somalia

ECONOMY
Currency ($ U.S. Equivalent): 2.07 birrs = $1
Per Capita Income/GNP: $140/$4.6 billion
Inflation Rate: 8.4%
Natural Resources: potash; salt; gold; copper; platinum
Agriculture: cereals; coffee; pulses; oil seeds; livestock
Industry: processed food; textiles; cement; building materials; hydroelectric power

FOREIGN TRADE
Exports: $333 million
Imports: $993 million

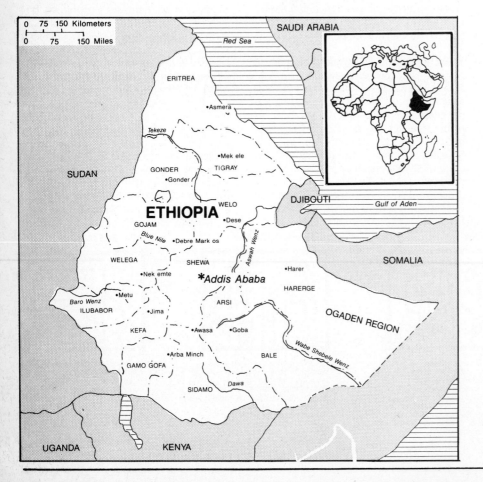

ETHIOPIA

Ethiopia, considered the poorest country in the world, has a long recorded history. Haile Selassie, the last emperor of Ethiopia, claimed he was descended from Solomon and the Queen of Sheba, and the history of the country has been traced from the Axum kingdom, founded in the first century A.D., to the military coup in 1974. This coup, which overthrew Haile Selassie, led to the demise of the ancient kingdom. Coup leaders later declared that the empire had become a Marxist-Leninist state. Many changes have taken place, yet old patterns persist.

THE COUP'S ORIGINS AND RESULTS

The past dominance of an Amhara ruling class in Ethiopia had developed through history, and regional aristocracies were built on peasant bases. The modernization of the Ethiopian kingdom had begun as far back as the mid-nineteenth century by Emperor Tewodros, and was continued by Menelik II in the late nineteenth century.

Haile Selassie gave Ethiopia the appearance of a constitutional state in the 1930s by establishing a Constitution, promoting some social reforms, opening Western schools, and supporting new construction in Addis Ababa, the capital city. In the 1950s and 1960s the regime began to be affected by new forces—such as the rise of nationalism throughout Africa, the impact of foreign capital, and the intrusion of military and economic advisors from the United States. Resistance to the emperor grew, especially in the university and among workers in Addis Ababa, teachers, and the military forces. Peoples such as the Tigray, the Somali, the Oromo, and the already nationalist Eritreans became more conscious of their different identities.

The coup itself was triggered by problems resulting from the sharp rise in food and oil prices and the terrible famine in Tigray and Wolo provinces in 1972–1973. It was said that 200,000 persons died during this famine. Meanwhile, conditions in the drought regions contrasted sharply with the growing wealth of the emperor and the urban upper class. Strikes, military mutinies, and peasant revolts reached their height in February 1974. In September a group of military officers deposed the emperor.

A Provisional Military Administrative Council (PMAC), a group of more than 120 military men known as the *Dergue* (Amharic for "committee"), took command. By the end of 1974 the Dergue had moved from a philosophy of "Ethiopia First" to "Ethiopian Socialism." The Dergue took drastic measures. Companies and lands were nationalized. A national campaign for development sent students into the countryside to assist in land re-

(United Nations photo by Y. Levy)

Most people in Ethiopia are engaged in agriculture and, to some extent, animal husbandry. However, urbanization is increasing.

Emperor Tewodros begins the conquest and development of modern Ethiopia **1855**	Ethiopia defeats Italian invaders at the Battle of Adowa **1896**	Fascist Italy invades Ethiopia and rules until 1941 **1936**

forms, to teach literacy, and to encourage the formation of active peasant associations, which remain important today. Associations called *kebeles* were also formed among workers in the cities.

However, the Dergue did not implement the plans for reconstruction, nor did it put a new people's government into effect, because it was unable to stabilize its own leadership and unable to agree on the groups that should be supported. Intense political rivalries, from 1974 to 1978, resulted in the executions of numerous individuals and the destruction of certain groups. An undetermined number of people lost their lives.

In 1978 Mengistu Haile Mariam came to power. He led the Commission for Organizing the Party of the Working People of Ethiopia (COPWE), and on the 10th anniversary of the Ethiopian revolution COPWE announced the formation of the Workers' Party of Ethiopia (WPE), a communist party, which now oversees government-sponsored national organizations. In 1987, under a new Constitution, voters chose members of the first National Shengo (Parliament), and Mengistu became president of a civilian government.

THE CURRENT SITUATION

The development of a socialist state has been delayed by crises as well as by personal political rivalries. The main crisis is civil war. There are liberation movements among the Tigray, the Oromo, the Somali, and the Eritreans. The government's answer to their ethnic pride and their desire for self-determination has been military repression. The size of the Ethiopian army was increased, often through conscription; the age of draftees was lowered to 19, and the government sought arms from abroad. The arms buildup led to a secret arms agreement with the Soviet Union in 1976, as well as a diplomatic realignment in 1977, whereby Ethiopia, once the ally of the United States, became closely attached to the Soviet Union. This move was to have many repercussions. The realignment caused the United States to look for other allies in the region, and U.S. support for Somalia (a former ally of the Soviet Union) and Kenya became substantial. The intensity of the warfare increased, and the resistance of those in opposition grew—now fueled by the Soviet arms that

the opposition captured from the Ethiopians.

The World Bank and the International Monetary Fund (IMF), influenced by the United States, withheld loans to Ethiopia. Consequently, for several years before 1981, Ethiopia received less aid than any of the UN-designated least developed countries (LDCs) from these organizations. During the drought of 1984–1985, however, relief agencies and individual governments came to the aid of Ethiopia. In spite of some criticism of methods of distribution and resettlement plans, these institutions and governments, including the United States, are working with Ethiopia to combat ongoing famine and to prevent future crises.

ECONOMIC PROBLEMS

Vast economic problems remain to be solved. Falling prices for coffee on the world market and the rising costs of imported goods compound the losses resulting from the civil wars and drought. Land reform has been a mixed blessing. Farmers guarded their harvests for themselves, while the city populations remained unfed. Recent changes offer higher prices for farmers and less governmental control. Although critics doubt the sincerity of the reforms and point to the financial strains of the war, others note that Ethiopia's is actually one of the most successfully managed economies in Africa. Inflation is kept low, industry operates at

(UNICEF photo)

Ethiopia's government has very limited financial resources and must depend on help from international agencies to cope with problems resulting from widespread drought.

| | The Eritrean liberation struggle begins **1961** | Famines in Tigray and Wolo provinces result in up to 200,000 deaths **1972–1973** | Emperor Haile Selassie is overthrown; the PMAC is established **1974** | Diplomatic realignment and a new arms agreement with the Soviet Union **1977** |

1980s

| Massive famine, resulting from drought and warfare | Tigray and Eritrean struggles intensify; many killed; cities captured and recaptured | Elections lead to civilian rule, with Mengistu as president |

100-percent capacity, and the growth rate is higher than most other African countries. The fact remains, though, that millions of people are in distress, and the escalating famine demands massive effort.

HISTORICAL CONTINUITIES

Features of the past continue to characterize, shape, and trouble the new Ethiopia. Perhaps most important is the heritage of ethnic diversity. The empire was a feudal kingdom, and ruling landed aristocrats in the various areas were local magnates rather than representatives of the central government. Local independence was maintained. The geographic variety of Ethiopia has helped to maintain the variety of languages and cultural traditions, but it has also worked against the consolidation and national integration of the different communities. Many groups have risen against the socialist state, which they claim is fascist.

The Eritrean movement is the oldest and strongest of the liberation movements. In 1945 Eritrea became independent of Italy and was put under Ethiopian jurisdiction as a federated territory. When the Ethiopian government abrogated Eritrea's status, armed struggle began in 1961. First under Haile Selassie and then the Dergue, the government resisted and fought Eritrean independence. The Eritrean People's Liberation Front (EPLF), the most active group, successfully resisted massive Ethiopian military campaigns in the 1980s and merged with the Eritrean Liberation Front in 1986. They have organized

a government and provide services in the liberated areas, and in 1986, for the first time, 100 nongovernmental organizations (NGOs) at the UN called for discussions to end the 25-year war.

Another persistent problem, the desire of ethnic Somali of the southeastern Ogaden region for reunification with Somalia, led to persistent insurgency and outright war between Ethiopia and Somalia in 1977–1978. Fighting over this area continues, despite an agreement signed in 1988.

The resistance of ethnic communities within Ethiopia to the new state is heightened by the failure of the leaders to give any power to these communities within the central government despite promises made in the new Constitution. The Amhara have always been the dominant rulers in the empire. Today they continue to be important, making up the majority in the ruling body.

The continuity of modern Ethiopia is also seen in religious life. Tradition claims that Christianity, in its unique Ethiopian form, was first introduced into the country in the fourth century A.D. It became allied to the emperor and the ruling class, and it developed distinctive national rituals, churches, and a special priestly class. Today, although the church is no longer a state church and church lands have been nationalized, the membership of the church continues to grow. Islam, too, has a long heritage in Ethiopia, and there is no evidence that this faith has been attacked since the new government came to power.

CONCLUSION

A most important characteristic of Ethiopia is its leadership role in continental Africa. During the colonial period Ethiopia was an example that inspired dominated peoples. The kingdom had defeated the Italians in 1896 and had maintained its independence, except for the period from 1936 to 1945 when Mussolini and Fascist Italy controlled the state. Ethiopia was a founding member of the United Nations and the home of the Organization of African Unity (OAU). Even today the headquarters of the OAU remains in Addis Ababa. Ethiopia played a leading role in maintaining the organization in 1982–1983, when conflicts over the Western Sahara and Chad threatened the OAU's destruction.

Attempts to reconcile with neighboring Sudan and Somalia have not been successful. In spite of discussions between government representatives, raids continue across the borders of southern Sudan and Somalia and Ethiopia, with each country providing material and moral support for the others' rebels.

More than 300,000 refugees are in Ethiopia because of conflicts in the region. Caught between opposing sides, with food now a weapon, millions starve.

DEVELOPMENT

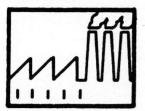

Land reform under the Dergue allowed peasants to control their own production, but the whole country does not benefit, and surpluses do not reach the cities. Almost 12 million people will have been reorganized in villages in the more fertile south by 1989.

FREEDOM

Political prisoners are still said to be held in Ethiopia, but human rights are more secure than in the terrible years from 1974–1978—especially 1977–1978, when arbitrary arrest, executions, and violence were widespread. Relatives of the former emperor are still detained, and in Eritrea, the level of violence is still high.

HEALTH/WELFARE

The per capita income is one of the lowest in the world, and 65% of the people are said to live below the poverty level. The deepest poverty is now in the urban areas. Many of those who were resettled are now self-sufficient in food.

ACHIEVEMENTS

Informal as well as formal education has been expanded in recent years. In 1979, an ambitious literacy campaign began, and at least ten million people in rural and urban areas have taken part. Fifteen languages are used. Villagization programs include new schools, roads, and housing.

Kenya (Republic of Kenya)

GEOGRAPHY

Area in Square Kilometers (Miles):
582,488 (224,900) (slightly smaller than Texas)
Capital (Population): Nairobi (1,200,000)
Climate: tropical to arid

PEOPLE

Population
Total: 21,044,000
Annual Growth Rate: 4%
Rural/Urban Population Ratio: 84/16
Languages: official: English, Kiswahili; others spoken: Kikuyu Luo, Kamba, Kipsigi, Maasai, Luhya, Gusii, Nandi, Somali, others

Health
Life Expectancy at Birth: 56 years male; 60 years female
Infant Death Rate (Ratio): 83/1,000
Average Caloric Intake: 88% of FAO minimum
Physicians Available (Ratio): 1/8,125

Religion(s)
38% Protestant; 28% traditional indigenous; 28% Catholic; 6% Muslim

Education
Adult Literacy Rate: 50%

COMMUNICATION

Telephones: 216,700
Newspapers: 4

CULTURE AND POLITICS

In the past as well as today, cultural activities in Kenya have been closely connected with politics, encouraging nationalism and revealing inequities. Events occurring at the Kamriitha Community Educational and Cultural Center illustrate this statement. The center was built by community efforts in Kamriithu, a Kenyan town of 10,000 people. The villagers developed a program at the center and operated it. The literacy committee organized a literacy study course, and the community organized dramas that illustrated the people's experiences and ideas. Ngugi wa Thiong'o was commissioned to write the first play—about the townspeople's own lives—and they discussed and criticized it as well as performed it in a theater that the town had built. The production was highly successful, but was banned, because the authorities felt it encouraged class conflict. Its potential for organizing peasants was a threat to the government. Ngugi was detained (he is now in exile). Later the center was closed and the theater destroyed.

TRANSPORTATION

Highways—Kilometers (Miles):
53,577 (33,217)
Railroads—Kilometers (Miles): 2,654 (1,645)
Commercial Airports: 2 international

GOVERNMENT

Type: republic; one-party state
Independence Date: December 12, 1963
Head of State: President Daniel arap Moi
Political Parties: Kenya African National Union
Suffrage: universal over 21

MILITARY

Number of Armed Forces: 14,750
Military Expenditures (% of Central Government Expenditures): $168,600,000 (8%)
Current Hostilities: border conflict with Uganda

ECONOMY

Currency ($ U.S. Equivalent): 15.87 Kenya shillings = $1
Per Capita Income/GNP: $309/$5.7 billion
Inflation Rate: 10.9%
Natural Resources: wildlife; land; soda ash; wattle
Agriculture: corn; wheat; rice; sugarcane; coffee; tea; sisal; pyrethrum; livestock
Industry: petroleum products; cement; beer; automobile assembly; food processing; tourism

FOREIGN TRADE

Exports: $1.2 billion
Imports: $1.6 billion

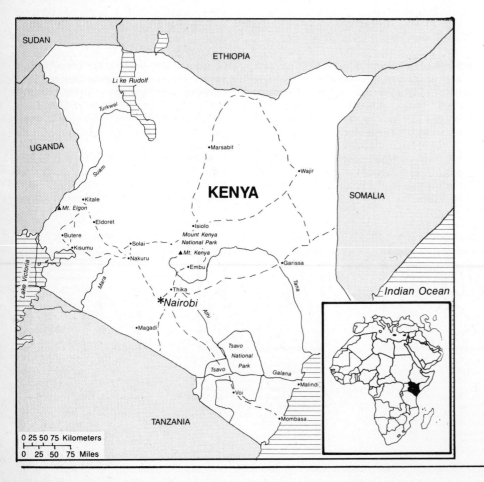

KENYA

Tom Mboya, Kenya's minister of economic development and planning in 1969, made these remarks in an article written for *The New York Times* a few months before his assassination:

> We suffered during our struggle for independence, but in many ways it was a simpler period than today. The present period is less dramatic. Nationalist sentiment must remain powerful, but it can no longer be sustained by slogans and the excitement of independence. Rather, it must itself sustain the population during the long process of development. For development will not come immediately. It is a process that requires time, planning, sacrifice, and work.

Someone observing Kenya today, years after Mboya's remarks, might agree with his sentiments. The quotation also raises questions about independence and development in contemporary Kenya.

KENYA'S PAST

The African peoples who are now citizens of Kenya were members of small-scale local societies in precolonial times. The Maasai, then as now, were herders who exchanged cattle for the crops of farmers such as the Kikuyu and Kamba. Organized Swahili city states developed on the coast. In the nineteenth century caravans of Swahili and Arab traders stimulated economic and political changes. However, the outsiders who had the greatest impact on the Kenya farmers and herders were the European settlers who came to Kenya as early as the first decade of the twentieth century.

By the 1930s the area of the temperate highlands near Nairobi had become "white man's country." More than 6 million acres of land—much of it the land of the Maasai—had been taken from the original owners, and many Africans had been moved to reserves. Kikuyu laborers, often migrants from the reserves, worked for the new owners—sometimes on lands that they had once farmed for themselves.

By the 1950s African grievances had been heightened by increased European settlement, growing African nationalism, and repression resulting from white fears. The movement called *Mau Mau* developed when a state of emergency was declared by the British colonial authorities. The freedom fighters, unassisted by any outside aid, fought the regime for 10 years. During this time 32 whites lost their lives, and 13,000 Kikuyu were killed. Eighty thousand Africans were de-

tained in detention camps by colonial authorities, and more than a million persons were resettled in controlled villages.

When political activity was finally allowed in Kenya, the person who emerged as a leader was the already-popular Jomo Kenyatta, who had been detained during the emergency and accused—without any evidence—of leading the resistance movement. Kenyatta, a charismatic leader, became prime minister and later president when Kenya gained independence. He led the country from 1963 until his death in 1978.

During the early years of Kenyatta's leadership the situation in Kenya looked promising. Kenyatta's government encouraged racial harmony, and the slogan *Harambee* ("Let Us Pull Together") was a call for people of all races to work together for Kenya's development. The political system seemed open, and there were (as there still are) regular elections. Land reforms provided plots to 1.5 million farmers, who made a little money from the production of cash crops, such as coffee, which received good prices on the world market in these years. A policy of Africanization opened businesses to Kenya entrepreneurs. Many new enterprises were begun—often developed with foreign capital. Kenya was called "the showcase of capitalism" and was compared to the similarly prospering Côte d'Ivoire in West Africa.

KENYA'S POLITICAL LIFE

According to news reports and general surveys of Kenya, "politics is king" in Kenya today. Daniel arap Moi, Kenyatta's successor, has sought to follow Kenyatta's policies and to use them in keeping his opponents and his followers in line. *Nyayoism* ("in the footsteps"—of Kenyatta) and "peace, love and unity" are the slogans of Moi's government; but, like his predecessor, Moi has consolidated his

power and detained and silenced opponents. Oginga Odinga, Kenyatta's (and now Moi's) political opponent, was detained for criticizing Kenyatta; and Charles Njono, a Kikuyu minister and powerful member of government, was suspended from office and the party for attempting to overthrow the government. In 1982 a constitutional amendment was passed making the Kenya African National Union (KANU) the only legal party—thus restraining opponents such as Odinga who had attempted to develop a second party. In 1986 Moi declared that KANU was "above" the government, the Parliament, and the judiciary. Within the party, there has been much dissension, and much competition for parliamentary seats. There have been Cabinet reshufflings, and new posts have been created that allow for increased patronage.

In August 1982 members of the Kenya Air Force attempted a coup against Moi's government. It did not succeed, but there was much violence in Nairobi. About 250 persons died, and approximately 1,500 were detained. The Air Force was disbanded. The university, whose students came out in support of the coup makers, was closed; it reopened in the summer of 1983, although campus unrest and closures emerged again in 1986 and 1987.

The coup and its aftermath have had a damaging effect on Kenya. Although Moi and the government recovered, the repercussions of this event are evident. Moi continually sought to consolidate his control and to silence critics. In response to international attention on human-rights abuses, Moi asserted Kenya's right to run its internal affairs; and in response to growing unrest, he called for elections in 1988. Church leaders and others criticized the method of choosing candidates, "queuing," because the public selection by voters leads to intimidation. As a result of this criticism, *Beyond*, a church maga-

		Mau Mau, a predominantly Kikuyu movement, resists colonial rule	Kenya gains independence under the leadership of Jomo Kenyatta	Tom Mboya, a leading trade unionist and government minister, is assassinated	Daniel arap Moi becomes president upon the death of Kenyatta
The British East African Protectorate is proclaimed 1895	British colonists begin to settle in the Highlands area 1900–1910	1952	1963	1969	1978

■ ■■■■■■■■■■■■■■■■ ■■■ ■■■■■■■■■■■■■■■■■ ■■■■■■■■■■■■■■■■■■■■ ■■■■■■■■■■■■■ ■■■■■■■■■■■■■■■■■■ ■■■■■■■■■■ 1980s

A coup by members of the Kenya Air Force is put down	Dissident activity, under the new name of Mwakenya, resurfaces	Parliamentary elections are held; many politicians are not reelected

zine, was banned. Political tensions led Moi to blame missionaries, Christian and Muslim fundamentalists, Libyans, and foreign researchers for the tensions.

Some parliamentarians lost seats in 1988, and Joseph Karanja replaced Mwai Kibaki as vice president. Some politicians want to abolish the secret ballot, but opposition by church officials forced Moi to postpone that decision.

Moi has opponents from the left and the right, with many Kikuyu—whose power eroded after Kenyatta's death—active in dissident groups. In spite of continued arrest, detention, and fines, opposition groups, sometimes with new names, resurface.

Members of an underground opposition group, Mwakenya (Union of Patriots for the Liberation of Kenya), have been detained, while others have escaped to exile. In 1987 Mwakenya joined with other dissident exiles to form the umbrella group United Movement for Democracy in Kenya (UMOJA), to "work for democratic change" in Kenya. Many Kenyans, however, when contrasting their country with their close neighbors' instability, value highly the strength and longevity of the party, trading political freedom for political stability.

EXAMINING THE SHOWCASE

Kenya, like other African countries, has been adversely affected by the conditions of the world economy. Until the late 1970s Kenya had one of the highest growth rates of the sub-Saharan African countries. Kenya is the most industrialized country of East Africa, and the cash crops that it exports are extensive and varied, thus buffering the nation's economy from the uncertainties of the world market. Nevertheless, the current low return for its cash crops abroad is one reason for Kenya's worsening economic situation.

The elite must take some responsibility for the problems of the Kenyan economy. They have spent their efforts in politicking; often they have used their wealth not for the advancement of production, but for the development of affluent lifestyles. Rather than struggling *for* development, they have struggled *over* what development there is. "Ten millionaires and ten million beggars" is how J. M. Kariuki, a reforming politician, described Kenya in the mid-1970s. The richest tenth of the population receive 40 percent of the wealth, while the poorest quarter of the people receive only 6 percent. The middle class has benefited from this unequal division of wealth and accusations of corruption abound. After months of rumors, a currency scandal surfaced in 1987. Bankers and coffee traders, mostly Asians, were arrested after an estimated $2.5 billion had been stashed in foreign banks from 1982–1984. Others were accused of bribing official investigators.

Foreign-owned industries and services are protected by the government, and they send their surplus earnings back to their own countries. Many enterprises are from the United States. U.S. corporations have played a large part in Kenya's economy and are part of a consortium that is providing loans to help Kenya meet its debts. And in spite of unrest, international donors have pledged to increase aid, praising Kenya's "open economy."

The U.S. government has also taken a special strategic interest in Kenya. In 1980 Kenya agreed to allow the United States to use the Nairobi Airport for its forces, and the port of Mombasa is a base for the U.S. Navy. Israel, too, has close relations with Kenya. The close ties to the United States and the presence of American military personnel have contributed to political tension in Kenya. A major source of foreign exchange, tourism, has declined in recent years. This decline has been attributed to the political unrest, increased government regulations and fees, and fear of Acquired Immune Deficiency Syndrome (AIDS).

CONCLUSION

Kenya celebrated its 25th anniversary of independence in 1988. There have been many achievements—in education and in agriculture, for instance. However, problems remain. The jobless in the cities are increasingly restless. Many of the gains of economic development are absorbed by Kenya's population growth—one of the highest in the world. Land reform has slowed down, and border tensions with Uganda simmer. Some believe that the promises of independence have been fulfilled; others, including some of the old freedom fighters, believe that Kenya has betrayed the goals of the earlier struggle.

DEVELOPMENT

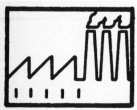

Kenya's game parks and safaris are well known in the Western world. Tourism is among the major sources of foreign exchange. It is a mixed blessing. The tourists who enrich the country use facilities and services geared to a wealthy enclave class, and promote a servant mentality.

FREEDOM

There are about 80 political prisoners in Kenyan jails, people are detained without trial, and some die in police custody, recent phenomena in Kenya. Parliament amended the Constitution to allow longer detentions without trial and to give the president the power to fire judges and members of the Public Service Commission.

HEALTH/WELFARE

Individual Kenyan communities have raised considerable amounts of money for self-help projects; politicians compete in pledging large amounts for the building of schools, clinics, and other developments. Other members of the community contribute what they can afford, and local citizens provide free labor for construction and maintenance.

ACHIEVEMENTS

Kenya has made great strides in education, restructuring the educational system to allow broader access to the university by opening a new university campus at Eldoret, and upgrading the Egerton Agricultural College and Kenyatta College to the status of full-fledged branches of the university.

Madagascar (Democratic Republic of Madagascar)

GEOGRAPHY
Area in Square Kilometers (Miles):
587,041 (226,658) (slightly smaller than Texas)
Capital (Population): Antananarivo (650,000)
Climate: tropical and moderate

PEOPLE
Population
Total: 10,568,000
Annual Growth Rate: 2.7%
Rural/Urban Population Ratio: 78/22
Languages: official: Malagasy; others spoken: French, others

Health
Life Expectancy at Birth: 46 years
Infant Death Rate (Ratio): 101/1,000
Average Caloric Intake: 111% of FAO minimum
Physicians Available (Ratio): 1/11,242

Religion(s)
51% Christian; 48% traditional indigenous; 1% Muslim

Education
Adult Literacy Rate: 53%

MALAGASY POETS

> What invisible rat
> comes from the walls of night
> gnaws at the milky cake of the moon?

Thus begins one of the poems of Jean-Joseph Rabearivelo (1901–1937), one of Malagasy's greatest twentieth-century poets. Like the poets who followed him, such as Jean Jacques Rebemananjara and Jacques Flavien Ranaivo, Rabearivelo wrote in French and was deeply affected by French poets, literature, and culture. Yet all of these poets were attached to local Malagasy forms and rhythms and were inspired by the *hainteny* form, which was so characteristic of the popular songs of the island. Several of the poems of Rabearivelo and Rananivo are reprinted in *A Book of African Verse*, edited by J. Reed and C. Wake (London, 1964).

COMMUNICATION
Telephones: 37,100
Newspapers: 7

TRANSPORTATION
Highways—Kilometers (Miles): 49,637 (30,774)
Railroads—Kilometers (Miles): 884 (549)
Commercial Airports: 3 international

GOVERNMENT
Type: republic; authority held by Supreme Revolutionary Council
Independence Date: June 26, 1960
Head of State: President (Colonel) Didier Ratsiraka
Political Parties: Advance Guard of Malagasy Revolution; Congress Party for Malagasy Independence; Movement for National Unity; Malagasy Christian Democratic Union; Militants for the Establishment of a Proletarian Regime; National Movement for Independence of Madagascar
Suffrage: universal over 18

MILITARY
Number of Armed Forces: 27,500
Military Expenditures (% of Central Government Expenditures): $114,400,000 (10.3%)
Current Hostilities: none

ECONOMY
Currency ($ U.S. Equivalent): 1,278 Malagasy francs = $1
Per Capita Income/GNP: $270/$2.6 billion
Inflation Rate: 9.8%
Natural Resources: graphite; chrome; coal; bauxite; ilmenite; tar sands; semiprecious stones; timber; mica; nickel
Agriculture: rice; livestock; coffee; vanilla; sugar; cloves; cotton; sisal; peanuts; tobacco
Industry: food processing; textiles; mining; paper; petroleum refining; automobile assembly; construction; cement; farming

FOREIGN TRADE
Exports: $328 million
Imports: $356 million

			Independence from France is achieved without armed struggle; Tsiranana becomes the first president		Didier Ratsiraka becomes president by military appointment
Merina rulers gain sovereignty over other peoples of the island **1828**	The French complete the conquest of the island **1904**	A revolt is suppressed by the French, with great loss of life **1947–1948**	**1960**	A coup leads to the fall of the First Malagasy Republic **1972**	**1975**

1980s

An attempted coup is foiled; the Indian Ocean Commission is established; Ratsiraka is reelected president

Pope John Paul II visits

Elections are postponed until 1989

MADAGASCAR

Madagascar, like the other island polities of the western Indian Ocean, lies on Africa's periphery. To a large extent, the nation has a separate history. Yet in modern times Malagasy peoples have become conscious of the concerns they share with Africans on the continent, and Madagascar is a full and active member of the Organization of African Unity (OAU).

The island's isolation and its early settlement by peoples from the Pacific have given Madagascar a distinctive character. The current population, while small, is very diverse. The Malayo-Polynesian peoples arrived in the early centuries A.D., and their descendants make up the majority of the 18 different Malagasy ethnic groups of the island.

FRENCH COLONIALISM

France claimed the island as a colonial territory in 1896 and spread its administration and language. New ways were selectively added to traditional patterns and were widely adopted. There were about 50,000 French residents by World War II. As opposition to colonialism developed during the mid-twentieth century, the French regime became more repressive. A revolt in 1947 was violently suppressed, resulting in many thousands of deaths. Its memory is still fresh in the minds of the country's people.

INDEPENDENCE

Madagascar gained its independence in 1960, when all of the member countries of the French Community became nations. The new government was led by Philibert Tsiranana and the Social Democratic Party (PSD). Its conservative stance led to uprisings among the peasants in southern Madagascar and disorder among workers and students in the capital. In 1972 Tsiranana gave controlling power to the popular General Gabriel Ramanantsoa; after much political disturbance, the military put Didier Ratsiraka in the office of the president in 1975.

RADICAL CHANGES

Since 1972 the system of government and the orientation of the country have changed. Ratsiraka's Charter, "the little red book," described the regime's new socialist and nonaligned approach. It continued some of the policies instituted by General Ramanantsoa—including efforts to stimulate and re-create the traditional agricultural village communities called the *fokonolona*, approximately 70,000 of which had been developed during General Ramanantsoa's administration.

In spite of its echoes of Marx and Mao, the Malagasy experiment is primarily an effort to revitalize Malagasy society. Many associations (like parties) are included in the ruling coalition, although all must be part of the National Front for the Defense of the Socialist Malagasy Revolution, an umbrella organization that encompasses all of the nation's political parties.

CURRENT PROBLEMS

Agriculture is a major Malagasy strength. Most of the people are rural, and a diverse group of crops are cultivated, including rice and yams. Important cash crops include vanilla (of which Madagascar provides more than half of the world's supply) and cloves. Unfortunately, natural disasters as well as the sluggish performance of the peasant fokonolona have limited the economy. Parastatals have been privatized and the currency devalued, leading to higher prices for fuel and transportation. These economic difficulties have led to a volatile political climate. The university was closed for months during 1986 and 1987 because of student protests, and political parties are active in preparation for 1989 elections. Victor Ramahatra became the new prime minister in 1988. Other Cabinet members retained their posts, in a government effort to ensure stability.

"OPEN HORIZONS"

Since 1972 the government has tried to break and limit the ties with France, renegotiating more advantageous terms with French companies and seeking support from other countries in both the East and West. Yet France remains Madagascar's major trading partner.

Ratsiraka has also worked to make the Indian Ocean free of foreign naval bases, has refused to lease such bases to either France or the United States, and continues to press—without success—for the withdrawal of the United States from Diego Garcia.

DEVELOPMENT

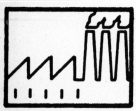

Madagascar has a fairly small population for its size. Only 5 % of the land is used for agriculture, indicating the potential for agricultural expansion. However, government efforts to open new lands to production have not been successful, and harvests have steadily declined.

FREEDOM

The Advance Guard of the Malagasy Revolution (AREMA) is the militant, well-organized government party of right- and left-wingers. Six political associations besides AREMA make up the National Front for the Defense of the Socialist Malagasy Revolution (NFDR). Political prisoners are detained without trial, and the press is not free.

HEALTH/WELFARE

"Better health for everyone" is a national goal. Ten percent of the national budget goes to the health services. UN agencies are supporting government efforts. There are relatively few Malagasy physicians in the country; many continue to practice in France.

ACHIEVEMENTS

A new wildlife preserve will allow the unique animals of Madagascar to survive and develop. Sixty-six species of land animals are found nowhere else on earth, and include the aye-aye, a nocturnal lemur which has bat ears, beaver teeth, and an elongated clawed finger, all of which serve the aye-aye in finding food.

Mauritius

GEOGRAPHY

Area in Square Kilometers (Miles):
1,865 (720) (about the size of Rhode Island)
Capital (Population): Port Louis (138,400)
Climate: subtropical; marine

PEOPLE

Population
Total: 1,100,000
Annual Growth Rate: 1.6%
Rural/Urban Population Ratio: 30/70
Languages: official: English; others spoken: French, Creole, Hindi, Urdu

Health
Life Expectancy at Birth: 69 years
Infant Death Rate (Ratio): 28/1,000
Average Caloric Intake: 122% of FAO minimum
Physicians Available (Ratio): 1/4,508

Religion(s)
51% Hindu; 30% Chrisitan; 16% Muslim; 3% other

Education
Adult Literacy Rate: 79%

COMMUNICATION

Telephones: 48,460
Newspapers: 7

DIEGO GARCIA

One the eve of the nation's independence, secret negotiations between British and Mauritian representatives resulted in Mauritius' sale of the island of Diego Garcia and neighboring atolls to the British for the small sum of $7 million. The inhabitants of Diego Garcia were completely ignored; moreover, they were subsequently moved to Mauritius in order to make room for a U.S. military base (which increased the militarization of the Indian Ocean). The people of Mauritius, through their government, have demanded the island's return. The United Kingdom and the United States have offered more money to former inhabitants of the island, and have agreed to their eventual return in an unspecified, but distant, future. The first National Congress of the ruling Socialist Militant Movement in 1986 called for the restoration of Mauritian sovereignty over Diego Garcia, "currently occupied by the American Army." Mauritian claims enjoy widespread support from the international community, but the issue remains unresolved.

TRANSPORTATION

Highways—Kilometers (Miles): 1,801 (1,116)
Railroads—Kilometers (Miles): none
Commercial Airports: 1 international

GOVERNMENT

Type: independent state; recognizes the British monarch as chief of state
Independence Date: March 12, 1968
Head of State: Prime Minister Aneerood Jugnauth; President Veerasamy Ringadoo
Political Parties: Mauritian Labor Party; Mauritian Militant Movement; Mauritian Socialist Party; others
Suffrage: universal over 18

MILITARY

Number of Armed Forces: no standing defense force
Military Expenditures (% of Central Government Expenditures): n/a
Current Hostilities: none

ECONOMY

Currency ($ U.S. Equivalent): 12.8 rupees = $1
Per Capita Income/GNP: $1,240/$957 million
Inflation Rate: 6.2%
Natural Resources: agricultural land
Agriculture: sugar; tea; tobacco
Industry: sugar production; consumer goods; labor-intensive goods for export; tourism

FOREIGN TRADE

Exports: $434 million
Imports: $529 million

| The Dutch claim, but abandon, Mauritius 1600s | French settlers and slaves arrive 1722 | The Treaty of Paris formally cedes Mauritius to the British 1814 | Slavery is abolished; South Asians arrive 1835 | Rioting on sugar estates shakes the political control of the Franco-Mauritian elite 1937 | An expanded franchise allows greater democracy 1948 | Independence 1968 | Labor unrest leads to the detention of MMM leaders 1971 | A cyclone destroys homes as well as much of the sugar crop 1979 | 1980s |

| The MMM-Socialist Party coalition sweeps the elections | The Socialist government is formed; Mauritius expels all Libyan diplomats | Party splits and realignments continue; the ruling party wins 65% of parliamentary seats |

MAURITIUS

Mauritius, "the sugary pearle of the Indian Ocean," was not permanently inhabited until 1722. Today more than a million people of South Asian, Euro-African, Chinese, and other origins live on the island nation. The major force behind this growth has been the labor and capital needs of the local sugar industry, which has always been the dominant influence on the island's development. In recent years 90 percent of the cultivated land has been planted with sugar. Sugar provides for nearly one-half of the nation's export earnings as well as about a third of its employment.

Although by regional standards most Mauritians enjoy a relatively good quality of life, dependency on sugar has had both social and economic costs. The price of imported food and other items as well as local wages have often risen faster than the international price of sugar, which has tended to fluctuate. In addition, major inequalities exist within the local sugar industry itself.

THE PEOPLE

The first sugar plantations were founded during the eighteenth century by French settlers, who used African slaves for labor. Approximately one-quarter of the Mauritian population are of mixed Euro-African (Creole) origin; a small percentage claim pure French descent. This latter group has traditionally formed the economic elite of the island. Today more than 55 percent of the agricultural land is comprised of 21 large Franco-Mauritian plantations, while the rest is divided between nearly 28,000 small land-holdings. French cultural influence remains strong. Most of the newspapers on the island are in French. However, most Mauritians speak a local, French-influenced, Creole language.

In 1810 Mauritius was occupied by the British, who remained and ruled the island until 1968. When the British abolished slavery in 1835, landowners turned to large-scale use of indentured laborers from what was then British India to work on the plantations. Today nearly two-thirds of the population are of South Asian descent.

POLITICS

Since 1886 Mauritius has maintained an uninterrupted record of parliamentary-style democracy, although the majority of the island population only achieved the right to vote after World War II. Ethnic divisions play an important political role, and this is often reflected in voting patterns. It is important to note, however, that ethnic constituency-building has not led, in recent years, to ethnic polarization. Other factors—such as class and ideology—have been important in shaping the character of political allegiance. All postindependence governments have been formed by coalitions.

In 1982 a coalition between the Marxist Mauritian Militant Movement (MMM) and the Socialist Party was elected by a landslide. Within months a split emerged between the two parties as well as within the MMM itself. New elections were held in 1983, and a coalition led by the Socialist Party, whose ranks had become enlarged by defections from the MMM, won. The current Socialist prime minister, Aneerood Jugnauth, was also the leader of the last government, but then he served as a member of the MMM. Mauritius will soon sever its remaining links with the British Crown and become a republic. Although electoral victories by the MMM in 1985 and scandals within the Socialist coalition threatened Jugnauth's government, the Socialists won a majority in 1987 elections.

POPULATION AND DEVELOPMENT

A major challenge facing any Mauritian government is the rising number of unemployed. The elimination of malaria after World War II triggered a population explosion on the island. By the early 1970s the population growth rate had fallen substantially, but the earlier baby boom put an increasing strain on the nation's job market. Despite the growth of light manufacturing, processing, and tourism, many are without work or are underemployed. The resulting low cost of labor and the open international policies of the government, as well as Mauritius' strategic location, have led to international competition for diplomatic and economic ties. Some of the countries in the race are Israel, Libya, and South Africa.

DEVELOPMENT

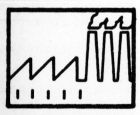

During the 1970s a number of new industries were attracted to Mauritius by the establishment of Export Processing Zones (EPZs), within which investors enjoy significant tax advantages. Although a modest success, the EPZs have not ended Mauritius' dependence on sugar or solved the growing problem of unemployment.

FREEDOM

Political pluralism and human rights are respected on Mauritius. The nation has more than 30 political parties, of which about a half-dozen are important at any given time.

HEALTH/WELFARE

Medical and most educational expenses are free. Food prices are heavily subsidized. Rising government deficits, however, threaten future social spending.

ACHIEVEMENTS

Perhaps Mauritius' most important modern achievement has been its successful efforts to reduce its birth rate. This has been brought about by government-backed family planning as well as by increased economic opportunities for women.

Rwanda (Republic of Rwanda)

GEOGRAPHY

Area in Square Kilometers (Miles):
26,338 (10, 169) (about the size of
Maryland)
Capital (Population): Kigali (150,000)
Climate: temperate

PEOPLE

Population
Total: 6,500,000
Annual Growth Rate: 3.2%
Rural/Urban Population Ratio: 95/5
Languages: official: French;
Kinyarwanda; other spoken: Kiswahili

Health
Life Expectancy at Birth: 44 years
Infant Death Rate (Ratio): 124/1,000
Average Caloric Intake: 94% of FAO
minimum
Physicians Available (Ratio): 1/25,151

Religion(s)
68% Christian; 23% traditional
indigenous; 9% Muslim

Education
Adult Literacy Rate: 37%

RWANDA'S HISTORIANS

A number of specialists were attached to the ruling dynasty of the
traditional kingdom of Rwanda, including several categories of official
historians. Each group was responsible for preserving particular materials. Some were genealogists who told the lists of kings and queens;
some told *ibisigo*, dynastic poems that glorified the rulers; and others
preserved secrets of the dynasty. This traditional knowledge was all
passed down orally, since the language was not written. Particular
families were responsible for passing this knowledge from one generation to another; it was memorized exactly. Such historical information is
different from the written sources upon which Western historians have
relied, but it is valid data that can be used in the reconstruction of
Rwanda's past.

COMMUNICATION

Telephones: 6,600
Newspapers: 1

TRANSPORTATION

Highways—Kilometers (Miles): 6,760
(4,191)
Railroads—Kilometers (Miles): none
Commercial Airports: 1 international

GOVERNMENT

Type: republic
Independence Date: July 1, 1962
Head of State: President (Major
General) Juvenal Habyarimana
Political Parties: National
Revolutionary Movement for
Development
Suffrage: universal for adults

MILITARY

Number of Armed Forces: 5,150
*Military Expenditures (% of Central
Government Expenditures):*
$22,000,000 (14%)
Current Hostilities: none

ECONOMY

Currency ($ U.S. Equivalent): 76
Rwanda francs = $1
Per Capita Income/GNP: $270/$1.7
billion
Inflation Rate: 5.8%
Natural Resources: tungsten; tin;
cassiterite
Agriculture: coffee; tea; pyrethrum;
beans; potatoes
Industry: food processing; mining;
light consumer goods

FOREIGN TRADE

Exports: $147 million
Imports: $202 million

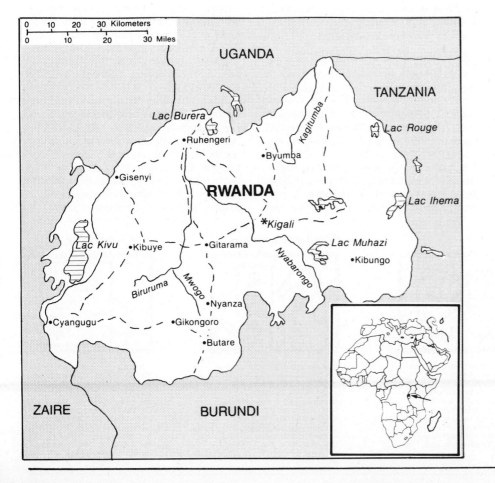

| Mwami Kigeri Rwabugiri expands and consolidates the kingdom 1860–1895 | Belguim rules Rwanda as a mandate of the League of Nations 1916 | The Hutu rebellion 1959 | Rwanda becomes independent; Gregoire Kayibana is president 1962 | Habyarimana seizes power 1973 | The National Revolutionary Movement for Development is formed 1975 | A new Constitution is approved in an nationwide referendum; Habyarimana is reelected president 1978 | 1980s |

| Unsuccessful coup attempt | Election for 50 members of parliament and for president; Habyarimana is the sole presidential candidate | Refugees from Burundi mass along the border |

RWANDA

In the beginning, according to a dynastic poem of Rwanda, the godlike ruler, Kigwa, fashioned a test by which to choose his successor. He gave each of his sons a bowl of milk to guard during the night. His son Gatwa drank the milk. Yahutu slept and spilled the milk. Only Gatutsi guarded it well.

The myth reflects a reality that Rwandans (Banyarwanda, as the inhabitants are sometimes called) have adhered to throughout their history: the Twa, pygmy peoples (1 percent of the population), have been the outcasts; the Hutu (89 percent) have been the servants; and the Tutsi (10 percent) have been the aristocrats. Hutu and Tutsi were linked through personal "cattle contracts," by which Hutu received cattle and protection and Tutsi received services. There were many other ties between these groups, whose members are still evenly distributed throughout the country. All of the people were subjects of the *mwami*, or king, who was very powerful and who headed a royal family that had a special status in Rwanda.

RADICAL CHANGES

This society no longer exists in its historical form, and the changes have been revolutionary. During the early decades of the twentieth century, when first the Germans (and later the Belgians) ruled through few administrators, primarily using the existing political system, traditional caste distinctions and royal prerogatives were maintained. New ideas and practices were

introduced through Catholic missions and schools and through the encouragement of growing cash crops, especially coffee. Even before the colonial era discontent was evident, due to the pressure of people and herds on already crowded lands. These problems increased with time.

The most radical developments occurred in the late 1950s and the early 1960s. Gradually, in the late 1950s, because of pressure from the United Nations (UN), Belgium began to introduce political opportunities to Rwandans. In 1959, after the death of the *mwami*, oppression by the Tutsi, who took power, led to bloody Hutu uprisings against the Tutsi. In 1961 Hutu leaders and the Hutu majority party, Parmehutu (the Hutu Emancipation Movement), gained support, won victories at the polls, and became the governors of Rwanda. The aforementioned uprisings and later Tutsi attacks and Hutu reactions in 1963–1964 caused thousands of deaths and the flight of tens of thousands to neighboring countries.

HABYARIMANA TAKES POWER

Major General Juvenal Habyarimana, a Hutu from the north, took power in a coup in 1973 and initiated the National Revolutionary Movement for Development (MRND) to bring together the hostile elements in the country. Habyarimana has maintained tight control over Rwanda, although a few opportunities for popular initiative have been evident. Voters have been given choices of electoral candidates; union activity is allowed, and

church publications are allowed to criticize the government.

Hostility between Hutu and Tutsi remains. Many Hutu and Tutsi left Rwanda during the upheavals of the late 1950s and 1960s and took up residence in nearby countries such as Burundi and Uganda. The extreme population pressure in Rwanda (one of Africa's most densely populated countries) has encouraged young people to migrate and has made the government reluctant to encourage those outside to return. Recent efforts to grant refugees the right to return to Rwanda, in order to give them a national status, have been rebuffed by the government. Rwanda hopes that the thousands of refugees in neighboring countries will be granted citizenship in their host countries.

Rwanda is also the host for refugees fleeing oppression or conflict in neighboring Burundi and Uganda. About 18,000 Hutu from Burundi were integrated into Rwandan society, although not given citizenship, but massacres of Hutu in 1988 caused an influx of more than 50,000 refugees from Burundi, overloading Rwanda's already strained economy.

DEVELOPMENT

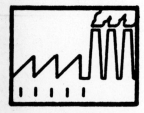

With the help of the European Economic Community, Rwanda is attempting to increase the variety of crops grown for export so it may become less dependent on coffee. Tea, tobacco, and pyrethrum are among the products whose growth is being encouraged.

FREEDOM

In recent years Rwandans have been able to choose from multiple candidates for Parliament, with lists compiled by provincial governors. In 1984 Habyarimana pardoned many prisoners and reduced others' sentences. On the 25th anniversary of independence in 1987, 4,000 prisoners were released.

HEALTH/WELFARE

The government recognizes that the high rate of population growth can eat up economic gains as well as increasing already severe pressures on land. A national population office was created, and resources committed to family planning were increased. Some question the reservation of large game reserves for European hunters, when farmland is scarce.

ACHIEVEMENTS

Abbe Alexis Kagame, a Rwandan Roman Catholic churchman and scholar, has written studies of traditional Rwanda poetry and has written poetry about many of the traditions and rituals. Some of his works have been composed in Kinyarwanda, the official language of Rwanda, and translated into French. He has gained an international reputation among scholars.

Seychelles (Republic of Seychelles)

GEOGRAPHY

Area in Square Kilometers (Miles):
435 (175) (about twice the size of
Washington, DC)
Capital (Population): Port Victoria
(23,012)
Climate: subtropical; marine

PEOPLE

Population
Total: 59,500
Annual Growth Rate: 1.2%
Rural/Urban Population Ratio: 63/37
Languages: official: English, French;
other spoken: Creole

Health
Life Expectancy at Birth: 66 years
Infant Death Rate (Ratio): 15/1,000
Average Caloric Intake: n/a
Physicians Available (Ratio): 1/1,750

Religion(s)
98% Christian; 2% other

Education
Adult Literacy Rate: 80%

THE NATIONAL YOUTH SERVICE

One of the most controversial programs of the Seychelles government
has been the National Youth Service (NYS), a mandatory work-study
camp for the nation's 16- and 17-year-olds. During the 2-year period of
enrollment, contact between the students and the outside world is quite
restricted. At the camp, practical training, politicization, and strict
social discipline are combined in an above-the-board attempt by the state
to mold a new Seychellois—one committed to egalitarian ideals and less
inclined toward alcoholism and other vices. The long-term effect of the
NYS remains an open question. The introduction of the program
provoked violent riots.

COMMUNICATION

Telephones: 4,521
Newspapers: 1

TRANSPORTATION

Highways—Kilometers (Miles): 259
(160)
Railroads—Kilometers (Miles): none
Commercial Airports: 1 international

GOVERNMENT

Type: republic
Independence Date: June 28, 1976
Head of State: President France
Albert René
Political Parties: Seychelles People's
Progressive Front
Suffrage: universal for adults

MILITARY

Number of Armed Forces: 1,000
*Military Expenditures (% of Central
Government Expenditures):* n/a
Current Hostilities: none

ECONOMY

Currency ($ U.S. Equivalent): 5.31
rupees = $1
Per Capita Income/GNP: $2,100/$140
million
Inflation Rate: 4%
Natural Resources: agricultural land;
fish
Agriculture: vanilla; coconuts;
cinnamon
Industry: tourism; copra and vanilla
processing; coconut oil; construction

FOREIGN TRADE

Exports: $4.5 million
Imports: $90 million

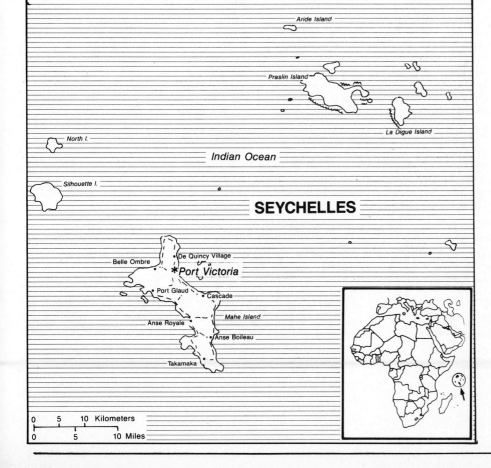

| French settlement begins 1771 | British rule is established 1814 | The British end slavery 1830 | Seychelles is detached from Mauritius by the British and made a Crown colony 1903 | Legislative Council with qualified suffrage is introduced 1948 | Universal suffrage 1967 | Independence 1976 | Coup of René against Mancham 1977 | 1980s |

| Mercenary coup attempt fails | Franco-Seychelles talks lead to greater political and economic cooperation between the two countries | René is reelected, unopposed; the third parliamentary elections since 1977 are held |

REPUBLIC OF THE SEYCHELLES

The Republic of the Seychelles consists of a series of archipelagos off the coast of East Africa. In recent years the lives of the Seychellois have been dramatically altered through rapid economic growth, political independence, and the establishment of a self-styled revolutionary socialist state. Behind this transformation has been the political rivalry of two very different, but equally controversial, leaders—James Mancham and Albert René— who together have guided the nation from an isolated colonial past into an uncertain future.

Although their existence was long known by Indian Ocean mariners, the Seychelles were not permanently inhabited until the arrival of French colonists and their slaves in 1771. In 1814 the British took over and controlled the territory until 1976.

ROOTS OF CONFLICT

Today's political struggle had its roots in 1963, when Mancham's Democratic Party and René's People's United Party were established. The former favored free enterprise and the retention of the British imperial connection; the latter advocated an independent socialist state. Electoral victories in 1970 and 1974 allowed Mancham, as chief minister, to pursue his dream of turning the Seychelles into "a little Switzerland" through policies designed to attract outside investment. Mancham was notably successful in promoting tourism, which fueled an economic boom. Between 1970 and 1980 per capita income rose from nearly $150 to over $1,700. At the same time, however, Mancham gained

a reputation in many quarters as a free-wheeling jetsetter who was indifferent to government detail. Some people believed Mancham's approach attracted capital from wealthy outsiders. His opponents, including the idealistic and outwardly austere René, saw Mancham's playboy lifestyle as a national embarrassment and contended that his administration was unconcerned with the impoverished majority of the population.

In 1974 Mancham, in an about-face, joined René in advocating the island's independence. The following year the Democratic Party, despite its parliamentary majority, set up a coalition government with the People's United Party. At midnight on June 28, 1976 the Seychelles became independent, with Mancham as president and René as prime minister. This was a curious union, given the differences in personality and politics between the two.

COUP BY RENÉ

On June 5, 1977, when Mancham was out of the country, René, with Tanzanian assistance, staged his successful "coup of sixty rifles," thus turning a temporary separation into a permanent one. A period of rule by decree gave way in 1979 to a new constitutional framework in which the People's Progressive Front, successor to the People's United Party, was recognized as the sole political voice.

The first years of René's rule were characterized by continuing prosperity, coupled with an impressive expansion of social-welfare programs. Nonetheless, enemies of the regime, both at home and abroad, were active in plotting its over-

throw. In 1981 a group of international mercenaries, who were believed to have had backing from Kenya and South Africa as well as exiled Seychellois, were forced to flee in a hijacked jet after a shootout with the new Seychelles Army. During the following spring, however, one-fifth of the army was itself detained without trial following another coup attempt.

In 1987 voters elected 23 members of Parliament, all members of the ruling party, in the third election since René came to power. The government continues to accuse foes in South Africa, Australia, and the United Kingdom of plotting aginst it.

THE ECONOMY

The coup and various attempted counter-coups have contributed to a recent decline in tourism, which in turn has depressed the economy. Although the Seychelles government is seeking to restore and expand tourism, it is also eager to diversify the nation's economic base by investing heavily in agriculture and fishing. Given the country's legal jurisdiction over some 400,000 square miles of excellent fishing waters, official attempts to build a modern seafood industry hold enormous potential, despite the problems of a shortage of skilled manpower and the threat of foreign poaching.

DEVELOPMENT

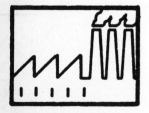

The government continues to pursue a flexible economic program designed to encourage healthy outside investment while promoting the growth of local government-owned companies. Some have expressed concern that foreign investors will use Seychelles to avoid sanctions against South Africa.

FREEDOM

Since the 1977 coup, press censorship, mail openings, preventive detention, forced exile, and political indoctrination of the youth have become a part of life. Disappearances of political opponents have been reported.

HEALTH/WELFARE

Under the new government, a national health program has been established; private practice has been abolished. Free-lunch programs have raised nutritional levels among the young. Education is also free up to age 14.

ACHIEVEMENTS

Under its current government, Seychelles has become a world leader in wildlife preservation. An important aspect of the nation's conservation efforts has been the designation of Aldrabra Island as an international wildlife refuge.

Somalia (Somali Democratic Republic)

GEOGRAPHY

Area in Square Kilometers (Miles):
638,000 (246,331) (slightly smaller
than Texas)
Capital (Population): Mogadishu
(700,000)
Climate: arid to semiarid

PEOPLE

Population
Total: 7,825,000
Annual Growth Rate: 9.6%
Rural/Urban Population Ratio: 70/30
Languages: official: Somali; other
spoken: Arabic, Oromo, Italian,
English, others

Health
Life Expectancy at Birth: 44 years
Infant Death Rate (Ratio): 163/1,000
Average Caloric Intake: 100% of FAO
minimum
Physicians Available (Ratio): 1/26,797

Religion(s)
99% Muslim; 1% other

Education
Adult Literacy Rate: 40%

SOMALIA AND THE SUPERPOWERS

The Horn of Africa is an interesting case study on the role of African
countries in superpower geopolitics. An ally of the Soviet Union until
1977, Somalia sought ties with the United States after Ethiopia became a
Soviet ally, and the United States valued strategic access to the Red Sea
and the Gulf states. A military accord was signed in 1980, and naval
facilities at Mogadishu and Berbera are used as staging areas for the U.S.
Rapid Deployment Force. Somalia has been a participant in U.S.-
organized war games since 1982. These close ties may explain why the
United States has not pressured Somalia on food-aid mismanagement
and human rights. Somalia is the third largest recipient of American aid
in Africa.

COMMUNICATION

Telephones: 6,000
Newspapers: 2

TRANSPORTATION

Highways—Kilometers (Miles): 17,215
(10,673)
Railroads—Kilometers (Miles): n/a
Commercial Airports: 1 international

GOVERNMENT

Type: republic; under military regime
Independence Date: July 1, 1960
Head of State: Major General
Mohamed Siad Barre
Political Parties: Somali
Revolutionary Socialist Party
Suffrage: universal for adults

MILITARY

Number of Armed Forces: 61.300
*Military Expenditures (% of Central
Government Expenditures):* n/a
Current Hostilities: border disputes
with Ethiopia; conflicts with
Ethiopian-backed Somali rebels

ECONOMY

Currency ($ U.S. Equivalent): 100
Somali shillings = $1
Per Capita Income/GNP: $300/$1.8
billion
Inflation Rate: 30%
Natural Resources: uranium; timber;
fish
Agriculture: livestock; bananas;
sugarcane; cotton; cereals
Industry: sugar refining; tuna and
beef canning; textiles; iron-rod plants;
petroleum refining

FOREIGN TRADE

Exports: $110 million
Imports: $470 million

British take
control of
northern regions
of present-day
Somalia
1886–1887

Italy establishes
a protectorate in
the eastern
areas of
present-day
Somalia
1889

The Somalia
Youth League is
founded; it
becomes a
nationalist party
1943

SOMALIA

Abundance and scarcity are never far apart; the rich and poor frequent the same house.

(Quoted by I. M. Lewis in The Somali Democracy)

This popular Somali proverb testifies to the delicate balance between subsistence and famine in a dry land. The majority of Somalia's people (80 percent) are pastoralists. The country, located on the horn of Africa, is best suited to a herding life. Ordinary people, knowledgeable about their environment, have adjusted their lives to it. Agriculture is possible in the area between the Juba and Shebelle rivers and in a portion of the north. There, people raise crops as well as keep animals. In the other areas, people move to secure good grazing for their herds of cattle, camels, sheep, and goats.

Such a lifestyle does not lend itself to city living. A half-dozen families may live in encampments and move as circumstances dictate. However, despite such small community groups, all Somali have clan relationships that extend over a large area. Moreover, Somalia is a country whose citizens, unlike those of most African countries, are virtually all of one group and speak Somali. Islam, the state religion, is also a binding feature, and Islamic culture and traditions as well as the faith are deep-rooted.

Somalia links Africa and Arabia, and Islam is one of the bridges. The nation's art and poetry also indicate shared influences; they are sophisticated forms of expression, familiar to everyone. In their richness and elaborateness, they contrast with and complement the spare environment and simplicity of home, clothing, and utensils. Traditional values of Somali ways of life have been maintained, but ecological changes and other influences, such as the policies of the current government, have affected Somali life and the Somali nation.

POLITICAL DEVELOPMENTS IN RECENT TIMES

Although Somali traditionally have shared a common language and lifestyle, colonial policies divided the people. For about 75 years the northern regions were governed by British forms of administration, while the southern and eastern portions were subject to Italian rule, language, and other influences. The different institutions colonialism imposed contributed to secession movements in the north, as people became dissatisfied with Somali government policies. This resistance escalated in 1987 and 1988.

Somalia became independent in 1960. In 1969 Siad Barre, the current president, came to power through a military coup. He introduced radical changes in governing concepts and organization that, in the beginning, appeared innovative and significant. Under Barre's leadership, a "scientific" socialism was to be built on an African base and not in conflict with Islam. Efforts were made to develop local councils, to initiate committees at the workplace, and to increase participation in government. New civil and labor codes were written. A new political party, the Somali Revolutionary Socialist Party (SRSP), was developed, and a Constitution was approved in a national referendum. The government program, including literacy education, was spread among nomadic groups through a rural development campaign in 1974–1975. Roads were built in order to encourage movement between regions. The theme was "Tribalism divides, socialism unites." Tribalism in this case stood for the divisions of clans.

Gradually, the promise of Barre's early years in office faded. Little was done to follow through the developments of the early 1970s. Indeed, Barre has bypassed the institutions he advocated. A national cult has grown up around the president, confirming other tendencies toward autocracy. The president took on emergency powers, relieved members of the governing council of their duties, and surrounded himself with clansmen and close kin, and isolated himself from the public.

IRREDENTISM AND RESISTANCE

Barre has also isolated Somalia in Africa by pursuing irredentism, policies that would unite all Somali peoples. Somali live in Kenya and Ethiopia, and some expatriate Somali want to join Somalia. Their aspirations have had some official support. Somali in Kenya and Ethiopia initiated guerrilla warfare in an attempt to free themselves from these countries so they could join Somalia. Bad relations

(United Nations photo)

Somali who had lived under the different administrations of the British and Italians in two colonial territories were united when independent Somalia was formed in 1960.

Somalia is formed through a merger of former British and Italian colonies under UN Trusteeship
1960

Siad Barre comes to power through an army coup; the Supreme Revolutionary Council is established
1969

The Ogaden war in Ethiopia results in Somalia's defeat
1977–1978

1980s

State of emergency; pact with the United States, a diplomatic realignment after Soviet ties dissolve

Resurgence of drought and famine; Barre is reelected, with 99.9% of the vote

Warfare in the north escalates

between Somalia and Kenya were eased in 1982, but the war in the Ogaden region of Ethiopia has been less easily solved. Ethnic Somali, backed by Somalia Army regulars, invaded the Ogaden region in 1977; a year-long war ensued. Defeated by Ethiopia, the Somali incursion was condemned by all members of the Organization of African Unity (OAU). Ground and air attacks across the borders of Ethiopia and Somalia continued in the 1980s. Although leaders from both countries met in 1987, the tensions remain.

The policy of irredentism has had other repercussions. It has committed the Barre regime to a massive buildup of the army and to negotiations for arms from the great powers. In the early years of the Barre government there were close ties between Somalia and the Soviet Union. Then, in 1977, in a diplomatic revolution, the Soviets became allied with Somalia's enemy, Ethiopia. As a result, Barre developed ties with the United States. U.S. Marines have conducted military exercises in Somalia, and the United States uses air and naval facilities developed by the Soviet Union at Berbera.

Somali resistance movements have developed outside the country. In 1982 the Democratic Front for the Salvation of Somalia, headquartered in Addis Ababa, and the London-based Somali National Movement agreed to unify their forces "against the fascist regime in Somalia," proposing a future democratic program. Somali rebels criticize Barre's economic policies and close ties to the United States.

In an attempt to court U.S. aid, Barre cracked down on dissidents and purged critics, espcially northerners, from government and the university. Many scientists and other intellectuals were detained and imprisoned in 1982, accused of leading and aiding the Somali National Movement. After 6 years of torture and detention without charges, trials convicted many northern intellectuals of treason. Two were sentenced to death. Pressure from international human-rights and scientific organizations led to a stay of execution.

In 1988 civil war escalated in the north. Thousands of refugees fled to Ethiopia to avoid the fighting. A Somali pilot, refusing to bomb civilians in Hargeisa, flew his plane to Djibouti.

REFUGEES IN SOMALIA

Somali life has been disrupted by droughts, warfare, and their repercussions. Somalia is a poor country. The drought of 1974–1975 led to the development of refugee camps—140,000 nomadic peoples were relocated to agricultural areas. There, people had to plan their lives anew. In the 1980s the drought affecting Ethiopia brought thousands of people into Somalia. At least 400,000 persons reside in refugee camps. Although some were returned to Ethiopia, drought and warfare there led to an influx of refugees from 1986 to 1988. Most of the refugees are women and children. Men leave the refugee camps to care for the herds that have not been decimated by the drought. In a plea for food aid in 1988, the government estimated that 3 million people were at risk for starvation. In addition, fighting in the northern region led to the deaths of 10,000 people, with an estimated 300,000 refugees fleeing to the Ogaden region of Ethiopia.

The situation has put pressure on Somalia's budget. But at the same time the refugee situation has meant a massive injection of outside aid, constituting up to one-third of the gross national product. In 1988 the United States rescheduled $33 million of Somalia's external debt. Somalia has been accused of inflating refugee figures and of diverting food aid to the army and private sales.

THE ECONOMY

Most people, even the refugees, continue to hold to the traditional herding life. Efforts to increase livestock production have had little success, but the export of livestock—especially cattle—to the Middle East is massive, involving more than 1.25 million animals yearly. Often the cattle are sold through private traders whose financial deals may not benefit the government; but they certainly aid large numbers of individuals. The migration of Somali workers to the Gulf states was an alternative source of employment, but the decline in oil production has limited this option. The events of the last 20 years, especially warfare and famine, have radically affected Somalia's pastoral economy and impeded efforts at development.

DEVELOPMENT

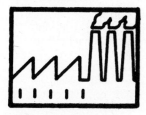

Barre announced $9 million of development projects. In 1987 Western donors pledged $435 million toward a requested $1-billion development program for Somalia.

FREEDOM

Freedoms are restricted in Somalia. The media are government-owned, and criticism of the government is prohibited. Although Barre released 1,700 prisoners in 1987, detentions without trial and torture of dissidents continue.

HEALTH/WELFARE

Oxfam America's solar pumps provide 60% to 70% of the water supply for refugees in the northwest area and are also used in traditional Islamic cooperatives, where they provide drinking water and irrigation for vegetable gardens.

ACHIEVEMENTS

The Somali language has effectively taken the place of colonial languages (English and Italian) as the official language. A written version of Somali was developed in the 1970s, and mass literacy campaigns were waged by teachers and students, who went out to teach nomadic citizens how to read and write.

Sudan (Democratic Republic of the Sudan)

GEOGRAPHY

Area in Square Kilometers (Miles):
2,504,530 (967,500) (about one-fourth the size of the United States)
Capital (Population): Khartoum (1,250,000)
Climate: desert in north to tropical in south

PEOPLE

Population
Total: 23,000,000
Annual Growth Rate: 2.7%
Rural/Urban Population Ratio: 65/35
Languages: official: Arabic; others spoken: Nuer, Dinka, Shilluki, Masalatis, Fur, Nubian, English, others

Health
Life Expectancy at Birth: 48 years male; 50 years female
Infant Death Rate (Ratio): 118/1,000
Average Caloric Intake: 99% of FAO minimum
Physicians Available (Ratio): 1/10,572

Religion(s)
73% Sunni Muslim in north; 18% traditional indigenous; 9% Christian

Education
Adult Literacy Rate: 20%

COMMUNICATION
Telephones: 68,800
Newspapers: 16

SUDAN'S CIVIL WAR

Sudan suffered 17 years of civil war before the southern regions were given autonomy in a 1972 cease-fire. Southern military officers were integrated into the regular army, and many progressed to the higher ranks. When Jaafar Nimeiri introduced Islamic Sharia law to replace the penal code in 1983 and reduced regional autonomy, armed resistance reemerged. The Sudanese People's Liberation Army (SPLA), led by Colonel John Garang, began guerrilla warfare in 1983. Garang, with a doctorate in economics, is the military and political leader of the resistance, a highly organized and experienced force which sought first the overthrow of Nimeiri and is now demanding a return to regional autonomy, withdrawal of Sharia, abrogation of all existing treaties, and new elections before peace talks begin. The well-organized rebels have prevented voting in the south and have disrupted delivery of relief supplies to the millions of Sudanese and refugee famine victims. Critics of the government charge that they in turn have militarized food convoys and have attacked civilian supporters of the SPLA.

TRANSPORTATION
Highways—Kilometers (Miles): 48,000 (29,760)
Railroads—Kilometers (Miles): 4,786 (2,967)
Commercial Airports: 5 international

GOVERNMENT
Type: republic
Independence Date: January 1, 1956
Head of State: Prime Minister Sadiq Al-Mahdi
Political Parties: currently 38 approved; strongest is Umma Party
Suffrage: universal for adults

MILITARY
Number of Armed Forces: 54,000
Military Expenditures (% of Central Government Expenditures): 1%
Current Hostilities: civil war

ECONOMY
Currency ($ U.S. Equivalent): 4.5 Sudanese pounds = $1
Per Capita Income/GNP: $361/$7.3 billion
Inflation Rate: 50%
Natural Resources: oil; iron ore; copper; chrome; other industrial metals
Agriculture: cotton; peanuts; sesame; gum arabic; sorghum; wheat
Industry: textiles; cement; cotton ginning; edible oils; distilling; pharmaceuticals

FOREIGN TRADE
Exports: $374 million
Imports: $771 million

Egypt invades Northern Sudan 1820	The Mahdist Revolt begins 1881	The Anglo-Egyptian Condominium begins 1899	Independence 1956	Nimeiri comes to power 1969	Hostilities end in southern Sudan 1972	1980s

Islamic Sharia law replaces the former penal code

The Army overthrows Nimeiri in a popular coup; Mahdi is elected a year later

Escalating civil war and famine

SUDAN

Sudan's diversity, vast size, and strategic location have long provided the nation with unique opportunities and potential liabilities. In the nineteenth century the area was under Turko-Egyptian rule, until an Islamic revolt in 1881. Anglo-Egyptian conquerors defeated the new theocratic state in 1898, and the United Kingdom dominated Sudan until its independence in 1956.

In 1969 Jaafar Nimeiri came to power in a military coup. He quickly moved to consolidate his power by eliminating challenges to his government from the Islamic right and the communist left. A declining economy, inflation, resistance in the south, close ties with the United States, and repression of dissent resulted in a 1985 military coup toppling Nimeiri. The coup preempted a brewing revolution. Within a year political parties were allowed to organize, and elections were held in 1986.

INTERNAL PROBLEMS

The historic tensions between northerners and southerners have flared since 1983 because of the neglect of development in the south, reduction of autonomy, and the replacement of Sudan's penal code with Islamic Sharia law.

Warfare in the south reemerged in 1983 and continues to disrupt political, social, and economic development. By 1988 the rebels, led by the Sudanese People's Liberation Army (SPLA), had the upper hand in the rural areas of the south. The government controlled only southern cities, which had become military garrisons as civilians fled the fighting. Both the government and the rebels prevented food aid from reaching civilians, using food as a weapon in a bitter struggle. Opponents have met regularly with government officials, but have not come to an agreement for a cease-fire. In addition to autonomy, the opposition demands the lifting of the state of emergency imposed in 1987 and the repeal of Sharia law. Despite earlier promises, pressures from Muslim fundamentalists have prevented Prime Minister Sadiq Al-Mahdi from returning to secular law. Pleas for peace from relief workers and church leaders met with resistance, but in mid-1988 the government conceded that famine relief could be directed to civilians.

ECONOMIC PROSPECTS

Sudan is still one of the poorest nations in the world. Development plans have been hindered by the inadequate transportation infrastructure, by the lack of foreign exchange, and by rampant inflation. In spite of its own weakness from drought and famine (more than 5 million at risk in 1988), Sudan welcomed refugees from Chad, Ethiopia, and Uganda. But by 1988 the government declared that Sudan could take no more refugees. The influx had put strains on Sudan's resources, and where facilities for refugees were adequate, local Sudanese resented the services provided to refugees.

Sudan has tremendous agricultural potential; however, it needs to find a means of developing that potential to get tangible results. Most development schemes for Sudan attempt to capitalize on the country's greatest resource: the waters of the Nile. Oil has been discovered in western and southern Sudan, in quantities believed sufficient to meet the country's domestic needs, but development is at a standstill because of attacks by rebel groups.

Sudan has a $10-billion foreign debt, and in 1986 the International Monetary Fund and the World Bank halted aid programs. Sudan has moved cautiously with economic reforms, in seeking new assistance from the IMF; and the government believes that unpopular austerity measures will be opposed by outspoken critics in their fledgling democracy.

FOREIGN RELATIONS

Sudan's vital geopolitical position is due not only to its location on the Nile and its intermediary role between African and Arab nations but also because it has borders with eight countries. Sudan has been courted by its neighbors and great powers alike. The Mahdi government has sought to maintain ties with Egypt and Saudi Arabia while seeking rapproachement with Libya (to neutralize Libyan support for southern rebels). Relations with Ethiopia and Chad remain strained, as those countries' rebels use Sudan as bases, and Sudan is shelled by the SPLA from within Ethiopia. The closer ties with Libya led to deteriorating U.S. relations, but Sudan seeks to conduct a balanced foreign policy; it is still a leading regional ally of the United States.

DEVELOPMENT

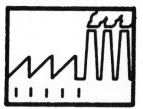

Sudan is moving to privatize some parastatals, and to reduce subsidies, and to increase payments to farmers in order to revitalize the economy and to qualify for IMF loans. If approved, the IMF plans to assist in irrigation, pesticide control, and the purchase of machinery.

FREEDOM

An outspoken and critical press developed after the 1985 coup, with many newspapers and weeklies covering a variety of issues. Some criticize the government for not acting on criticism, and others charge that the government supports the killing of civilians, especially Dinka, in the south.

HEALTH/WELFARE

Sudan's population is growing at one of the highest rates in the world. Infant mortality is also high. The Sudanese Family Planning Association has played a pioneering role in educating women to the dangers of repeated pregnancies. The association hopes the government will establish a family-planning program and a national population policy.

ACHIEVEMENTS

Sudan, home to the largest number of refugees in the world, has been noted for its hospitality and support for refugees fleeing war and famine in the region. This openness has put a serious strain on resources, and may cause tensions if economic conditions deteriorate.

Tanzania (United Republic of Tanzania)

GEOGRAPHY

Area in Square Kilometers (Miles):
939,652 (363,950) (more than twice the size of California)
Capital (Population): Dar es Salaam (1,400,000); Dodoma (political)
Climate: tropical; arid; temperate

PEOPLE

Population
Total: 23,200,000
Annual Growth Rate: 3.2%
Rural/Urban Population Ratio: 80/20
Languages: official: Kiswahili; others spoken: Chagga, Gogo, Ha, Haya, Luo, Maasai, Hindu, Arabic, English, others

Health
Life Expectancy at Birth: 52 years
Infant Death Rate (Ratio): 110/1,000
Average Caloric Intake: 87% of FAO minimum
Physicians Available (Ratio): 1/21,784

Religion(s)
35% traditional indigenous; 35% Muslim; 30% Christian

Education
Adult Literacy Rate: 80%

COMMUNICATION

Telephones: 99,000
Newspapers: 3

THE SWAHILI COAST

A trading coastal culture, African based with Arabian influence, developed over hundreds of years on the East African coast. For 2,000 years merchants from the Mediterranean and the Middle East traded along the coast of East Africa. Eventually, the mingling of Bantu-speaking peoples with Arab culture created the Swahili, an Afro-Arab people with their own African-based language. Based in cities on islands and along the coast, they traded with Arabia, Persia, India, and China, and eventually with the interior of what are now known as Kenya and Tanzania. Converted to Islam and also Arabic speaking, these cosmopolitan peoples traded interior produce for porcelain, spices, and textiles from all over the world, and created an impressive written and oral literature. They still play an important role in the political and commercial life of Tanazania.

TRANSPORTATION

Highways—Kilometers (Miles):
45,202 (28,025)
Railroads—Kilometers (Miles): 3,569 (2,212)
Commercial Airports: 3 international

GOVERNMENT

Type: republic
Independence Date: December 9, 1961
Head of State: President Ali Hassan Mwinyi
Political Parties: Chama Cha Mapinduzi (Revolutionary Party)
Suffrage: universal over 18

MILITARY

Number of Armed Forces: 38,350
Military Expenditures (% of Central Government Expenditures): $179,000,000 (9%)
Current Hostilities: none

ECONOMY

Currency ($ U.S. Equivalent): 93 Tanzanian shillings = $1
Per Capita Income/GNP: $200/$4.1 billion
Inflation Rate: 35.8%
Natural Resources: hydroelectric potential; unexploited iron and coal; gem stones; gold; natural gas
Agriculture: cotton; coffee; sisal; tea; tobacco; wheat; cashews; livestock; cloves
Industry: agricultural processing; diamond mining; oil refining; shoes; cement; textiles; wood products

FOREIGN TRADE

Exports: $255 million
Imports: $1 billion

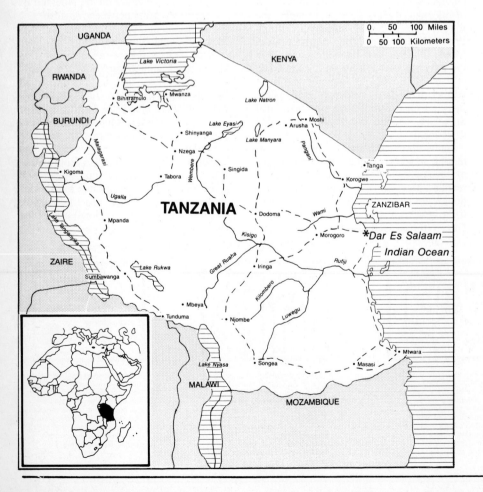

TANZANIA

The development of a country is brought about by people, not by money. Money, and the wealth it represents, is the result and not the basis of development. The four prerequisites of development are different. They are i. People; ii. Land; iii. Good Policies; iv. Good Leadership.

The Arusha Declaration, from which this quotation is taken, has been the cornerstone of Tanzanian socialism since 1967. Tanzania's first president, Julius Nyerere, as well as this program for development have been widely admired. The aim of Tanzanian socialism has been to build on Tanzanian communal values and the people's self-reliance. The Arusha Declaration declares that Tanzanians should determine their own future. Loans, foreign aid, and outside investment may contribute—but may not be central—to development. It is the people's hard work, intelligence, and democratic cooperation that advance their development.

Two decades have passed since the Arusha Declaration was set forth. During those years Tanzania has continued to strive toward the declaration's goals.

MEETING ARUSHA'S GOALS

In 1967 Tanzania, a country that had been independent for 6 years and which had joined with Zanzibar in 1964, was one of the poorest countries in the world. Today Tanzania is still a poor country, but the well-being of Tanzanians has increased and the other goals of equality and democracy espoused in the Arusha Declaration have been realized to some extent. At the same time there have also been failures.

One of the major government efforts has been the creation of ujamaa villages. *Ujamaa* is the Swahili word for "family-hood," and the aim of the villages is to build on the traditional values of the Tanzanian family. Historically, rural peoples in Tanzania lived either as pastoralists in temporary settlements or as farmers in scattered individual households. In the late 1960s people were encouraged to move to the ujamaa villages and form new communities that would cooperate in production and be better served by government social agencies. Now there are more than 8,000 ujamaa villages in Tanzania. However, the revolution in living patterns has not been easy to achieve, nor has it achieved all that was hoped for. Not everyone was willing to make the move. In the 1970s the government began to use force to achieve villagization. The process aroused resistance and dampened the ujamaa spirit.

(United Nations photo by B. Wolff)

Freighters anchor at Dar es Salaam harbor in Tanzania. Trade and communications are important links in the development of a nation.

Despite these problems, many of the goals of Arusha have been achieved. There has been increased participation by people in their governance and efforts to advance equality and to improve the public welfare. Village assemblies and councils, partly appointed and partly elected, were established by law in all new villages. The Revolutionary Party of Tanzania—Chama Cha Mapinduzi (CCM)—formed by the union of the Tanganyika African National Union (TANU) and the Afro-Shirazi Party of Zanzibar, encouraged internal criticism as well as competition for office. In 1980 more than half of the 84 members of Parliament seeking reelection were voted out of office. A new party constitution in 1982 provided for secret balloting for major offices. Government and party powers were separated, and efforts were made to avoid concentration of power at the top. The party, nevertheless, still is the power behind the government and determines both candidates and national policies.

The government sought to spread the benefits of development to the countryside as well as to the cities. Income distribution among civil servants became more equitable. Accumulation of capital is illegal, and hoarding and black-market activities are considered "economic sabotage." Women's rights are promoted. There were special efforts to increase female enrollment in secondary schools, and the government used its appointive powers to ensure that 20 percent of the village council members are women. These policies brought praise from many, but opposition from some Muslim leaders, especially in Zanzibar.

Life is better in many ways for ordinary Tanzanians. Education and health care have improved and are more readily available, adult literacy is high, and life expectancy has risen. Nearly 40 percent of all villages have access to clean water. Infant mortality rates are lower, and clinics are more accessible.

Yet despite these improvements and the efforts made toward meeting socialist goals, other goals seem far away. Tanzania remains one of the 25 least developed countries in the world. Social services are better, but people are poorer. Prospects look dim. The national wealth is more equally distributed, but it is no bigger.

The sultan of Oman transfers capital to Zanzibar as Arab commercial activity increases **1820**	Germany declares a protectorate over the area **1885**	The Maji Maji rebellion unites many ethnic groups against German rule **1905–1906**	Tanganyika becomes a League of Nations mandate under the United Kingdom **1919**	Tanganyika becomes independent; Nyerere is the leader **1961**	Tanzania is formed of Tanganyika and Zanzibar **1964**	The Arusha Declaration establishes a Tanzanian socialist program for development **1967**	A Tanzanian invasion force enters Uganda **1979**

1980s

Nyerere retires; Mwinyi succeeds as president

Tanzania accepts IMF conditions and loans

Tensions with the CCM over unrest in Zanzibar

Moreover, self-reliance has not been achieved, and the advances that have been made have depended on foreign aid, of which Tanzania receives more than almost any other African country. Nyerere's policies came under criticism as enthusiasm waned, but he consistently based decisions on his ideology of African socialism.

THE ECONOMY

Some blame Tanzania's circumstances on government inefficiency and mistakes in management, as well as on other domestic factors. Yet the economic problems facing Tanzania are similar to those facing other African countries. The conditions of world trade have deteriorated; cash-crop exports have declined in price. In 1981, for instance, coffee was getting only one-third of what it had been worth a year earlier. Meanwhile imports such as oil, which absorbs half the foreign exchange, and needed equipment are more expensive than they were in 1967. People may work hard, as Arusha exhorts, yet their increased production of crops may not give them as large a return as earlier, smaller harvests did.

During the early 1980s Tanzania lacked the money to buy needed imports. Industries slowed to an estimated 30 percent of their capacity because they lack machinery, raw materials, or spare parts. Some closed. The transportation system—so vital to the scattered Tanzanian population—especially suffered. Basic necessities, including food, were in short supply, and people in need turned to smuggling or the black market.

Agriculture is the basis of the economy, and yet, as has been noted, cash crops grown for export do not offer satisfactory sources of foreign exchange. Indeed, the government, concerned about the food crisis, encouraged farmers to turn from cash crops to food production.

Other options for exports do not seem viable. There are few mineral resources, although discoveries of natural-gas reserves may someday bring in wealth. Industries neither satisfy consumer needs at home nor provide products to sell abroad.

The Tanzanian government responded to the 1980s economic crisis by formulating a National Economic Survival Plan (NESP). There were crackdowns on economic exploiters, recognition of earlier mistakes and mismanagement, and small-scale farming ventures revitalized. Cooperatives were restored, and some state plantations have been turned over to private hands.

While promoting an openness to new solutions, Tanzania has struggled, with difficulty, to keep its socialist goals. After resisting International Monetary Fund conditions for loans, Tanzania began an IMF reform program in 1986. By 1988 import restrictions had been reduced, the workforce cut back, and salaries reduced. Some subsidies were also reduced, and the shilling lost 75 percent of its value. These policies increased imports, restocked shelves, and began to reduce the debt. But combined with reduced revenues from Tanzania's export crops, they have also had negative effects. Prices of goods skyrocketed, and the minimum wage was $10 per month, down from $20.

As bureaucrats also struggled to make ends meet, official corruption rose. The high cost of imported medicines has meant that health care has declined, especially affecting women and children.

TIMES OF TRANSITION

Political controversy, opposition to Nyerere's long stay in power, and the declining zest for pursuing goals all accompanied the increased economic hardship and led to criticism and a coup attempt in 1983. Following the small number of African heads of state who have retired after long tenure, Nyerere retired in 1983, as planned. He remains as head of the party and still has a strong hand in Tanzanian politics. His successor, Ali Hassan Mwinyi, the former president of Zanzibar, was elected in 1985. Unrest in Zanzibar and Pemba in 1985 and 1986, because of political and religious discontent, led to the ouster of 6 Zanzibar politicians from the CCM in 1988. The Tanzanian leadership must balance Zanzibar's need for autonomy with national unity and party control. Yet though buffeted by an international economy it cannot control, lack of natural resources, and the demands of its citizenry, Tanzania continues to strive toward the goals of the Arusha Declaration.

DEVELOPMENT

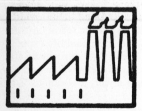

More than 1,700 health centers and dispensaries were built in Tanzania after independence, but these gains are threatened by strains on the economy. In an effort to promote self-reliance and indigenous resources, Tanzania annually gives an award for scientific achievement. The 1988 winners were two teachers.

FREEDOM

On the 25th anniversary of independence 1,000 prisoners were granted amnesty. In the midst of difficult times, government has continued to allow, and sometimes to encourage, criticism of its policies, while clamping down on "economic sabotage."

HEALTH/WELFARE

Tanzania has made great advances in education, health care, and literacy. Universal Primary Literacy (UPE) was established, and a national literacy campaign was very successful. Tanzania is the most literate nation in Africa.

ACHIEVEMENTS

Tanzania has played a leading role in advancing all-African causes in African and international forums. Nyerere and Tanzania spearheaded efforts of the Frontline States in the liberation struggles of Southern Africa. Hundreds of thousands of refugees have been welcomed in Tanzania and have been offered permanent homes and citizenship.

Uganda (Republic of Uganda)

GEOGRAPHY

Area in Square Kilometers (Miles): 235,885 (91,076) (slightly smaller than Oregon)
Capital (Population): Kampala (331,000)
Climate: tropical to semiarid

PEOPLE

Population
Total: 16,800,000
Annual Growth Rate: 3.2%
Rural/Urban Population Ratio: 92/8
Languages: official: English; others spoken: Kiswahili, Luganda, Iteso, Soga, Acholi, Lugbara, Nyakole Nyoro, others

Health
Life Expectancy at Birth: 49 years male; 53 years female
Infant Death Rate (Ratio): 113/1,000
Average Caloric Intake: 83% of FAO minimum
Physicians Available (Ratio): 1/25,633

Religion(s)
50% Christian; 40% traditional indigenous; 10% Muslim

Education
Adult Literacy Rate: 52%

COMMUNICATION

Telephones: 48,880
Newspapers: 5

SONG OF LAWINO

Song of Lawino, a "poetic novel" by Ugandan poet and novelist Okot p'Bitek, has been popular in the Western world as well as in Africa. First written in the Acholi language, it has been translated into English by the author and depicts a "modern" Ugandan man who has assumed Western values. The story is told through the eyes of his African wife, who is not Western-educated but is wiser than he. The views she presents illustrate how sensible many traditional African ways are. For example, in one passage, the wife says: "Listen/My husband,/In the wisdom of the Acoli/Time is not stupidly split up/Into seconds and minutes, . . ./It does not resemble/A loaf of millet bread/Surrounded by hungry youths/From a hunt./It does not get finished/Like vegetables in the dish. . . ."

TRANSPORTATION

Highways—Kilometers (Miles): 7,582 (4,700)
Railroads—Kilometers (Miles): 1,286 (797)
Commercial Airports: 1 international

GOVERNMENT

Type: republic; under control of the National Resistance Council
Independence Date: October 9, 1962
Head of State: President Yoweri Kaguta Museveni
Political Parties: National Resistance Movement; Nationalist Liberal Party; Democratic Party; Conservative Party; Uganda People's Congress
Suffrage: universal for adults

MILITARY

Number of Armed Forces: 20,000
Military Expenditures (% of Central Government Expenditures): n/a
Current Hostilities: internal conflicts

ECONOMY

Currency ($ U.S. Equivalent): 60 Uganda shillings = $1
Per Capita Income/GNP: $240/$6.2 billion
Inflation Rate: 16%
Natural Resources: copper; other minerals
Agriculture: coffee; tea; cotton
Industry: processed agricultural coods; copper; cement; shoes; fertilizer; steel; beverages

FOREIGN TRADE

Exports: $380 million
Imports: $509 million

Establishment of the oldest Ugandan kingdom, Bunyoro, followed by the formation of Baganda and other kingdoms **1500**	Kabaka Metesa I of Baganda welcomes British explorer H.M. Stanley **1870s**	A British protectorate over Uganda is proclaimed **1893**	An agreement gives Baganda special status in the British protectorate **1900**

UGANDA

After 2 decades of repressive rule, violence, and unrest, Uganda struggles for peace, reconciliation, and normalcy. A land rich in natural and human resources, Uganda suffered dreadfully under Idi Amin and his legacy of chaos and violence.

THE TRADITIONAL INHERITANCE

Uganda is located in the area of the Great Lakes of East Africa and includes the volcanic Ruwenzori Mountains. It has been said that in Uganda you can drop anything into the soil and it will grow. The country's political heritage is also rich. Complex kingdoms such as Baganda, Bunyoro, Ankole, and Toro stretched back to the fifteenth and sixteenth centuries. These kingdoms were characterized by elaborate institutions and rituals; a variety of officials, including oral historians; a ruling class that was often cattle-holding; and systems of client-patron relations. Early European visitors were impressed by the kingdoms and their seeming similarities to early European feudal monarchies. When the British took over the region they maintained the Baganda kingdom and allowed the Baganda *Kabaka*, or ruler, and his chiefs to rule under British "protection."

During the colonial years the Bagandans (citizens of Baganda), who today still maintain a feeling of pride in their own achievements and advancements, shaped political conditions to their best advantage—and to the disadvantage of neighboring kingdoms such as the Bunyoro. During the nineteenth century many of the peoples of the region began questioning long-standing beliefs and values and therefore were receptive to the new Christian faith as well as to Islam, and to the educational opportunities that the mission schools offered. As a result, Ugandans, and especially Bagandans, learned many of the skills needed by the new state after independence. Unfortunately, Bagandans used their new skills to serve Baganda rather than the larger Ugandan state. This threat of Bagandan dominance was to raise opposition and conflict.

In the 1950s the Bagandan royal government, recognizing that Bagandans were a minority within the colonial state and fearing that Baganda's interests would suffer after independence, sought to se-cede from the proposed new nation. Although this did not happen, Baganda did manage to procure federal status (which gave Baganda a certain amount of independence) under the first Constitution, and a limited federal position was granted to the other indigenous kingdoms.

In the years following independence Milton Obote, prime minister and head of the majority Ugandan People's Congress (UPC)—and not a Bagandan—developed a more unified government, though he had to use force against the Bagandans in order to do so. The move increased opposition to his rule inside and outside of his party. The socialist program that Obote

(World Bank/Y. Nagata)

Uganda has maintained a steady performance in agriculture, but officials want to diversify away from coffee, the leading cash crop.

developed also met resistance. In 1971, when Obote was out of the country, the armed forces under General Idi Amin seized power.

THE DESTRUCTIVENESS OF AMIN'S RULE

Deaths, violations of basic human rights, threats to ordinary security, and the de-struction of a promising economic base characterized Idi Amin's 8 years in power. It is estimated that there were from 50,000 to 300,000 arbitrary killings. Many of those killed were well-known and respected leaders, such as the Anglican Archbishop of Uganda Janani Luwum and the former Chief Justice and Prime Minister Benedicto Kiwanuka.

Other aspects of Amin's rule shaped the current situation in Uganda. The assets of all Asian noncitizens were taken over, and 40,000 Asians fled the country. British firms were nationalized. The wealth that came into government hands as a result of these takeovers was used to reward the military and gain support for Amin's regime. Amin destroyed the old administrative system in Uganda and instituted 10 provinces, each headed by a military governor who was literally a warlord. The army changed and grew as troops who were suspect were dropped and outsiders such as Sudanese and Zairois were added. It became an army of occupation, 25,000 strong, rather than a source of security.

Development had no place in Amin's Uganda. The economy was destroyed. Peasant farmers survived by abandoning cash-crop production and turning to subsistence agriculture. By 1979 industries were producing at only 15 percent of capacity, and the factories that manufactured equipment such as hoes had no steel. Outsiders—including the British, Israelis, the United States, Arab countries, Libya, and others—continued to trade with Amin's Uganda, providing materials to the elite who participated in his government. Amin's officials stole from the farmers, smuggled out cash crops through a highly organized network, received plunder, or—like many others—fled to neighboring countries.

AMIN'S DEFEAT

Resistance movements existed within Amin's Uganda, but they were not successful. Individual critics were forcibly silenced. Striking workers, student protestors, and rebel ethnic groups directed their efforts against the regime, and assassination and coup attempts were frequent. None of these efforts led to the end of Amin's rule. Tanzanian troops finally invaded Uganda and deposed Amin. The war began after Amin's troops attacked Tanzania, late in 1978. Ugandan exiles in

Kabaka of Baganda is exiled to the United Kingdom by the British for espousing Bagandan independence **1953**	Uganda becomes independent **1962**	Obote introduces a new unitary Constitution and forces Bagandan compliance **1966**	Amin seizes power **1971**	Amin invades Tanzania **1978**	Tanzania invades Uganda and overturns Amin's government **1979**

1980s

Obote's UPC wins in the first elections since 1962; an army coup topples Obote

The NRM takes power, under Yoweri Museveni

Recovery produces slow gains, while unrest continues

Tanzania—including A. Milton Obote—took part in the war of liberation in 1979.

The campaign was successful. A demoralized army was defeated, and Amin fled—first to Libya and then to Saudi Arabia. Yet the challenge of national recovery was greater than the challenge of Amin's defeat.

THE NEW GOVERNMENT

In March 1979, during the fighting, representatives of 19 exile groups met at Moshi in Tanzania and formed the Uganda National Liberation Front. A provisional government grew from this organization with Ususf Lule, a Bagandan and former chancellor of the University of Makerere, as president. Objections to his authoritarian rule led to his forced resignation, and his successor, Godfrey Binaisa, was soon removed in a dispute over presidential powers. A military commission took over and administered elections in 1980. Milton Obote won those elections, but opposition parties charged that the elections were rigged. This victory did not lead to a peaceful and prosperous Uganda. Political slogans emphasized reconciliation and reconstruction, but political violence and economic problems recurred.

RECONCILIATION FAILS

Under Obote, arrest, detention, and torture of civilians by the military continued, and, some charged, escalated. Because arrests by the army are illegal, the Obote government refused to acknowledge the arrest and disappearance of hundreds of civilians. The Democratic Party was bitterly critical of the government's practices, charging that more Ugandans were killed in 1982 than in any year of Amin's rule. Opposition legislators were murdered, and journalists were detained. One opposition party went into exile and formed a guerrilla resistance movement. Other resistance groups, such as the National Resistance Movement (NRM), developed in the south as well as in the west Nile area, Amin's home area.

Opposition to Obote led in July 1985 to an army coup, staged by General Tito Okello. Obote fled to exile in Kenya and then Zambia, and the new government released more than 1,200 political prisoners. Although reconciliation talks with the NRM began soon after, the resistance continued their struggle and by January 1986 had control of Kampala, with Yoweri Museveni as president.

RECONSTRUCTION

Museveni inherited debts, low levels of industrial and agricultural productivity, a lack of necessities, and the corruption that accompanies scarcity. International Monetary Fund (IMF) negotiations led to the devaluation of the currency and debt rescheduling. The debt was reduced, and the real gross national product rose. Food production increased, and the percentage of export crops, including the traditionally strong crops, cotton and coffee, grew, although smuggling continues. Asian citizens were invited to return home and were assured that their properties would be returned.

By 1988 the NRM had made progress in many areas, but it still faced rebel activity and banditry in the north and east. While agricultural production has increased elsewhere, these areas still face violence against civilians, scarcity of food and services, and overcrowded urban areas when farmers flee to cities, leaving crops untended. Despite negotiations with opposition leaders and a government amnesty program, random groups of armed men roam rural areas, stealing from and killing civilians. Areas with a police presence have fared better and are returning to normal, but some estimate that more than 1 million people may be displaced and in need of assistance.

The government also faced opposition from rebels led by religious leader Alice Lakwena and border clashes with Kenya over trade disagreements. Although President Museveni and Kenya's President Daniel arap Moi met late in 1987 to diffuse the tensions, transport of goods, debts, and electric power were still affected by these disagreements well into 1988. The chaos, violence, human-rights abuses, and instability of the last 20 years, however, have left a burdensome legacy.

DEVELOPMENT

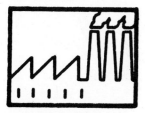

Food production has improved in many areas, but insecurity and violence have obstructed the recovery of agriculture, preventing harvesting and impeding transportation.

FREEDOM

Under both Amin and Obote, thousands of civilians were detained, tortured, killed, or disappeared. Many fled to neighboring countries, while others were displaced within Uganda. More than 1,200 persons were released after the 1985 coup. Detentions without trial, killings and harrassment of civilians by both rebels and soldiers continue, although matters have improved since 1987.

HEALTH/WELFARE

Recovery programs concentrate on projects such as the rehabilitation of hospitals, but overcrowding and rural unrest hamper efforts. The spread of AIDS also challenges Uganda's fragile recovery.

ACHIEVEMENTS

The NRM has made a commitment to raising women's status and standard of living. There are two women Cabinet ministers and three deputy ministers. Women's organizations are being encouraged and the government plans to increase women's access to education and credit. Women are members of Resistance Committees, grassroots political units.

Southern Africa

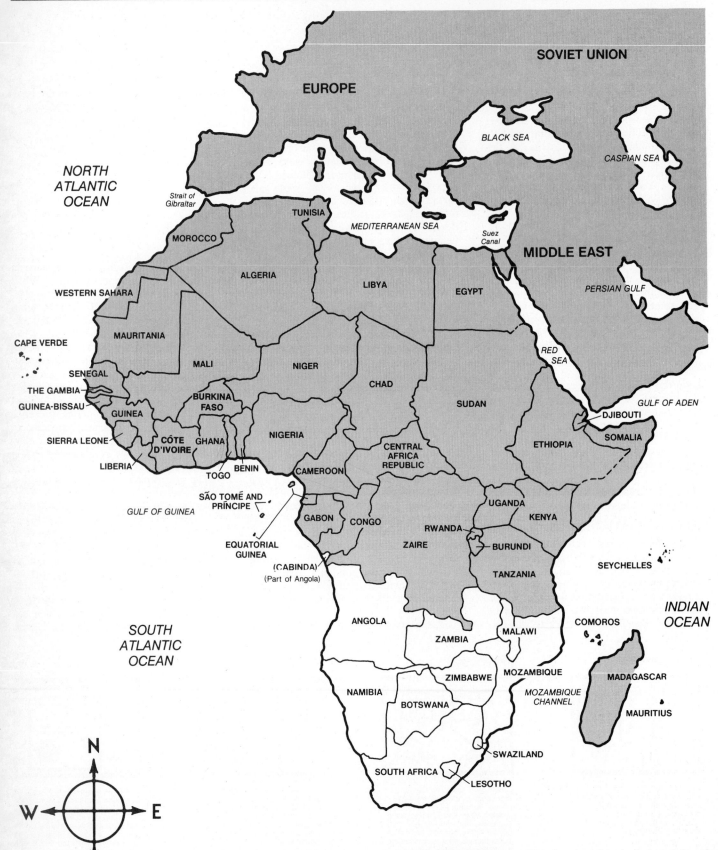

The countries of Southern Africa have been deeply influenced by South Africa's industrial and military power and alienated by its racial policies.

120

Southern Africa: Destabilization Obstructs True Independence

Southern Africa—which includes Angola, Zambia, Malawi, Mozambique, Zimbabwe, South Africa and its colony Namibia, Lesotho, Botswana, and Swaziland—is a region of savannas and desert (the Namib), plateaus, and a Mediterranean climate that encourages comparisons between this area and North Africa. It is not so much the geographic features, however, as the peoples and their past interactions that give the region its identity. It is history that provides the keys for understanding the forces that both unite and divide Southern Africa.

The peoples of the region include the first inhabitants (hunters and gatherers such as the Khoisan speakers who now live in the dry regions of Namibia and South Africa), the many Bantu-speaking groups who came into the region in the first millennium A.D., and white settlers who arrived later. The continuing impact of the settlers and their communities has made much of Southern Africa what it is today.

EUROPEAN MIGRATION AND DOMINANCE

From A.D. 1000 to 1500 Bantu speakers migrated into Central, East, and Southern Africa. By the sixteenth century the entire region was populated by a variety of ethnic groups practicing both agriculture and pastoralism. The Khoi-khoi and San occupied the southernmost tip of the continent, while the Swazi, Tswana, Xhosa, Zulu, and Ndebele, among others, occupied the remainder of the region.

In the seventeenth century whites from Holland settled at the Cape of Good Hope. Their population gradually expanded, moving into the interior and eastward along the coast, conquering and enslaving some of their African neighbors. The British took over these settlements beginning in 1795, and English colonists began arriving in 1820. In the 1820s Shaka, the Zulu leader, was engaged in nation building and conquest. His wars stimulated the movement of vast numbers of people from the eastern areas of present-day South Africa to the west and north. Many current residents of Mozambique, Malawi, Zimbabwe, and even Tanzania are descended from the Africans who came north and settled during that time. The whole area still bears the marks of that revolution, called the Mfecane.

The conservative Dutch-descended Boers, or Afrikaners, ancestors of the white leaders in South Africa today, trekked inland in the 1830s to found Boer nations, which were free from British control. Later, when gold and diamonds were discovered, white miners and entrepreneurs traveled to the Transvaal, spreading out in the regions around Johannesburg and Pretoria and moving farther north. In 1890 a "column of pioneers" of Cecil Rhodes' British South Africa Company made their way to present-day Zimbabwe. Others spread to Zambia. British traders, missionaries, and other settlers came separately to the area that is now known as Malawi. The territories of present-day Angola and Mozambique were also settled by white colonists from Portugal.

By 1900 all of these areas were under the colonial rule of either the United Kingdom or Portugal, while Germany controlled present-day Namibia. South Africa had the largest white population, and the Afrikaner and British settlers there had the longest heritage. Although defeated in a war with the

(United Nations photo by Alon Reininger)

Countries throughout Southern Africa are developing projects to employ laborers who otherwise migrate to South Africa, a pattern established in colonial times. This worker is building a highway in Lesotho.

British (1899–1902), these settlers were able to gain virtual independence in 1910. With their rich natural resources and outside aid as well as their own skills, they were able to industrialize and develop in ways that far surpassed the other colonies of the region. This development depended on the black labor from throughout the area. Migrants came from Portuguese as well as British territories to serve the South African economy. Meanwhile policies of land reservation, labor regulation, and discrimination could be found in varying degrees in all these territories. Portugal's white colonists claimed to follow policies different from the British—more readily accepting blacks as equals once they were "civilized"—but the results were the same: there was power for whites and little advancement of the colonized peoples.

NATIONS BECOME INDEPENDENT

During the 1950s and 1960s all of the countries of Southern Africa were affected by the "winds of change" (as British Prime Minister Harold Macmillan described the forces of flux in Africa in the 1960s), but the struggle for national independence was slow and hard. In the countries with small settler groups, however, the movements for independence had more success. First Malawi and Zambia, then Lesotho, Swaziland, and Botswana, became recognized as independent nations. The area was polarized between liberated and unliberated countries. In 1974 a military revolt in Portugal brought statehood to Mozambique and Angola, after a long armed struggle by liberation forces. Finally, in 1980, after a protracted armed struggle, Zimbabwe became free. South Africa stood alone, a white-minority-ruled state with its unwilling satellite, Namibia, confronting independent black governments.

Today contrast between apartheid South Africa and the black states remains. Yet every part of the region is deeply influenced by South Africa. Neighboring countries hope to free themselves from its powerful presence. The attachments fashioned in the past are economic as well as historical. Roads and rails lead to Johannesburg and Capetown, where expatriate African workers have worked in the industries and mines for generations. The countries of the north use the infrastructure for their exports and import South African-manufactured goods and food that they do not produce.

Destabilizing policies and violence practiced by South Africa have been even more disturbing than the region's economic dependence on the country. Independent black states are hostile to South Africa's apartheid policies, and

(United Nations photo)

Angolan youths celebrated when the nation became independent in 1974.

they have provided havens for South Africa's exiles who have built bases for liberation struggles in these countries. South Africa's armed forces have attacked supposed bases and encouraged insurgency within the independent states. In spite of security agreements signed between South Africa and Mozambique and Angola in 1984, South Africa has continued to attack its neighbors with impunity.

Opposition to South Africa has stimulated movements for economic integration among the other countries. Nine countries, including Tanzania in East Africa, have joined together in the Southern African Development Coordination Conference (SADCC) to free themselves from dependence on South Africa and to cooperate on projects of economic development.

In this essay we look more closely at these features of the Southern African region: the threat of South Africa and its relationships with its neighbors, the historic regional economic dependence on that country, the widespread impact of food shortages, and the efforts to develop viable regional alternatives to dependence upon South Africa.

SOUTH AFRICA'S MILITARY POWER AND DESTABILIZING POLICIES

South Africa is a superpower, and its influence in the southern part of the African continent reflects the vast difference between its development and that of its neighbors. South Africa's generals compare their country's status to the role of the Soviet Union in Eastern Europe or Israel in the Middle East. Its militarization is recent but growing. Despite the United Nations' arms embargo of South Africa, established in 1977, the country's military establishment has been able to secure both arms and sophisticated technology from the West in order to develop its own military industry. South Africa is almost self-sufficient in arms, with a vast and advanced arsenal of weapons and a possible nuclear capacity. In 1978 South Africa imported 75 percent of its weapons; today it imports only 5 percent. South Africa currently exports armaments worldwide, supplying weapons to both Iran and Iraq, for example.

South Africa now spends 20 percent of its budget on the military. The army numbers more than 100,000, and the reserve consists of most white males under age 55, many of whom are on call against urban insurgents at home while the army itself fights the forces of the South West African People's Organization (SWAPO) in Namibia and Angola.

All of the countries in Southern Africa share an unwilling acquaintance with South Africa's military strength and suffer from its impact. South Africa has directed military attacks against any country harboring South African exiles who support the African National Congress (ANC) or any other movement of resistance against South Africa, and it destroys infrastructures that might lead to economic independence from South Africa. Angola, Lesotho, Mozambique, Botswana, Zambia, and Zimbabwe have been bombarded by South African planes.

South Africa has supported rebel movements within

(United Nations photo)

Followers of Steven Biko left South Africa after the Soweto riots and after his death. They added to the numbers and spirit of the South African liberation movement.

neighboring states. These movements have directed their attacks against the rail lines and oil depots so essential to the well-being of these developing economies. In Angola, the South African Air Force has protected the National Union for the Total Independence of Angola (UNITA) in its attacks on railroads, including the Benguela railroad, which is used by Zambia and Zimbabwe. South African troops led ground assaults with UNITA against Angola. Since 1980 the Mozambique National Resistance (MNR, also known as Renamo), funded and led by South Africans, has attacked the ports and oil depots at Maputo, Mozambique; and it has conducted a brutal war against civilians and social services in the rural areas. South African air bases near the Zimbabwe border will enable South Africa to attack four countries by air.

There are conflicts within Southern African countries that South Africa can heighten. Some Zimbabweans have claimed that the dissident movements in Zimbabwe's Matabeleland were encouraged by South Africa, and Lesotho authorities have accused South Africa of manipulating the antigovernment Lesotho Liberation Army. There are other signs of South African intrusion. The assassinations of anti-apartheid foes Joe Gqabi and Ruth First, South Africans living in exile, appear to have been engineered by South Africa, and many in Southern Africa believe that South Africa was responsible for the death of Mozambican President Samora Machel in 1986.

Prime Minister Pieter Botha has expressed South Africa's desire to make nonaggression pacts with neighboring states. The first of these agreements was signed between Swaziland and South Africa in 1982. In 1984 South Africa and Mozambique signed a nonaggression pact, the Nkomati Accords. Mozambique agreed to limit acts against South Africa by ANC representatives in Mozambique, and the South African government pledged to withdraw support from the MNR fighters in Mozambique. A less formal agreement with Angola aimed to limit Angolan aid to SWAPO forces from Namibia and South Africa's assistance to the antigovernment UNITA movement in Angola.

Soon, however, South Africa violated the accords. Since 1985 South African and American assistance to UNITA has increased, and South African soldiers have been involved in raids on Angolan villages, cities, and oil installations. Renamo continued to destabilize Mozambique, and South African forces continued raids against neighboring countries. The South African Defense Force (SADF) officially admits to assassinating 146 people in raids on neighbors since 1981. This figure, however, ignores the more than 100,000 killed by the MNR in Mozambique, and the hundreds of thousands impaired, maimed, and starving because of regional wars.

Blaming its neighbors for continued African National Congress attacks on South Africa, the South African government justifies violence against its neighbors. These countries continue their diplomatic and moral support for the ANC, while discouraging military excursions from their borders. Many observers note that ANC training and military actions increasingly originate from within South Africa.

FACTORS OF DEPENDENCE

Regional dependence on South Africa has forced many of its neighbors to take a cautious attitude toward South African political refugees, even though they may refuse South African pacts. Seventy-five percent of Southern Africa's rail lines are South African. Fifty percent of Zambia's traffic, as well as many of Zimbabwe's exports, move over these rails. Tanzanian and Zimbabwean troops now protect the pipelines and oil depots in Mozambique for these reasons. It is not surprising that Zimbabwe does not allow the ANC to launch attacks on South Africa from within its boundaries.

Dependence goes both ways, however. The countries of the region also trade with South Africa, as do many other African countries farther north. Economically, South Africa is the most developed country on the continent, with manufactured goods and agricultural surpluses that Africa needs. Nearly every African country imports South African goods and crops. South Africa also is dependent on its neighbors for labor, markets, and transportation outlets.

Lesotho and Swaziland, which are surrounded by South Africa, and Botswana, which borders South Africa on the

(United Nations photo by Jerry Frank)

South Africa's economic and military dominance overshadows the region's planning.

north, are especially bound to South Africa (although since 1986 Lesotho and Swaziland are no longer tied to the South African currency, the rand). These countries have been the recipients of South Africa's expertise: South Africa is building a railroad in Botswana, and a water project in Lesotho is South African-financed. But both projects will also benefit South Africa, through increased rail traffic to the country and through the water resources it will gain from the Orange River. These projects illustrate the readiness of South Africa's apartheid system to increase regional dependence, gain resources for itself, and, increasingly, to circumvent economic sanctions.

Migrant laborers who come to work in South Africa increase these interdependencies. Laborers from Mozambique, Lesotho, and Malawi migrated to the mines of South Africa as early as the 1890s; they were driven by colonial taxation policies or were recruited by employers and their agents. The pattern continued after independence. Although South Africa's neighbors are trying to create more jobs for their workers at home, tens of thousands still migrate to South Africa for jobs.

This is not a tie that is easy to break. For instance, more than 40 percent of Lesotho's national income depends on wages from abroad. These governments unwillingly maintain the pattern because the foreign exchange that migrants provide buys needed imports—one of the most essential of which is food. Ironically, limited food production in the region has been connected to the migration of agricultural

laborers to the mines, and to the destabilization efforts of South Africa. Lack of rainfall has historically been a problem in this region, and in the 1980s the problems of food supply were greatly increased by drought and warfare.

THE FOOD CRISIS

Famine and food shortages in Southern Africa are a result of drought in the 1980s and continued warfare against civilians, especially in Angola and Mozambique. The drought in Southern Africa neither lasted as long nor was as widely publicized as was the drought of West Africa or the Horn, yet it was no less destructive. Although some countries—such as Zimbabwe, Mozambique, and Botswana, as well as areas of South Africa—suffered more than others, the same features of the crisis were found everywhere: water reserves were depleted; cattle and game, historically a dominant characteristic of this region, died; and crop production declined, often by a half or a third.

Maize and cereal production suffered everywhere. Many countries, including Zimbabwe and South Africa, usually exporters, had to import food themselves. In South Africa, there were noticeable contrasts between white areas, where irrigation saved crops, and black homelands, which had no such facilities and depended on the "foreign aid" of the white government. The projects that South Africa has planned to secure further water resources for itself may rob the rivers on which the Sotho and Zulu peoples depend. Estimates of human suffering during the 1980s ranged in the

(UN photo)

Ovahimbo herdsman quenches his thirst at a stream at Epembe, Kaokoland in Namibia.

millions: more than half a million each were affected in Angola, Lesotho, and Botswana (half of its population), and 2 million were malnourished in Mozambique.

Cereal production in the region was up 40 percent in 1988, after a bad harvest in 1987. Zimbabwe was not only able to export but also to send gifts of food to Tanzania and Ethiopia. Recognized internationally for its achievements in food production, Zimbabwe raised the outcome of peasant production from 8 percent at independence in 1980 to 64 percent in 1987.

Regional destabilization and warfare have meant continued famine in Angola and Mozambique, despite improved rainfall. In 1987 there were 4.6 million at risk for starvation in Mozambique, and 2.7 million in Angola. Malawi faced food shortages because of the presence of 500,000 refugees fleeing warfare in Mozambique. Food security in the region awaits peace.

THE SOUTHERN AFRICAN DEVELOPMENT COORDINATION CONFERENCE

A recently established cooperative effort among Southern African states may help to coordinate food assistance as well as to loosen the ties with South Africa and lessen the threat from that country. Southern Africa's black states recognize that they can only break out of South Africa's "constellation" if they can find alternative sources of foreign exchange and other trading partners, increase their mutual infrastructure, and develop their energy sources. They are trying to cooperate on these tasks. The Southern African Development Coordination Conference (SADCC) was established by an agreement signed in 1980.

Several of the states, known as the Frontline States, have coordinated their foreign-relations policies in the past and played important roles in the liberation of Zimbabwe and the continuing effort to extract Namibia from South Africa's grasp. The states of Angola, Botswana, Mozambique, Zambia, and Zimbabwe, as well as Tanzania, took steps to control the world distribution of news. They "in principle" banned journalists who report to bureaus in South Africa. South Africa seldom permits journalists from Frontline States to report from within its boundaries, and the authorities in South Africa have passed laws to severely restrict reporting on events in that country. The independent African states want to encourage international media organizations to establish full-time bureaus in their countries.

The SADCC members are doing more than just talking. They are working at practical tasks to exploit the vast potential of their countries. Each country has been assigned an area for research and planning. Angola is responsible for

(World Bank photo)

Regional planning, such as the building of the Kariba dam, is critical to the development of independent economies.

energy, Mozambique for transport and communication, and Tanzania for industry. A macroeconomic survey of the members was conducted, each research sector has a long-term plan, and Scandinavian countries and the European Economic Community concluded accords with SADCC. To improve its image in the region, the United States approved aid to SADCC in 1987. Recent successes include the total telecommunications independence from South Africa; new electricity grids, which offer power to Botswana and Swaziland; and alternative roads, which carry 30 percent of Malawian goods north through Tanzania. Regional military cooperation aims to protect rail and oil lines to expedite the exports of the landlocked countries.

The organization faces problems besides the threat of South Africa and food shortages. The world recession and related problems of low export and high import prices affect all of the SADCC members. Moreover, the ideologies of the states differ, ranging from the socialism of Tanzania, Mozambique, and Angola to the capitalist orientations of Zambia and Malawi. Malawi's diplomatic and other relations with South Africa have met with strong regional disapproval. Disagreements related to these differences may develop as SADCC advances, especially as outside capital and transnational corporations become involved. Yet SADCC's economic needs and the importance of countering South Africa's power take precedence over these differences at present. SADCC countries are determined to prevent fissures and to avoid such dangers as an overloaded bureaucracy and substantial debts. Moreover, financial donors should be attracted by goals of SADCC, by the possibility of giving financial assistance multilaterally, and by the practical achievements that the conference has already recorded. Financial backing will have important political as well as economic benefits for the independent states of Southern Africa.

(United Nations photo)

In recent years apartheid, the South African government's policy of racial discrimination, has caused increasing unrest among blacks.

Angola (People's Republic of Angola)

GEOGRAPHY

Area in Square Kilometers (Miles):
1,246,699 (481,351) (larger than Texas
and California combined)
Capital (Population): Luanda
(1,000,000)
Climate: tropical and subtropical

PEOPLE

Population
Total: 8,971,000
Annual Growth Rate: 2.5%
Rural/Urban Population Ratio: 79/21
Languages: official: Portuguese;
others spoken: Ovimbundu,
Kimbundu, Bakongo

Health
Life Expectancy at Birth: 42 years
male; 44 years female
Infant Death Rate (Ratio): 200/1,000
Average Caloric Intake: 83% of FAO
minimum
Physicians Available (Ratio): 1/1,834

Religion(s)
84% traditional indigenous; 12%
Roman Catholic; 4% Protestant

Education
Adult Literacy Rate: 30%

COMMUNICATION

Telephones: 40,000
Newspapers: 1

INTERNATIONAL INTERVENTION AND DIPLOMACY

After years of warfare, peace negotiations again became a reality for
Angola in 1988. Although South Africa had first invaded Angola in
1975, South Africa acknowledged for the first time in 1987 that its troops
were fighting in Angola. War weary, the parties directly involved began
meeting in 1987, with pressure brought to bear by the United Nations,
the United States, and the Soviet Union.

The international diplomatic negotiators can claim some credit, but it
appears that South Africa did not come to the bargaining table until
military options had failed to defeat the Angolan government. Most
observers agree that the prospect of a long-term quagmire, not a desire
for reconciliation, induced South Africa to negotiate for peace. Many in
the region doubt the sincerity of the South Africans, since they have
made agreements before and not abided by them.

TRANSPORTATION

Highways—Kilometers (Miles):
73,828 (45,877)
Railroads—Kilometers (Miles): 3,189
(1,982)
Commercial Airports: 2 international

GOVERNMENT

Type: Marxist people's republic; one-
party rule
Independence Date: November 11,
1975
Head of State: President Jose
Edouardo dos Santos
Political Parties: Popular Movement
for the Liberation of Angola-Labor
Party
Suffrage: universal for adults

MILITARY

Number of Armed Forces: 52,750
*Military Expenditures (% of Central
Government Expenditures):* n/a
Current Hostilities: civil war; attacks
by South Africa

ECONOMY

Currency ($ U.S. Equivalent): 30
kwanzas = $1
Per Capita Income/GNP: $500/$3.5
billion
Inflation Rate: n/a
Natural Resources: oil; diamonds;
manganese; gold; uranium
Agriculture: coffee; sisal; corn;
cotton; sugar; manioc; tobacco;
bananas; plantains
Industry: oil; diamond mining;
fish processing; brewing; tobacco;
sugar processing; textiles; cement;
food processing; construction

FOREIGN TRADE

Exports: $1.4 billion
Imports: $1.1 billion

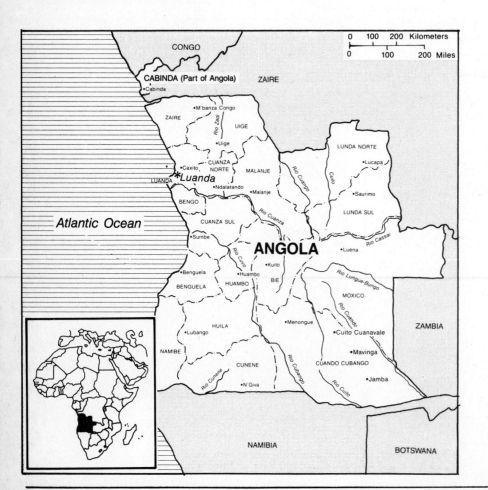

ANGOLA

Angola has had a long history of contact with Western countries, but such contact has not bettered the lives of its citizens. The nation's beginnings were ominous. The Portuguese first made contact with peoples of the Kongo State in the northern area of present-day Angola in 1483. After the Kongo rulers developed relations with the Portuguese government, Jesuit missionaries arrived; rulers were baptized and schools were established. Even the art of the time reflected the Portuguese influence. However, Portuguese slave traders soon destroyed these promising beginnings, and the slave trade became the predominant institution connecting Angolans and Westerners during the sixteenth, seventeenth, and eighteenth centuries. Meanwhile the Portuguese expanded among the kingdoms of the south, wreaking devastation.

Aside from the slave trade, the Portuguese presence had little impact in earlier times. Then, in the late nineteenth and early twentieth centuries, Portuguese penetration increased and Portuguese settlement was encouraged. Three hundred thousand Portuguese settlers were living in Angola in the 1960s when the liberation war began. Coffee plantations and diamond mining in Angola had contributed to Portugal's development and had depended on the forced labor of Angolans. Although the Portuguese claimed that they encouraged Angolans to learn Portuguese and to practice Catholicism and Portuguese ways of life (thus becoming "assimilated" and equal to their colonizers), fewer than 1 percent of Angolans had achieved this status by the middle of the twentieth century.

Angola is potentially one of the richest countries in Africa, but both the heritage of colonialism and the circumstances since independence have prevented Angolans from fully developing their economic as well as human potential. World conditions and a heritage of war have held back the nation.

A HERITAGE OF WAR

The liberation struggle against the Portuguese began with a powerful rebellion in 1961 and lasted for 13 years. In many ways, it was a constructive struggle. Members of the Popular Movement of the Liberation of Angola (MPLA) were deeply influenced by Marxist ideology and worked to develop new structures and new attitudes among the populations of liberated zones. Women as well as men took an active part in the war and the decision making. Although the MPLA military efforts did not reach the major population centers, by the 1970s the MPLA had the support of most of the regions. However, there were divisions among the liberation fighters. The National Front for the Liberation of Angola (FLNA), a primarily northern movement, and the National Union for the Total Independence of Angola (UNITA), based in the southeast, were never reconciled to MPLA leadership.

When the popular revolution in Portugal in 1974 led to the decolonization of that country's overseas territories, Angola became independent under MPLA. Its leaders, however, were immediately engaged in a new war, following an invasion by South Africa. It was not until 1976 that the MPLA government could claim to have defeated the South African forces, and they were able to do so only with the assistance of Cuban forces, which have remained in the country since that time.

South African aggression did not end in 1976. Namibia, which borders Angola on the south, is illegally claimed by South Africa. Seventy thousand refugees from Namibia have settled in camps in southern Angola, and the South West African People's Organization (SWAPO) has established bases there.

South African troops have stepped up their attacks on SWAPO bases and Angolan civilian targets. In 1984 talks between Angola and South Africa led to an agreement for the withdrawal of South African troops and SWAPO, and for the formation of a joint monitoring commission. However, South African air and ground attacks and logistical and human support for UNITA did not decrease. As Angolan government forces went on the offensive against UNITA, South Africa provided more air attacks and up to 8,000 troops.

UNITA has been fighting against the MPLA government since 1975. Led by Jonas Savimbi—a Marxist first dependent on the Chinese and then on South African and U.S. aid (many Angolans consider him an opportunist)—UNITA was nearly destroyed in 1976. With U.S. ($30 million in 1988, including Stinger missiles) and South African assistance, it now controls much of the rural areas of the country, including some of the most fertile agricultural regions. Savimbi has gained international recognition through visits to the United States and Portugal.

British, Czechoslovak, Philippine, and other expatriates employed by the Angolan government have been taken hostage and released only after direct negotiations between UNITA and their countries have take place. Assisted by advertising firms in the United States and Europe, Savimbi has carried out extensive public-relations campaigns. Foreign journalists have been encouraged to visit and report on this "state within a state."

GOVERNMENT SURVIVAL

The MPLA government is recognized by all countries in the world, with the exception of the United States and South Africa. Nonetheless, the government has spent most of its existence fighting for survival. The wars against South Africa and UNITA have eaten up much of the budget; and the problems of world recession as well as internal destruction have meant that the needs of the population are great, but the means to satisfy those needs are small. The government has tried to restore the economy by depending on elected committees of peasants and workers, yet practical problems remain.

The major source of government revenues is oil, pumped daily by various oil companies, including Gulf and Texaco. Half of the return goes to Angola, providing 90 percent of its export earnings. The government is concentrating on a major expansion of the oil industry. Production is expected to increase, but the decline in the price of oil means drastically reduced oil revenues, which are needed for arms to defeat South Africa and UNITA and for development that will counteract the devastation of war.

Other sources of wealth appear less

(United Nations photo by J. P. Laffont)
The war for independence from Portugal led to the creation of a one-party state.

		Queen Nzinga defends the Mbundu kindoms against the Portuguese 1640					South African-initiated air and ground incursions into Angola 1976	President Agostinho Neto dies; dos Santos becomes president 1979
The Kongo State develops 1400	The Kongo State is contacted by the Portuguese 1483		The MPLA is founded in Luanda 1956	The national war of liberation begins 1961	Angolan independence from Portugal 1975			

1980s

President dos Santos assumes emergency powers; South African air and ground incursions into Angola	Savimbi visits the United States; U.S. "material and moral" support for UNITA resumes	Massive losses on the battlefield speed peace negotiations

promising. All earnings are below pre-independence levels. Prices for diamonds, Angola's second major mineral enterprise, have declined; and production of coffee, the major cash crop, has been drastically reduced, as many coffee plantations are untended. Industrial production has also dropped since independence, in part because of the departure of Portuguese residents, many of whom had technical skills. Now only about 10,000 Portuguese remain as Angolan citizens. Railroads, such as the independently owned Benguela line, need new engines and are disrupted by UNITA attacks, which sometimes reduce traffic by 90 percent.

Even more serious is the decline in food production. The turmoil of recent years has displaced approximately half a million people. Another 350,000 refugees are in Zaire and Zambia. Farmers have not been able to plant their crops, and harvests have declined. Not only has the government been forced to import 90 percent of Angola's food, but it has had to spend needed foreign exchange to do so. Faced with widespread hunger, appeals for food aid in 1988 netted pledges of $75 million in needed assistance.

President Jose Edouardo dos Santos was given emergency powers to deal with the crisis. The MPLA government has committed itself to productivity and efficiency in the economic sphere, but has been forced to use many of its resources to defend its sovereignty. Oil revenues and massive Soviet aid ($1 billion) have been committed to supporting minimal services and to carrying out the war. In general,

despite the attention given to the Cuban presence in the country, Angola has shown a nonaligned approach in its world trading relations and in its acceptance of advisors—depending on partners as varied as Brazil, Japan, Portugal, the Soviet Union, and Cuba. Four-fifths of Angola's trade is with the West. Western bankers and businessmen have found that Angola is a reliable partner that pays its bills on time and honors its contracts. The government has tried to avoid borrowing, and this has kept the country out of debt. However, Angola has not been able to avoid the repercussions of the recent world recession, and austerity measures are in effect.

CONCLUSION

Angola's hardships will be lessened when the negotiations over Namibia are completed and that country moves to independence. The United States and South Africa have linked movement toward Namibian independence to the withdrawal of the approximately 40,000 Cuban troops currently in Angola. However, Angola and Cuba have agreed that the troops should stay until South Africa withdraws from Namibia and Angolan sovereignty is secure. Escalation of the fighting in 1987 and 1988 led to a revival of negotiations for a peace settlement between South Africa and Angola and a plan for independence for Namibia. In 1988 representatives of Angola, Cuba, South Africa, and the United States conducted negotiations to begin withdrawal of troops from Angola and to implement United Nations Resolution 435 for Namibian independence.

In fierce battles in the spring of 1988, especially around the garrison town of Cuito Cuanavale, Cuban troops entered the fighting directly, a first since 1976. In response to a South African invasion assisted by UNITA troops, Cuban troops helped well-trained Angolan government forces to prevent a South African victory. Although the battle appeared to be a stalemate, South African losses, especially among whites, created controversy and resistance at home. Several hundred black South African troops refused to serve in Angola, and white conscripts publicly defied the draft.

In 1988 South Africa began withdrawal of its troops from Angola and agreed to begin implementation of the UN plan, to coincide with Namibian elections in 1989. The pace of the Cuban withdrawal remained a sticking point, but all parties to the negotiations continued to meet.

"No one can stop the rain," wrote Angola's first president Augustino Neto in one of the poems he composed in jail in 1960. Tired of warfare, yet skeptical of the prospects for peace, Angolans look toward a day when their vast resources can be used for development, not war.

DEVELOPMENT

The tiny enclave of Cabinda, separated from Angola by a 25-mile strip of land, is home to about 85,000 people. Gulf Oil Corporation pumps thousands of barrels of oil daily from its offshore fields, with royalties paid to the government in Luanda. Government and Cuban troops maintain garrisons to protect residents and the oil facilities.

FREEDOM

The MPLA party organs direct activities in Angola, but there have been efforts to increase popular political participation in recent years. Spies and supporters of opposition groups have been convicted by military courts, and some opponents are detained without trial.

HEALTH/WELFARE

Chaos and uncertainty in areas of conflict have reduced prospects for health care. Thousands of displaced persons are unable to farm, creating hunger and destroying services. Civilians, especially children, have suffered greatly. Angola, along with Mozambique, has the world's highest number of orphans and amputees.

ACHIEVEMENTS

Despite the current turmoil, Angola has been able to improve its educational system. Eighty-two percent of the primary-school-age population are enrolled in school, and basic literacy programs have been expanded. Important educational programs exist at SWAPO refugee camps in the south.

Botswana (Republic of Botswana)

GEOGRAPHY

Area in Square Kilometers (Miles): 600,372 (231,804) (about the size of Texas)
Capital (Population): Gaborone (96,000)
Climate: arid; semiarid

PEOPLE

Population
Total: 1,220,000
Annual Growth Rate: 3.3%
Rural/Urban Population Ratio: 79/21
Languages: official: Setswana, English; other spoken: Khoisan

Health
Life Expectancy at Birth: 63 years
Infant Death Rate (Ratio): 63/1,000
Average Caloric Intake: 90% of FAO minimum
Physicians Available (Ratio): 1/6,780

Religion(s)
85% traditional indigenous; 15% Christian

Education
Adult Literacy Rate: 71%

THE KGOTLA

By tradition, all political and judicial decision making within a Tswana community has to be aired in an open public forum known as the *kgotla*. This institution, somewhat analogous to the proverbial New England town meeting, has long served as a foundation of Tswana democratic ideals, as expressed in this common axiom: "A chief is a chief by the people." Politicians running for office in Botswana today know that they must visit and speak with kgotlas in their areas. There are uban counterparts to the traditional kgotla. "Freedom squares" are locations in Botswana's urban areas where various party candidates speak out on issues to crowds of onlookers. This heritage of debate and democracy may explain the strength and success of Botswana as a functioning parliamentary democracy.

COMMUNICATION

Telephones: 11,700
Newspapers: 3

TRANSPORTATION

Highways—Kilometers (Miles): 10,784 (6,701)
Railroads—Kilometers (Miles): 726 (451)
Commercial Airports: 3 international

GOVERNMENT

Type: parliamentary republic
Independence Date: September 30, 1966
Head of State: President Quett K.J. Masire
Political Parties: Botswana Democratic Party; Botswana National Front; Botswana People's Party; Botswana Independence Party
Suffrage: universal over 21

MILITARY

Number of Armed Forces: 3,260
Military Expenditures (% of Central Government Expenditures): $28,700,000 (1.8%)
Current Hostilities: attacks by South Africa

ECONOMY

Currency ($ U.S. Equivalent): 0.40 pulas = $1
Per Capita Income/GNP: $920/$900 million
Inflation Rate: 10%
Natural Resources: diamonds; copper; nickel; salt; soda ash; potash; coal
Agriculture: livestock; sorghum; corn; millet; cowpeas; beans
Industry: diamonds; copper; nickel; salt; soda ash; potash; frozen beef; tourism

FOREIGN TRADE

Exports: $653 million
Imports: $535 million

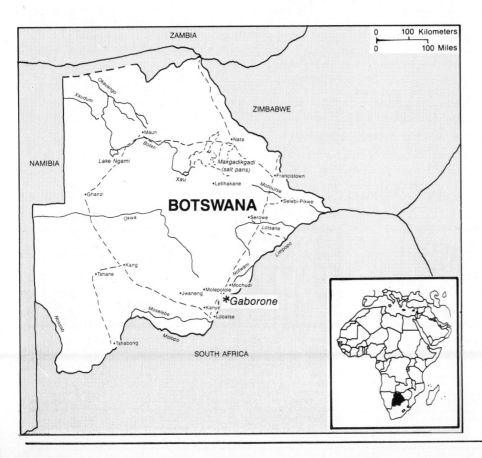

Tswana establish themselves in Southern Africa 1400s	Invading groups of Nguni and Southern Sotho threaten the Tswana 1820s	Afrikaners begin to encroach on Tswana land north of the Orange River 1839	The British establish colonial rule over Botswana 1885	Botswana gains independence 1966

1980s

Seretse Khama, the nation's first president, dies in office	General elections in which the Botswana Democratic Party wins a large majority	South African raids kill Botswana citizens and South African exiles; tough new security laws are passed

THE REPUBLIC OF BOTSWANA

Botswana, an arid country about the size of Texas, has been the Cinderella story of postcolonial Africa. The country emerged from 80 years of not-so-benign British colonial neglect in 1966 as a drought-stricken, underdeveloped backwater with a per capita income of only $69. In the 2 decades since this less-than-auspicious beginning, however, the nation's economy has grown at an annual rate averaging 13 percent, one of the world's highest. Social services have gradually been expanded, and Botswana's success has gradually been translated into a better standard of living for the majority of its population. Yet the country also remains vulnerable to the uncertainties of international markets, the problems of weather, and the designs of its powerful neighbor, South Africa.

Most of Botswana's citizens are Tswana, a group that is also represented in the population of South Africa. A number of minority groups also exists, but there has been relatively little ethnic conflict during contemporary times. A notable characteristic of the Tswana is their historic preference for living in large settlements with populations of 10,000 or more. In the past these communities centered around crops, cattle, and trade. A radical transformation took place in the late nineteenth century, when colonial taxes and economic decline stimulated the growth of migrant labor to the mines and industries of South Africa. In many regions, migrant earnings remain the major source of income.

DEVASTATING DROUGHT

The standard Tswana greeting, "*pula*" ("rain"), reflects the traditional significance attached to water in a society prone to its periodic scarcity. The country suffered severe drought in the mid-1980s, which—despite the availability of underground water supplies—had a devastating effect on both crops and livestock. Small-scale agropastoralists were particularly hard-hit.

The cattle industry is an important part of the economy, dominating the agricultural sector. The Lobatse slaughterhouse, which opened in 1954, stimulated the growth of the cattle industry. An outbreak of foot and mouth disease in the late 1970s led to a marketing decline, and revived production was threatened by the 1980s drought. Botswana's cattle population declined during that time from 3 million to 2 million.

Mining is the most important aspect of the economy. Since independence the rapid expansion of local mining activity has fostered Botswana's internal growth. The dominance of South African capital in most new enterprises has caused concern, but the Botswana government has a good record of maximizing its share of benefits. The Selebi-Pikwe nickel/copper mine is the nation's largest employer and accounts for roughly 25 percent of the country's export earnings.

THE SOUTH AFRICA PROBLEM

South Africa remains a lingering problem. For many years, refugees from racist oppression have found a haven in Botswana, but the country has been a target of South Africa's regional destabilization since 1985. South African commandos attacked Gabarone, killing South African refugees and Botswana citizens alike, most recently in 1988. In response, Botswana has tightened security and protested at international forums. A weak neighbor with a small population, Botswana cannot afford sanctions against South Africa, but it has urged other nations to do so. The nation has maintained its principled opposition to apartheid and has been promoting majority rule as a member of the Frontline States, but South African pressure to deny refuge to apartheid foes is likely to continue.

Since independence, Botswana has survived as one of the few multi-party democracies in Africa. The nation's record in human rights is spotless. Its liberal character and ongoing concern for social justice have made Botswana a symbol of peace and progress for people of all races in Southern Africa.

DEVELOPMENT

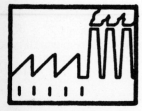

Botswana has used its revenues to improve the lives of its citizens and is an active member of SADCC, recently signing an agreement with Zaire, Zimbabwe, Tanzania, and Mozambique to develop and preserve the 1,400-mile Zambezi River.

FREEDOM

Botswana's reputation for tolerating pluralism has been reinforced by the publication of two privately owned daily newspapers—The Examiner and Botswana Guardian. The government-owned Botswana Daily News continues to air criticisms by opposition groups. Some critics fear that new seccurity laws may be used to stifle dissent.

HEALTH/WELFARE

Most of Botswana's citizens now live within 10 miles of health-care facilities, and there are hundreds of new schools. Many students have been sent abroad for training as health professionals. Efforts are underway to seek better services for the Basarawa, traditionally hunters and gatherers, without destroying their lifestyles and sense of identity.

ACHIEVEMENTS

The Tswana are renowned as innovators. In 1909 one of Africa's first indigenous government-owned corporations was founded in northern Botswana. More recently researchers have succeeded in developing a light, low-cost plow/planter/cultivator that could have a significant impact on peasant farming in Central and Southern Africa.

Lesotho (Kingdom of Lesotho)

GEOGRAPHY

Area in Square Kilometers (Miles):
30,344 (11,716) (about the size of
Maryland)
Capital (Population): Maseru
(80,200)
Climate: temperate

PEOPLE

Population
Total: 1,681,000
Annual Growth Rate: 2.5%
Rural/Urban Population Ratio: 88/12
Languages: official: English, Sesotho;
others spoken: Xhosa, Zulu

Health
Life Expectancy at Birth: 54 years
Infant Death Rate (Ratio): 98/1,000
Average Caloric Intake: 107% of FAO
minimum
Physicians Available (Ratio): 1/12,280

Religion(s)
70% Christian; 30% traditional
indigenous

Education
Adult Literacy Rate: 59%

COMMUNICATION

Telephones: 4,500
Newspapers: 3

THE SESOTHO LANGUAGE

Since the mid-nineteenth century Sesotho has been a leading literary language in Africa. Basotho writers have produced a wealth of prose, poetry, and nonfiction in their vernacular. The *Leselinyane La Lesotho*, first published in 1863, is sub-Saharan Africa's oldest continuous vernacular newspaper. Thomas Mofolo's play *Chaka* and Paulas Mopeli's novel *Blanket Boy* are among the many works that have been translated for international audiences. Sesotho also continues to be a major medium in music, journalism, and broadcasting. The South African government has promoted a separate Sesotho alphabet for use among Sotho peoples living in South Africa; this has created one more barrier for South Africans who have tried to encourage reconvergence among various regional dialects.

TRANSPORTATION

Highways—Kilometers (Miles): 4,033
(2,506)
Railroads—Kilometers (Miles): 1.6
(0.994)
Commercial Airports: 1 international

GOVERNMENT

Type: constitutional monarchy
Independence Date: October 4, 1966
Head of State: King Moshoeshoe II;
Major General Justinus Lekhanya
(prime minister and head of
governing Military Council)
Political Parties: banned in 1986
Suffrage: universal over 21

MILITARY

Number of Armed Forces: 1,500
*Military Expenditures (% of Central
Government Expenditures):* 6.5%
Current Hostilities: none

ECONOMY

Currency ($ U.S. Equivalent): 2.12
malotis = $1
Per Capita Income/GNP: $520/$730
million
Inflation Rate: 17%
Natural Resources: diamonds; water;
agricultural and grazing land
Agriculture: mohair; corn; wheat;
sorghum; peas; beans; potatoes;
asparagus; sheep; cattle
Industry: carpets; woolen apparel;
candle making; pottery; jewelry;
tapestries; tourism; mining

FOREIGN TRADE

Exports: $121 million
Imports: $326 million

133

		The Sotho successfully fight to preserve local autonomy under the British 1870–1881		The elections and Constitution are declared void by Jonathan 1970		The Lesotho Liberation Army begins a sabotage campaign 1979
Lesotho emerges as a leading state in Southern Africa 1820s	Afrikaners annex half of Lesotho 1866		Independence is restored 1966		An uprising against the government fails 1974	1980s

South African raids on Maseru; Lesotho refuses to sign a security agreement with South Africa

A military coup overthrows Jonathan

Amid fears of violence, Pope John Paul II's visit is a disappointment

THE KINGDOM OF LESOTHO

The beauty of its snow-topped mountains has led visitors to proclaim Lesotho the "Switzerland of Africa." Unlike its European namesake, however, this small, independent enclave in the heart of South Africa has recently enjoyed neither peace nor prosperity. Listed by the United Nations as one of the world's least developed countries, each year the lack of opportunity at home causes half of Lesotho's adult males to seek employment in South Africa. Foreign aid and a share of customs collected by South Africa are the next largest sources of revenue. A small-scale local insurgency campaign as well as escalating tensions with South Africa and its homeland client states have added to the burden of chronic underdevelopment.

A HOMOGENEOUS NATION

Lesotho is one of the most ethnically homogeneous nations in Africa; almost all of its citizens are Sotho. The country's emergence and survival were largely the product of the diplomatic and military prowess of its nineteenth-century chiefs, especially the great founder Moshoeshoe. During the 1860s warfare with South African whites led to the loss of land and people, as well as an acceptance of British overrule. For nearly a century the British preserved the country, but they taxed the inhabitants and generally neglected their interests. Consequently, Lesotho remains dependent on its neighbor, South Africa. However, despite South African attempts to incorporate the country politically as well as economically, Lesotho's independence was restored by the British in 1966.

Lesotho's politicians were bitterly divided at independence, and opposition leaders boycotted the ceremony. In 1970 Prime Minister Leabua Jonathan of the ruling National Party nullified an election won by the rival Congress Party, and he suspended the Constitution. A multiparty Interim National Assembly was appointed in 1973 but failed to bring about a reconciliation. Since 1979 there has been an escalating opposition campaign within the country, carried out by the Lesotho Liberation Army (LLA), an armed faction of the Congress Party. The government maintained that this group was aided and abetted by South Africa as part of that country's regional destabilization efforts. Cancellation of planned elections, a South African raid on Maseru, and a South African trade embargo led to a military coup ousting Jonathan in 1986. Major General Justinus Lekhanya became the new prime minister.

Politics in Lesotho are complex. The Roman Catholic Church has put pressure on the government to return to civilian rule, and it is known that some military leaders want to return to the barracks. South Africa prefers a civilian government. Some in the military support the king, who leans toward a more feudal political structure. The African National Congress (ANC) of South Africa, still influential in Lesotho, also appears to support the king.

SOUTH AFRICA'S POWER

While consistent in its opposition to apartheid, the government recognizes the necessity for limited cooperation with South Africa. Producers of wool (the nation's largest export after labor) must rely on South African marketing boards. South African interests are also heavily involved in Lesotho's small tourist and diamond industries. The Lesotho National Development Corporation actively seeks to attract further South African investment. The Highland Water Scheme has great hydroelectric potential for South African industry, creating another reason for South Africa's interest in Lesotho politics.

South Africa has used economic and military pressure on Lesotho. In 1974 oil deliveries were cut back, and 10,000 Sotho migrant workers were fired. In 1982 and 1985 South Africa raided the capital, Maseru, killing Sotho citizens as well as South African refugees. And in 1986 the total South African trade embargo because of Lesotho support for the ANC contributed to the overthrow of Prime Minister Jonathan. Sixty ANC members were expelled after the coup, with South Africa pressing for more expulsions.

In 1988, when armed men captured a busload of pilgrims on their way to see Pope John Paul II, Lesotho looked for help to South African commandos, who attacked the bus, killing the hijackers and one passenger. As long as Lesotho is surrounded by and dependent on an apartheid South Africa, its economic and political freedom will be limited.

DEVELOPMENT

A major governmental priority is the improvement of internal communications. Currently many communities are also accessible via South Africa. An international airport is also being built.

FREEDOM

Since the suspension of the constitution there have been allegations of human-rights abuses and killings, many of which have involved the nation's paramilitary Police Mobile Unit, which has close ties to South Africa. After the 1986 military coup a general amnesty for political prisoners was granted, but political activity has been banned.

HEALTH/WELFARE

With many young men away in the mines of South Africa, much of the resident population relies on subsistence agriculture. Despite efforts to boost production, malnutrition, aggravated by drought, is a serious problem.

ACHIEVEMENTS

Lesotho has long been known for the high quality of its schools, which for more than a century and a half have trained many of the leading citizens of Southern Africa. The national university at Roma was established in 1945 and for a while served as the main campus of the University of Botswana, Lesotho, and Swaziland, until it resumed its autonomous status in 1976.

Malawi (Republic of Malawi)

GEOGRAPHY

Area in Square Kilometers (Miles):
118,484 (45,747) (about the size of
Pennsylvania)
Capital (Population): Lilongwe
(202,000)
Climate: subtropical

PEOPLE

Population
Total: 8,063,000
Annual Growth Rate: 2.6%
Rural/Urban Population Ratio: 88/12
Languages: official: Chichewa,
English; others spoken: Nyanja, Yao,
Sena, Tumbuka, others

Health
Life Expectancy at Birth: 43 years
male; 45 years female
Infant Death Rate (Ratio): 172/1,000
Average Caloric Intake: 97% of FAO
minimum
Physicians Available (Ratio): 1/53,000

Religion(s)
traditional indigenous; Chistian;
Muslim

JOHN CHILEMBWE

In 1915 John Chilembwe of Nyasaland (now Malawi) "struck a blow"
against British colonialism and died in the attempt. Chilembwe was a
Christian minister who had studied in South Africa as well as in the
United States. He had returned home to establish the Providence
Industrial Mission and to build a great church. His feelings against the
British settlers developed from the injustices he had seen: European
takeover of lands for plantations, poor working conditions for laborers,
increased taxation, and, especially, the recruitment of Africans to fight
and die in World War I. He rallied a few followers and planned an
uprising, which led to the deaths of three settlers and imprisonment or
death of the Africans involved or suspected of involvement. Chilembwe
appears to have planned his martyrdom. This uprising was the first
effort in Southern Africa to resist colonialism and yet maintain many of
the aspects of society that had developed from its influence.

Education
Adult Literacy Rate: 25%

COMMUNICATION

Telephones: 28,800
Newspapers: 2

TRANSPORTATION

Highways—Kilometers (Miles): 11,311
(7,028)
Railroads—Kilometers (Miles): 754
(470)
Commercial Airports: 2 international

GOVERNMENT

Type: republic; one-party state
Independence Date: July 6, 1964
Head of State: President-for-Life
H. Kamuzu Banda
Political Parties: Malawi Congress
Party
Suffrage: universal over 21

MILITARY

Number of Armed Forces: 5,000
*Military Expenditures (% of Central
Government Expenditures):* n/a
Current Hostilities: none

ECONOMY

Currency ($ U.S. Equivalent): 2.47
kwachas = $1
Per Capita Income/GNP: $175/$1.1
billion
Inflation Rate: 8.8%
Natural Resources: limestone;
uranium potential
Agriculture: tobacco; tea; sugar;
corn; peanuts
Industry: food; beverages; tobacco;
textiles; footwear

FOREIGN TRADE

Exports: $271 million
Imports: $291 million

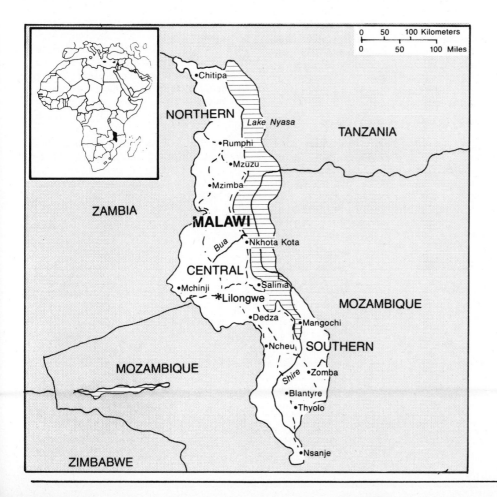

| Malawi trading kingdoms develop **1500s** | Explorer David Livingstone arrives along Lake Malawi; missionaries follow **1859** | The British protectorate of Nyasaland (present-day Malawi) is declared **1891** | Reverend John Chilembwe and followers rise against settlers and are suppressed **1915** | The Nyasaland African Congress, the first nationalist movement, is formed **1944** | Independence under the leadership of Hastings Banda **1964** | Diplomatic ties are established with South Africa **1967** | Banda becomes president-for-life **1971** | **1980s** |

| Austerity budget bans new government development projects; creditors reschedule debts | Death sentences of the Chirwas are commuted to life imprisonment | Support for Renamo declines; influx of Mozambique refugees is accompanied by drought and food shortages |

MALAWI

Malawi is a beautiful country that is little known to outsiders because it rarely appears in the news. Foreign journalists are not often allowed in the country. What little we learn from the media comes from government sources or exiles in opposition. Thus one must construct the reality from opposing images.

President-for-Life Dr. Ngwazi Hastings Kamuzu Banda, now in his eighties, has developed and maintained an unusually tight rein over the government and the nation. Cabinet reshufflings limit the development of possible power bases by rising politicians. Anyone—even Banda's close associates—who receives too much public praise or attention may be suspect, imprisoned, or prone to "accidents." No successor has been designated, and those who are suggested have reason to worry.

DISSIDENT GROUPS

Dissident groups based outside the country began to be formed in 1964—the very year of independence—when six senior ministers were dismissed or resigned after protesting slow Africanization and accommodation to South Africa. Currently there are three liberation groups outside Malawi: the Malawi Freedom Movement (MAFREMO), the Socialist League of Malawi (LESOMA), and the Congress for the Second Republic. Members of these opposition groups are in danger from Banda's regime even when they are in other countries.

The president, while ruthless, has been politically astute and seems to have the respect and support of ordinary citizens. There is no evidence of rebellions, strikes,

or refugee movements to other countries. Government controls are evident. Migration to the cities is restricted, and the government oversees popular groups.

RURAL LIFE

Life seems to have improved for the farmers who make up the majority of Malawi's inhabitants. They have been served by projects initiated and aided by government and by outside agencies. Self-reliance has been encouraged. The country is fortunate to have some of the most fertile soil of the region, but since 1987 drought, growth of cash crops, and over half a million refugees from Mozambique have strained Malawi food supplies.

The country remains very poor, and figures for health care, life expectancy, and infant mortality have not improved. While workers, such as those on the tea plantations, have complained about conditions without achieving any results, some citizens have benefited more than others from the economy. The owners of tea, tobacco, and sugar estates, rather than ordinary farmers, have gained from the influx of aid into the country. Ministers of government and higher civil servants, as well as President Banda, have accumulated wealth and land.

A CONSERVATIVE COURSE

Banda has kept Malawi on a conservative course in its foreign policy. Early in his presidency he established diplomatic relations with South Africa, and he has accepted loans and exchanged visits with South African leaders. Two-thirds of Malawi's exports are sold to South Africa, and one-third of its imports are from that

country. In recent years the country has developed better relations with its neighbors such as Zambia, including full diplomatic relations with Tanzania. In 1986 Renamo raids on Mozambique were initiated from Malawi, but under economic and diplomatic pressure from fellow Southern African Development Coordination Conference (SADCC) members, Malawi flushed Renamo guerrillas from its borders. When Renamo forces entered Mozambique, increased military pressure by Mozambique, Zimbabwe, and Zambian troops led in 1987 and 1988 to a large increase in refugees entering Malawi.

Despite what sources describe as cautious policies and good financial management, Malawi, like many other African nations, has suffered financially from the recent world recession as well as the problems accompanying the rising prices of industrial goods and the declining prices of oil, raw materials, and cash crops.

Both officials and rural peasants have welcomed Mozambican refugees, sharing food and resources, and international agencies have responded with assistance. But until peace comes to the Southern Africa region, Malawi, like its neighbors, will struggle for true economic independence and prosperity.

DEVELOPMENT

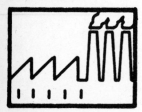

Educational opportunities have increased greatly in recent years, but secondary schools are limited to an elite group. The Kamuzu Academy, which opened in 1981, hires foreign teachers and trains students who will attend universities abroad.

FREEDOM

The climate of suspicion in Malawi resulting from President Banda's fear of opposition has led to arbitrary arrests and numerous detentions without charges. For example, poet Jack Mapanje was arrested without charges in 1987, and his book was banned.

HEALTH/WELFARE

Integrated health, administrative, and agricultural services are being developed in each of four target areas of the country. Malawi still has one of the highest child death rates in the world. More than 50% of children under age 5 are stunted by malnutrition.

ACHIEVEMENTS

To provide piped water to villagers, several thousand miles of pipes were laid from hills to plains, and 4,000 standpipes were installed. A groundwater program will supply 30,000 more Malawians with clean water. In 1987 Malawi won the first prize in the International Year of Shelter for the Homeless.

Mozambique (People's Republic of Mozambique)

GEOGRAPHY
Area in Square Kilometers (Miles):
786,762 (303,769) (about twice the size of California)
Capital (Population): Maputo (886,000)
Climate: tropical to subtropical

PEOPLE
Population
Total: 15,259,000
Annual Growth Rate: 2.7%
Rural/Urban Population Ratio: 91/9
Languages: official: Portuguese; others spoken: Yao, Tubbuka, Batonga, Makua

Health
Life Expectancy at Birth: 47 years
Infant Death Rate (Ratio): 158/1,000
Average Caloric Intake: 78% of FAO minimum
Physicians Available (Ratio): 1/48,028

Religion(s)
65% traditional indigenous; 22% Christian; 11% Muslim; 2% other

Education
Adult Literacy Rate: 38%

COMMUNICATION
Telephones: 51,600
Newspapers: 3

SOUTH AFRICA AND MOZAMBIQUE'S REBELS

The Mozambique National Resistance (MNR), also known as Renamo, was first organized under white Rhodesian auspices in 1975–1976 to prevent Mozambican assistance to the liberation forces in Zimbabwe. When Zimbabwe became independent in 1980, Renamo headquarters was transferred to Transvaal in South Africa.

Renamo targets civilians, rural infrastructure, agriculture, and food convoys. Captured documents and testimony from former members of Renamo indicate long-standing South African support for the Renamo attacks in Mozambique. Although some visible assistance was curtailed after the Nkomati Accords in 1984, South African military personnel, air force supply drops, and, some say, leadership of the movement, have continued. It appears that Renamo leaders are divided over whether to seek more assistance from right-wing groups in the United States and Europe or to keep the South African ties.

TRANSPORTATION
Highways—Kilometers (Miles): 26,498 (16,465)
Railroads—Kilometers (Miles): 3,436 (2,135)
Commercial Airports: 3 international

GOVERNMENT
Type: republic
Independence Date: June 25, 1975
Head of State: President Joaquim Chissano
Political Parties: Mozambique Liberation Front (FRELIMO)
Suffrage: not yet established

MILITARY
Number of Armed Forces: 50,000 (with advisors from Cuba, China, Soviet Union, and East Germany)
Military Expenditures (% of Central Government Expenditures): $157,800,000 (32%)
Current Hostilities: rebel attacks; attacks by South Africa

ECONOMY
Currency ($ U.S. Equivalent): 40.3 meticais = $1
Per Capita Income/GNP: $220/$1.3 billion
Inflation Rate: n/a
Natural Resources: coal; iron ore; tantalite; flourite; timber
Agriculture: cotton; tobacco; cashews; sugar; tea; copra; sisal; subsistence crops
Industry: processed foods; textiles; beverages; refined oil; chemicals; tobacco; cement; glass

FOREIGN TRADE
Exports: $90 million
Imports: $525 million

MOZAMBIQUE

Mozambique is under siege. Ordinary life is difficult—even desperate—for many people in Mozambique today. Extensive drought and other natural disasters have been compounded by years of war. Many people are hungry, must move to survive, are separated from their loved ones, and barter because of lack of money. These circumstances interfere with the new society that Mozambique has been seeking to build since independence.

"Let us make the entire country into a school where everybody learns and everybody teaches." Independent Mozambique has been a country where everyone is encouraged to contribute ideas to the building of the nation. Dynamic democratic responsibility is actively practiced. Not only are leaders elected to their positions, but the people themselves participate in making decisions.

In a small and growing number of communal villages, citizens work together to develop productive communities. Worker councils are found in factories; participatory committees exist in towns. Ordinary people with some training run the 300 people's courts, which make an "offensive for legality," especially in the rural areas. Civilian militias, which include women members, are active throughout the country in defense of their villages. In the schools, students are involved in formal lessons, but they also decide among themselves how they will work collectively to solve some of the very real problems of the community. There is much social pressure, but there is also much enthusiasm throughout the society for learning and teaching.

Mozambique has a Marxist-Leninist socialist government, and the Mozambique Liberation Front (FRELIMO), which has about 100,000 members, is the legal political party. The government controls the press, puts limits on the rights of assembly, and oversees all organizations. Yet ordinary people play an important role in criticizing government policy and making suggestions for future development. More than two-thirds of the party members are workers, peasants, and soldiers. Meetings that Central Committee members hold in the countryside arouse lively criticism and discussion.

Samora Machel became president after independence in 1974, and he was a charismatic leader. He and his administration were responsive to criticism and to the needs of ordinary people. Government was flexible in its policies and was able to recognize mistakes and change course. The people's stores, taken over by the government when the owners fled in 1974, were given back to private ownership because they did not operate effectively. The 1983 party Congress discussed the failings of the state farms and determined that small local communal farming efforts should be stressed in the future. Members agreed to encourage private agricultural enterprise, which had formerly been banned.

Machel and the government also responded quickly to complaints about the brutality of security forces and corruption of bureaucrats. A major "clean-up" campaign took place in 1982 and 1983; police officers and civil servants were brought to trial. In line with Mozambique's "teaching and learning" approach, those accused of brutality and corruption were often sent to isolated "re-education camps" rather than to prison. There was no evidence of a wealthy elite class.

THE PROBLEMS FACING MOZAMBICANS

"In fact we are not a developing country. We are an underdeveloping country. . . . We are getting poorer and poorer each year," stated Minister of Information José Luis Cabaco. Mozambique is very poor, and although the people work together to improve their circumstances, progress is not evident. Mozambique is not naturally wealthy; except for coal, there are no extensive mineral deposits. The predominantly rural population is sparsely distributed. Agriculture is the mainstay of the economy, but at the time of independence less than 10 percent of the arable land was cultivated. Foods and cash crops—including cotton, sugar, tea, and, especially, cashew nuts—have been hard hit by droughts, cyclones, and floods. The state farms lowered, rather than increased, production of crops such as rice and the world recession meant that prices for exports dropped, while prices of imports rose.

Its heritage also holds Mozambique back. The country was under Portuguese rule for more than 400 years, until the revolution of 1974 in Portugal brought freedom to the colonies as well. Despite Portuguese claims that African peoples of its "overseas territories" were given opportunities for advancement, this was not the reality. At the time of independence, only 10 percent of the population could read and write Portuguese or other lan-

The fourth Congress of Mozambique's ruling FRELIMO party moved away from large development projects in favor of smaller projects and grass-roots socialism.

| Portuguese explorers land in Mozambique 1497 | Mozambican laborers begin migrating to South African mines 1800–1890 | FRELIMO liberation movement officially launched 1962 | FRELIMO's leader, Eduardo Mondlane, killed by parcel bomb 1969 | Liberation struggle successful when Portuguese revolution brings independence 1975 |

1980s

South African commando unit attacks Maputo; increased Renamo attacks on civilian and military targets

Machel is killed in an air crash; Chissano becomes president

Mozambique increases diplomatic efforts for peace in the region

guages. The struggle for independence under FRELIMO during the 1960s and early 1970s encouraged unity, but it could not increase the standard of living. After 1974, 250,000 Portuguese residents emigrated, taking their skills and capital with them. Only 10,000 citizens of Mozambique are of Portuguese origin today, and they have the same rights as other citizens. There are Portuguese and Asian Mozambicans among the Cabinet members.

The most significant barrier to progress has been the rural terrorism of the Mozambique National Resistance (MNR). Anywhere from 10,000 to 20,000 Renamo fighters operate in a majority of the provinces. Although these fighters have tried to appeal to traditional beliefs and spirit mediums, they do not have a popular following in Mozambique, and they have no specific plan for improving people's lives. They attack health centers, schools, and rural infrastructures, force young boys to join their ranks, and try to create fear by using torture. Renamo has attacked vital transport links and fuel depots, facilities that serve Malawi and Zimbabwe as well as Mozambique, and has also interfered with famine relief. The economy has been critically affected by the war, with food production devastated and budget priorities focused on defense, and services such as health care and education suffering the most. More than 3 million people were at risk for starvation in 1988. At great risk, peasants walk hours to farm crops during daylight hours, but Renamo attacks on civilians and farms drive many into exile.

A severe challenge was the death of

President Samora Machel in a mysterious plane crash in 1986. More than 30 aides and Cabinet ministers also died in the crash. Mozambicans held South Africa responsible and closed ranks with their leaders around their new president, former Foreign Minister Joaquim Chissano. Chissano has continued the policies of his predecessor, defending Mozambique from Renamo attacks and seeking regional solutions to Mozambique's problems.

REGIONAL STRATEGIES

In 1984 Mozambique signed a nonaggression pact with South Africa, a state with which it has had hostile relations. In this pact, South Africa agreed to stop support for Renamo, and Mozambique agreed to prohibit African National Congress (ANC) bases that would have taken action against South Africa. The ANC, while maintaining activity in South Africa itself, has been limited in Mozambique. Few members were allowed to stay, despite Mozambique's continuing diplomatic and moral support for the liberation struggle.

Even though Chissano met with South Africa's President Botha in 1988 to press for South Africa to withdraw its support for Renamo, warfare continued and even escalated. Renamo attacks have reached into the capital of Maputo, and 15,000 Zimbabwean soldiers assist Mozambicans in capturing rebel bases and guarding rail links to the coast. Studies estimate that more than 100,000 civilians have been killed by Renamo attacks, while 2 million to 3 million people are displaced within Mozambique and more than 1 million have fled to Malawi and Zimbabwe.

With limited Western assistance and the

Zimbabwe soldiers, security in the north improved somewhat in 1988, enabling 47,000 people to return to their lands. Wherever Mozambicans have returned to their villages, they have begun farming and rebuilt schools and clinics, determined to survive.

The major change in Mozambique's foreign relations—besides the ambiguous relationship with South Africe—is its relationship with the United States. Despite pressure from right-wing groups, the U.S. government lifted its ban on direct economic aid to Mozambique, appointed a new ambassador, and condemned Renamo attacks on civilians. Mozambique is seeking Western investment and has instituted economic measures to comply with International Monetary Fund and World Bank loan conditions.

CONCLUSION

Since 1984 Mozambique has sought to maintain a real independence. Recent events—such as famine, the attacks of Renamo, the Nkomati Accords, and the death of Machel—have restrained and influenced the country's actions. As noted in many tributes to the late Samora Machel, the popular expression of the liberation struggle is still applicable: *A Luta Continua* ("The Struggle Continues").

DEVELOPMENT

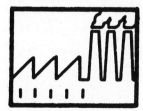

To maintain minimum services and recover from wartime destruction, Mozambique relies on the commitment of its citizens and international assistance. Mozambique works with relief agencies to keep food supplies moving and to rebuild agriculture and health services.

FREEDOM

Mozambique established campaigns against abuses by the security forces and against corruption, as a response to popular complaints. Chissano offered an amnesty to Renamo rebels in 1987 urging them to rejoin Mozambican society.

HEALTH/WELFARE

Medical care for everyone has been a government priority. The immunization campaign that vaccinated 95% of Mozambicans against measles, tuberculosis, tetanus, and smallpox has begun to have positive results. Civil strife and attacks on health services and food shortages have drastically curtailed health-care goals.

ACHIEVEMENTS

Women have played an increasingly important role in the government and economy of Mozambique. One hundred and five of the 667 members of the Fourth Annual Congress in 1983 were women. The Organization of Mozambican Women has had a major influence in bettering women's conditions.

Namibia

GEOGRAPHY

Area in Square Kilometers (Miles): 824,292 (318,261) (slightly smaller than Texas and Oklahoma combined)
Capital (Population): Windhoek (110,600)
Climate: arid; semiarid

PEOPLE

Population
Total: 1,184,000
Annual Growth Rate: 2.7%
Rural/Urban Population Ratio: n/a
Languages: official: English, Afrikaans; others spoken: Ouambo, Kavango, Nama/Damara, Herero, Khoisan, German

Health
Life Expectancy at Birth: 41 years
Infant Death Rate (Ratio): 120/1,000
Average Caloric Intake: n/a
Physicians Available (Ratio): 1/4,736

Religion(s)
more than 50% traditional indigenous; less than 50% Christian

Education
Adult Literacy Rate: 99% whites; 28% others

"APPROACHING INDEPENDENCE?"

Many Namibians and others in the region are cautiously optimistic that independence may soon become a reality. Successes on the battlefield and diplomatic negotiations accelerated movement toward independence in 1988. SWAPO victories and South African losses in Angola and Namibia led to increased costs, both financially and in human lives, especially among white soldiers. Both black and white soldiers have refused to fight in Angola and Namibia, raising the political costs to South Africa. More than 70,000 Namibian students carried out a boycott of classes for 4 months in 1988, with the support of their parents, mine workers, and churches. They demanded the removal of military bases from the vicinity of schools, the end of attacks on students, and elimination of apartheid education. Students then fled by the thousands across the border to Angola. After many meetings, representatives of the United States, Cuba, Angola, and South Africa agreed to a troop withdrawal and UN-supervised elections during 1989. Differences remained over the timing and numbers of Cuban troop withdrawals from Angola, a condition insisted upon by South Africa and the United States.

COMMUNICATION

Telephones: 69,300
Newspapers: 3

TRANSPORTATION

Highways—Kilometers (Miles): 54,500 (33,866)
Railroads—Kilometers (Miles): 2,340 (1,454)
Commercial Airports: 4 international

GOVERNMENT

Type: under South African administration
Independence Date: none
Head of State: Pieter Botha (president of South Africa); Louis Pievaar (administrator-general)
Political Parties: Action Front for the Preservation of the Turnhalle Principles; Federal Party; Democratic Turnhalle Alliance; South West Africa People's Organization; United Democratic Party
Suffrage: universal within ethnically based governments

MILITARY

Number of Armed Forces: 50,000 South African and South African-trained troops
Military Expenditures (% of Central Government Expenditures): n/a
Current Hostilities: internal conflicts with African liberation groups such as SWAPO, which fields 6,000–8,000 forces

ECONOMY

Currency ($ U.S. Equivalent): 2.24 South African rands = $1
Per Capita Income/GNP: $789/$860 million
Inflation Rate: 16%
Natural Resources: diamonds; copper; lead; zinc; uranium; silver; cadmium; lithium; coal; possible oil reserves; fish
Agriculture: corn; millet; sorghum; livestock
Industry: meat canning; dairy products; leather tanning; textiles; clothing; mineral concentrates

FOREIGN TRADE

Exports: $462 million
Imports: $488 million

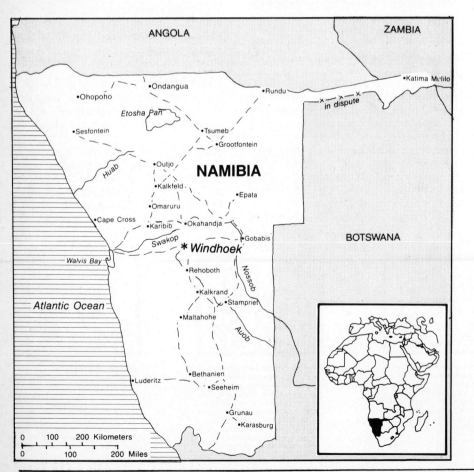

Germany is given rights to colonize Namibia at the Conference of Berlin 1884–1885	Herero, Nama, and Damara rebellions against German rule 1904–1907	South Africa assumes League of Nations mandate 1920	The UN General Assembly revokes the South African mandate; SWAPO begins war for independence 1966	Bantustans, or "homelands," created by South Africa 1968	A massive strike paralyzes the economy 1971	The Western Five contact group is formed to negotiate for South African withdrawal from Namibia 1977	An internal government is formed by South Africa 1978

1980s

The first SWAPO rally in Namibia in 5 years attracts 13,000 people

Mineworkers strike in support of student boycotts to demand an end to war and removal of South African bases

Negotiations for independence accelerate and move forward, under UN auspices

NAMIBIA

This sparsely populated and arid country is a focal point of current political strife in Southern Africa. Its people, numbering about 1.1 million, half belonging to one of the Ovambo ethnic groups, are dominated by a minority of 75,000 whites (mostly Afrikaners and Germans) through policies of *apartheid* (separateness) which are implemented by South Africa. Such domination is currently being challenged by the South West Africa People's Organization (SWAPO), which is waging a war of independence against the South African occupation of the country.

Early travelers' accounts show regular trade between the various ethnic groups. From the late 1700s onward the country was strongly influenced by South Africa—first through market demands, and later by direct South African control. The expanding Cape Colony of South Africa initially siphoned off many traditional forms of wealth, such as cattle, to the growing economies of Europe, and created a demand for new goods, such as ostrich feathers and ivory.

Namibia was officially a German colony from 1884 to 1919. During this time land began to be taken from Namibians for use by white settlers. In response to this, there were a number of uprisings against colonial authority, and these culminated in the Herero and Nama War of 1904–1907. The response by the German Colonial Office was devastating. An expeditionary force sent to suppress the rebellion caused the deaths of 70 percent (92,258) of the Herero, Damara, and Nama peoples.

At the end of World War I the colony was mandated to South Africa by the League of Nations as a trust territory. South Africa violated the terms of the mandate by introducing apartheid and by developing the economy for its own benefit. The battle was joined by the United Nations, when, at its inception, it took over administration of League of Nations mandates. In 1966 the UN revoked South Africa's mandate, making continued South African presence in Namibia illegal. UN diplomatic efforts aimed at ending South African occupation and bringing about independence, but Western support of South Africa impeded progress.

At present the country is embroiled in a war of liberation against South Africa, led by SWAPO. This organization has sought an end to South African rule of Namibia and to apartheid. At first its tactics were peaceful, consisting of protests and appeals to local authorities, foreign governments, and the UN. But in 1959 police opened fire on members of a peaceful crowd gathered to protest their forced removal to a new ghetto. Thirteen persons died, and 53 were wounded. In response SWAPO made plans for a guerrilla war, which it initiated in 1966. Over the years the stakes—in terms of numbers of troops and sophistication of equipment—have steadily increased on both sides, with South Africa escalating from armed police to an army of occupation, sometimes 70,000 strong.

To maintain its hold on Namibia, South Africa has employed a variety of tactics, both internally and internationally. Since 1975 South Africa has arranged political conferences, based on representation of race and ethnicity, to create internal change. Because SWAPO rejects representation along ethnic lines, it refused to participate. In 1985 a "new" transitional government was formed, which was also rejected as a puppet government by SWAPO, Namibian nationalists, and most church groups. They demand the implementation of UN Resolution 435, which calls for withdrawal of South African troops, internationally supervised elections, and independence. West Germany, France, the United Kingdom, Canada, and the United States (called the Western Five contact group) negotiated unsuccessfully for South African withdrawal from Namibia.

War weary, South Africa, Angola, Cuba, and the United States began negotiations for independence in 1988. As Cuban troops engaged South African soldiers in southern Angola, and SWAPO and Angolan troops improved their skills in 1987–1988, South African casualties mounted; the South Africans were forced to withdraw to Namibian bases. Many black South African and Namibian conscripts refused to fight, and white deaths began to create opposition within South Africa. Cautiously optimistic, Namibians saw South African troops begin their withdrawal in 1988, with the UN independence plan scheduled to begin in 1989.

DEVELOPMENT

Namibia's mineral wealth is concentrated in the hands of whites, both South African and European. The war cost of $400 million per year and apartheid policies have meant that little is spent on services to benefit the majority of Namibians. Namibia's current $750 million debt may be another reason for South African willingness to cut ties to Namibia.

FREEDOM

Political opponents are detained and tortured and have no rights, and church and newspaper offices have been burned and bombed. Since 1986 South African atrocities aimed at civilians have increased, including gruesome torture and harassment.

HEALTH/WELFARE

Unemployment among blacks has always been high. A severe drought in the 1980s decimated what little agricultural output blacks could produce. Poverty and malnutrition are extremely widespread, and educational expenditures are racially skewed, with white children receiving 4 times as much as black children. SWAPO training camps in Angola educate thousands of exiled children.

ACHIEVEMENTS

Namibian churches, unions, and students have been united in recent years in their support for the independence struggle and their demands for an end to South African occupation and the war against the Namibian people.

South Africa (Republic of South Africa)

GEOGRAPHY
Area in Square Kilometers (Miles):
1,222,480 (437,872) (about twice the
size of Texas)
Capital (Population): Pretoria
(administrative) (822,000); Cape
Town (legislative) (1,900,000);
Bloemfontein (judicial) (231,000)
Climate: temperate; semiarid; arid

PEOPLE
Population
Total: 35,625,000
Annual Growth Rate: 2.9%
Rural/Urban Population Ratio: 45/55
Languages: official: Afrikaans,
English; others spoken: Xhosa, Zulu,
Sesotho, Tswana, other Bantu
languages

Health
Life Expectancy at Birth: 63 years*
Infant Death Rate (Ratio): blacks
94/1,000; whites 14.9/1,000
Average Caloric Intake: 116% of FAO
minimum*
Physicians Available (Ratio): 1/1,583*

Religion(s)
81% Christian; 19% Hindu and
Muslim

Education
Adult Literacy Rate: blacks 50%;
whites 99%

THE AFRICAN NATIONAL CONGRESS

The African National Congress (ANC) was founded in 1912, in response
to the taking of land from Africans and the introduction of "pass laws"
controlling their employment and movement. For 50 years members
carried on peaceful resistance to apartheid by organizing protest
marches, supporting workers' demands and strike actions, and creating
independent schools and services. ANC goals are expressed in the
Freedom Charter, which states that "South Africa belongs to all who
live in it, black and white . . ." and calls for "one man, one vote" and
the abolition of the color bar. These beliefs caused the arrest of
thousands and the trial of ANC leaders for treason. When the ANC was
banned and Nelson Mandela, Walter Sisulu, and others were sentenced
to life imprisonment, the ANC went underground in the 1960s, planning
sabotage against military and political targets and organizing resistance.
The ANC and Nelson Mandela, its leader, gained supporters and stature
as South African repression escalated during the 1980s.

COMMUNICATION
Telephones: 2,750,000
Newspapers: 23

TRANSPORTATION
Highways—Kilometers (Miles):
229,090 (142,356)
Railroads—Kilometers (Miles): 35,434
(22,018)
Commercial Airports: 3 international

GOVERNMENT
Type: republic
Independence Date: May 31, 1910
Head of State: President Pieter W.
Botha
Political Parties: National Party;
Progressive Federal Party; New
Republic Party; Conservative Party;
Labour Party; Afrikaans Weerstand
Beweging; Cape Democrats
Suffrage: whites; Asians and
Coloureds over 18 vote only for
chambers which have no power;
blacks (72% of the population) have
no vote

MILITARY
Number of Armed Forces: 106,000
standing; 320,000 ready reserves;
150,000 paramilitary commando
volunteers; 60,000 police; ANC has
an estimated 10,000 trained guerrillas
*Military Expenditures (% of Central
Government Expenditures):*
$2,900,000 (3.7%)
Current Hostilities: civil war with
African nationalists in South Africa
and Namibia

ECONOMY
Currency ($ U.S. Equivalent): 2.24
rands = $1
Per Capita Income/GNP:
$4,000*/$112 billion
Inflation Rate: 12.3%
Natural Resources: gold; diamonds;
mineral ores; uranium; fish
Agriculture: corn; wool; wheat;
surgarcane; tobacco; citrus fruits
Industry: mining; automobile
assembly; metal working; machinery;
textiles; iron and steel; chemicals

FOREIGN TRADE
Exports: $18.4 billion
Imports: $15.3 billion

*Figures for blacks and whites, when
separated, vary greatly.

SOUTH AFRICA

South Africa is one country, but two worlds. One, the minority white world, is affluent, healthy, well educated, and in charge. The nonwhite world is poor, malnourished, poorly educated, and controlled. The minority white government of South Africa, following a policy of *apartheid* (separateness), maintains the division of these two worlds while exerting control over the nonwhite world. In the workplace, the marketplace, the street, and other places where people meet, whites can always dominate.

THE SYSTEM OF APARTHEID

The system of apartheid in South Africa has a long history. The laws implementing the separation of whites and nonwhites began after the Nationalist Party came to power in 1948, but the system of apartheid was built on early-twentieth-century events and laws. Some claim that racial discrimination started as far back as 1652, when the first Dutch settlers came to the Cape. A few of the keystones of the system include racial classification, the establishment of *bantustans* ("homelands"), the restrictions of the Group Areas Act, job classification, a pass system, and a vast array of security legislation, which is backed up by force.

In South Africa, every citizen is classified according to race. The arbitrary divisions set up by the Race Classification Act are: White, Coloured, Asian, and Bantu. Only about 17 percent of the population are whites; the Coloured are of mixed races. The Asians, the smallest group, number approximately 800,000 and are descendants of the Indian people who first came to South Africa in 1860. The vast majority of South Africans are classified as Bantu-speaking Africans; they belong to many different groups, including the Tswana, Sotho, Zulu, and Xhosa.

Today in South Africa this classification by race determines every aspect of one's life from birth to death. Thousands of laws determine the limits of achievement and action if one is not white.

Apartheid, or separate development, means more than different laws for different "races." No black is considered a citizen of South Africa, and no black can vote for the South African government. Every black person is supposed to be a citizen of his or her "nation." Asians and Coloureds who have no homelands in South Africa have limited rights in South Africa. A set of 10 bantustans have been devised for the African majority. Supposedly, these homelands are built around some of the areas where different peoples have historically lived. Only 13 percent of the land of South Africa, however, has

been allocated to these homelands, where 70 percent of the people are expected to live. Most of the land is poor, eroded, and far from industry and resources. These reserves provide a pool of cheap labor for the South African system. Many of the residents must leave to work in the mines, farms, and factories of South Africa.

Every black person is considered a citizen of a homeland, and the South African government intends that all homelands should become independent. Some of the bantustans have already received supposed independence. Transkei, Ciskei, Venda, and Bophuthatswana, for example, have elected black governments and have developed their own budgets and their own laws. Yet their independence is a facade covering both continuing South African influence and the continuing dependence of these underdeveloped areas on South Africa. No outside country has recognized their independence.

Meanwhile almost half of the Africans

who are considered citizens of these homelands live in the "white" areas of the country, and the white areas have been isolated from the poverty, repression, and increasing unrest in the black townships. Although the government does its best to restrict press coverage of this unrest, since 1985 it has become harder to deny black resistance. Whites feel threatened by the general international hostility against South Africa and consider themselves beleaguered by its hostile neighbors. South African whites generally believe that military action against these neighbors is acceptable and will be successful. (As more whites saw action in the townships and on South Africa's borders, however, and as the white death toll rose in the late 1980s, white conscripts increasingly refused military service. Some were sentenced to the maximum of 6 years in prison for their refusal.)

Africans have a very different view. The changes that whites call "reforms"

(United Nations photo)

The system of apartheid makes it impossible for most black South Africans to share in South Africa's economic prosperity.

are seen by blacks as cosmetic and insignificant. Blacks believe that all so-called progress has been backward rather than forward, and many feel trapped in a prison where whites hold the keys. They are "dying by installments," as one person put it. They see little opportunity to control their own lives, and many believe that violence is the answer.

Until recently, black South Africans had to carry passes that included their work permits (wives and children come to cities illegally to be with the working men, whom they might otherwise see for only a few weeks a year). Each year several hundred thousand people were apprehended for pass-law violations, and most were shipped back to the homelands. The government abolished the pass laws in 1986, but identity cards will be issued for all, and "influx control" will continue.

A large number of Africans (25 percent) have the "right" through employment, marriage, or birth to be in urban areas or "white" South Africa. All must have jobs. These blacks, as well as Coloured and Asian people, are restricted as to where they can live by the Group Areas Act. In this program, "racial reshuffling" occurs as the increased demand by all groups for housing leads to the reclassification of different sections of cities, and as historically legal black settlements—"black spots"—are removed from the countryside. Squatter settlements, which spring up outside cities such as Pretoria and Cape Town, include "legal" residents for whom no "legal" housing is available, as well as "illegal" men, women, and children who can be shipped back home. An estimated 3.5 million "illegal" persons have been resettled in camps in or on the borders of the homelands, in conditions similar to or worse than those of least developed countries all over the world.

The sophisticated and advanced economy of South Africa—built on the mining of gold (the major export product), diamonds, and other raw materials—is dependent on black labor. Yet black workers in the vast array of industries and mines are legally restricted in the jobs that they can hold; and even with recent advances, the pay that they receive is far less than that of white workers. Foreign companies, including many from the United States, have profited from this unequal treatment—even though such discrimination may be against the law in their own countries. Employers readily admit that white South Africa cannot maintain its industrial development without the labor force from Transkei and other bantustans. There is a scarcity of skilled labor in modern South Africa, which authorities try to solve through the encouragement of white immigration rather than through the training of black South Africans.

(United Nations photo)

Women chop wood in Transkei, one of the so-called black homelands in South Africa. The UN General Assembly has condemned the creation of such areas, asserting that they are a means of perpetuating apartheid.

IS THE SYSTEM CHANGING?

During 1982–1983 there was much publicity and some optimism expressed about possible changes in the apartheid system. Yet the moves to liberalize the system were limited and have since been accompanied by ever-increasing control, development of power by the government, and severe repression against all critics.

A bill passed in the white Parliament in 1983 and approved by the white electorate brought Asian and Coloured representatives into the South African government, but only in their own separate chambers. The bill also gave increased powers to the president, who is the head of state under the revised government. Significantly, the proposed government system completely excluded blacks and was designed to divide the majority by offering limited political participation to Asians and Coloureds. Although the Coloured Labor Party accepted the proposed measure, many Coloureds and Asians were deeply opposed and organized with blacks against it.

White unity is still strong, but it is becoming fragmented. White South African society is very complex. Many right-wing whites are also deeply opposed to reforms, which they believe will "open the flood gates" for change. A Conservative Party has been formed by those who have broken with the Nationalists over this issue, and right-wing ideologues, with Nazi sympathies, formed the Afrikaner Resistance Movement. In their virulent opposition to perceived reforms, they have challenged the Nationalist Party and broken up its rallies. Meanwhile, the white Progressive Federal Party (PFP), which is opposed to apartheid policies, remains a tiny minority. Several PFP leaders resigned from Parliament in 1986, stating that their roles there could no longer contribute to change. They are working among whites to build support for a postapartheid society. A new party, the Cape Democrats, composed of whites opposed to apartheid, was formed in 1988.

The Nationalist Party hoped to gain support for its policies with a good showing in the October 1988 elections. The Conservative Party, however, gained seats; and among blacks, pressured to turn out to vote for segregated local elections, the turnout was abysmally low.

Other moves of the government have done away with "petty" apartheid regulations in South Africa without disturbing the major outlines of apartheid. Signs announcing separate facilities have been taken down at telephones, park benches, and rest rooms. The Hilton Hotel is now open to anyone who can afford it. Unequal income-tax regulations have been abolished; blacks no longer pay more taxes than do whites.

Yet such changes are cosmetic while the reality of apartheid policies continue. Thus, the courts say that people cannot be moved from residences in the wrong area unless alternative housing exists—but this alternative housing may be like the township for Cape Town workers, which will require a 40-mile commute to work. The government has allocated money for black education, but schooling remains segregated, and the funds for educating whites are nearly 9 times larger than those made available for blacks.

There have been changes for black workers, but increased repression in the late 1980s may turn back gains. Job reservation laws were eliminated for most blue-collar workers, and many skilled jobs are now held by blacks in industries other than mining. In 1979 black unions in industries became legal, and miners were allowed to form unions as well; and in 1982 the government declared that such unions need not register with the government. There are now about 1 million workers in the nonracial independent unions, and more join each year. Hundreds of strikes have occurred yearly, with union leaders negotiating with management for modest wage increases. Thirty-four unions joined together in 1985 to form the Congress of South African Trade Unions (COSATU), to increase labor's influence within South Africa. Labor has taken an increasingly significant role in the struggle for workers' rights, and in the broader fight to end apartheid.

This active role has gained wages and concessions from owners, following large strikes in 1987 and 1988, but has also angered the government. Some COSATU leaders have been detained or killed. Their activities have been restricted and their offices bombed in efforts to counteract their growing influence among workers and political activists, and restrictive labor legislation proposed in 1988 would take back many of the gains made in the 1980s. Both the move toward reform and the increasingly violent repression have led to increased actions by blacks and to a broader resistance against the government.

BLACK INDEPENDENT ACTION AND RESISTANCE

The opportunities for independent action for blacks in South Africa are limited, but repression and despair have brought increased opposition to apartheid, at the risk of death. Although protests against the system of apartheid have as long a history as the system itself, organizations and avenues of protest have been closed off. During the 1950s many organizations—including the African National Congress (ANC), founded in 1912—joined in nonviolent protests against the system, but their positive achievements, such as the development of the influential Freedom Charter and the widespread acceptance of its goals, did not change apartheid.

The year 1960 was a crucial one for protesters. Police fired at participants in a peaceful demonstration at Sharpeville, and more than 60 persons were killed. The government assumed emergency powers, banned the ANC as well as the more recently formed Pan African Congress (PAC), and made even mild protests difficult. The Black Consciousness Movement, which developed during the early 1970s, led by Steve Biko, aroused the black youth of South Africa. But after student riots in Soweto (a Johannesburg suburb) the government suppressed the movement, and Biko was killed while in jail. Many young people fled South Africa, and a new generation of resistance began.

Youths and their supporters were radicalized by the events of the late 1970s, resulting in the rebellion and violence of the 1980s. The Azanian People's Organization (AZAPO) was revitalized by leaders released from prison or who returned from being banned. AZAPO is allowed to exist, but the organization is as closely watched as other possible arenas of African resistance. Another organization is *Inkatha*, a movement started by Zulu Chief Gatsha Buthelezi, who maintains a dialogue with the white government.

New and lively local newspapers in black communities have provided a focus for community and union publicity. Yet it is difficult for them to survive. The major commercial black newspapers, the *Mail* and the *Sunday Mail*, were banned in 1981 and forced out of business. There are more than 100 laws with which newspapers must comply, dealing with how the news is to be reported, and by whom. Violating these laws can bring about a newspaper's demise. As opposition to the government escalates, press restrictions increase. Now no reports of events are allowed unless they are approved by the government; no reports of violence in the townships may be described or shown. Newspapers that present any views contrary to the government can be suspended or banned without legal recourse. Journalists and editors, such as *New Nation*'s Zwelake Sisulu, have been imprisoned without charges.

Churches have been centers of black initiative and independence for many

Migration of Bantu speakers into Southern Africa 1000–1500	The first settlement of Dutch people in the Cape of Good Hope area 1652	The British gain possession of the Cape Colony 1815	Shaka develops the Zulu nation and sets in motion the wars and migrations known as the Mfecane 1820s

years. These churches have included not only the established Christian churches, which are part of worldwide communions, but also the great variety of independent African Christian churches, which have deep roots in South Africa. The South African Council of Churches (SACC), led by Bishop Desmond Tutu until his election as Anglican archbishop of South Africa, is a significant organization. Tutu has spoken out against apartheid, and practical programs have been established by SACC for some of apartheid's victims. As black rebellion and government intransigence have escalated, the churches have spoken out for change, with Tutu calling for economic sanctions in 1986. Though other groups have been silenced, the churches have remained one area of resistance to government policies.

Some groups are trying to unify the forces that oppose the regime. The United Democratic Front (UDF), initiated by Reverend Allan Boesak, a theologian, among others, rallied groups against the government proposals for constitutional reform. Another front, the National Forum, was organized by leaders of AZAPO. As their voices have become more outspoken, UDF leaders have been detained, charged with treason, and some murdered. With most of their leaders in detention, new restrictions in 1988 prohibited the UDF and 16 other organizations from carrying out any activities. UDF headquarters, along with other anti-apartheid groups such as the SACC and the South African Catholic Bishops Conference, have been bombed.

Peaceful protest seems an ineffectual

recourse against the apparently immovable forces in power, but the weapons of violence are extraordinarily difficult for blacks to acquire. The violence that ensued during the demonstration at Sharpeville in 1960 and the resulting repression in the early 1960s convinced many people, including ANC leader Nelson Mandela, who has been jailed for more than 25 years, that they would have to resort to violence. Yet it has been used with restraint. For instance, the Spear of the Nation, the military wing of the ANC, sought to destroy strategic South African targets while carefully avoiding the taking of human lives. In 1985 ANC President Oliver Tambo stated that government violence against blacks has caused the ANC to rethink this policy. Some ANC sympathizers within South Africa have taken up violence against civilian targets, but bombings and attacks during the 1988 elections were focused on targets such as police stations.

The apartheid system is maintained by a net of antiterrorist, anticommunist security legislation, which is wide enough and vague enough to catch anyone suspected of opposition to the system. The legal right of the security forces to detain persons without charging them has been especially effective in crushing opposition to apartheid. As repression and rebellion have escalated in the 1980s, the security forces have increased powers and immunity from legal challenge. The military can rely on sophisticated weaponry, and all white males are required to put in 2 years of service and later serve as reserves, although, as noted earlier, increasing numbers are refusing service.

From 1984 to 1986 more than 2,000 were killed as the army and police broke up demonstrations, funerals, and even church services. Many black youths believe that they have nothing to lose and have risked their lives to defy restrictive laws and the apartheid state.

The year 1985 was a turning point in the escalation. Arrests and bannings of black leaders led to calls to make the townships "ungovernable." Pretoria declared a state of emergency for 36 districts in July, and there were more than 1,500 arrests during the first 2 weeks. By June 1986 the entire country was declared in a state of emergency. Rock-throwing youths were shot by police and soldiers; 25,000 to 30,000 people have been detained since 1986, more

(United Nations photo by Milton Grant)

Resistance groups have gained international recognition in their struggle against the South African regime.

The Boer War: the British fight the Afrikaners (Boers) **1899–1902**	The Union of South Africa gives rights of self-government to whites **1910**	The African National Congress is founded **1912**	The Nationalist Party comes to power on an apartheid platform **1948**	The Sharpeville Massacre: police fire on demonstration; more than 60 deaths result **1960**	Soweto riots are sparked off by student protests **1976**

1980s

Bishop Desmond Tutu is awarded the Nobel Peace Prize	Nationwide state of emergency; arrests, bannings, escalation of violence	Anti-apartheid leaders are detained or silenced; the ANC meets with whites outside South Africa

than 7,000 of them children. Studies estimate that 83 percent of South African detainees are tortured while in jail; more than 100 died in detention. In Natal province, the government stood by as more than 800 people died between 1986 and 1988, as Inkatha members tried to force blacks to join their organization.

As leaders are killed, detained, or banned, others take up leadership. Millions of workers participate in strikes; and unions, community groups, and churches have picked up the struggle as their leaders are routinely detained or forced underground. Maintaining such leadership will be difficult. South African death squads around the world have killed or injured ANC officials and sympathizers in London and Paris as well as in the Southern African cities of Harare, Gaborone, and Maputo. In spite of these attacks, the ANC continues to advocate a nonracial democratic unitary state and has met with representatives of white South African institutions. It also has launched a campaign to become the sole representative of the South African people.

CONCLUSION

Increased violence is assured, and South Africa will use all of its power to keep anti-apartheid forces in line. Their strategies to maintain white power and supremacy will continue to include the nurturing of a black middle class with an interest in the system; piecemeal cosmetic reforms; fostering division among blacks; and, of course, military force. The South African government can marshall all of the resources of this advanced industrialized state to maintain military dominance and totalitarian control over resistant peoples, and it has support from outside countries as well. Blacks cannot possess arms—even black police officers are not allowed to use them—yet few whites are without them. The policies of South Africa within the Southern African region (described in the regional essay) operate to cut off secret arms flows from the north and to punish governments that sympathize with liberation. However, it is clear from their rising militancy that black South Africans will not accept anything less than majority rule.

The world community has condemned apartheid, and as violence has escalated, international calls for comprehensive economic sanctions increase. In many countries, anti-apartheid work is carried out by independent groups. Recognizing South Africa's dependence on foreign investment, many groups in the United States and the Europe have worked on campaigns to persuade foreign investors to get out of South Africa. Cultural and sports boycotts have publicized the evils of the system.

Yet many governments continue to meet South Africa's needs. Loans from the International Monetary Fund and private banks in the 1980s helped South Africa to survive the world recession. In spite of increased pressure from anti-apartheid lobbyists, many U.S. banks still lend to South Africa. Export regulations to South Africa were softened under the Reagan administration, and South Africa was able to secure needed specialized equipment.

Several European countries have instituted sanctions, and in 1986 the U.S. Congress passed sanctions legislation over a Reagan veto, but South Africa has managed, with the help of its friends, to build up a superior arsenal of arms.

The effects of the sanctions are debatable. The South African government and its supporters in the United States and Europe maintain that South Africa is not hurt and that black workers suffer more from economic sanctions. Others, however, point out that the U.S. sanctions bill of 1986 has been weakly enforced and that the United Nations arms embargo of 1977 has been broken by Western allies of South Africa. Even so, evidence is mounting that the South African economy has suffered, with whites feeling the economic squeeze and a majority of blacks in support of sanctions. Rent boycotts, the falling rand, and a negative balance of white immigration have weakened the South African economy. President Pieter Botha's overtures to South Africa's neighbors are seen by many as attempts to increase sanctions-busting, already an established practice in countries such as Swaziland.

The interactions of the entire world help to maintain the two worlds of South Africa. However, it will be the actions of its own people that determine the future of the country.

DEVELOPMENT

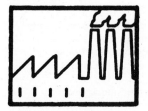

In defiance of the government, groups of businesspeople, academics, journalists, students, and sports officials have met with members of the ANC in independent African countries to discuss political and economic views, the current struggle, the role of boycotts, and South Africa's future.

FREEDOM

Banning, detention, and death are common punishments for speaking out against apartheid. Children as young as age 7 have been detained; demonstrators have been shot. Under the state of emergency, the press may report only what is approved by the government. Torture, killings, and bombings of anti-apartheid groups escalated in 1988.

HEALTH/WELFARE

Higher education for black South Africans, like primary and secondary education for blacks, is inferior to that of whites. Blacks cannot attend white universities, except under special circumstances. Student boycotts and armed soldiers at schools have squelched education.

ACHIEVEMENTS

As government-selected black leaders step down and security and services are reduced in the black townships, local "people's governments" are emerging. At risk to their lives, block representatives join in larger committees to make decisions for the townships, and communities attempt to educate the youth.

Swaziland (Kingdom of Swaziland)

GEOGRAPHY

Area in Square Kilometers (Miles):
17,366 (6,704) (slightly smaller than
New Jersey
Capital (Population): Mbabane
(administrative) (51,000); Lobanta
(legislative)
Climate: temperate; subtropical;
semiarid

PEOPLE

Population
Total: 757,000
Annual Growth Rate: 2.5%
Rural/Urban Population Ratio: 74/26
Languages: official: English, Siswati;
others spoken: Zulu, Sesotho, Nguni

Health
Life Expectancy at Birth: 47 years
male; 50 years female
Infant Death Rate (Ratio): 156/1,000
Average Caloric Intake: 97% of FAO
minimum
Physicians Available (Ratio): 1/8,750

Religion(s)
53% Christian; 47% traditional
indigenous

Education
Adult Literacy Rate: 65%

COMMUNICATION

Telephones: 10,700
Newspapers: 1

NCWALA

Visitors to Swaziland are frequently impressed by the pageantry associated with many of its state occasions. The most important ceremonies take place during the lunar *Ncwala* month in December and January. This is a time when the nation reaffirms its bonds with the royal house. As the month begins, runners are sent to collect water from the ocean and various rivers, thus reestablishing their historic association with the Swazi. The main festival lasts for 6 days and includes the king's tasting of the first fruits, blessings to the ancestors, and prayers for rain. During the entire period there is much ritual dancing—the most important of which is performed on the fourth day by the king and other members of royalty.

TRANSPORTATION

Highways—Kilometers (Miles): 3,450
(2,193)
Railroads—Kilometers (Miles): 292
(181)
Commercial Airports: 1 international

GOVERNMENT

Type: monarchy
Independence Date: September 6,
1968
Head of State: King Mswati III
Political Parties: Imbokodvo National
Movement: Ngwane National Liberty
Congress; Swaziland Progressive
Party; Swaziland United Front
Suffrage: universal for adults

MILITARY

Number of Armed Forces: 2,700
*Military Expenditures (% of Central
Government Expenditures):* n/a
Current Hostilities: none

ECONOMY

Currency ($ U.S. Equivalent): 2.12
emalangenis = $1
Per Capita Income/GNP: $790/$490
million
Inflation Rate: 21%
Natural Resources: iron ore; asbestos;
coal; timber
Agriculture: corn; livestock;
sugarcane; citrus fruits; cotton; rice;
pineapples
Industry: milled sugar; cotton;
processed meat and wood; tourism;
chemicals; machinery, beverages;
consumer goods; paper milling;
mining

FOREIGN TRADE

Exports: $174 million
Imports: $322 billion

| Zulu and South African whites encroach on Swazi territory **1800s** | A protectorate is established by the British **1900** | Independence is restored **1968** | Parliament is dissolved **1973** | **1980s** |

King Sobuza dies; King Mswati III is crowned and soon dissolves the Liqoqo

New elections strengthen the king and retain ties to South Africa

New factories engage in "sanctions-busting," bringing economic growth to Swaziland

SWAZILAND

Swaziland is a small, landlocked kingdom sandwiched between the much larger states of Mozambique and South Africa. Many casual observers have tended to look upon the country as a peaceful island of "traditional" Africa that is seemingly immune to the continent's contemporary conflicts. An extended power struggle following the death of the long-reigning King Sobuza II as well as a deal involving the possible transfer of territory and citizens from South Africa have, however, shattered such illusions.

EXTERNAL PRESSURES

Since the late eighteenth century the fortunes of Swaziland have been subject to external pressures. From 1900 until the restoration of independence in 1968 the kingdom existed as a British protectorate, despite sustained pressure for its transfer to South Africa's jurisdiction. Local white settlers, who at the time made up only 2 percent of the population but who controlled more than two-thirds of the protectorate's land, supported this proposed transfer.

Throughout the colonial period the ruling House of Dlamini, which was led by the energetic Sobuza II after 1921, successfully served as a rallying point for national self-assertion—a factor that no doubt contributed to the overwhelming popularity of the royalist *Imbokodvo* party in the elections of 1964, 1967, and 1972. In 1973 Sobuza dissolved the Parliament and repealed the Westminster-style Constitution, characterizing it as "un-Swazi." In 1979 a new, nonpartisan Parliament was

chosen. However, preeminent authority has remained with the king and his advisory council, the *Liqoqo*.

Sobuza's death in 1982 left many wondering if Swaziland's unique monarchist institutions would survive. A prolonged power struggle increased tensions within the ruling order. The Liqoqo appointed both a new prime minister, Prince Bhekimpi, and a new Queen Regent, Ntombi. Prince Makhosetive, Ntombi's teenage son, was installed as King Mswati III in 1986, at the age of 18. Ntombi removed rivals with modernizing tendencies, but the new king dissolved the Liqoqo, possibly to reduce conservative influence and establish his own authority.

One of the major challenges facing any Swazi government is the nature of its relations with its powerful neighbor, South Africa. Under Sobuza, Swaziland managed to maintain its political autonomy while recognizing its economic dependence on South Africa. The delicate relationship has been altered because of a nonaggression pact between the two countries and a proposed land deal. As a result of the nonaggression pact, Swazi security forces have moved forcefully against suspected African National Congress (ANC) activists. In 1987 ANC officials were killed in Swaziland, most probably by South African agents. The land deal, now aborted, would have transferred lands from two South African "homelands" to Swaziland, giving the country access to the sea. The South African government cancelled the agreement after protests from the affected population within South

Africa, yet despite this setback, cooperation between the two governments continues.

THE ECONOMY

Swaziland's economy, like its politics, is the product of both internal and external initiatives. Since independence the nation has enjoyed a high rate of economic growth led by the expansion and diversification of agriculture. Success in agriculture has promoted the development of secondary industries, such as a sugar refinery and a paper mill. There has also been increased exploitation of coal and asbestos; and tourism, which depends on weekend traffic from South Africa, is another source of revenue.

Swazi development has relied on capital-intensive (rather than labor-intensive) projects. These projects have increased the disparities in local wealth and have meant continued dependence on South African investment. Since 1986, factories have been established so that companies can avoid international sanctions against South Africa. Swaziland is not an island apart; it is part of the continent, a microcosm of contemporary Africa, illustrating both the continent's problems and its progress.

DEVELOPMENT

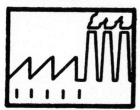

Swazi workers and their government have become a component of efforts to avoid economic sanctions against South Africa. Factories in Swaziland relabel some goods produced in South Africa as "Made in Swaziland" and ship them through South Africa to the United States.

FREEDOM

The current political order restricts many forms of opposition, though its defenders claim that local councils, *Tikhudlas*, allow for popular participation in decision making. There have been few reports of serious human-rights violations, and political prisoners detained during the royal power struggle were released in 1985.

HEALTH/WELFARE

Primary-school enrollment now approaches 100%, although quality has not kept pace with quantity, according to the government's own evaluations. The country's low life expectancy and high child-mortality rate are attributed to an overemphasis on curative, rather than preventive, medicine.

ACHIEVEMENTS

Under Sobuza II, Swaziland welcomed South African refugees and supported the ANC. Since 1984, however, some refugees have been returned to South Africa, police have rounded up suspected ANC guerrillas, and many refugees have had to leave for other countries such as Tanzania.

Zambia (Republic of Zambia)

GEOGRAPHY

Area in Square Kilometers (Miles):
752,972 (290,724) (slightly larger
than Texas)
Capital (Population): Lusaka
(641,000)
Climate: tropical to subtropical

PEOPLE

Population
Total: 7,770,000
Annual Growth Rate: 3.1%
Rural/Urban Population Ratio: 51/49
Languages: official: English; others
spoken: Bemba, Nyanja, Tonga, Lozi,
others

Health
Life Expectancy at Birth: 47 years
Infant Death Rate (Ratio): 107/1,000
Average Caloric Intake: 90% of FAO
minimum
Physicians Available (Ratio): 1/8,104

Religion(s)
51% Christian; 48% traditional
indigenous; 1% Hindu and Muslim

Education
Adult Literacy Rate: 54%

COPPER: ZAMBIA'S MONOCULTURE

Zambia, like many other African countries, has depended on the
earnings of one export (in Zambia's case, copper) for most of its
revenues. This means that national revenue is almost completely dependent on external factors—demand and world prices. Copper provided 87
percent of Zambia's exports. During the 1970s the price of copper
dropped drastically. After a peak output of 683,000 tons per year in the
mid-1970s, production in 1984–1985 was 525,411 tons. With the mining
sector faced with continued decline in prices and with exhaustion of
reserves, copper production was down a further 12 percent in
1985–1986. Although prices rose in 1987, outdated equipment and
diminished production capacity prevented Zambia from taking advantage of the rise. Coping with a rising national debt and development
needs is made made more difficult by this lack of a diversified economy.
Since 1985 Zambia has tried to diversify by promoting agriculture, but
investment is needed to provide technical assistance and infrastructure.

COMMUNICATION

Telephones: 60,500
Newspapers: 2

TRANSPORTATION

Highways—Kilometers (Miles):
36,809 (22,872)
Railroads—Kilometers (Miles): 2,014
(1,251)
Commercial Airports: 2 international

GOVERNMENT

Type: republic
Independence Date: October 24, 1964
Head of State: President Kenneth
David Kaunda
Political Parties: United National
Independence Party
Suffrage: universal for adults

MILITARY

Number of Armed Forces: 15,500
*Military Expenditures (% of Central
Government Expenditures):* n/a
Current Hostilities: none

ECONOMY

Currency ($ U.S. Equivalent): 8.33
kwachas = $1
Per Capita Income/GNP: $570/$2.3
billion
Inflation Rate: 20%
Natural Resources: copper; zinc;
lead; cobalt; coal
Agriculture: corn; tobacco; cotton;
peanuts; sugarcane
Industry: foodstuffs; beverages;
chemicals; textiles; fertilizer

FOREIGN TRADE

Exports: $431 million
Imports: $714 million

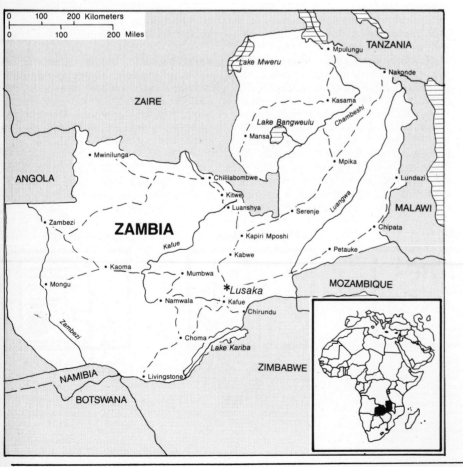

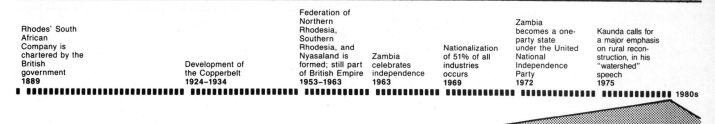

Rhodes' South African Company is chartered by the British government
1889

Development of the Copperbelt
1924–1934

Federation of Northern Rhodesia, Southern Rhodesia, and Nyasaland is formed; still part of British Empire
1953–1963

Zambia celebrates independence
1963

Nationalization of 51% of all industries occurs
1969

Zambia becomes a one-party state under the United National Independence Party
1972

Kaunda calls for a major emphasis on rural reconstruction, in his "watershed" speech
1975

1980s

South African raids on Zambia

IMF conditions lead to riots; more than 30 are killed

Rumors abound of Kaunda's retirement as the economy deteriorates

ZAMBIA

Kenneth Kaunda, the leader of Zambia's independence movement during the 1950s and 1960s and the president of Zambia since 1964, has often expressed his concern to maintain contact with citizens and their problems and to use government power for the people's welfare. External factors and internal changes have increased the challenge of these goals.

URBAN MIGRATION

Approximately 49 percent of Zambia's nearly 8 million people live in towns and cities. Peoples from all of the 70 or more different ethnic groups, speaking as many different languages (and often English as well), come to the cities to visit or to stay with relatives and friends. Migration to the towns is expected to increase in the future. This is not surprising, for while life in the cities is hard, life in the countryside is even harder. Rural farmers make less than one-third of the wages of urban workers. Even if the visitor does not find a job in the city—and jobs are hard to find—there are still reasons for coming. Schools, health facilities, and good water are more readily available.

The urban population in Zambia is so high because copper mines stimulated the development of such centers during the past century. White settlers came to the present-day Copperbelt in the late nineteenth century to search for minerals. The British South Africa Company, founded by Cecil Rhodes and chartered by the British government, received concessions

from chiefs and claimed the lands. Of the more than 30,000 expatriates in the country today, most are connected with the industry. Copper became the source of Zambia's prosperity, but the prices of copper and cobalt, the second major mineral, have declined on the world market, causing economic crisis.

ECONOMIC WOES

Zambians also suffered economic hardship in the 1970s when Zambia supported the liberation struggles of Angolans and Mozambicans against Portugal and of Zimbabweans against the Rhodesian government. Zambia took a leading role in the economic boycott of Rhodesia.

When Zimbabwe became independent in 1980 it was expected that Zambia's economic situation would improve. This did not happen. In addition to the unfavorable conditions of the world market, South Africa's destabilizing tactics continued to affect Zambia—interfering with its rail lines, for instance. Problems of mismanagement on the home front contributed to an economic situation that has been described as "in disarray." Debts mount, infrastructure is in disrepair, and the quality of life is steadily deteriorating.

"HUMANISM" IS ESPOUSED

The Zambian government seeks answers to these economic problems. President Kaunda espouses a moderate Christian "humanism" akin to Western liberalism. However, he has added a socialist compo-

nent. Kaunda stressed the importance of rural development, yet problems of the rural areas worsen. Economic difficulties have led to an international debt which amounted to $6 billion by 1988. Negotiations with the International Monetary Fund led to currency devaluations, an austerity budget, cuts in food subsidies for urban dwellers, and rising prices.

In opposition to the rising price of maize, the worst riots since independence occurred in the Copperbelt in 1986, leaving at least 30 dead. Kaunda cancelled the price rise. Efforts to diversify the economy by increasing agricultural outputs of maize, tobacco, sugar, wheat, dairy and beef are hampered by the lack of new technology and fertilizer, and by disease.

ZAMBIA AND AFRICAN AFFAIRS

Kaunda has taken a leading role in seeking peace for the Southern African region. He has met with South African leaders, brought together the opposing parties in Angola and Namibia, and welcomed refugees. Kaunda has played a prominent role in the Southern African Development Coordination Conference, and his support for the African National Congress has led to air attacks on Zambia.

DEVELOPMENT

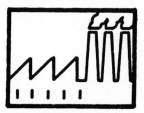

Higher producer prices for agriculture, technical assistance, and rural-resettlement schemes are part of government efforts to raise agricultural production. The agricultural sector has shown growth. However, financial inputs are needed, and much maize is smuggled over the border to Zaire, reducing Zambia's potential for recovery.

FREEDOM

Amnesty International reports that opponents of the government are detained without trial, tortured, and the death penalty is maintained. A 1988 crackdown on the black market was perceived by many as an anti-Asian political move in an election year.

HEALTH/WELFARE

The rise in the price of maize and fertilizers affect the cost of living. Kaunda has emphasized his continuing "moral obligation to lift the living standards of the people" but has stressed the need to raise prices to acquire foreign exchange, necessary to revive industries now working at only 40% capacity.

ACHIEVEMENTS

Zambia's educational system was very deficient at the time of independence, and there were fewer than 100 Zambian college graduates. The University of Zambia, founded through contributions from all over the country, had 312 students in 1966 but more than 4,000 by the 1980s.

Zimbabwe

GEOGRAPHY

Area in Square Kilometers (Miles):
390,759 (150,873) (slightly smaller than Montana)
Capital (Population): Harare (730,000)
Climate: subtropical

PEOPLE

Population
Total: 9,987,000
Annual Growth Rate: 3.5%
Rural/Urban Population Ratio: 75/25
Languages: official: English; others spoken: Shona, Ndebele, others

Health
Life Expectancy at Birth: 58 years male; 61 years female
Infant Death Rate (Ratio): 77/1,000
Average Caloric Intake: 86% of FAO minimum
Physicians Available (Ratio): 1/12,340

Religion(s)
75% Christian; 24% traditional indigenous; 1% Muslim

Education
Adult Literacy Rate: 50%

ZIMBABWE'S AGRICULTURAL SUCCESS STORY

In 1988 the New York-based Hunger Project awarded Zimbabwean President Robert Mugabe its Africa Prize for Leadership for the Sustainable End of Hunger. While recognizing the importance of leadership, though, most acknowledge that credit for the success of Zimbabwe's food production lies with the peasant, communal, and commercial farmers. Peasant farmers have boosted their maize production 1,000 percent since independence, with their share of agricultural production rising from a share of 8 percent to 64 percent. White commercial farmers also increased their output by 300 percent. Government loans, building of grain depots for storage, and improved roads, as well as resettlment for landless Zimbabweans, have encouraged thousands to increase productivity. The UN Food and Agriculture Organization (FAO) has targeted women farmers and encourages cooperative projects.

COMMUNICATION

Telephones: 214,000
Newspapers: 2

TRANSPORTATION

Highways—Kilometers (Miles):
85,237 (52,964)
Railroads—Kilometers (Miles): 2,743 (1,704)
Commercial Airports: 2 international

GOVERNMENT

Type: one-party socialist state
Independence Date: April 18, 1980
Head of State: Executive President Robert Mugabe
Political Parties: Zimbabwe African National Union and Zimbabwe African People's Union (merged); others
Suffrage: universal over 18

MILITARY

Number of Armed Forces: 41,000
Military Expenditures (% of Central Government Expenditures): $464,800,000 (6.2%)
Current Hostilities: none

ECONOMY

Currency ($ U.S. Equivalent): 1.72 Zimbabwe dollars = $1
Per Capita Income/GNP: $275/$4.7 billion
Inflation Rate: 16.2%
Natural Resources: gold; chrome ore; coal; copper; nickel; iron ore; silver; asbestos
Agriculture: tobacco; corn; sugar; cotton; livestock
Industry: mining; steel; textiles

FOREIGN TRADE

Exports: $1.3 billion
Imports: $1.0 billion

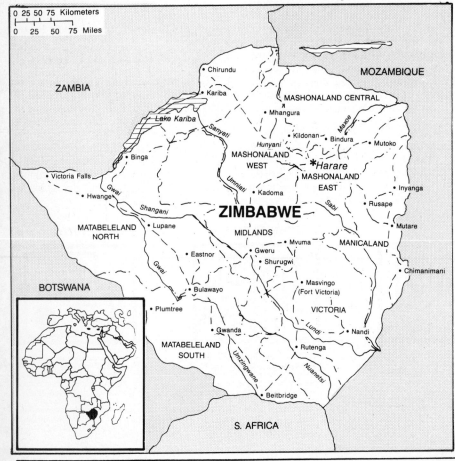

ZIMBABWE

The independent republic of Zimbabwe was born on April 7, 1980. Its birth had been prolonged, painful, and difficult. The new country emerged from years of hardship and violence in a cruel war. Before the creation of Zimbabwe the country was called Rhodesia, after Cecil Rhodes, the nineteenth-century British entrepreneur. Whereas the name of the new state is intended to symbolize the aspirations of the African majority, the name Rhodesia rallied those who believed in the privileges of a small minority—white Rhodesians—who defined themselves as the sole representatives of the nation.

The home of powerful trading and agricultural states since the fifteenth century, Zimbabwe attracted white settlers and miners from South Africa in 1890. After 34 years of British South Africa Company administration, what was then called Southern Rhodesia became a self-governing British Crown colony. "Self-government" was, however, virtually confined to a white electorate, only 3 percent of the population. In 1953 Southern Rhodesia became the focal point of a federation of British colonial territories, which the settlers hoped might develop into a dominion such as Canada or South Africa. White immigration was encouraged; white domination was the goal.

The federation collapsed when the United Kingdom acknowledged the right of two of its members to secede after African nationalist movements there became too strong to contain. These territories are now the independent states of Malawi and Zambia.

WHITE RHODESIANS SEEK INDEPENDENCE

In Rhodesia, the settlers feared that the reforms that the federation inspired would lead to majority rule. They rallied around the Rhodesia Front Party, which rejected any prospect of change and led the country to a Unilateral Declaration of Independence (UDI) in 1965. At first it appeared that they might achieve their objective. On the south, Rhodesia was bordered by a sympathetic South African government, and it was flanked by two Portuguese colonies, Angola and Mozambique, where the occupying power was committed to war against any African nationalist movement. In this context, a United Nations-sponsored economic and arms boycott, although it weakened the economy, proved inadequate to topple the Rhodesia Front under its determined leader, Ian Smith. After years of peaceful protests, African nationalists decided in 1966 to turn to armed struggle in the countryside to achieve their aim of majority rule. Supported by peasant farmers throughout the country, the armed struggle lasted 14 years.

The tide began to turn as fighting intensified in Mozambique and that colony became independent following the collapse of the Portuguese dictatorship in 1974. Despite taking much punishment from the Rhodesian Army, Mozambique authorities gave effective support to a growing Zimbabwe guerrilla struggle as it rallied the rural African population to threaten the Smith regime. For the African fighters, the war was a second *Chimurenga* (a Shona expression meaning "fighting in which everyone joins"), inspired by the unsuccessful risings of the African majority against white settlers from 1895 to 1897. One of the executed leaders of the uprising, Nehanda, a spirit medium, died "singing and shouting that her children would return to free the people."

INTERNAL SETTLEMENT FAILS

The Rhodesian Army could not defeat the liberation forces, and the government came under pressure from the West to come to a settlement. At first an "internal settlement" excluding those nationalists fighting in the bush was instituted, in 1978; but, despite the presence of an African prime minister, Bishop Abel Muzorewa, this failed to halt the nationalists' military attacks. Finally, in 1979, all of the belligerent parties met at Lancaster House in London to agree on a ceasefire and to set up a national election, which resulted in a great victory for African nationalists. A majority of seats was won by the Zimbabwe African National Union-Patriotic Front (ZANU-PF), with the Zimbabwe African People's Union (ZAPU), led by Joshua Nkomo, an important politician since the 1950s, winning a small number of seats. ZANU leader Robert Mugabe became the first prime minister of independent Zimbabwe in 1980.

FORMIDABLE PROBLEMS

The political, economic, and social problems inherited by the Mugabe government were, and still are, formidable. Until independence there were really "two nations" in Rhodesia: black and white. Segregation in most areas of life, such as housing and

(United Nations photo)

During the armed struggle of the 1970s the minority Rhodesian government resettled many Africans in controlled villages.

the state school system, was the norm, and African facilities were vastly inferior to white facilities. Approximately half of the national territory was reserved for whites only. On "white" land, a prosperous capitalist agriculture, which was based on growing maize and tobacco for export as well as a diversified mix of crops for domestic consumption, flourished.

The workforce for these plantations, together with the large number of domestic servants, constituted a particularly impoverished and oppressed portion of the population. On "black" land, the Tribal Trust Lands, most of the soil was poor and dry; there were few roads and communications facilities. Most of the adult population had to work in the "white" part of the country much of the time. While skilled Africans found few job opportunities until the labor shortage during the 1970s war became overwhelming, everything was done to encourage white immigration. Indeed, the majority of whites resident in 1980 were the products of post-World War II immigration from the United Kingdom and South Africa, a large minority coming after UDI.

WHITES CONTROL THE ECONOMY

The new government could not entirely dismantle the privileged settler world, partly because after UDI, whites had created what was by African standards a relatively prosperous and self-sufficient economy. It could not simply be destroyed without great national loss. Zimbabwe was the most industrialized nation between Egypt and South Africa. The Mugabe government was careful to prevent white disaffection from negatively affecting the economy.

Also, the Lancaster House agreement essentially tied Mugabe's hands. Private property is legally enshrined in Zimbabwe and cannot be confiscated without generous compensation. Socialism certainly remains the government's long-term goal, but Zimbabwe remains a capitalist country with a socialist-inclined government. For 7 years after independence one-fifth of the seats in Parliament were retained by the small white minority, but in 1987 the Parliament abolished seats reserved by race. As a gesture of reassurance to the white community (and some say to the white regime in South Africa), the black members of the assembly appointed white businesspeople to 11 out of the 20 seats previously reserved for whites.

ACHIEVING POLITICAL UNITY

The split between Mugabe's ZANU and Nkomo's ZAPU has been a serious prob-

lem. ZANU broke away from ZAPU in 1963 over personal and tactical disagreements rather than issues of principle. The result was open fighting in the African township of the capital, Salisbury (now named Harare). ZAPU had originally been the dominant national movement, but the military success of ZANU under its brilliant commander, the late Josiah Tongogara, won over many people.

During the war many attempts were made—in vain—to reunite ZANU and ZAPU. Only briefly after the ceasefire did they agree to form a "Patriotic Front" for negotiating with Ian Smith and international forces. Although both parties wanted to function on a national basis, the 1980 election revealed that ZAPU strength had largely become limited to the southwestern portion of the country and to the Ndebele-speaking minority of the population.

There were strong tensions. Nkomo and several ZAPU men initially received ministerial appointments. However, discoveries of secret arms caches, which the government claimed ZAPU intended to hoard until the right moment for a coup, strained relations and led to Nkomo's dismissal in February 1982. Late in 1982 and

again in early 1984 the North Korean-trained Fifth Brigade of the Zimbabwean Army was dispatched to the southwest, the ZAPU stronghold, where many incidents of violence had been reported. Still armed, ZAPU dissidents operated there, and the government's aggressive response alienated Ndebele even further. In March 1983, after a raid on his home, Nkomo fled across the border to Botswana, where many Ndebele refugees had gathered. He remained out of the country until August, when he returned and resumed his seat in Parliament. In early 1984 human-rights violations by the army were taken up by a closed committee and later detailed in a report of the Catholic Church.

Attempts at unity accelerated in 1985 and 1986, but tensions and rivalries remained. In elections after independence, ZANU increased its majority and Mugabe called the results a mandate for one-party rule, a long-held goal of ZANU. Continued unrest, attacks by ZANU supporters on ZAPU offices and individuals, and accusations of human-rights abuses hampered efforts at unity.

Aware that disunity could be exploited by South Africa in its regional destabilization efforts, Mugabe pressed for unity, in

(Oxfam America photo)

These children attend school, but they also contribute time and labor to the vital tasks of food production, often in school gardens.

(United Nations photo by P. Heath Hoeffel)

These Zimbabwean students are on their way to harvest a cotton crop in the eastern part of the country.

Heyday of the
gold trade and
Great Zimbabwe
1400s–1500s

The Ndebele
state emerges in
Zimbabwe
1837

The Pioneer
Column: arrival
of the white
settlers
1890

spite of continued violent attacks by rebels on church members, white farmers, and missionaries in 1987 and 1988. With an agreement to include Joshua Nkomo in the Cabinet, the government reopened ZAPU offices and lifted a ban on meetings of opposition leaders in December 1987. Mugabe became the first executive president, for a 6-year term, in 1987, and Nkomo became a joint vice president in ZANU, with Deputy Prime Minister Simon Muzenda. On the eighth anniversary of independence in April 1988 Mugabe offered an amnesty to armed dissidents. By the end of May, more than 120 (of an estimated 150) had turned themselves in to join in reconciliation efforts.

SOUTH AFRICAN RELATIONS

The conflict between ZANU and ZAPU in Zimbabwe made for a difficult security situation. Zimbabwe and South Africa have poor relations. The South African government, which once backed Ian Smith, supported Muzorewa in the national elections and was stunned by Mugabe's victory. It is difficult for the South African regime to accept a government led by Africans with socialist ideals, who came to power through an effective guerrilla campaign against an allied white minority regime.

At the same time Zimbabwe is in need of good economic relations with South Africa. Trade links with South Africa intensified during the UDI period, and South African investment became very sizable in Zimbabwe. Zimbabwe has firmly opposed South African domestic policies and has worked to establish closer economic ties with such neighbors as Mozambique, as an alternative to continued dependence on its neighbor to the south. Zimbabwe permits only a modest civilian presence of the African National Congress (ANC) and other South African liberation organizations within its borders, but it is a strong supporter of majority rule at international forums. Zimbabwe has sacrificed to assist Mozambique against the Renamo rebel movement (large numbers of Zimbabwe troops protect railways and defend villages in Mozambique), is leading the international call for economic sanctions, and is prepared to suffer the consequences affecting its own economy. South Africa has attacked homes and offices in the capital Harare; has built an air base along the Zimbabwean border; and, many believe, has supported the armed dissidents.

MEETING THE CHALLENGE

Readjusting an unequal social and economic system and creating unity were the greatest challenges facing independent

(Oxfam America photo)

In Zimbabwean organizations, as in many African institutions, decisions are often made by consensus, arrived at after long discussions.

Chimurenga: rising against the white intruders ending in repression by whites
1895–1897

Southern Rhodesia is proclaimed a British Crown colony
1924

Unilateral Declaration of Independence
1965

Armed struggle begins
1966

Elections following cease-fire bring victory to ZANU-PF and an end to the war

1980s

National elections give ZANU a large majority; Parliament abolishes reservation of seats by race

Mugabe becomes executive president and offers a unity settlement to ZAPU

Increased economic independence from South Africa; support for embattled Mozambique

Zimbabwe. In the first year after independence the economic situation of Zimbabwe was favorable enough to allow for a large measure of optimism in the new state's ability to meet the challenges ahead. With the lifting of sanctions, mineral, maize, and tobacco exports expanded and import restrictions were eased. Workers' incomes rose, and a minimum wage, which covered even farm employees, was introduced for the first time. The rise in purchasing power benefited industry.

Zimbabwe had hopes that foreign investment and aid would pay for an ambitious scheme to buy out many white farmers and to settle African peasants on their land. There was a rapid expansion in educational and rural health facilities, while Africans began to enter the civil service in large numbers. However, much of the aid promised during independence negotiations was not forthcoming. Deteriorating conditions in the early 1980s slowed progress. The stagnation in world trade has brought down the value of Zimbabwean exports and forced the government to control imports strictly.

The most severe drought in a century reduced agricultural production, but rains in 1984 and 1985 increased maize production. Government policies and determined citizens further raised agricultural production in the late 1980s.

Foreign investment has been slow in coming to Zimbabwe because of the nation's security problems; foreign-aid grants were disappointingly small. The United States, although at first Zimbabwe's principal source of aid, periodically reduced assistance because of budget and political considerations. As in other parts of the world, the Reagan administration expected aid recipients to support U.S. foreign-policy decisions. In 1983 Zimbabwe's refusal to support the American position on the Korean Airline incident, Zimbabwe's co-sponsorship of the UN condemnation of the American invasion of Grenada, and criticism of U.S. policy toward South Africa led to aid reductions in 1986. In response, Mugabe stated, "When we fought for our independence, we never meant to sell it at all." In 1988 $5 million in American aid was restored.

During its first years in power the ZANU government was able to promote some significant reforms, but it acted with surprising caution, given its commitment to revolutionary change. Without money promised by Western governments, and moving cautiously to buy out white commercial farmers, efforts at land reform lagged. (At the same time some ministers and high officials began to acquire large farms and other properties while enriching themselves.) More than 40,000 families have been resettled and given land, and their productivity has greatly increased with assistance from the government. The goal at independence of settling 162,000 families, however, is far from being achieved. Loans, extension services, and a commitment to rural infrastructures and facilities such as roads, grain depots, schools, and health facilities have made rural areas more attractive and, therefore, productive. Since independence, primary-school enrollment has increased 300 percent and secondary enrollment 500 percent; and the infant mortality rate, seen as an indicator of general welfare, has been reduced 40 percent.

ZIMBABWE'S ACCOMPLISHMENTS

The difficulties Zimbabwe faces should not overshadow its accomplishments. First, the success of the war created an unprecedented sense of public confidence in the possibility of developing a democracy. Second, in a short time Zimbabwe has succeeded in providing a minimum of welfare benefits—notably in health and education—to the majority of its people. Finally, Zimbabwe has so far been able to offer to its racially mixed population a peaceful nonracist solution to the bitter conflict between the "two nations." The majority of white citizens remain in the country, although their numbers diminished after independence.

ZANU and Mugabe see the one-party state as the solution for problems of unity and development. If political unity can be fostered, economic growth sustained, and South African aggression and destabilization checked, Zimbabwe can move toward the equitable society promised during the revolutionary struggle.

DEVELOPMENT

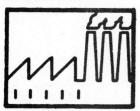

Peasant production has increased dramatically since independence, creating grain reserves and providing exports for the region. The work of communal farmers has been recognized both within Zimbabwe and internationally.

FREEDOM

In the early 1980s Amnesty International and groups within Zimbabwe accused the government of the torture and killing of opponents in Matabeleland. Since 1987 government troops and police have restricted themselves to tracking rebels and have reduced civilian harassment. The government released the last political prisoners in 1988.

HEALTH/WELFARE

Zimbabwe has hosted several international conferences on the health and welfare of children, and provides support for training and assistance for traditional midwives. Combining traditional skills with contemporary medical knowledge, midwives assist women in rural areas, where 75% of Zimbabweans live.

ACHIEVEMENTS

In spite of the bitter liberation struggle, drought, and continued South African hostility, Zimbabwe has continued agricultural production, made peace with the white community, and assisted its neighbors in their struggles. A strong leader in SADCC, the OAU, and the Non-Aligned Movement, Zimbabwe sets a positive example for the region and the continent.

Articles from the World Press

Annotated Table of Contents for Articles

Topic Guide to Articles

TOPIC AREA	TREATED AS AN ISSUE IN:	TOPIC AREA	TREATED AS AN ISSUE IN:
AIDS	7. AIDS in Africa—Plague or Propaganda?	Economic Development	3. The Slow Progress of Africa's Recovery 4. Cooperation Pays Off 6. Rethinking Higher Education 9. Ecowas: Standing Together 13. Walking the Economic Line in Nigeria 17. Heading Off the Prospect of Famine 18. Kenya Woos Outside Cash to Stoke New Jobs 19. Harvests Under Fire 22. Experimenting with Capitalism 24. The Horatio Algers of South Africa 25. Zambia's Autonomous Adjustment
Agriculture	3. The Slow Progress of Africa's Recovery 5. Food: Finding Solutions to the Crisis 11. Credit the Farmer for More Food 17. Heading Off the Prospect of Famine 19. Harvests Under Fire 25. Zambia's Autonomous Adjustment		
Apartheid	19. Harvests Under Fire 20. Polls Menace Pretoria's Neighbors 26. Art on the Frontlines	Economic Investment	3. The Slow Progress of Africa's Recovery 6. Rethinking Higher Education 11. Credit the Farmer for More Food 18. Kenya Woos Outside Cash to Stoke New Jobs 22. Experimenting with Capitalism 25. Zambia's Autonomous Adjustment
Arts	1. BaKongo Cosmology 8. African Cinema 26. Art on the Frontlines		
Border Disputes	15. Resolution Condemns Violence	Economy	3. The Slow Progress of Africa's Recovery 9. Ecowas: Standing Together 13. Walking the Economic Line in Nigeria 19. Harvests Under Fire 23. "We Are Stronger" 24. The Horatio Algers of South Africa
Cinema	8. African Cinema		
Civil War	14. The Right to Choose 15. Resolution Condemns Violence 16. Sudan Reeling From Disasters 21. South African Connections		
Class	15. Resolution Condemns Violence 16. Sudan Reeling From Disasters 19. Harvests Under Fire 21. South African Connections	Education	4. Cooperation Pays Off 6. Rethinking Higher Education
		Environment	5. Food: Finding Solutions to the Crisis
Cultural Roots	1. BaKongo Cosmology 8. African Cinema 14. The Right to Choose 26. Art on the Frontlines	Famine	3. The Slow Progress of Africa's Recovery 5. Food: Finding Solutions to the Crisis 12. The Cloud Over Africa Is Locusts 16. Sudan Reeling From Disasters 17. Heading Off the Prospect of Famine 25. Zambia's Autonomous Adjustment
Current Leaders	10. Hanging on to a "Revolution" 25. Zambia's Autonomous Adjustment		
Debt	2. Struggle for Dignity 3. The Slow Progress of Africa's Recovery 25. Zambia's Autonomous Adjustment	Foreign Aid	3. The Slow Progress of Africa's Recovery 9. Ecowas: Standing Together 11. Credit the Farmer for More Food 19. Harvests Under Fire
Drought	5. Food: Finding Solutions to the Crisis 11. Credit the Farmer for More Food 16. Sudan Reeling From Disasters 17. Heading Off the Prospect of Famine		

TOPIC AREA	TREATED AS AN ISSUE IN:	TOPIC AREA	TREATED AS AN ISSUE IN:
Foreign Investment	18. Kenya Woos Outside Cash to Stoke New Jobs 22. Experimenting with Capitalism 25. Zambia's Autonomous Adjustment	**Philosophy**	1. BaKongo Cosmology
		Politics	10. Hanging on to a "Revolution" 14. The Right to Choose 20. Polls Menace Pretoria's Neighbors
Foreign Relations	18. Kenya Woos Outside Cash to Stoke New Jobs 25. Zambia's Autonomous Adjustment	**Political Reform**	10. Hanging on to a "Revolution"
Foreign Trade	9. Ecowas: Standing Together 18. Kenya Woos Outside Cash to Stoke New Jobs	**Private Enterprise**	24. The Horatio Algers of South Africa
		Race	15. Resolution Condemns Violence 19. Harvests Under Fire 21. South African Connections
Health and Welfare	7. AIDS in Africa—Plague or Propaganda? 15. Resolution Condemns Violence 16. Sudan Reeling From Disasters	**Refugees**	14. The Right to Choose 15. Resolution Condemns Violence
History	1. BaKongo Cosmology	**Religion**	1. BaKongo Cosmology
Human Rights	2. Struggle for Dignity 4. Cooperation Pays Off 14. The Right to Choose 15. Resolution Condemns Violence 16. Sudan Reeling From Disasters	**Science**	1. BaKongo Cosmology
		Theater	26. Art on the Frontlines
		Turmoil	10. Hanging on to a "Revolution" 14. The Right to Choose 15. Resolution Condemns Violence 16. Sudan Reeling From Disasters
Independence	2. Struggle for Dignity 14. The Right to Choose 15. Resolution Condemns Violence		
		Trade	3. The Slow Progress of Africa's Recovery
Labor	4. Cooperation Pays Off 22. Experimenting with Capitalism 23. "We Are Stronger"	**Violence**	10. Hanging on to a "Revolution" 15. Resolution Condemns Violence 16. Sudan Reeling From Disasters 19. Harvests Under Fire 20. Polls Menace Pretoria's Neighbors 21. South African Connections
Music and Art	8. African Cinema 26. Art on the Frontlines		
Natural Disasters	12. The Cloud Over Africa Is Locusts 16. Sudan Reeling From Disasters	**Women**	4. Cooperation Pays Off
Natural Resources	3. The Slow Progress of Africa's Recovery 13. Walking the Economic Line in Nigeria 25. Zambia's Autonomous Adjustment	**Youth**	4. Cooperation Pays Off

Article 1

The World & I
SEPTEMBER 1988

BAKONGO
COSMOLOGY

Complex ideas of the universe from the heart of Africa were little recognized until recent decades

Wyatt MacGaffey

European visitors to Africa have often been reluctant to credit the people they meet with the capacity for abstract or systematic thought. In the 1880s, travelers and missionaries with experience of the Lower Congo believed "the ideas of the natives" amounted to no more than "a ruinous heap." Said one, "There is no coherence in their beliefs, and their ideas about cosmogony are very nebulous." Anthropologists have concurred: "One would seek in vain in [Kongo] culture for large and coherent conceptions and structures such as would give the human reality they incarnate the prestige accorded in Africa and elsewhere to other civilizations."

Yet, some African civilizations have indeed earned prestige for the complexity of their cosmologies and the refinement of their moral and symbolic systems. The ideas of the Dogon of Mali and the related Bamana (Bambara), noted also for their sculptures, have been studied for decades by a school of anthropology founded by Marcel Griaule. The Dogon had a graded series of initiation lodges in which wisdom was progressively revealed to a religious elite. In the best-known of his publications, *Conversations with Ogotemmeli*, Griaule describes how the Dogon assigned a learned elder to explain the origin and mysteries of the universe to him.

But where no hierarchy of religious elite existed —such as in the Lower Congo—there was no social basis for the development and authentication of cosmological knowledge. We also expect to learn about a cosmology from myths and to recognize myths by the miraculous events that occur in them, in which sacred beings and divine heroes shape the world. But in Lower Congo we find no narratives of this kind.

Instead of asking whether the BaKongo or any other people have a cosmology, we could assume that they must have one, because all social interaction necessarily presupposes some ordering of the world in space and time, specifying the place of human actors within it. If two Americans meet, for example, they are usually unaware that they think anything about "cosmology" or that, if they did, it would have any relevance to their interaction. Nevertheless, to interact at all, they must know or assume certain fundamental things about each other. It is necessary to know, for example, whether the person one is addressing is alive or dead. Usually that is no problem, though it is possible to be mistaken; comedies and thrillers both exploit the shock value of such mistakes. The difference between life and death also has serious public consequences, since a live person has civil rights and legal responsibilities that a dead person does not.

The difference between life and death is not a given in nature, however; that is, it is not in all cases a simple matter of observation. In the last two decades, Americans have repeatedly asked their courts and legislatures to decide just what the difference is. The beginning of life is as difficult to identify as the end and has given rise to as many controversies. The language used by parties to these disputes is often overtly religious, in a denominational sense, but even if it is not, their emotional tone and their feeling that these issues are fundamental tell us that we are in the domain of religion.

Cosmological distinctions about the order of the universe, the place of humankind within it, and the nature and varieties of human beings vary from one society to another. They may or may not be true in some scientific sense. Since they are fundamental to social life and experience, it is difficult if not impossible for the members of the society to step outside their assumptions, which they take to be given realities, or to imagine what life would be like in a different universe.

Kongo cosmology

The BaKongo, who live in the western Zaire province of Lower Zaire (called in colonial times Lower Congo) and in adjacent parts of both northwestern Angola and the People's Republic of Congo, may number some three million people. Their territory, on the Atlantic threshold of the Zaire basin—the heart of Africa—has been deeply influenced by relations with Europe going back more than five hundred years to the first arrival of Portuguese ships on the coast in 1483. After the creation of

ELISOFON ARCHIVES: NATIONAL MUSEUM OF AFRICAN ART

Traditional BaKongo wood carvings. *Photo on left page:* A crouching figure on a round bell. *Above:* Carved head for an ivory staff.

the colony of the Belgian Congo in 1908, most Kongo men, and many women, went to school, became Catholics or Protestants, and entered wage labor. Their political party, Abako, led by Joseph Kasa-Vubu, was one of the most effective forces in the fight for national independence, obtained in 1960. In Zaire today they are among the best educated and most influential groups.

In 1970, most BaKongo believed that the universe is divided into the two worlds of the living and the dead, separated by water and related to each other in such a way that when the sun sets among the living it rises among the dead. The movement of human life resembles that of the sun, in that after being born into this world and spending a lifetime in it, the soul passes into another existence in the alternate world. The other world is very much like this one. In fact, it is in a sense identical to it, since after dark, when the living go to sleep, the dead wake up and go about their daily occupations in what they think of as day, in the same houses that the living use, cultivating the same fields and cooking at the same hearth. There are also differences, however; in some ways the dead contrast with the living. Since they are older and can see in our world as well as their own, they are more powerful, They do not suffer from disease as we do, and they have become white rather than black.

Kongo cosmology is in fact more complex than this, but the sketch suffices to suggest that the fundamental concepts of time, life, death, and race are entirely different from those taken for granted by Americans or Europeans. In this cosmology, since the land of the dead is like another village, and not really very far away, it is remarkable rather than epoch-making that individuals may be able to go there and return to this world, to die and rise again from the dead.

The land of the dead is the village cemetery in the adjacent forest, but it can also be entered through certain caves and deep pools. The water that divides the worlds may be any pool or stream—the Zaire River or the Atlantic Ocean. In one of the most powerful applications of this cosmology, America, the land on the other side of the ocean, is the land of the dead to which Africans go when they die, changing their skins and becoming white.

The cosmology of divided worlds is an abstract model that enables the BaKongo to comprehend and interpret the facts of history and geography, human social experience, and relations of power. As we shall see, they use it to understand international relations, a dispute between two villages, or their own dreams. As the grammar of their thinking, it has not itself, until recently, been the object of their intellectual scrutiny. As an interpretive schema, it is mobilized when the urgencies of events demand it, and it may be applied differently by different individuals, drawing different conclusions.

The Kongo cosmology was first set out in print by Fu-kiau kia Bunseki in 1969, in a short work entitled *The MuKongo and the World in Which He Circulates,* written in KiKongo and published with a French translation. Fu-kiau, a young man with a good secondary education, was prompted to write by his conversations with the anthropologist J.M. Janzen. Fu-kiau was not a hoary Ogotemmeli steeped in tradition, but a man whose contact with outsiders was such that he could appreciate their problem in understanding the Kongo perspective. A diagram of the universe, similar to Fu-kiau's and labeled in KiKongo, has been found in use among Afro-Cubans in Cuba.

Fragmentary elements of Kongo cosmology have long been discussed, only to be relegated to footnotes as oddities instead of being taken seriously as parts of the missing system of Kongo religion. Europeans, representing a civilization that sees itself as obviously superior to all others in its moral, scientific, and political achievements, have natural-

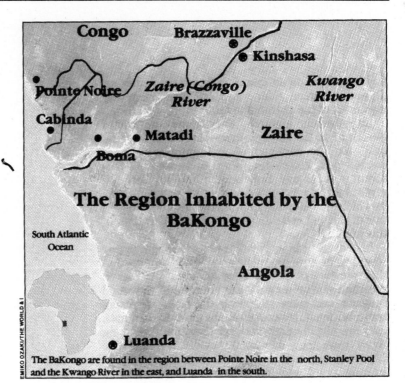

The Region Inhabited by the BaKongo

The BaKongo are found in the region between Pointe Noire in the north, Stanley Pool and the Kwango River in the east, and Luanda in the south.

ly been reluctant to admit that they were seen by Congolese as spirits of the dead, their morality as witchcraft, their science as magic, and their politics as cannibalism. It is still more difficult to admit that there may be some truth to this perspective.

Personal experiences

Kongo cosmological thinking was brought home to me personally when my wife and I lived in Matadi, the main port of Zaire, situated at the head of navigation on the Zaire estuary. It had about 180,000 inhabitants in 1970, many of them sailors who regularly traveled to Antwerp, New York, Houston, and even Japan on Belgian and Zairean merchant ships. Many more worked in the docks, and most of them had opportunities for contacts of various sorts with the crews of foreign ships. The town was also the seat of Protestant and Catholic missions established there since its founding in the 1880s. My host was a relatively prosperous man, an electrician, who could afford to keep a substantial household, including two wives and twelve children.

As I walked across the marketplaces of the town, I would be followed by a murmur of explanation from one marketwoman to another. *"Ndombe kena!* He's black!" People would tell the story: My host, the electrician had formerly owned a bar. To raise money for it, he had sold me his nephew, by witchcraft, to persons unspecified (missionaries, perhaps), who had transported me to America. I had become white in the land of the dead, had made good to the point of being able to marry a white lady, and had now come back to demand a reckoning; that explained why I was living in my "uncle's" house without paying any rent, why I was willing to eat local food, spoke authentic KiKongo and asked all those questions about local tradition—I was trying to recover my roots.

Sometimes people would put the question to me directly, in French or KiKongo: "Monsieur, is it true that you are black?" Others brought me photographs of recently deceased relatives to ask how they were getting on in the States. I had to reply that unfortunately we had so many immigrants arriving in America every day that it was hard to keep track of them all. Not everybody thought the same way. My host and his wives insisted to their friends that I was a *real* white man, and students from the secondary school, upwardly mobile all, noting my nondescript clothes and the fact that I went about on foot, would sometimes sneer at me as a bankrupt, poor white.

Even these skeptics had not really abandoned the traditional cosmology; the land of the dead has its native population, people whose ancestors were always white, in addition to those who have been imported as slaves by witchcraft. "Monsieur, were your ancestors black or white?" A matter of common puzzlement is the skin-change: Does it happen immediately or gradually? A black American evangelist visiting Kinshasa was asked about his light-brown color; how did he get that way? Embarrassed to recall a presumptive history of plantation miscegenation, he said that it came gradually, and his questioner went away satisfied.

The view of myself that I encountered in Matadi was not new to me. Five years before, I had lived in the village of Mbanza Manteke which, though rural, is no more remote from contact with Europe than is Matadi. A famous Protestant mission was established there in 1879, and since the turn of the century its male inhabitants have worked in cities like Kinshasa or Matadi. It gradually became clear that people expected me to take a siesta at noon, not just because that had been the habit of the missionaries when they lived there, but because for white people, as the BaKongo saw it, noon was really midnight, so of course they needed to sleep. Likewise, the European custom of sea-bathing was understood as a means of restoring one's health by contact with home base, as it were, the land beyond the water. My neighbors would call me "dead man" and laugh, somewhat uneasily.

At that time—1964—the U.S. government saw itself as engaged in a struggle with the Russians for the hearts and minds of the Congolese. The United States Information Agency took care to provide local newspapers with accounts, in French, of the presidential elections, in order to demonstrate the virtues of democracy. Some of the villagers read these

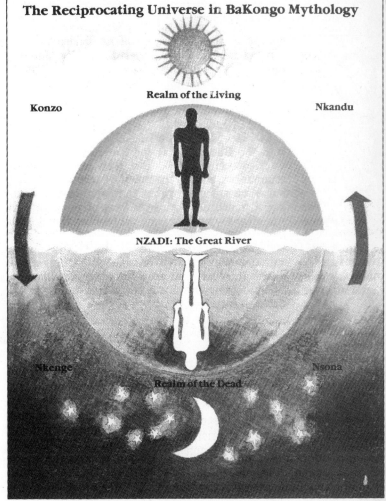

The Reciprocating Universe in BaKongo Mythology

Realm of the Living

Konzo

Nkandu

NZADI: The Great River

Nkenge

Nsona

Realm of the Dead

EMIKO OZAKI/THE WORLD & I

accounts with great interest and asked me questions to further their understanding. It turned out that they interpreted what they read in terms of their cosmology, in which not only the universe but any part of it may be thought of as divided into two opposed worlds. They gathered that Mr. Johnson, representing North America and therefore a white man, was contending with Mr. Goldwater, a black man, the leader of South America.

At the same time, they knew all about Sputnik, alerted by radio, and they would draw my attention to satellites passing overhead. They greatly admired both the Russians and the Americans, who could produce such marvels. But they had no use for communists, such as the Belgians, who were nothing but witches and incapable, they were sure, of building so much as a railroad locomotive. Later, the Americans were to be congratulated on flying to the moon, something Kongo magicians could also do, but the trouble with magicians was that one was never sure they were not up to mischief with their remarkable feats. Just what were the Americans doing on the moon, anyway? I was never able to answer this question satisfactorily.

Rituals and dreams

Cosmology is revealed not only in such personal experiences but also through the analysis of rituals. Kongo rituals proceed in a space that has first been laid out as a microcosm, sometimes by drawing a diagram on the ground. The simplest and most common diagram is a cross, not to be confused with the Christian cross. A person taking an oath, for example, may mark a cross in the dirt with his finger, then stand on it to swear. The transverse line corresponds to the boundary between the worlds; the intersecting one, to the path of forces moving between them. In some of the complex rituals performed in precolonial times, initiates were described as spending several days, weeks, or even months in the land of the dead under the water. What in fact they did was to spend the time in a specially built enclosure or distant camp. When they emerged from seclusion, they were considered to have been reborn, able to speak the secret languages of the dead and endowed with miraculous powers.

Their cosmology is so necessary to the organization of their culture and so taken for granted by them that the BaKongo do not recognize it as a topic or "problem." Conversely, once we have been alerted to it, the evidences of it are everywhere. The cosmology that the foreigner finds surprising is treated merely as the setting for transitory ingenuities, as in the riddle, "What black man went to Europe and became white?" Answer: a manioc root left soaking in the water for three days (to remove the acid) and then peeled.

In dreams, the soul may see something of the other world, so dreams are taken seriously as glimpses and warnings of the occult forces at work in our lives. To dream of trucks, trains, or ships is a sinister warning that someone will be "traveling." In the 1930s, when trains were new to the country, people would go down to the station to watch for recently deceased relatives passing through on their way to Matadi and beyond. Only people with special sinister powers, however, are actually active in the night world, while their bodies lie asleep in bed. They include witches, and also chiefs, who must have powers like those of witches in order to be able to defend the community against them.

Kongo history through Kongo eyes

The BaKongo tell no stories of the kind that the Western ear recognizes immediately as myths. In a cyclical or reciprocating universe such as Fu-kiau describes, one would not expect to find an account of its origin. What one does hear, in many hotly contested versions, are the

A typical inland BaKongo village.

stories of the origins of the clans in Mbanza Kongo. Mbanza Kongo, located in what is now northern Angola, was the capital of the Kingdom of Kongo when the Portuguese visited it at the end of the fifteenth century. The kingdom disintegrated after the battle of Mbwila in 1665, the capital itself being reduced to no more than an important village to which the legendary majesty of the past still faintly clung.

In modern Kongo, everyone derives his or her social position from membership in his or her mother's descent group or clan. Clan membership specifies the range of partners it is possible to marry and indicates where one has rights to land and residence. In asserting a claim to land or to political office, the head of a clan recites its tradition of origin, in which it usually appears that the founding chief left Mbanza Kongo, crossed the great river (*nzadi*), and arrived at the clan's present territory where, there being no other inhabitants, he "swept up the droppings of the elephant" and founded his own *mbanza*, or central place. The story tells his magical deeds, such as crossing the river on a raffia mat. It reports what clans he met along the way, whose sister he married, and so on. The representatives of other clans are supposed to be able to confirm the truth of these events and thus the property rights that the story legitimates.

Since, in a general sense, such stories might well be true, historians have generally treated them as accounts of actual migrations in which the BaKongo dispersed over their present territory from their original home. Scholars assumed that the river was the Zaire (Nzadi) and dismissed the magical events as accretions on a historical core. In fact, the supernatural references are among a number of clues showing that the stories are the missing myths, that they are narrative versions of the model of the divided worlds of the Kongo universe. In both the stories and the model, the essential movement in time is a crossing from one world to the other across the water that divides them.

The slave trade and the Christian missions

From the mid-seventeenth century to about 1890, the history of Kongo is bound up with the slave trade. Trials for ritual offenses, often violations of cult rules specially designed to trap the unwary, fed a thriving internal trade in slaves. Political losers and troublemakers could be sold to another village nearer the coast, with replacements acquired from further inland. At the coast, European slave traders established depots by treaty with chiefs who could guarantee orderly conditions of business and a steady supply of slaves in exchange for guns, cloth, liquor, and other goods.

This trade is understood by modern BaKongo as witchcraft; or rather, "witchcraft" is, among other things, what the BaKongo call slave trading. Witches, who are one's evilly intentioned neighbors, acquire sinister powers from the other world that enable them to operate "at night," that is, in unseen, occult ways. They steal the souls of victims, often relatives, who in the daylight world will be seen to die shortly afterwards. These souls may be eaten by members of the witch's coven, each of whom is obliged to provide a meal for the others in turn. This belief is the basis for stories interpreted by foreigners as cannibalism; there was never any actual cannibalism among the BaKongo.

Instead of being "eaten," stolen souls may be sold for an unholy profit, which explains, in Kongo eyes, why some people get rich. Victims should be sold, like slaves, at some distance, so that they cannot make their way home. Most victims of witchcraft end up in America, where they are supposedly put to work in factories making textiles and automobiles. Their souls would go to America anyway, after a normal death, but witchcraft sends them there prematurely.

Described and understood as witchcraft, the slave trade is believed to have persisted into the twentieth century. All relations with Europe and America, collectively referred to as *Mputu,* are understood in the same way. When Protestant missionaries arrived in the 1880s, they were seen as practicing a new form of the same trade. To be converted meant to be initiated into a magical conspiracy, similar to the traditional cults, in which the initiates learned how

to become powerful and wealthy. In exchange, as in other cults offering sinister competitive advantage over one's neighbors, the converts had to hand over the souls of one or more relatives. These victims the missionaries kept stored, it was believed, in attics, trunks, or boxes, until the time came to ship them to America. In 1912, when a certain Swedish missionary began to build a brick house, the local people said, "It's all over, he's building a warehouse for souls." And when schoolchildren began to learn the French terms for parts of the body, many people fled as far away as Brazzaville.

Despite this dubious reputation, the Protestants did win many converts. So did the Catholics, who came later, so that since the 1930s virtually all BaKongo have been Christians. Nevertheless the reputation exists. In 1980, in Kisangani, about one thousand miles northeast of Kongo territory, rumor explained the recent arrival of Baha'i missionaries in that area by saying that the government had incurred an enormous foreign debt in building the new international airport there and had had to allow a new group to harvest souls in order to pay it off.

The economics of imperialism

The production of export goods by local labor, organized by the Belgians in the earliest stages of colonial rule, continued the same extortion of souls by other means. I was told in 1970 that ivory and rubber, the principal exports at the turn of the century, were merely the containers for souls being shipped overseas. Later on, when the cultivation of urena was introduced (and required), the fact that some people's bundles of fiber weighed surprisingly heavy when sold to Belgian traders proved that the victims of witchcraft had been stowed in them. Amid the nationalist fervor of 1960, a Kongo newspaper published an article, in French, demanding the immediate return of all Kongo people who had been transformed into a chemical product as merchandise.

It was believed in 1970, in Matadi and elsewhere in Lower Congo, that some individuals, willing to do anything to get to America and become rich, would volunteer for this traffic. They would enter into an agreement with a foreign technician about to go home on leave and eager to do a little business on the side, such that he would take them with him to sell in Mputu. Industrial accidents in the port of Matadi were popularly explained in this way. Elsewhere I was told of certain deep pools into which ambitious persons anxious to reach the land of the dead would throw themselves, to return later as newly arrived but "locally made" white technicians or managers.

In the office of a certain magical healer, I was told a whole colonial history. The office was a murky little shed in Matadi; around the walls hung various obscure bundles, a small stuffed crocodile, a turtle shell, and a calendar from the Dime Savings Bank of Brookline. On the healer's desk stood a glass full of ballpoint pens awaiting medication so that their schoolboy owners would be able to pass their examinations. The story:

This trade was not created by black people but by the Catholic missionary. From the time of our ancestors it was our custom to sell people, but they did not die entirely. They were sold to the Portuguese, who stuffed them into ships for transportation to Belgium. When they arrived there, the Belgians sent out a notice to all the nations, saying, "What shall we do with these people? for they are worthless." Then the Protestant missionary said, "It is not proper to kill them; they should be sent to an island with water on every side, where they will die of hunger, and that will be the end of them." So they signed an agreement and put the people on ships and cast them away on an island where there was a forest with no food in it, and the sea on every side.

But truly God does not sleep. He gave them civilization, and skyscrapers sprang up, and food appeared, and every needful thing. When the Belgians came to see what had happened, they found nothing but skyscrapers, with no room anymore to plant food. And so it is to this day.

So the Catholic priest considered that something else should be done, saying, "This time, when we buy someone, we had better finish him off for good." When a man dies he has no means of knowing he is going to Belgium. Lots of people when they have been traded have the idea that now they are going to be rich, they will have their own magic. But when one has gone to Europe, that's where his name is; as for a return here, there is none—he wants the white man's ways.

Later the priest, seeing how things were, sent a message to the colonial government, saying, "The medicines the people use, which give them power, should be taken away." So now in Belgium they have a whole house full of our things, though they have no idea how to use them.

It would be a mistake to treat this story as fantastic or even simply wrong. Despite the unfamiliar idiom, we can recognize in it references to both Manhattan and the Royal Museum of Central Africa at Tervuren in Belgium. More importantly, the story conveys a far more accurate picture of the extraction of labor from Africa for the benefit of the developed world than does the usual self-serving account of Europe's "civilizing mission" and the white man's burden.

The sources of cosmology

A system of belief does not descend ready-made from the sky, nor can we explain either its origin or its present strength by saying that it is a relic of the traditional past. Their cosmology seems real to the BaKongo because they live it; their daily experience confirms it. If we examine that same life sociologically, we find that the sociological models of political organization and marital alliance exhibit the same structure as the cosmology.

Every free man or woman belongs to a matrilineal clan, a group whose members trace their descent from an original female ancestor. The group is exogamous, meaning that everyone must look to some other group for a spouse. In practice, the members of any one clan marry into many other clans, but if we were to construct a model of the marriage system, it would be necessary to show only one other clan in order to demonstrate the principle. The marital alliance extends into other matters as well. For example, every group

A symbolic power-figure made of wood and iron nails.

ELISOFON ARCHIVES: NATIONAL MUSEUM OF AFRICAN ART

needs at least one other to testify to the truth of its traditions and its property claims. Though every individual belongs with his mother in one group, his father necessarily belongs to the other, where he has certain religious and political functions to fulfill, and so on.

This simple, egalitarian model is well established in Kongo thought and expressed in a variety of proverbs, such as "Where the needle goes, the thread follows," and "Whence the pig escaped, they return the piglet." It is also embodied in a number of figures of speech, found among many Central African peoples, that describe the relationship between two clans as being like the two banks of a river. The role of a married woman in linking them is compared to that of a canoe going to and fro. The similarity to the model of the reciprocating universe is clinched by the term *nzadi*, which means not only "large river" but "in-law." Hence the riddle, "What large river is full to overflowing, but we don't fall in?"

The reciprocating universe is thus real to BaKongo because they literally live it.

In 1921, Simon Kimbangu arose as a prophet in Lower Congo, preaching the Gospel, healing the sick and casting out witchcraft. So began one of the best-known African religious movements of modern times, surviving Belgian repression through several decades and giving rise to many variants. One of the strongest Kimbanguist themes concerns the expected return of the "King of the Americans." A hymn says, "When the King of the Americans comes, to announce the King of Kongo, our sufferings will have been noticed."

Not understanding Kongo cosmology, the Belgians took this millenarian expectation literally, attributing it to the nefarious influence of Marcus Garvey or of the American government, eager to take over the Belgian colony. In fact it meant that BaKongo expected the hand of God, working through his prophet Kimbangu, to turn the world upside down, so that the ancestors from across the water (the Americans) would return, and disease and oppression would end. Similar ideas guided popular understanding as national independence approached in 1960. Many people thought they would become white, and some of them knocked politely on the doors of European residences asking to see the kind of accommodations they would be moving into. The Europeans thought them naive, as no doubt in a sense they were, though not in the sense that was attributed to them.

A longer discussion would show that the whole cosmology is intriguingly more complex than I have shown here. Like other cosmologies, Kongo ideas of the universe are not in a simple sense either true or false. Component propositions may be refutable, but the system, as part of the fabric of a way of life, is self-confirming. As that way of life changes, so will it become implicit in the cosmology. Such a process happens not because of any universal tendency but because of particular local events. More and more BaKongo individually live urban, bureaucratic lives to which the clan system is becoming irrelevant. More radically, the government of Zaire has taken legal, economic, and political steps to destroy local social structures such as the one described here.□

—————— **Additional Reading** ——————

Wyatt MacGaffey, *Religion and Society in Central Africa*, Chicago, 1986.

Robert Farris Thompson and Joseph Cornet, *The Four Moments of the Sun: Kongo Art in Two Worlds*, Washington, 1981.

Wyatt MacGaffey is John R. Coleman Professor of Social Sciences at Haverford College.

Article 2

WEST AFRICA
November 21-27 1988

Struggle for dignity

By a correspondent

AFRICA, at the fortieth anniversary of the United Nations Universal Declaration of Human Rights, is in a sorry state. Most things being relative, it must quickly be asserted that Africa is not unique in this situation. The lot of mankind is definitely divisible, with a minority enjoying the fullest rights, even in excess, while the majority of humans steadily increase in their numbers, and seemingly in inverse proportion to the rights they enjoy.

Some would argue that as the fingers on the hand are not of equal length, so must humans have lives of unequal length and quality. Others would piously add that the meek shall inherit the earth. On which note, the cynics would proclaim: the poor shall have land rights in the afterlife.

Africa, the cradle of earthly civilisation, looms largest in the statistics of poverty, illiteracy, and disease. The dominant media of the world have succeeded in fixing Africa in the 'international consciousness' as the home of the backward section of humanity, with leaders to match. Many people unwittingly share the apartheid line of argument: Look what Africans do to themselves with their independence'. Many Africans

ARTICLE 19

By BILL DAY
Detroit Free Press

themselves believe, even if they won't admit it, that white people's civilisation is superior. But that is part of the inculcated self-hate.

Frederico Mayor, the Unesco director-general, recently took the opportunity of the impending fortieth anniversary of the human rights declaration to appeal to all heads of state and government, education ministers and educators (perhaps he meant to include health ministers as well). He said: "Every man, woman and child in this world must know that no one should be subject to discrimination, be it based on race, colour, sex, language, religion, political opinion, national or social origin, property, birth, or other status. No one may be held in slavery or servitude. No one may be subjected to torture or to cruel, inhuman or degrading treatment or punishment".

This is precisely the catalogue of daily violations that occurs in innumerable countries. The only problem is to establish the hierarchy of responsibility, and draw up a plan of corrective, affirmative action. It would be understandable, although incorrect, for Africans to point the index finger at colonialism as the root cause of contemporary problems. But many Africans have dismissed this argument which gives an alibi for their governments. The negative impact of colonialism must figure in any serious analysis, but must not obliterate the divisions in African societies before and after imperialism. One must also be aware of the political and material bonds between cer-

tain African governments and certain foreign powers, be they governmental in form, or financial in nature.

The colonising countries themselves have a long history of human rights violations perpetrated by the rulers against the ruled. And the conquest of certain rights has been the fruit of long centuries. There is an argument over what exactly produced developments in the rights of peoples, whether economic forces were solely or primarily responsible. Two examples are the evolution of voting rights according to gender and class, and the raising of living standards in the latter stages of industrial revolution in order to have a more quiescent and productive working class.

There is, however, the inescapable fact that it is people of a certain consciousness — perhaps even the objective alliance between the most intelligent rich people, the middle classes with ample consciences, and the militant defenders of the human rights of workers — who have been the human agents for improvement.

But there is also the fact of the relative value of the existence of Bills of Rights, constitutions, and the paper paraphernalia of human rights (included the United Nations' own hallowed document). The argument goes that they are the guarantee of recourse to laws that exist; that the framework enables laws to be enforced. But some countries do not have constitutions — Britain is one kind of example. Some countries have constitutions whose noble provisions have no practical mean-

ing. And most important of all, governments of the day can change the laws and amend constitutions.

Many African countries have fine constitutions; but they also have laws that suggest a permanent state of emergency, enabling them to detain people indefinitely without charge or trial, literally 'at the pleasure' of the leadership, if not to say plainly that it is often the bitter fruit of nervous whims and malicious caprices. The Thatcher government in Britain is under current criticism for eroding trade union and press freedoms. The Reagan regime has been attacked in detail for reversing during its eight-year tenure the civil and human rights gains of the 1960s.

Indeed, the political programmes of such governments — commonly known as right-wing or conservative — tend to liberate the impersonal market forces and leave people to enjoy those human rights they can afford.

This is where the contemporary tide of structural adjustment programmes enters the picture. The free-market doctrines that underpin the IMF and World Bank programmes are criticised for reversing the social and economic gains made by African countries since independence. Political gains are also eroded when the rise of opposition to the adjustment policies threatens the stability of governments. Hence the persuasive argument that Africa's variety of dictatorships — military; military-cum-civilian; single party; president-for-life, etc — is ideally suited for the task of implementing economic programmes that are designed to lubricate the movement of finance capital rather than ameliorate the lives of ordinary people.

It was no surprise that among the charges laid against the IMF and World Bank during their September 'trial' in Berlin was that they and the governments implementing their policies were in violation of the Universal Declaration of Human Rights. A look at the list of rights and freedoms in the human rights covenants (see box) would suggest that peoples' rights are being sacrificed on the altar of positive indices of macroeconomic growth.

The growing concern of the main managers of the international economic system has been to write into the adjustment programmes some measures to 'alleviate' what they claim to be their 'short-term' impact. Ghana's Pamscad programme — which aims to 'mitigate the social costs of adjustment' — is being implemented in a political climate that rolls storm clouds over anybody who wishes to question the whole adjustment programme. The foreign and local managers, it would seem, are increasingly concerned with the *political* costs of structural adjustment. That is why a new form of social welfare is being developed on an international scale, seeking to adjust the old structures of aid and dependency in order to meet contemporary requirements.

This is why education and information appear to be at the sharp end of the debate. Education because it is the foundation on which people make rational choices that affect their destiny. Information because its dissemination — in quality and quantity — is the foundation for the broad development of the greatest number of people. Information and education may, in fact, be rolled into one global and ever expanding corpus of human experience and invention.

The combination of information, education and action is that which best combats the greedy paranoia of tyranny. That is why organisations exist like Amnesty International, Article 19, Index on Censorship, Human Rights Watch, InterRights, the US Lawyers Committees, the African Jurists' Association, the various national and local organisations de-

voted to defending human rights. And that is why it becomes increasingly necessary to protect the human rights watchers.

Their particular problem is finding themselves in the role of acting as the conscience of governments. They are the bell-ringers and the town criers. They are obliged to shout aloud that the regime has no clothes. But they face two major problems. The first is how to publicise the nakedness of the regime. The local press is nearly always a tool of the regime, living with the same fears for personal security as the rest of the population. There is such a degree of inherent instability in African regimes that open criticism is one step, or one decree away from subversion.

And that is the second problem. Any recourse to foreign media and international human rights organisations too often leads to charges of subversion, and of being in the pay of foreign intelligence agencies. African countries are on the whole far removed from the Latin American death squads. But they tend to throw people into prison for rather long periods of time without charge or trial.

A roll call of Africa's leaders and gov-

ernments would not be very impressive in terms of their respect for the UN list of human rights. Against another set of criteria, many of them would emerge as lauded guarantors of political stability, and valued friends of one foreign power or the other. There is little point in making a catalogue here of African country violators of human rights. Amnesty International's 1988 report, for example, finds grounds to mention 45 African countries. And its list concentrates on civil and political rights. We can safely declare that until the majority of Africa's people enjoy basic standards of health, personal security, and civil rights, all the countries are in violation of the Universal Declaration.

But whatever the regime in Africa, there is always the patient, courageous work of obliging the government to obey the existing laws, seeking promulgation of new laws which improve life for the majority of people. This is the basic struggle for the dignity and respect that most people believe to be their birthright. And this is an important part of the way forward for a strong Africa, united in its action for healthy, educated and productive Africans.   WA

WEST AFRICA
September 19-25 1988

Article 3

The slow progress of Africa's recovery

Patrick Smith reports on the background to the UN Special Session on Africa which began last week.

THE UNITED NATIONS General Assembly's special session on Africa, which started on September 12 to review progress on the region's five-year recovery programme launched in 1986, faces a mountain of data indicating that far from improving, economic and social conditions in Africa are getting worse. Delegates to the two-week assembly will be debating a report by the UN Secretary-General Javier Perez de Cuellar which shows that per capita income in Africa has fallen further since the launch of the programme, the debt burden has increased and is likely to rise still further,

while the last two years have seen more cuts in imports which are crucial to economic recovery.

The UN review of the recovery programme comes at a time when the price levels of some of Africa's principal export commodities are at their lowest level — in real terms — for 50 years, while the region falls deeper into debt. The UN Conference of Trade and Development (Unctad) estimates that by the year 2010 Latin American debt will be, on present trends, about 83 per cent of its total export income while Africa's will be over 280 per cent.

Perez de Cuellar described Africa's debt burden ". . . as one of the most important factors constraining recovery and development in the continent". The region's total external debt had risen to $218bn by the end of 1987, according to the UN's Economic Commission for Africa. That is three times the region's export earnings, which is a considerable deterioration since 1985 when Africa's debt was twice its annual export earnings.

Unless there are some dramatic new initiatives African countries will have to devote an increasing proportion of their export earnings to debt service; in 1987 debt service was estimated at about $27bn to $29bn for the region, and is projected to reach $45bn a year by 1995. The combined effects of this debt service burden, decline in export earnings, together with drought and structural constraints in the domestic economies has ". . . outweighed the positive influence of policy reforms", de Cuellar said.

This sober assessment of Africa's economic progress, or lack of it, calls into question the reciprocity on which the UN Programme of Action for African Economic Recovery and Development (UN-PAAERD) was launched. UN-PAAERD was a compact under which African governments committed themselves to wide-ranging economic reforms while the international community pledged to provide additional financial support.

To a great extent, African governments have fulfilled their side of the bargain. The UN review shows the impact of devaluation and cuts in public spending — two of the key policies in the 'reform programe' packages — on African economies. African exchange rates, which were higher than those of any other developing region in the early 1980s, are now the lowest in the world, having fallen by an average of 55 per cent in the last three years, while the governments' budgetary deficits have been cut by nearly a third.

Coming on top of existing social and economic deprivation, this has meant "severe personal hardship" for hundreds of millions, de Cuellar said. Infant and child deaths in Africa are increasing yearly and are projected by Unicef to total 50m in the period 1985 to 2000.

So, while African governments have implemented the promised policy reforms, the international community's pledges of increased capital flows and concessional finance have not restored growth nor even prevented further deterioration. Several initiatives — the World Bank's Special Facility for Africa, the IMF's Structural Adjustment Facility, the Baker Plan and the repeated rescheduling of debt repayments — have been undertaken with mixed results. But the general conclusion is that they have not gone far enough.

Some initiatives, like Ghana's Programme of Actions to Mitigate the Social Costs of Adjustment (Pamscad), have succeeded in focusing attention on the scale of the economic and social problems facing those African countries which have adopted adjustment programmes, but the economic and social programmes launched in response to the crisis have not kept pace with the deepening crisis.

In real terms, net resource flows to Africa have virtually stagnated. At $22.9bn in 1987 they were some 2.3 per cent higher than in 1986, but were still 2.2 per cent lower 1985. Private commercial credits have been almost negligible for the past five years and even official export credits have fallen off sharply. Official Development Assistance (ODA) from the member countries of the OECD's Development Assistance Committee, Opec countries and the multilateral institutions rose in nominal terms in 1987, but the UN review points out that this reflects no increase over 1986 levels.

Despite these grim statistics, de Cuellar urged African governments "to continue the process of policy re-orientation and reform aimed at accelerating recovery and improving the performance of their economies". At the same time, de Cuellar urged the international community to back the programmes more effectively, in particular for countries to step up the level of Official Development Assistance.

Apart from this call, de Cuellar also argues for a series of new initiatives to increase Africa's export earnings. Most apposite perhaps, in view of the recent price crashes in the commodity markets, is the call for a Common Fund for Commodities which is designed to help commodity-dependent countries finance export diversification. Africa is terribly dependent upon primary commodities as a source of foreign earnings; about 90 per cent of all exports from sub-Saharan Africa are primary commodities.

Any dip in commodity prices, therefore

The export of primary commodities is not the ticket to the future for ailing economies.

has an immediate effect on the region's ability to import its agricultural inputs, industrial plant and machinery, medical supplies, fuel and even wood. A fall of about $19bn in the region's earnings from commodity exports in 1986 (about a third of its $64bn income the previous year) dealt a devastating blow to development plans and investment in diversification.

The proximate reason for the fall in commodity prices is a glut of produce as each African country tries to boost output. And these African countries are increasingly competing not just amongst themselves for the export markets but with other developing countries — Africa's coffee producers compete with the mega-debtors and coffee growers of Latin America; Africa's oil palm producers compete with the growing productivity of oil palm growers in South East Asia; while Africa's cocoa producers have to contend with growing competition from both Latin America and Asia.

Clearly the export of primary commodities is not the ticket to the future for Africa's ailing economies.

But development of alternatives and investment in the diversification of industries, along with the construction of the required infrastructure and implementation of training programmes, is at best a medium-term process and one that is unlikely to start until the countries involved can achieve some economic equilibrium, between external demands and local needs. In the meantime, Africa should at least be able to process more of its commodities, the UN review says.

The UN report also argues for a substantial increase in the IMF's Compensatory Financing Facility (CFF) which has failed to provide anything near the level of support necessary to offset Africa's losses as export prices tumble.

While de Cuellar welcomed the Toronto Summit's menu of options he urged that they should be "translated in the immediate future into concrete, broadly applicable and substantial debt relief measures that would reduce the stock of debt in Africa . . ." However the Toronto measures — even if they were implemented immediately — would only help the poorest of Africa's debtors while several countries with substantial debt burdens, like Côte d'Ivoire and Nigeria, would not be affected.

Such countries which fell into the middle-income category of developing countries were supposed to benefit from the much vaunted Baker Plan outlined almost three years ago by the former US Treasury Secretary James Baker. The thrust of the plan was the return of debtor countries to credit worthiness through growth-oriented economic policies supported by new loans from the commercial banks and the multilateral organisations such as the World Bank and the IMF.

Even in distinctly un-radical quarters like the World Bank and IMF, there is a view that the plan is unrealistic given the self-interest of the banks who are predominantly concerned to minimise their exposure to heavily indebted countries.

Indeed the managing director of the IMF, Michel Camdessus, has sharply criticised the banks for not lending enough and taking too long to do it — "Last year net bank lending to countries with debt servicing problems was negligible at best; the two years before it was negative". In turn banks say that it is fine for Camdessus to criticise them for not increasing their exposure when his own organisation is a net recipient of funds from many of the still chronically indebted countries.

Banks also argue the "new money" elements in the Baker Plan are being applied unevenly; they are especially angry about what they call 'free riders', that is banks which never put up new money but benefit from the interest payments. A recent rescheduling agreement with Côte d'Ivoire, which is written under French law and has yet to go into effect, punishes the 'free riders' by stopping service on the debt, for banks which do not up new money.

However, the commercial banks show every sign of disliking the Unctad alternative (or compliment) to the Baker Plan even more. The Unctad plan, detailed in this year's report, calls for a 30 per cent once-for-all cut in commercial bank debt for the 15 most indebted countries. The Unctad case is that if these savings were ploughed in to export diversification while the efficiency of investment is improved, the main debtor countries — including Côte d'Ivoire and Nigeria — would be better able to service the remainder of their debt.

The carrot for the industrialised countries, the Unctad economists argue, is that a reduction in the commercial debt of these countries would provide an extra fillip to world trade and help to improve the US trade balance. Such a programme of debt relief would stimulate annual increases over the 1987 level of $18bn in net import demand from debtor countries; some $6bn of this could be used to buy US products.

Predictably the banks and other members of the international financial establishment have been luke warm towards the plan. They prefer market mechanisms, such as exit bonds and debt to equity swaps, as a means of reducing the debt stock. However, the Unctad proposal indicates there is no shortage of radical ideas to alleviate the debt crisis, of which several will be under contention during the UN General Assembly's review of UN-PAAERD. ◼

Article 4

AFRICA NEWS
November 28, 1988

Cooperation Pays Off

Six days a week, Selina Adjebeng-Asem rises at 5 a.m., and she rarely goes to bed before 1 a.m. In the 20 hours that constitute her work day, the Ghanaian sociologist and mother of three teaches classes to 350 undergraduates at Nigeria's Ife University, makes four round-trips to her children's schools to deliver them to morning and afternoon classes – feeding them lunch in between – does the family shopping, cooks an evening meal, checks her children's homework before putting them to bed, and, finally, burns the midnight oil with academic chores like writing and reading. On Saturdays, Asem rests. "That is my day," she says, smiling. "Nobody better talk to me."

As daunting as Asem's schedule may seem, her position as one of Africa's highly educated professional women relieves her of the arduous physical labor that is a constant feature of most African women's lives. And Asem is the first to insist that she is not unique, even among the women in her socio-economic class. "All average working women [in west Africa] are doing what I'm doing," she says. "They wake at about 5 and are asleep, at the earliest, by 11. We cope somehow, and we hope that nature will continue to be good to us so that we can survive."

At the annual African Studies Association conference in Chicago last month, Asem joined other scholars in examining some of the problems faced by African women, along with the strategies some are using to better their lot.

Across the board, according to the participants at the Chicago meeting, African women tend to be better off when they cooperate with each other, formally or informally. In Ghana, for instance, University of Michigan anthropologist Gracia Clark founded a women's agricultural cooperative whose members have combined government encouragement, sage financial advice and traditional social structures to run a successful business.

The Hadasko ("hard working") Women Farmers' Association was born in 1981, when an official from Ghana's National Council for Women and Development visited Damongo, in the northwestern district of Gonja. The official recommended that the women of Damongo form a cooperative in order to take advantage of government funds that were available to collective farms. Under Flt. Lt. Jerry Rawlings, Ghana's government has favored the agricultural sector of the economy, and there has been a strong push toward getting more women involved in farming.

The Hadasko association, which grows cassava and processes it into gari, a staple food in many parts of Ghana, has quadrupled its membership to 200 women in seven years. It operates without men and without outside assistance because the women – who, traditionally, have been ineligible for bank loans because they don't own property – have found strength in their reputation. Although the cooperative will guarantee to repay a bank loan taken out by a member, it automatically ousts any member who defaults on a loan without good cause. Thus, the project has earned a reputation among local bankers as an excellent risk. And that trend, according to Gracia Clark, applies to women's cooperatives in other parts of Ghana. "Banks lend to women and like lending to women," Clark says, "because women pay the money back."

Hadasko is also successful, Clark says, because it draws upon Damongo's existing power structure. First, the group poses no threat to local men because farming was never a "male domain." And second, the association institutionalizes a pre-existing relationship between the community's women. The cooperative is split into work groups of five to ten members each, and within each group, women help each other, not only with work-related tasks, but with childbirth, domestic problems and other personal matters. Each group is led by a respected, generally older, member of the community – a woman who would traditionally be looked to as an advisor.

Finally, of course, Hadasko has succeeded because the Ghanaian government encourages such initiatives. But even in Kenya, where

Almasy-Vauthey/Unesco

Primary schoolchildren in Lagos, Nigeria. At many African secondary schools, boys outnumber girls by almost two to one.

authorities have been less willing to support women's groups, Hilarie Kelly of UCLA founded a nomadic group whose women come together under the aegis of a sacred ritual to cooperate on economic projects and to work out problems.

The Orma, Muslim cattle-herders who live near Kenya's border with Somalia, are gradually settling into a more sedentary life style that, Kelly says, affords women "more occasion for cooperative labor and leisure." But settling into villages has also meant an increase in interpersonal tensions, and since Islam, as the Orma practice it, does not encourage women to gather to discuss problems, Orma women have turned to an institution that pre-dates their community's conversion to Islam.

The *gaas eba* (meaning "blessed shade," and so named because meetings are held under trees) is led by women elders, and it has so much power as a ritual expression of the woman's "role in regulating the sacred forces behind fertility, rain, milk production, peace and tranquility," Kelly says, that "men cannot prevent their wives from attending." But, even though Orma women also acknowledge the ritual importance of *gaas eba*, the institution is evolving, in

some neighborhoods, into a series of regularly held meetings where women can address various secular concerns. The *gaas eba* serves as a conduit for complaints from women to male village elders; and sometimes, Kelly says, a women's *gaas eba* receives permission to punish an "especially offensive or abusive husband whose behavior is taken as an insult against all women, as thus against domestic peace."

The *gaas eba* has also, in some cases, spawned women's cooperatives for the sale of milk. Some of these are now competing successfully with other cattle-herding groups, and even with the government's Kenya Cooperative Creameries.

While the Ghanaian and Kenya collectives highlight the power women can seize when they work together, there are few national women's initiatives active in Africa. Many African governments have established organs for the consideration of women's issues, but so far, little impact has been made on the daily lives of women on the continent.

One Kenyan academic at the Chicago conference blamed women themselves for not pushing their own concerns at the national level.

"Where were the women's organizations?" the academic asked, after explaining that a law that would have made wife-beating illegal in Kenya was thrown out of court because it was "traditional" for men to "discipline" their wives. Citing the recent decision by Kenya's ruling Kenya African National Union to take the once-powerful women's organization called *Maendeleo Ya Wanawake* under its mantle, the academic complained that other such groups "have not taken the lead in helping women either to seize the rights they do have or to fight for others."

Selina Adjebeng-Asem, who spoke at a recent gathering Duke University in North Carolina, agrees that women must take the lead and help themselves. But she insists that attempts to "liberate" African women are doomed to failure unless men are also liberated.

"I belong to a number of organizations that are women-based," Asem says, "but I don't think that is where the problem lies. The problem lies in the society. We would be defeating our purpose by making it just a feminine issue. The only reason we ask women to get involved is because it concerns us, and men are not going to go out of their way to look at our problem. But when it becomes a mainstream problem, then men are going to look at it."

Asem's particular interest is in gender inequalities in the Nigerian work force, and she believes that more women must get more education in order to break into technical fields in significant numbers.

"People will tell you that we don't have a women's problem in Nigeria," Asem says. "I mean, nobody is discriminating against any woman. If you can get education, you can get a job. And if I have a faculty position and have the same qualifications as [a man], I get the same salary. There's no discrimination."

But the problem for many Nigerian girls, Asem says, is getting the education in the first place. Many families place great emphasis on educating sons, but keep their daughters at home "cleaning and doing dishes and helping Mommy take care of the babies." Other girls, especially the daughters of Nigeria's Yoruba trading women, often leave school young in order to join their mothers in the street markets.

When educating children represents a financial sacrifice – as it does for more and more African parents as the continent's debt crisis deepens – school fees are allocated to sons. "There is something in our community," Asem says, referring to west Africa, "that believes that male stands for power, stands for continuity. So even women want to educate their male children more than their female children – because they will carry the family line. They are the symbols of the family."

According to Asem, not only does the drop-out rate for Nigerian girls increase as they go further in school, but those women who do complete degrees are "sexually segregated" into "female ghettoes" like nursing, teaching and clerical work. She and the other members of a professional women's group make regular visits to secondary schools, where they talk to first-year female students about the opportunities that are available in technical fields.

Asem admits that the task of sensitizing the next generation of west Africans—male and female—to women's issues won't be easy. The pressure on women to conform to existing norms is "incredible," Asem says. Most of her women students are afraid that if they get all the education they want and need to compete with men for high-level jobs, they will be unable to find husbands when they are ready to marry. And in Africa, Asem says, "a woman must marry. A woman must have children."

But Asem thinks Africa's current economic woes may actually help women decide to go on in school. "I hope and believe that all these inflationary trends are going to make men accept more qualified women as wives. I think that the woman who has more education and a fatter pay packet will stand a better chance of getting a husband than the one that stops by the way." Asem also counsels women to get more education as a hedge against failed marriages, since women often bear primary responsibility for providing for their children.

While Asem doesn't think Nigeria needs a "women's movement" on the Western model, she does believe that individual women can affect a lasting change in the way society views women's roles.

"Who makes society but us?" Asem asks. "And who can change society but us? You just stick your neck out and say, 'I'm not doing this,' 'I'm going to go ahead and do that.' Believe me, by the time two or three people have become deviates, society is bound to accept us for what we are."

"Just go ahead and do exactly what you want to do," Asem advises her students, male and female. "Just do it."

Yosef Hadar/World Bank

Women planting groundnuts at a seed multiplication farm in Nigeria.

Article 5

AFRICA REPORT
September-October 1988

AGRICULTURE

FOOD
Finding Solutions to the
CRISIS

The cover story of this issue is food and agriculture in Africa. Though blessed with an abundance of arable land and a population which is primarily agrarian, the African continent lags woefully behind the rest of the world in its ability to grow enough food to meet the needs of its expanding population. Beginning with the director-general of the International Institute of Tropical Agriculture, who outlines a strategy to address the food crisis, we examine why Africa is not feeding itself, analyzing the agricultural sectors of a sampling of countries. Poverty, not lack of resolve, emerges as the key impediment to Africa's agricultural development.

BEDE N. OKIGBO
Bede N. Okigbo is director-general of the International Institute of Tropical Agriculture in Ibadan, Nigeria.

Most African countries are still unable to produce enough food to satisfy increasing demand due to population growth, urbanization, and other pressures of modernization. Africa, which has area of about 30.3 million square kilometers and is second only in area to Asia, has potential resources to produce more food than its current population requires. However, many physical, biological, socio-economic, and technological constraints constitute almost intractable obstacles to increased agricultural productivity. Moreover, in addition to the food crisis, sub-Saharan Africa also faces demographic, environmental, economic, and political crises.

Traditional African agriculture has al-ready undergone changes, with some increases in agricultural productivity. Although the shifting cultivation and related fallow systems on which African traditional agricultural production systems are based were once ecologically sound and economically viable, they have become increasingly outmoded and unable to satisfy escalating demands for food, feed, industrial raw materials, and other products.

All these call for good understanding of the continent's environmental resources and traditional resource management strategies and systems as a basis for planning, formulating policies, and establishing priorities and strategies in research aimed at developing appropriate technologies for more efficient management, processing, and better utilization of the enormous but not unlimited resources of this vast continent.

> Traditional African agriculture has already undergone changes, with some increases in agricultural productivity.

Africa has tried to adopt resource management strategies, agricultural production systems, and technologies developed elsewhere. But these have either been unsuccessful or very disappointing, especially in agricultural production. Sub-Saharan Africa currently lacks capabilities for executing research of sufficient scope, intensity, and continuity necessary for developing efficient, permanent,

Irrigation scheme, Sourou Valley, Burkina Faso: More effort and resources should be given to irrigation in increasing food production

and sustainable agricultural production systems and component technologies that ensure attainment of annual growth rates of 3-4 percent in agricultural and/or food production. Without such growth rates, food self-sufficiency or security cannot be assured.

It is for this reason that the international agricultural research centers (IARCs) have been founded and mandated to conduct problem-oriented research and training that assist national institutions to quantitatively and qualitatively increase food production. But it is obvious that with very weak national agricultural research systems that lack the critical manpower resources and are inadequately and erratically funded, poor extension services, and ineffective linkage with the farmer, full advantage cannot be taken of developments at the IARCs in finding effective solutions to Africa's food and agricultural crisis by the year 2000.

The following recommendations are guidelines for finding solutions to the above problems. Agricultural development is a long-term and continuous exercise. Therefore, all governments should be committed to allocating enough re-

sources to agricultural development and should ensure that priority is given to policies and strategies aimed at achieving this goal.

Efficient management of our agricultural and natural resources requires adequate knowledge of the African environment and its natural resources, traditional management, and production and utilization systems as a basis for determining priorities and strategies in research and development.

This can best be achieved through balanced allocation of resources to basic, strategic, applied, and adaptive research programs that are effectively linked with training, extension, and the farmer.

In all studies, a multidisciplinary approach should be adhered to as is done in farming systems research that involves interaction of physical, chemical, biological, and social sciences. There is need for regional cooperation and effective linkage with IARCs in attempts to develop capabilities for generating appropriate technologies for increasing agricultural production at the individual or local country level.

In tackling the African food crisis and in all activities aimed at achieving food self-

sufficiency and security, priority should be given to increased production of commodities for which a given country has ecological and/or economic advantage and not for all food items that are imported. There is room for planned international trade among African countries and more cooperation aimed at regional rather than national self-sufficiency.

There is need for higher priority to be given to selected underutilized African food plants and multi-use species since their integration with major staples ensures greater sustainability of production, broadening of the food base, better food quality, and more efficient utilization of resources.

A multiple land use strategy should be adhered to so as to ensure that the limited land available is efficiently utilized to satisfy demand for agriculture, forestry, roads and airports, markets, etc. An element should be integrated watershed development which ensures that crops are grown in the landscape in toposequences in which they are most adapted. This will facilitate greater use of much of the 20 million hectares of hydromorphic soils in Africa. Moreover, more effort and resources should be given to realization of the potential of irrigation in increasing food production in sub-Saharan Africa.

It is the duty of African researchers to ensure relevance and also contribute to facilitating adoption of new technologies through greater emphasis on on-farm research linked with extension and users, rather than conduction of research as an academic exercise or as an intellectually prestigious ritual.

There are a host of policy issues which must be addressed if increased agricultural production is to be attained. These include:

• giving high priority to problems of the majority of small farmers;
• determining the extent of government participation in direct production, which is often not successful;
• giving meaningful balance between cash commodities and subsistence agriculture;
• striking a meaningful balance between agricultural and industrial development;
• finding ways of ensuring adequate rural infrastructural development and provision of incentives to farmers;
• provision for planning multiple land use and finding ways to increase farm size;

• ensuring complementarity in development among various ecological zones.

Finally, it is unlikely that the critical level of agricultural research needed for developing technologies for increasing agricultural productivity can be adequately funded on a continuing basis as long as debt burdens of African countries persist. It is therefore recommended that funds needed for agricultural research be deducted from the debt-servicing charges for individual African countries until they have the capability of producing enough food to meet demand. ◯

Article 6

AFRICA NEWS
November 30, 1987

RETHINKING HIGHER EDUCATION

Studying French at a teachers college in Nigeria

United Nations

Arusha, Tanzania—The economic stagnation and decline confronting the continent of Africa has plunged African higher education into its worst crisis since the advent of independence in the late 1950s and early 1960s.

African educators—many of whom work in institutions so severely strapped by foreign currency shortages that they are unable to buy basic materials such as laboratory equipment and books—came together with government officials and aid donors here in late September to plot strategies to address the crisis.

"The harsh economic circumstances afflicting our countries," threaten African universities with "strangulation," according to Zambian Minister of Higher Education Lameck Goma. Many students are left "undereducated," and the situation has caused "overcrowding, poor teaching, impoverished research and frustrated, embittered students and staff," Goma told the Arusha meeting of the East and Southern Africa Universities Research Program (ESAURP).

One response to the current situation generated heated debate at the ESAURP gathering: a controversial, to date "confidential" – yet widely circulated – draft of a World Bank paper on "Education Policies for Sub-Saharan Africa: Adjustment, Revitalization and Expansion." A summary of the draft was quoted at a meeting of African university vice-chancellors, presidents and regents in Harare, Zimbabwe last January 19. More formal presentations were made to African education ministers in Addis Ababa, Ethiopia and Abengourou, Cote d'Ivoire in late January and early February.

The report says African universities generally cost more to operate than they should, offer weak programs, pour resources into fields that do not promote development and use money that could benefit more people if spent on primary schools.

The study also states that many under-equipped institutions are producing "biologists who have not done a dissection, physicists who have never measured an electric current..., lawyers who do not have access to recent judicial opinions [and] medical doctors whose only knowledge of laboratory test procedures is from hearing them described in a lecture hall."

David Wiley, director of African Studies at Michigan State University, paints the picture in similarly gloomy terms. Because libraries cannot afford to keep pace with current literature, many African students are unable to do basic research in their fields – and

Students in Nursing Training School in Niamey, Niger.

United Nations

they cannot hope to build on past advances unless they know about them.

The American Association for the Advancement of Science, with distribution assistance from the U.S. Information Agency (USIA), is providing African universities with scientific journals to ameliorate the shortages, but Wiley says many more foreign donors must get involved in providing basic funds for libraries and laboratories.

Most experts offer similar diagnoses of the larger problems faced by higher education in Africa. The average, underfunded African university lacks the resources needed to properly meet urgent needs in education, research and social service. But as is the case in the broader African economic crisis, proposed cures vary radically.

The World Bank paper prescribes some surgery: cut the number of

students and faculty, curtail academic programs that don't directly contribute to development, charge more university costs to students, tighten admission standards, close some campuses and merge duplicate programs.

The study recommends that part of the savings be used to provide more rigorous education to the remaining university students and to selectively expand development-oriented research and training programs. The remainder, the study says, should be used to improve primary schools – which, according to World Bank researchers, offer the best return on education investments.

Many African scholars have denounced the proposals, saying they smack of neocolonialism. If adopted, the measures would make it impossible for Africa to replace foreign technicians with local skilled personnel and plunge the continent into "a

GLOBAL STUDIES: AFRICA

state of dependency for all times," according to University of Zimbabwe Vice-Chancellor Walter Kamba. "We would be colonies forever," Kamba warned at the Harare meeting, "going back to the developed countries and saying, 'We can't cope.'"

Aklilu Habte, the former president of the University of Addis Ababa who is currently serving as the World Bank's special advisor on human resources development for Africa, counters that the Bank paper has been widely misunderstood and that most of the furor has arisen because the study was quoted out of context in Harare. Aklilu says the Bank is encouraging the funding of primary schools partly because literacy will lead to equality and partly in the hope that governments will be pressured by increased numbers of primary school graduates into revamping their secondary school systems along more cost-efficient lines, using correspondence courses and phasing out most boarding schools.

But Aklilu insists that a reconsideration of the importance of primary and secondary education does not mean abandonment of universities. "After making great strides between 1960 and 1984, African universities have declined in the past three years," Aklilu notes, because the governments are unable to provide enough money to keep facilities and materials current. "Our interest is in recruiting alternative forms of funding," and not in cutting university programs that have real benefit in the African situation.

The World Bank paper suggests that one way to retain programs may be to regionalize them. "Some countries have only 5,000 students in the university," Aklilu says, "but each little university has some of the same courses of study," and regional institutions would save on faculty salaries, materials and infrastructures.

Wiley believes that the identity crisis of higher education is rooted in its colonial history. Modeled after European universities and developed as elite institutions, African universities were not expected to participate in the development process.

"In 1961, when I first set foot on the campus of the University of Ibadan in Nigeria – the premier university of Africa's most populous nation – the Department of Classics was the largest department," Wiley recalls.

He says that African education officials have become interested in the pattern of land-grant universities in the U.S., where faculty spend time out in the field and the teaching and research programs at their schools reflect the concrete needs of communities – especially in agriculture, education and health. "Clearly, at this time in history," Wiley says, "the African university has a greater capacity than any foreign institution to conduct research that is responsive to the continent's development needs."

Mesfin Wolde-Mariam, a retired University of Addis Ababa professor who is currently a Fulbright Fellow at Michigan State, says Africans must "be taught to think logically about development problems," and that this process must begin at the primary school level. "Even mathematics shouldn't be taught in the abstract," Wolde-Mariam says. "Everything we teach should be applied to our lives."

According to Wolde-Mariam, the western educational system is inappropriate for Africa on all levels. Children, he says, should not focus on exams "so they can put a label on their foreheads and say 'I have done this,'" but instead, should be taught that the reason for learning anything is to apply it to their lives. Even arts education, as currently taught, could be done away with on that basis. "Art comes from experience," Wolde-Mariam says when challenged about the seemingly utilitarian nature of his plan. "If third world musicians are trained in the first world, whose music will they play?"

Wolde-Mariam believes the Bank recommendations do not go far enough to separate African education from its counterparts in the west. Other critics say the study is based on an overly narrow cost-benefit analysis that ignores both the economic advantage of replacing high-paid foreign advisors with local personnel and the broader social advantage of producing a cadre of university-trained citizens.

The study is on firmer ground, these academics say, when it insists that college students should pay more toward their education. Accord-

Many institutions are producing physicists who have never measured an electric current, lawyers who do not have access to recent judicial opinions and doctors whose only knowledge of laboratory test procedures is from hearing them described in a lecture hall.

For Wolde-Mariam, the ideal African education would be similar to the land grant model, except that instead of experts residing in the field, students would be there, addressing development problems as they arose, gaining "education by experience." He agrees with the World Bank paper's recommendations for slashing current programs and thinks universities ought to be decentralized, with only a small cadre of experts at one central location to provide advice and to do advanced research for scholars and students working in the field.

ing to the World Bank's Aklilu, African universities – most of which provide free tuition, room and board – cannot afford to bear the brunt of the costs any longer.

Cutting subsidies is, however, fraught with political difficulties, as officials in Ghana experienced when university students struck earlier this year to protest just that. Loan programs – another World Bank proposal already adopted by several African nations – only work when the money is repaid. The programs in place have faced enormous collection problems when the students graduate.

Aklilu denies that instituting charges for advanced studies will necessarily handicap qualified poor students in relation to their wealthier peers. He says African universities should look at the way colleges in the U.S. distribute scholarship money on the basis of need.

The fate of the plan will depend partly on the response from the foreign donors Aklilu cites as vital to its success. Foreign aid now contributes substantially to African higher education, and much more is needed if African governments are to relieve themselves of burdensome education subsidies.

At the ESAURP meeting, African universities received a relatively positive response to their requests for continued – even expanded – funding.

The most favorable response came from two Scandinavian countries – which have, in recent years, supplanted the U.S. and Britain as top foreign aid donors in many southern African nations.

Norway and Sweden have traditionally focused aid on the poorest of the poor: rural primary schools, not universities; midwives and village health workers, not urban medical centers. In the World Bank study, Sweden is the one donor praised for tilting away from higher education.

Today, however, aid officials from both countries are placing new stress on helping Africa build advanced institutions that can replace foreign donors in planning and developing basic services.

Olaf Kran, Tanzanian representative for Norad, Norway's overseas development agency, said his group is gradually shifting more funds into higher education. Swedish International Development Agency President Carl Tham said his government also expects to increase higher education spending, "especially in southern Africa, where it strengthens nations under siege from apartheid."

Nor are all U.S. funders cutting back spending on higher education. David Court, the Rockefeller Foundation's regional representative in Nairobi, says the foundation is

Prescription for Africa's Schools

World Bank Report No. 6934 on "Education Policies for Sub-Saharan Africa: Adjustment, Revitalization and Expansion" offers seven recommendations to improve elementary schooling and refocus secondary and tertiary education:
• Increase education's share of total (public and private) expenditures – currently averaging 4% to 5% of most African national incomes – by 1% or more.
• Spend the new money on primary schools, where modest increases in spending on textbooks and other instructional materials – up to $5 per pupil at the primary level from a current average of 60 cents – are the most cost-effective means for improving education. Reducing class size, improving teacher training or introducing sophisticated technology would have far less impact.
• Reduce secondary school costs and expand services – especially to female students and those in rural areas – by using more correspondence courses and phasing out expensive boarding schools.
• Compel students and their families to pay more of the cost of post-secondary education. Reduce staff size at universities, cut scholarships, close some programs and tighten admission standards; but selectively increase spending in some fields that "directly support economic development."
• Improve programs for "selecting, training and supervising school managers, and enhance institutional autonomy." Develop achievement tests that measure the performance of schools and let supervisors and communities see the results.
• Adopt "short term, painful measures of adjustment" needed to free funds for improving educational quality: encourage expansion of private schools, impose fees for some public schools, control secondary and post-secondary school spending. Use savings to increase spending on instructional materials, testing, maintenance of schools and new equipment.
• Shift foreign aid priorities to emphasize primary education while encouraging donors to set up schemes for recurrent grants rather than one-time capital expenditures. Make future aid partially dependent upon the African nations' performance in restructuring educational priorities.

planning wide-ranging programs of support for institutions as diverse as the rapidly growing University of Zimbabwe – widely recognized as the region's most successful – and war-ravaged Makerere University in Uganda. Court maintains that in the philanthropic community, where funding fashions change almost as fast as clothing styles, there is a need to return to an old and currently unfashionable emphasis on general support for development of strong third world universities.

Michigan State's Wiley echoes Court's sentiments, recommending a continuing emphasis on Ph.D.-level training in scarce skill areas. And he urges, along with Wolde-Mariam, that particular attention be paid to the applied aspect of an academic discipline rather than to the theoretical alone – such as support for agronomists who are developing climate-appropriate crops and immunologists who are pioneering new vaccines for diseases endemic in Africa. Finally, the Michigan State professor recommends an increase in donor support for programs to provide African solutions to uniquely African problems, citing the work being done by Kenyan Professor Thomas Odhiambo, director of the International Center of Insect Physiology and Ecology, to increase food production and health standards in rural areas. Wiley maintains that it would be a grave mistake for African universities to abandon the forms of advanced scientific research their own scholars are best equipped to do.

As the debate about the best way forward continues, African educators and governments find themselves at a crossroads between European-style higher education and the fledgling attempts being made – in the face of economic pressure that cannot be ignored – to address Africa's needs on Africa's terms. The direction they will take is unknown, but what does seem clear is that the higher education boom, which lasted for over two decades and saw a 20-fold increase in the numbers of Africans attending university, is over.

– Steve Askin, with Sally Baker

Article 7

UJEST AFRICA
November 7-13 1988

Aids in Africa — plague or propaganda?

Mary Harper

SOMEWHERE in the world, someone becomes infected with the Human Immunodeficiency Virus (HIV) every minute. The World Health Organisation (WHO) estimates that between five and 10 million people have the virus worldwide, and with the number of cases doubling about once a year, 100m people are expected to be infected by 1992.

Acquired Immune Deficiency Syndrome (Aids), which is caused by the HIV virus, is in many ways a unique health challenge. The infection is invisible, and 'remains silent' for an average eight years before manifesting itself as 'full-blown Aids' which, in all known cases, has proved fatal. There is no vaccine and no cure, and as HIV is mainly spread by sexual contact, it is often difficult to discuss freely. Although patterns of spread, symptoms of the disease, and even the virus itself, are different in different parts of the world, (for instance, the HIV-2 virus in West Africa), Aids has now reached every corner of the globe. It is no longer confined to certain 'high-risk groups' but affects men, women and children.

The last few weeks have seen two major developments in the battle against Aids. The Panos Institute in London has published *Aids and the Third World,* a dossier written by Renée Sabatier, containing the most comprehensive, balanced and up-to-date account of Aids available today. In perfect complement to this, the International Planned Parenthood Federation (IPPF) has recently compiled *Preventing a Crisis,* a manual designed to help family planning workers to disseminate information and actively encourage 'safe sex' as a way of preventing the spread of Aids.

Both Panos and the IPPF condemn reports that Africa is the birthplace of Aids or that it is more riddled with the disease than anywhere else, as ill-informed and racist. According to the WHO's September 1988 figures, Congo, which has the highest

concentration of reported Aids cases in Africa, comes fourth in the world Aids prevalence list, closely followed by the USA. Zaire, which has received a notoriously bad press with Kinshasa being re-christened as 'Aidsville', and its brothels as 'sidagogues', ranks 57th on the list.

In Africa, the Aids virus spreads heterosexually, unlike in Western Europe and the USA where it is still mainly transmitted homosexually or through intravenous drug use. HIV in Africa affects men and women equally and, as a result, a new generation of 'Aids babies' is being born. Aids has become well and truly a family disease. One hypothesis that has been put forward to explain this epidemiological pattern makes a link between Aids and the relatively high incidence of other sexually transmissible diseases (STDs) in Africa, particularly the urban areas. It is thought that ulcers and sores caused by STDs may facilitate the transmission of the HIV virus from one person to the next.

Like the tenacious theories put forward as explanations for the heterosexual spread of HIV in Africa, the whole Aids pandemic is shrouded in mystery and uncertainty. There is no reliable information on Aids and by the time one message has perco-

lated its way down to the general population, it is out of date and a new one is already on its way to replace it. Because of the confusion surrounding Aids, reactions to the disease tend to be irrational and hysterical. Time and again, countries have responded in similar ways when they are confronted with their first Aids cases. The initial reaction is to bury their heads in the sand — it was not until President Kaunda's son, Masuzyo, died of Aids in October 1987 that the government acknowledged the existence of the disease in Zambia.

Following the stage of denial and delay comes an outburst of panic. As the plague mentality develops, the search for scape-

---

HIV in Africa affects men and women equally and as a result a new generation of 'Aids babies' is being born.

---

goats begins, heralding the start of a new epidemic of blame and counter-blame. With the Aids crisis, some very ugly prejudices have re-emerged. Along with Hai-

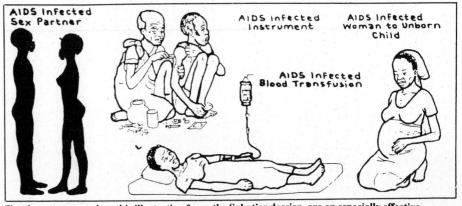

Simple cartoons, such as this illustration from the Sabatier dossier, are an especially effective means of education.

tians, homosexuals, and prostitutes, Africans have been singled out as the guilty party in the Aids pandemic.

Africans have suffered heavily at the hands of the press. The September 21, 1986 issue of *The Sunday Telegraph* ran a front-page article with the headline 'African Aids deadly threat to Britain'. The article said there was a positive duty to discriminate on racial grounds because Black Africa has a uniquely bad record. The effect of this, and other articles which took statistics from one Nairobi suburb where 80 per cent of prostitutes are HIV-positive as representative of the country as a whole, not only offended African countries politically, but had serious economic repercussions as well. The 25 per cent drop in Zambia's tourist revenues between 1985 and 1986 has been attributed to the bad Aids press it received in Europe. Africans have been discriminated against by immigration laws – Cyprus insists that all African students have an Aids test before entering the country. Press reports indicate that South Africa has extended apartheid to Aids by making foreign black applicants for work have an HIV-antibody test.

One reason why Africa has been the focus of so much of the 'blame' for Aids is the HIV tests carried out on old blood samples by European and American doctors, often without consultation with their African colleagues. Sixty-six per cent of all tests carried out on 1972-1973 blood samples taken from Ugandan children came out as HIV- positive, and similarly alarming statistics emerged throughout Central Africa. It has since been proved that a large number of these tests were 'false positives', with many negative tests showing up as HIV-positive because the blood had been damaged by heat and the testing facilities were inadequate.

It is still part of many people's 'general knowledge' on Aids that the disease originated in the African green monkey and was then passed on to human beings. Earlier this year, this theory was firmly and finally disproved, and it has now been relegated to the growing world of Aids mythology. The origins of Aids remain obscure and are likely to stay that way. But the damage has been done – several African countries refuse to participate in Aids conferences in protest against the labelling of Africa as the birthplace of the disease. Inevitably there have been waves of counter-blame with Aids being stamped as a capitalist disease or, according to one Lagos prostitute, a white man's disease.

Throughout the world, fear is being used as a motivation for change, with a doomsday mentality permeating Aids awareness campaigns. The skull and cross-bones is

raised, and, according to Gill Gordon of IPPF, sex becomes equated with death. The main effect of presenting Aids in this way has been to marginalise it and drive it underground. Panos and the IPPF have set about undoing the damage done by these aggressive campaigns by adopting a more compassionate approach aimed at integration rather than segregation. IPPF in particular, aims to present Aids as yet another STD, albeit a more deadly one, rather than as a totally new and separate disease.

Aids has not occurred in a vacuum — worldwide there are Family Planning Associations with organisational structures suitable for tackling the problem of Aids. There are whole armies of family planning workers who, with additional training, could spearhead Aids prevention campaigns. Creating separate Aids centres is not only expensive, but shines the spotlight on Aids patients, increasing their vulnerability to discrimination and persecution.

Although there is no vaccine and no cure for Aids, it is a containable disease. Aids is not like the nuclear bomb: something we learn to live with, but can do very little about. And the solution does not have to be as extreme as in Cuba which has a policy of complusory testing for all its citizens, with those found HIV-positive being put into quarantine. Apart from the impossibility of locking away all 10 million of the WHO-estimated HIV-infected people, testing is very expensive, costing between $1 and $8 for a preliminary test, and between $30 and $75 for a confirmatory test, which is much more than the annual per capita health spending in many Aids-affected African countries.

According to Renée Sabatier, education is the single most important weapon against Aids that we possess. Education is more than a matter of supplying people with information, for Aids-prevention boils down to individuals helping themselves by changing their sexual behaviour. People need to be given information and the power or motivation to act on it. Education can work to prevent the spread of Aids as it has done in some areas of Uganda where intensive action-oriented education campaigns have actually brought about a drop in infection rates. Education cannot work if people are not even supplied with information to act upon such as in Nigeria where, according to Renée Sabatier, 80 per cent of rural people have never heard of Aids.

While governments and the media ping-pong back and forth between fear and complacency, family planning associations throughout the world are waging a more regularised and steady war against the spread of HIV. This is no simple matter, for

not only is information about Aids often cloudy or out-of-date, but there are a whole host of cultural differences and sensitivities surrounding the issue of sexual behaviour. There is no universal approach to Aids education—telling people to insist on monogamy is pointless in a society where polygamy is the norm. So far, condoms are the best form of 'safe sex' available, although they are by no means 100 per cent 'safe', and are best if used with a spermicide containing nonoxynol 9 or menfagol which help to de-activate the HIV virus. Condoms in Africa are not taken very seriously because they often break due to poor quality or deterioration in sunlight. Another problem with condoms is that women often lack the power to insist that their partners wear them; prostitutes are often paid more money for sex without a condom.

IPPF believes it is especially important to aim education at youth, before they start being sexually active so that they will form a reservoir of healthy parents and an insurance for future generations. Uganda has been particularly active in this area, and has included Aids education in its primary and secondary school curricula. Prostitutes are another 'target group' for education as they are particularly at risk. In Accra, two projects have been started which supply prostitutes with free condoms, or enable them to escape from their profession by providing them with funds to set up small businesses.

The problem of how to tell people about Aids has been particularly well-tackled in Africa where information is often presented in a comprehensible, unthreatening and familiar way. One especially effective way is through popular media such as music, drama, cartoons and films. In Guinea-Bissau for instance, where 80 per cent of the population is illiterate, an Aids song contest was held in 1987. The ever famous 'grand maitre' Franco and his OK Jazz band of Zaire have made an album called *Attention Na Sida* which will probably reach more people in Africa than many government campaigns. ▪

Copies of *Aids and the Third World* by Renee Sabatier are available from The Panos Institute, 8 Alfred Place, London WC1E 7EB at a price of £5.95. The *Preventing a Crisis* manual produced by Gill Gordon and Tony Klouda is available from The AIDS Prevention Unit, International Planned Parenthood Foundation, P.O. Box 759, Inner Circle, Regent's Park, London NW1 4LQ at a price of $7 (or £4 in the UK only) including postage.

The UNESCO Courier,
March 1988.

Article 8

African Cinema

A young and relatively unknown art

Tereza Wagner and Claude Ondobo

TEREZA WAGNER, *of Peru, specialises in the anthropology of contemporary arts and cultures. Since 1979 she has been a staff member of the Section for the Promotion of the Arts in Unesco's Culture and Communication Sector, with special responsibility for programmes dealing with cinema, architecture and the plastic arts.*

CLAUDE ONDOBO, *of Cameroon, former journalist and communications teacher, is currently a specialist with Unesco's International Programme for the Development of Communication (IPDC).*

ALL African wisdom is to be found in oral culture—in words, speech, symbols and rhythm. So the highest form of artistic expression is storytelling: not merely the narrative as such, but the whole scene of storyteller and audience, with pauses and rhythm and concrete ways of representing the word. There is a strong similarity between African stories and the language of film, and it is not surprising that African cinema, born only thirty years ago, should already have produced some first-rate film-makers and films which rank with the great classics of world cinema.

But although this cinema is important in the eyes of connoisseurs and film buffs, it is still relatively unknown to a wider audience, whether at home or abroad, since it has developed in isolation, virtually without help from the outside world, sure of its inspiration, its strength and its rights. For this very reason, despite the crisis affecting the film world everywhere, African cinema today is indispensable, since its aesthetic, its themes and its symbols are like an influx of new blood. African film-making carries within itself the seeds of a renewal of cinematographic language. Apart from the similarity between the latter and African storytelling, African civilization possesses another feature which links it with the language of film: the fact that the imaginary and the real are placed on an equal footing.

Cinema, which is the art of metaphorical representation of human situations and feelings, has a language of absolutes. It brooks no half-measures and never says anything that does not signify: in this it differs from literature. This makes it an art with a close grip on reality, traditionally an art of entertainment but, besides, an area for reflection on all the social, political and cultural problems which arise in a particular society. In Africa, modernity and tradition seem incompatible, more so than anywhere else. African cinema is striving to find a point of convergence between these two types of society. This is true, above all, of the first generation of African film-makers. African cinema uses the tradition/modernity dichotomy to illustrate political issues as well as cultural and psychological themes.

This opposition between the modern world and the world of the ancestors is a constantly recurring theme in the works of two of the founding fathers of African cinema, Ousmane Sembène, from Senegal, who is also a novelist, and the late Oumarou Ganda, from Niger. The latter began his career as an actor with Jean Rouch, the French film-maker and pioneer of *cinéma-vérité*, a movement which had a profound influence on *cinéma d'auteur*, or the distinctively personal style of film-directing, in the 1960s.

Ousmane Sembène, aware of the cultural and political role that any creative artist has a duty to assume in society, became a film director the better to attain his chosen objectives. He very quickly realized that, in Africa, films reached a wider audience than literature. His films, like his books, take a shrewd look at the past and present attitudes of the peoples of Africa. With rare courage and lucidity, this man strives through his work to denounce vacillating, cowardly or ineffectual behaviour on the part of those who are motivated by greed for profit and glory, masquerading as religious faith and respect for tradition. Conversely, women and the younger generation are bearers of the hope that some day a fine, strong African society will emerge.

Whereas for Sembène the two cultures, traditional and modern, must blend into a single culture, in order to eliminate both the ignorance behind a blind respect for tradition and the powerlessness that is often engendered by a false concept of modernity, Oumarou Ganda made a painful choice in favour of village life. However, he was well aware that village life cannot remain set apart from economic and cultural developments. His analysis therefore coincides to some extent with that of Ousmane Sembène.

Other pioneers of African cinema are the late Paulin Soumanou Vieyra, from Senegal, and the Ivorians Timité Bassori and Désiré Ecaré, all three trained in Paris; Ruy Guerra, from Mozambique, who worked mainly in Brazil; and the self-taught Mustapha Alassane, from Niger, to mention only the best known.

The first full-length African feature film, *La Noire de ...*("Black Girl"), was made in 1966 by Ousmane Sembène. Based on a minor news item, this film traces the reasons which induce a young Senegalese domestic servant, working for some former *coopérants* (French Peace Corps workers) who have settled in Antibes, to commit suicide. The film's symbolism is powerful, and in some respects recalls the tragedy of the slave trade. African film-makers are aware of the weight of their history and the disasters of submission, and until the late 1970s they used films on mythological, fictional and documentary subjects, and also cartoons, as a means of describing all aspects of what it is to be African: in everyday life (*Borom sarret*—"The Building Site"—a short film made in 1962 by Ousmane Sembène), in relations with the West (*F.V.V.A.,* 1972, by Mustapha Alassane), in dreams and weaknesses (*Le wazzon polygame,* a medium-length film made in 1971 by Oumarou Ganda), and in the battle for freedom (*Soleil O,* 1969, by Med Hondo).

Between 1975 and 1980, some very interesting film-makers joined the ranks of the pioneers: the Malian Souleymane Cissé, trained, like Sembène, in the USSR; the marvellous Gaston Kaboré from Burkina Faso, trained in Paris; the Senegalese Djibil Diop, director of only one full-length feature film, *Touki-Bouki,* but which is regarded as one of the most important products of the national film industry; Safi Faye, the first African woman to distinguish herself as a talented film-maker, Johnson Traoré, trained in Paris; the Guinean Moussa Kemoko Diakité, trained in the Federal Republic of Germany; the Gabonese Pierre Marie Dong and Philippe Mory, both trained in France; the Congolese Sébastien Kamba, also trained in France; the Cameroonian Daniel Kamwa and the Mauritanian Med Hondo, already mentioned, both of whom came to the cinema from the theatre; and, lastly, the film director, novelist, playwright and producer, the Nigerian Ola Balogun, also trained in Paris. This second generation of film-makers won international recognition for African cinema.

The historical film emerged in Africa in the 1980s, addressing new themes which do not necessarily stem from the modernity/ tradition dichotomy. This is true, for example, of the very fine full-length films of Gaston Kaboré, including *Wend Kuuni* ("The Gift of God", 1982), and that of Souleymane Cissé, *Yeelen* ("The Light", 1987), which won the Jury Prize at the 1987 Cannes Festival. *Wend Kuuni* is a psychological drama which tells the story of a child who is abandoned by his family and becomes autistic. But this inner silence cannot remain impervious to the warmth of fellowship emanating from the community. *Yeelen* is a dramatic work in which a father's jealousy of his son, who is to be initiated into sacred knowledge, locks the two in mortal combat. The action of these two films unfolds in traditional societies where the conflict

between tradition and modernity is no longer used as a frame of reference.

If the historical film is proving more and more attractive to African film-makers, it is because this type of subject affords an opportunity to describe the religious, political and social order of rural communities and to show their solidarity in the face of adversity, while drawing attention to village philosophy and ethics.

Thus Med Hondo's very beautiful *Saraaunia* (1986), or *Emitaï* ("Thunder God", 1971) and *Ceddo* ("Outsiders", 1977) by Ousmane Sembène, highlight the life of village communities in their struggles against foreign invaders, whether military as in the first two films, or religious as in the third. The social order, which has been destroyed by the modern world, is particularly well portrayed in these films. In *Saïtane* (1973), by Oumarou Ganda, the harmonious balance of power collapses very swiftly when such occurrences as adultery or incest (as in *Niaye*, 1965, by Ousmane Sembène) start to influence the behaviour of those who hold these powers in trust. It is nevertheless remarkable to observe that, once the drama has been worked out, the rigour of tradition restores order. In *Yeelen*, the confrontation between father and son causes natural disasters as well as serious economic and social disruption. But the story ends with a prophecy foretelling that a day will come when the Bambara will once again be a great nation.

While the themes represented in African films are for the most part universal, the unity of time, space and rhythm found in them is

resolutely a part of African culture and civilization. Time, like space, is elastic, and does not place a frame around the action. Events occur as if the eternity of the gods had dawned on Earth, and as if, despite the thousand-and-one preoccupations of everyday life, time did not matter. Just like the wide, generous open space of the African landscape, time cannot be hemmed in by man and it takes its natural course, independently of human activities. By contrast, the rhythm of these films is beaten out by human hands. In counterpoint to time and space, rhythm is provided by movement, by the most mundane gestures, or by speech, which always takes on an oracular tone. This is what makes it altogether human.

In *Lettre paysanne* ("Letter from the Country", 1975), by Safi Faye, we watch the everyday life of the film-maker's own village during the winter months. Work in the fields in the mornings, the midday meal-break, as day follows day, punctuated by scenes under the palaver tree and snatches of conversation, all of which are strands imperceptibly weaving the fabric of the film. The beauty of the countryside, the peace of the natural world, the weight of time, although strongly present, do not obscure the questions of survival that the village must face, and do not deflect any of the criticism that may be aroused by traditional customs, manners and morals.

Set against this highly political and intellectual form of cinema, there is also the commercial cinema of the English-speaking countries. The Nigerian Ola Balogun, who is probably the only African

film-maker to have directed and produced more than ten full-length feature films, has had a run of successes with works adapted from Yoruba theatre, in which marvellous stories unfold in a universe of music and dance. His output also includes works of a mythological nature, such as *The Black Goddess* (1979), or political films like *Cry Freedom* (1980), a protest against colonization. These works are, nevertheless, closer to Western cinema than those of the French-speaking African countries.

Although the wealth and complexity of African cinema cannot be denied, it is nevertheless not equipped to compete against the powerful world film industry. Two major obstacles stand in its way: technique and funding. This cinema emerged and developed virtually without support of any kind, whether financial, political, cultural or technical. Thirty years later, the working conditions of film-makers are still extremely precarious. Indeed, cinema came late to the African continent, at a time when "maximum technical know-how" has become necessary in order to make a film with universal appeal. *Yeelen* by Souleymane Cissé shows that, with adequate funding and techniques, a film can emerge from the ghetto in which African cinema is at present languishing. Since mainly experimental and art films are being produced, the African economic sector has not concerned itself with setting up a film industry. But the growing interest shown by international producers in this *cinéma d'auteur* will, perhaps, result in a breakthrough.

AFRICA NEWS
July 11, 1988

Article 9

Ecowas: Standing Together

The impact of last month's 11th summit of the Economic Community of West African States is already being felt in the region. Three nations have acted on a unanimous resolution asking members of the

community, known as Ecowas, to outlaw the importation of toxic waste, and leaders of other states have reaffirmed their hopes for unity in west Africa.

Though the June 24–25 meeting in

Lome, Togo was billed more as an opportunity for heads of state from the 16-nation group to promote solidarity in economic policies, at least a third of the proceedings revolved around the waste issue, which ex-

Heads of state arriving in Lome, Togo for summit meeting.

ploded onto the international scene last month (see *Africa News*, June 13). From the opening remarks by host President Gnassingbe Eyadema of Togo to statements made by various leaders upon returning home, the condemnation of countries that accept toxic materials—and those that try to dump them in Africa—was a persistent theme.

"Our efforts for the economic development of our states and for the progress of our peoples will be in vain if we do not ... preserve the lives of our peoples and our environment," Eyadema said. To that end, Nigeria proposed that the group set up a "dump watch," with members pooling and sharing information about ships that might try to bring toxic waste into the region. That initiative was made more urgent when it was learned that virtually every nation on the west African coast has been approached as a possible recipient of hazardous materials.

The conference adopted a resolution "vigorously condemning" toxic waste dumping and confirming that "all 16 west African states have

agreed to promulgate laws" to end the practice. The same resolution mildly chided waste-producers by asking that the industrialized countries "take the necessary steps to see to the safe elimination of their nuclear and industrial waste and to prevent their exportation to other nations."

The government of Nigeria introduced a similar resolution at the Organization of African Unity summit in May. Last month, Nigerian officials were infuriated by the discovery of a private deal between companies in Nigeria and Italy that resulted in the dumping of noxious, possibly radioactive, waste in Koko, a town in Nigeria's Bendel state. The Nigerian weekly, *Newswatch*, said in its June 27 issue that people in Koko were storing drinking water in the

empty Italian drums, which were marked "R" – for "radioactive," according to the magazine.

As Nigerian President Ibrahim Babangida – who stepped down as Ecowas chair after three terms – and the other leaders met, the Italian company retrieved what it could of its waste on Nigerian government orders. Some Nigerian officials have demanded the death penalty for anyone found to be implicated in such schemes.

While Liberia announced that it had turned down three requests to take on industrial waste, Cote d'Ivoire passed laws meting out severe penalties for involvement with dumping. A government statement on the issue largely summed up the Ecowas position: "We cannot accept that at a time when industrialized

We must do what we can to ease the tension and to create the confidence necessary for peace and cooperation.

nations refuse to buy our commodities at reasonable prices, these same countries are selling us death for ourselves and our children."

Though economic matters were somewhat overshadowed by the waste furor, the Ecowas conference did grapple with some longstanding problems, such as debt, trade liberalization and organizational funding.

While President Eyadema lauded "the latest proposals made at the Toronto summit [of the seven leading industrialized countries] with a view to lightening the debt burden of the poorest countries," he also noted that the continent recorded a net loss of $31 billion in 1986. He laid the blame squarely on the shoulders of wealthy Western nations.

"Africa, which needs capital for its development," received only $18 billion in public development aid in 1986, Eyadema said, and the continent "thus transferred to the rich and industrialized countries of the North

$16 billion out of its meager resources."

"It is also known," the president continued, "that in 1986 African countries transferred three and a half times more money to the International Monetary Fund than what they received from that institution in 1985."

"One wonders," he mused, "who is aiding whom in the long run."

The World Bank and the African Development Bank have committed to major funding of Ecowas development projects through the Ecowas Fund for Cooperative Compensation and Development. But Eyadema told his listeners that while they can take the funding as a vote of confidence in regional integration efforts, Ecowas nations "must also count on our own capabilities to find internal resources to finance priority projects."

Finding the resources to fund itself has been a sore spot for Ecowas since its inception. Organization officials say only Nigeria and Togo are up to date in their payments to the development fund, with Cote d'Ivoire

and Burkina Faso—one of the region's poorest countries—not far behind.

The fund was supposed to be financed in two series of payments, one beginning in 1978 and the other last July. *West Africa* magazine says only 11 of the 16 Ecowas members have paid their full share of the 1978 bill; the others are hopelessly behind in the latest drive. A report by the fund's general secretary chided members who had not contributed in ten years. "Liberia's name came up often" in the report, *West Africa* says.

In a closed-door session, Burkina Faso President Blaise Compaore demanded explanations from those who were in arrears to the fund, and he reportedly got firm commitments for payment from some. But that tough stance was not reflected in the final communique, which said, "The member states have renewed their earlier commitment to acquit themselves of their financial obligations to the community's institutions."

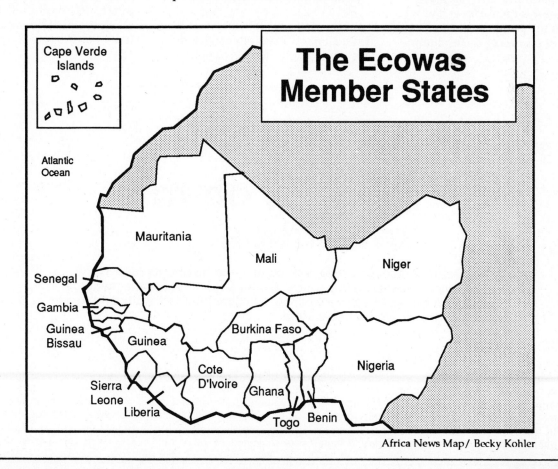

The Ecowas Member States

Cape Verde Islands

Atlantic Ocean

Mauritania

Mali

Niger

Senegal

Gambia

Guinea Bissau

Guinea

Burkina Faso

Cote D'Ivoire

Ghana

Nigeria

Sierra Leone

Liberia

Togo

Benin

Africa News Map/ Becky Kohler

With an unprecedented 15 heads of state present for the meeting, Ecowas was in a unique position to reaffirm its original goals. The communique reiterated the organization's commitment to:

• liberalize trade, eventually eliminating tariffs between member nations and leading to some pooling of resources;

• create a west African common market similar to the European Economic Community;

• form a united front against lender nations when renegotiating foreign debt financing;

• legalize free movement of citizens between one Ecowas state and another;

• create a common currency for the region; and

• improve telecommunications and road systems to link member states.

Ecowas is about five years behind in its timetable for reaching those goals, and newly elected chair Sir Dawda Jawara of Gambia remarked in his acceptance speech that progress "has been painfully slow, as year after year new targets are set and we move from the problematic to what is in danger of becoming the unattainable."

But last month's meeting may have paved the way for some improvement. If nothing else, it began the process of binding a few old wounds.

> *In 1986, African countries transferred three and a half times more money to the International Monetary Fund than they received in 1985.*

At Nigeria's urging, Ghanaian head of state Jerry J. Rawlings attended the summit. He only stayed a few hours, but his greeting from President Eyadema – who two years ago accused the Rawlings government of aiding anti-Togolese "terrorists" in a coup plot – was warm, and he was the crowd favorite on the streets of Lome.

Rawlings said he had also taken the opportunity to begin settling old "misunderstandings" with President Felix Houphouet-Boigny of Cote d'Ivoire and Nigerian President Ibrahim Babangida. "We must do what we can to ease up the tension and to create the confidence necessary for peace and cooperation," Rawlings said as he departed.

Finally, the summit was successful as a symbol of west African commitment to unity. In echoing the OAU resolution condemning toxic waste dumping – and especially in the honored-guest status accorded President Mobutu Sese Seko of Zaire, who observed the meeting in his capacity as chair of the Central African Economic Community – Ecowas made a distinct statement. As President Abdou Diouf of Senegal put it, "We have built a bridge ... along the path [toward] the construction of an African economic community."

WEST AFRICA
September 5-11 1988

Article 10

Hanging on to a 'revolution'

President Samuel Doe may well go down in history as leader of a revolution against the Americo-Liberian oligarchy, but his methods for staying in power are attracting criticism internationally and from within Liberia, writes Eddie Momoh.

IN 1985, Amnesty International, the London-based human rights organisation, reported that political trials in Liberia did not conform to internationally accepted standards of fairness. For example, in 1981, Mr Samuel Doe publicly accused the vice-chairman of the People's Redemption Council (PRC), Major-General Thomas Weh-Syen and four others of plotting to assassinate himself and other members of the PRC. A 'supreme military tribunal' was convened to carry out an *in camera* "fact-finding investigation" which was to be followed by a trial at which defence counsel would be present. However, according to Amnesty International, on August 13, 1981, the tribunal sentenced the five to death, although it

'We live with corruption' — Doe

Excerpts from a recent interview given by President Doe to a special correspondent:

On corruption . . .

We can minimise corruption but we cannot eradicate it. This is impossible. People in my country have a way of doing things . . . some feel they cannot do without eating government money. However, when such people are caught we deal with them. I cannot promise anyone that corruption will be wiped out in the Liberian society . . . that would be unrealistic on my part. We have to live with corruption. We were born long after corruption started so I believe we will die with corruption.

On attempts to remove him from power . . .

People believe because I am President of Liberia, they also have the right to become president of this country. Our society is one in which people like to imitate one another. For example if you have a nice Afro haircut, I might try to have the same without caring to know whether the cut will fit my hair. The same is the case for those who believe they have the right to become president because Samuel Doe is president. These people will do everything to remove me. They think to become president (of a country) is an easy job; for them the (attraction) is when you become president, everybody looks up to you.

On attempts on his life . . .

No (laugh). I am not afraid. I believe because I was duly elected; I have a mandate to serve the Liberian people for six years. So why should I be afraid?

On military indiscipline . . .

I think we have some of the best-trained soldiers here. I cannot agree with you that they have invaded the university campuses to beat up students. What we should direct our attention at is the widespread indiscipline in the schools and universities. Our students have been taking advantage of the high level of freedom they enjoy in this country. The incident you refer to had to do with students' refusal to sit their examinations in spite of the fact that the decision to do so had been taken by the examination board. The students say they ought to fix their own time for the examinations and decided to hold a demonstration. Now instead of the demonstration taking place within their campus, they decided to go on the town and disrupt the peace. I was told this resulted in widescale looting and vandalism. The police intervened but the matter got out of hand; so we had to order the soldiers to quieten the situation.

On relations with Sierra Leone . . .

We still enjoy a very good relationship with the government of Sierra Leone except that we had been disappointed about the position taken by President Momoh when last month we sent home some Sierra Leoneans who wanted to return. I think as a colleague and neighbour, the first thing President Momoh should have done over that incident was to send his foreign minister here to obtain our side of the story rather than turning to the press to let his feelings be known.

I have no knowledge of his allegations that soldiers had beaten and detained Sierra Leoneans at the Executive Mansion. We don't imprison people here . . . you can even go out and see for yourself whether anyone is locked up here at the Mansion. We respect the rule of law in our country and love foreigners. All we had done was to ask some people that if they wanted to continue to live in this country, they should regularise their documents. We did not deport them. In any case, President Momoh and myself are doing everything to resolve the unfortunate situation.

On his love for playing football . . .

I started playing football back in 1963 and have since done so even after becoming President. I could have been playing the game much more in public but my duties as President do not allow this. So rather, we have organised ourselves here at the Executive Mansion to play football from time to time.

The game has not only helped me to excercise but has given me the opportunity to meet with some of my old friends. They tell me what my people think about me and what they want me to do for the country. Some ask me for favours like paying hospital bills for their girl friends or school fees for their children. I give a few hundred dollars here and there now and again. Football is the only sport I know . . . It is not true that people are afraid to tackle me . . . It is part of the game if they can throw me down, but sometimes my security boys do not like this.

---

had been officially instituted only as a panel of inquiry. They were executed the following morning.

Amnesty International adds that within four years the PRC has executed at least 50 people, 32 of them for political offences. Amnesty says in most cases executions had been carried out without any formal trial, citing the case of Lieutenant-Colonel Moses Flanzamaton, the Executive Mansion guard who was executed in 1986 for allegedly attempting to assassinate President Doe. Also in 1981, 14 lower-rank soldiers were arrested and accused of plotting to overthrow the government. The 14 were tried before a special military tribunal without defence counsel; 13 of the soldiers were sentenced to death. Amnesty appealed to the authorities to commute their sentences but, within a few days, all 13 soldiers were secretly executed at the Post Stockade prison.

Within the last two years, there have been persistent reports of secret executions within the Executive Mansion, although the government continues in its denials. But since the abortive coup in November 1985, there is evidence to suggest that either soldiers attached to the Executive Mansion have taken the law into their own hands, or that there has been some form of state-sponsored killing by sections of the security forces.

In 1985, Mr Patrick Kugmeh, Mr Doe's press secretary, reported that Charles Gbenyon, the television producer, died "after a gun he was carrying on him accidentally went off", adding that the incident occurred when "security officers took him to the Executive Mansion for questioning". This contrasted sharply with accounts by relatives of Charles Gbenyon. They claimed Gbenyon was dragged to the Executive Mansion where soldiers fell upon him after the President himself had given the orders to "go finish him". The Gbenyons' account appears to match those by independent sources in Monrovia and the implication of a comment made by Jesse B. Karnlly, the Assistant Minister of Information in charge of public affairs. In a *West Africa* interview shortly after the abortive coup in 1985, Karnlly said of Gbenyon: "He was one of those young men who never listened to advice". Last March, the government reported that Mr Joe Kaipaye, one of the alleged leaders of a coup plot, fell from the sixth floor of the Executive Mansion. Information minister, Emmanuel Bowier said Kaipaye had committed suicide.

Last month, Sierra Leoneans who were expelled from Liberia told the local press that some of them had been detained and tortured at the Executive Mansion. The Liberian government denied these allegations.

Sources say the Executive Mansion has become something of a political melting pot where security officials and politicians compete fiercely for prominence and continually manoeuvre for positions or for the attention of the President. On top of the list are Mr Alvin Jones, the Minister of State for Presidential Affairs and close relation of President Doe; Johnny Kpor, Assistant Minister for Administration, and Yancy Peter Flah, also an assistant minister with special presidential duties.

All three are from Doe's Krahn tribe. Below them are Johnny Taylor, an Assistant Minister for Public Affairs, Veronica Deagor, Assistant Minister for Economic Affairs, and Mr Patrick Kugmeh, Mr Doe's diminutive press secretary.

Also prominent are officials of the Executive Mansion Guard (EMG), the G-2 and the Special Anti-Terrorist Unit (SATU). Satu is an offshoot of the Executive Mansion Guard with special training in hand-to-hand combat. Both the EMG and Satu are President Doe's personal militia, permanently based at the Executive Mansion. The EMG is about 800-strong and well-armed, chiefly with US-made M16s. The Satu is an elite unit supervised by Israeli officers. Its members are reputedly brutal and were responsible for the killing and raping when they invaded the University of Liberia campus in 1985.

The current trial of William Gabriel Kpolleh and nine others is the latest in a series of treason trials since Mr Doe seized power, further underlining the state of political uncertainty prevailing in Liberia. The uncertainty goes back to 1980, to the very composition of the men who seized power. They were all either NCOs or ordinary soldiers who had no leadership experience of any sort. In this way, the new People's Redemption Council (PRC) not only lacked the intellectual requirements of their position but their general inexperience was to determine the future behaviour of the regime.

To correct the imbalance, some members of the Movement for Justice in Africa (Moja) and the Progressive Alliance of Liberia (PAL) were promptly appointed to serve as mentors to their ill-educated masters. But cracks soon emerged and the inevitable sorting-out of this disparate band resulted in the first bloody feuding within the new government, leading to the execution of Thomas Weh-Syen.

The execution of Weh-Syen, who was generally regarded as the champion of the regime's radicals, was a major political and psychological blow, and was the beginning of the demise of the radicals. Togba-Nah Tipoteh, Moja leader and finance minister, decided not to return to Liberia from an official trip to Côte d'Ivoire, and other radicals in the PRC were either demoted or sacked.

The subsequent retreat from any kind of radicalism was assisted by the Reagan administration's attitude. Mr Richard Swing, the then US ambassador in Monrovia, reportedly advised Washington of a strong Libyan influence in the new Liberia (after Doe had established diplomatic relations with Tripoli and visited revolutionary Ethiopia). He warned that unless the US was able to arrest it, the influence was set to undermine US interests not only in Liberia, but also in the West African subregion. Promptly, Washington announced a record aid package of nearly $80m, the highest in the region. The day after Swing met with Doe for several hours, Liberia broke off diplomatic relations with Libya, and students who were already in Addis Ababa learning how to conduct mass literacy campaigns were ordered back home.

With the flow of US dollars came the inevitable use of state power as a mechanism for personal enrichment. Doe himself rapidly metamorphosed from an undernourished-looking soldier in ill-fitting battle fatigues into a plump, immaculately suited figure with a fashionable Afro-cut. Within three years, the PRC had fragmented. The leftward lean-

were fraudulent? The answer lies in the fact that Washington was nervous about the competing interests opposing Doe. It adopted the posture of sticking with 'the devil you know', and felt it could still control Doe.

But as the scale of the election-rigging became clearer, Washington felt hugely embarrassed and the question among State Department officials was how to present a credible policy option to a hostile Congress which had doubts about Doe's brand of democracy.

One of the options was to remove Samuel Doe and replace him with Jackson Doe (no relation), leader of the Liberia Action Party (LAP), which was widely believed to have won the elections. This theory fitted well with the thinking among some major opposition elements who were determined that Doe should not be allowed to take office.

Nicholas Podier, Thomas Quiwonkpa, Samuel K. Doe and Thomas Weh-Syen.

ing intellectuals of Moja were the first to go, followed by some of Doe's closest military friends, who were either executed or still cannot be accounted for.

In 1984 when democratic elections were announced, the radicals attempted a political comeback, but Mr Doe prevented them. He refused to recognise the Liberian People's Party (LPP) and told the Liberian people that it was communist. But it was all part of his design to hang onto power, legitimising himself as president by holding elections. That elections took place at all, let alone that opposition parties were eventually allowed to contest them, was due more to US pressure than to Doe's commitment to democracy. By every independent account, the elections were rigged.

Why then did the US say the elections were fair when everyone was saying they

But in November 1985, the Quiwonkpa coup went disastrously wrong partly because Washington did not let the Israelis know what was going on. Israel had by then only recently established diplomatic relations with Liberia and Israeli officers were already training members of the National Security Service, so that when the attempted coup took place, it was an opportunity for Israel to present itself as a reliable friend of the government. According to some accounts, the Israelis jammed the communications of the coup-makers and effectively controlled communications between the Executive Mansion and Doe's cousin, Brigadier-General Edward Smith, then head of the para-military force near the airport which swept into Monrovia and took the relaxed and prematurely jubilant Quiwonkpa forces by surprise.

The failure of that coup, its bloody aftermath, and subsequent events, have raised the question of whether Doe can unite the country and improve the economy. Liberia is today more divided than ever before. Corruption is widespread and salaries of civil servants are months behind schedule. Although the country nominally uses US dollars as its currency, the government continues to flood the market with $5 coins, the so-called "Doe dollars", which are worthless elsewhere. Virtually all foreign lending institutions have cut off Liberia's credit and even the massive US aid programme may be reduced in the coming months. There is continued unrest in the schools and universities. Liberia is tense.

Like the late President Zia of Pakistan, Doe has made more enemies than his officials would care to admit. President Doe still has four years before his present term expires but it is unclear how he hopes to survive given the continued state of political uncertainty in the country. ▨

INTERNATIONAL AGRICULTURAL DEVELOPMENT
MARCH/APRIL 1988

Article 11

Africa is littered with credit schemes for small-scale farmers that have not worked. A fund in the west African country Mali is working; IAD looks at how it operates

CREDIT THE FARMER FOR MORE FOOD

"Give credit to small-scale farmers round here? You must be joking. I've tried it...they just pocket the money; you never see it again".

The German businessman in Mali was expressing a widely-held view of the credit prospects of Africa's poorer farmers. So many schemes have failed, so many hopes dashed.

But a fund that has been operating for three years in an eastern part of Mali—a country which ranks with Ethiopia and Burkina Faso as one of very Africa's poorest countries—is turning conventional wisdom on its head. The $9 million Village Development Fund Project (VDFP) in Segou region, makes low interest loans to peasant farmers and enjoys a repayment rate that any financial institution would envy—100%.

The fund is almost wholly financed by the U.N.'s Rome-based International Fund for Agricultural Development (IFAD) which has found that putting credit into the hands of small-scale farmers is one of the best ways of releasing their potential to grow more food.

The project area lies in the Segou region, some 150 miles north-east of the capital Bamako. It is a semi-arid, desperately poor region, with poor soil, few natural resources, little rainfall, a declining stock of trees but a great deal of sand. Illiteracy among villagers borders on 100%; there are few effective government services.

Agriculture is mainly subsistence; chief crops are millet, sorghum, fonio (a mili/sorghum type grain with good drought-resistance) and, to a lesser extent, cowpea. Vegetables include potato, cabbage, onions and tomatoes. Groundnuts and peanuts are grown in some villages. Cattle are kept by people who can afford them.

Although set up only 3 years ago the VDFP is clearly benefitting village communities. The project gives low interest credit to farmers in 85 of the region's 439 villages to help them buy draught oxen, sheep and goats, agricultural tools and fertiliser. Loans are chanelled to them through Mali's Banque nationale de developpement agricole (National Bank for Agricultural Development).

Farmers are charged annual interest of 9% with repayments due over a 5-year period. Those who want a loan put their proposal to a meeting of the village community—and it is an assembly of the whole village that has the final say and who are then responsible for repayment.

A community seeking a loan has itself to put down 10% of the value of the money it wants to borrow. So far the VDFP has loaned just over $1 million to around 3000 farmers in 85 villages, making the average loan about $350.

Over two-thirds of the money borrowed has been used to purchase draught animals which, in turn, have helped farmers to considerably extend the area under crops.

> "In one of the very poorest areas of Africa more food is being produced for both rural and urban communities"

Eligible

Villages are selected for inclusion in the project if they satisfy certain criteria. VDFP manager, Mr. Abdoul Kader Maiga says that a community must have a record of being trustworthy, it must have social cohesion, with people cooperating together well and it must have a good record of paying its taxes (the government imposes a flat rate tax on all villagers); it must also have the potential to expand the cropping area.

"It is the willingness of people to take advantage of the credit that we are looking for", says Mr. Maiga. "And the project makes it clear that the poorest in the village must gain—if that is not agreed, then there is no loan. Often the poor cannot afford animals and work for the richer members of the village. Receiving credit from the fund enables them to set up on their own."

Women farmers—so often overlooked in Africa—have, he says, received loans for gardening activities, also for goats to try to increase milk supplies.

First

In a small village called Sinebougou, some 30 miles from Segou, the president of the village committee, Mr. Demba Diallo, was one of the first farmers to receive a loan from the VDFP. Mr. Diallo, whose chief crop is millet, used a $600 loan to purchase 3 oxen, a plough and several bags of fertiliser.

Before receiving the loan he ploughed by hand and could not farm more than 5 hectares, only about half his land area. Now he says that his oxen enable him to crop double that area and cover 10 hectares. In the first two years after taking the loan the fertiliser helped to increase the yield of his millet from 600 kg. to 800 kg. a hectare. His total harvest was over 4 tons a year higher. Some of the extra food he kept for his extended family of 20 people; some he sold in nearby towns.

In total the farmers of Sinebougou village have received 40 oxen from the fund which has enabled them to double the area under crops.

Many other villages, covered by the project report similar increases. In one of the very poorest areas of Africa more food is therefore being produced for both rural and urban communities.

The project also makes loans available to help people to diversify away from dependence on agriculture and so have more security when drought strikes. Loans have been made for setting up village shops, blacksmith work, carpentry, trading animals, and for selling salt (which is often difficult to obtain) sugar and petroleum.

Social aspects are also important. The VDFP has encouraged villagers to improve literacy skills and health care. Some villages now have their first ever literate people.

Problems

The project's innovative nature has brought its own problems. "It's different from most development projects" says Mr. Maiga "and some people have not come to terms with that".

The VDFP is supposed to have an *applied research* component, to be carried out under the supervision of existing government institutions. But no research is taking place because of a conflict between the fund and the government institutes. "The researchers come to us with the ideas which were basically top down" says Mr. Maiga; "the project did not want that; we want basic research to be done on farmers fields and for progress to be built up from there".

Problems also arose for a *seed multiplication centre* which again was due to be part of the project. "The existing seed centre at Babougou wanted to develop seeds for big farmers not poorer farmers" says Mr. Maiga, "we want to develop drought resistant seeds which will help safeguard yields when drought strikes". Mini-seed multiplication centres have now been established in different villages.

The project interest in improving *health* brought a clash with the Ministry of Health over the best way to go about this. It was eventually agreed that the VDFP should help to train volunteer primary health care workers. "The project has made a big

Two oxen and a multi-cultivator has enabled this farmer to double the land he crops
John Madeley

When Success brings Problems

Mali peasant farmer Mr. Lassine Coulibaly last year enjoyed a big increase in his harvest of peanuts. With the help of a loan from the IFAD funded Segou based Village Development Fund he increased his output *five-fold* — from 8 sacks, each of 65 kilos, to 40 sacks.

He was delighted with the big jump. Other farmers in his village of Blan also enjoyed substantial increases in their peanut harvests

In the neighbouring village of Dofounou it was a similar story. This village was one of the very first to join the project 3 years ago. With the help of oxen, agricultural equipment and fertiliser, purchased on credit under the project, they enjoyed substantial crop increases in their first two years. Harvests of millet, peanuts, groundnuts and cowpea were all significantly higher.

But for Lassine Coulibaly, the farmers in his village, in Dofounou and other villages in the Segou region there was a sizable snag. The additional millet was certainly welcome—some they ate in the village, some they sold in nearby towns.

For peanuts, groundnuts and cowpea, however, it was a different story. When they came to sell these products *there was simply no market*. To be precise there was a small local demand, but no market for the bulk of what they produced.

The farmers, all of whom are peasant small-scale farmers, naturally wonder what is going on. And they are worried. All have borrowed money to buy inputs to increase output and, as they cannot sell many of the nuts, repayments are a struggle.

In Dofounou village the farmers have sized up the situation. "The problem is one of over-production", says the village president Mr. Adana Samake.

Not enough thought

The problem is also that too little thought has gone into a vital stage of the food chain. When the project was devised it seemed a good idea to encourage farmers to increase thee output of cash crops and give them a regular cash income—in what had previously been predominantly subsistence villages. They needed cash to pay back the loan from the project.

But no one thought hard enough about a market for these extra crops. It was just assumed there would be a market

A project document states "all incremental production not consumed on the farm would easily be absorbed on the regional or Mali domestic market and/or neighbouring countries". *This has proved to be wildly optimistic and completely unfounded.*

Project manager Mr. Abdoul Kadar Maiga has tried hard to find markets both in Mali and abroad. So far he has had little success. When local traders were approached to buy nuts they offered only a very low price. Again the price offered for cowpea was so low that it did not cover the costs of production.

Attempts have been made to sell the surplus in other regions but there is limited purchasing power within Mali to buy.

Foreign buyers have told Mr. Maiga that the quantities involved are not large enough for them to buy. Available, for example, are 1000 tons of surplus cowpea. To the small farmers of Segou region, this sounds a hefty amount; foreign buyers say it is not enough.

Storage

Adding to the villagers' problems is the fact that they have no adequate storage facilities for their surplus foods. This is something to which the project is now turning its attention.

In the meantime some of the farmers are cutting their losses by eating the surpluses themselves. But this does not help them to re-pay their loans

At the end of February this year the farmers were due to re-pay. "It will be difficult" admitted an Dofounou farmer. Drought in last year's planting season, and subsequently lower harvests last October, caused many men to leave the village. This makes re-payment—for which the whole village is responsible—even harder.

"Disaster"

"Increased output, no market" can spell disaster for poor farmers. The lesson of the Village Development Fund Project in Mali is that markets have be carefully tested and found *before* farmers are encouraged to increase output of market bound food.

It cannot just be assumed that firm markets exist. Peasant farmers cannot survive on imaginary markets. An integrated approach is vital in a project of this kind.

Meanwhile, Lassine Coulibaly, like hundreds of other farmers in the Segou region, can only hope that those markets will turn up.

impact on health" claims Mr. Maiga, "every village now has it own drugstore."

Drought

The biggest immediate problem for the region's villages is the erratic rains which fell last July and August, when farmers plant their seeds. Harvests in most villages range from 50% to only 2% of normal.

Their village, home to 1,100 people, is not untypical—the millet harvest was only 2% of normal. Villagers grow vegetables and have 4 tons of millet in store. But with 8 months to the next cereal harvest the villagers have a critical problem. People say that their vegetables—which they can water—could stand between life and death.

As the threat of famine grows, people are leaving villages to begin a long walk to search for food and work in other areas of Mali and in neighbouring countries. Whilst some exodus takes place every year, the

The farmers of Dofounou village. Nearly all have substantially increased their output of peanuts—their only problem now is where to sell them

farmers to buy food in the emergency—the snag is that the cost of food has rocketed and there is not much around.

To date all the repayments due under the project have been made. But a question mark hangs over this year's repayments. The weather could mean delay—and the VDFP does allow for a delay because of "weather calamities".

Success

Why is the Mali project working when most others in Africa have failed? "Most credit schemes for small-scale farmers have not worked because they were too flexible", believes Abdoul Maiga; "extensions to re-payment periods were granted too easily and the farmers got away with too much".

"We realise when there is a genuine need for an extension of the re-payment period", he says.

The VDFP is working well because villages had to satisfy fairly strict criteria before they could be included in the project. Villages that seemed financially shaky and who posed a re-payment risk have been excluded. The fund aims to extend loans to a further 75 villages within two years. But well over half will still be excluded.

The project's careful selection of villages is undoubtedly a key reason for its success; it is also a reason why credit schemes have yet to prove they can reach people in the very neediest villages as the following article explains.

movement is now exceptionally heavy; from some villages about half the people have already left.

In a village like Sinebougou, where yields were half of normal, the extra area under crops has shielded people from the effects of drought; it means that the villagers are now eating whereas

previously they might have ended up famine victims.

"We are sending an SOS for help" said a farmer in one village. The chief problem facing many farmers is how to make their repayments. The lower harvests have given them no little or no surplus to sell. The VDFP is making loans available for

---

Article 12

NEW YORK TIMES
INTERNATIONAL
FRIDAY, NOVEMBER 11, 1988

The Cloud Over Africa Is Locusts

By JAMES BROOKE
Special to The New York Times

M'PAL, Senegal — Dieye Rawaan pumped pesticide powder and his seven children banged pots and pans, but the cloud kept descending: millions of desert locusts seeking fresh vegetation.

A few hours later, the cloud lifted, having consumed its weight in crops. Below stretched a panorama of bare millet stalks and leafless peanut plants chewed to stubble.

"It's as if they cut my fields with scissors," the still-dazed Senegalese farmer murmured recently, nudging several bright yellow locust carcasses with his plastic thong.

From the Atlantic Ocean to the Red Sea, the worst locust plague in 30 years is gnawing through Africa's farm lands. The plague has given rise to an eradication effort that includes satellite images sent by telefax machines and squadrons of helicopters and crop dusters spraying the latest generation of pesticides.

A Helpful Wind

But in the war against this ancient pest, the greatest battle was not won this year by high technology but by an arm of nature revered by farmers since biblical times: a powerful wind.

Early last month, as billions of locusts threatened to descend from the deserts of Mauritania into the rich farming regions of Senegal, a strong wind sprang up and pushed most of the swarms out to sea.

First, they infested the Cape Verde Islands. Then ships at sea radioed sightings from the mid-Atlantic. Finally, on Oct. 15, the first surviving swarms straggled into the Caribbean, borne on the shoulders of Hurricane Joan.

"It is the first time in contemporary history that the locusts crossed the Atlantic," said Rafik Skaf, an entomologist who has fought locusts in Africa since 1950. "The fact that they can cross the Atlantic in five days, and then lay eggs, shows that they have enormous vitality."

Dr. Skaf, who came out of retirement this year to combat the locust plague, predicted that desert locusts will not survive long in the moist environment of the Caribbean.

Spread of Pest Feared

But the same fatal combination of strong winds and strong genes recently allowed the pests to establish footholds in semiarid areas east of Africa. In recent weeks, they moved into Saudi Arabia, Kuwait, Iraq and Iran.

"Next it will be Pakistan and India that will be invaded," predicted Dr. Skaf, who works out of Dakar, Senegal, as the West Africa locust control coordinator for the United Nations Food and Agriculture Organization.

Eventually, the locusts could infest as many as 60 third-world countries, said Robert Huesmann, director of the Desert Locust Task Force of the United States Agency for International Development.

At an emergency locust conference attended by 35 countries late in October, King Hassan II of Morocco proposed the creation of a United Nations "green helmet" task force that would be empowered to range freely across national boundaries to combat locust swarms.

For Morocco, such a solution is too late. Early in November, locusts swarmed over the natural barrier of the Atlas Mountains and descended for the first time in years into the fertile farming lands of the Sous valley.

U.S. Gives $40 Million

"A pilot told me he was flying at 8,000

feet over the Atlas and he looked out his window and saw a swarm flying right alongside him," said George Carner, deputy director of the American aid mission in Dakar.

This year, the United States has given about $40 million toward locust control in Africa, including two crop dusting planes that arrived in Senegal in the first week in November.

But experts estimate that African governments may need to spend $250 million a year to limit crop damages by the locusts. So far this year, 5.6 million acres in Africa have been treated against locusts, and the infestation is spreading.

Dr. Skaf said the plague could last as long as a decade and would probably be ended only by a chance combination of natural forces: wind, rain and drought.

Control Programs Cut

The entire calamity could have been averted two years ago for a small part of the $250 million sum.

In 1986 and 1987, the seeds of today's global problem grew unchecked in remote areas torn by war: Eritrea Province in Ethiopia, northern Chad and the southern Sudan.

But even if the breeding areas were accessible to central government control, most African countries were complacent about the threat. Africa's last major infestation ended in the early 1960's. In the subsequent, largely locust-free decades, Africa's locust control programs were reduced to skeletal operations.

Untouched by central government control and fed by vegetation from ample rains, the locusts steadily multiplied in 1986 and 1987. Eventually, overcrowded and running short of food, they started swarming.

As in a scene from a science fiction movie, these pinkish clouds rise with the warming air of the midmorning and move windborne across the African landscape, blocking the sun.

"It's like flying through a blizzard with very big flakes," said Pierre Lambert, a 33-year-old pilot from Montreal, who flies spraying missions here for a Canadian aid program. Caught recently in a swarm in Mauritania, he

was forced to make an emergency landing because locust carcasses clogged the cooling vents of his single-engine plane.

20 Billion in One Swarm

In Algeria this spring, one swarm grew to cover 150 square miles, about 20 billion insects. Since locusts eat their weight in food each day, this swarm was capable of devouring 40,000 tons of food a day, enough to feed 20,000 people for a year.

In the farming area near here, several car accidents were caused by cars skidding on locusts that carpeted Senegal's coastal highway. The locusts were "hoppers," wingless larva that march in bands.

"What we are doing now can't stop the invasion," Dr. Skaf said as he watched a lime green army of hoppers march silently but inexorably across the floor of a millet field here.

Traditionally, African peasants dug trenches and buried the hoppers as they marched over the top. Today, scientists prefer pesticides.

Dr. Skaf, a veteran of many campaigns, advocates spraying crisscross strips of dieldrin in desert areas. With this tactic, the roving locust bands cross a dieldrin zone and die.

But dieldrin is now banned in the United States and many other countries because it is a long-lasting pesticide that enters the food chain and ends up in milk and food consumed by humans. In some African countries, people eat fried locusts.

Consequently, the Western donors have pledged not to use dieldrin in the locust campaign in the third world.

"The dieldrin would be in their fish, in their meat," said Stanlislaw Manikowski, a Canadian entomologist here who works with Dr. Skaf. "And who would the third-world countries accuse? The industrialized countries that gave it to them."

Instead of dieldrin, the crop dusting planes spray fenithrion or malathion, both weaker and shorter-lived pesticides.

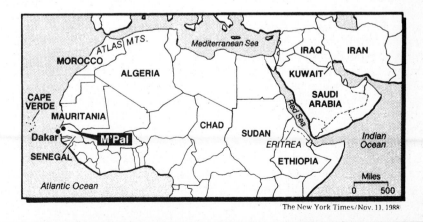

The New York Times/Nov. 11, 1988

AFRICA NEWS
October 31, 1988

Article 13

Walking the Economic Line in Nigeria

United Nations

Construction projects, like this railroad, have been funded by international loans.

With one eye on a restive populous and the other on Western financial institutions, the government of Nigeria is treading a narrow course of economic reforms that it hopes will prove its credit worthiness without leading to public revolt.

The problem for President Ibrahim Babangida, as for the leaders of all the third world's heavily indebted nations, is that international lenders require extensive economic restructuring before they will agree to schemes—such as rescheduling payments—that can ease a country's debt burden. But because the reforms almost always slash social programs, reduce subsidies on essential goods like food and fuel, and cut the ordinary person's purchasing power, they can lead to widespread protest.

Nigerian newspapers and magazines are calling attention to the country's similarities with Algeria, where unrest that began October 4 has left several hundred people dead and injured, most of them shot by army troops. Both Nigeria and Algeria are heavily dependent on the world price of oil, which has slumped from over $40 a barrel early this decade to less than $10 a barrel in recent weeks. And both countries have rejected economic controls imposed by the International Monetary Fund (IMF), which would have been a condition for receiving any new loan money from major international agencies.

But like Algeria, Nigeria has put into place its own program which is, in many cases, stricter than the IMF would have demanded. The goal is to rescue Nigeria's economy from its downward spiral by cutting imports, boosting exports, attracting investments and eliminating waste and inefficiency. The result has been hard times, especially for Nigeria's poor.

Until the oil boom ended in 1980, petroleum exports accounted for over 90% of Nigeria's revenues and for 85% of its foreign exchange earnings. Those funds supported not only an extensive building program throughout the country – and a lavish lifestyle for a conspicuous elite – but also a range of social programs that

World Bank

Since Nigeria is not subject to an internationally imposed austerity program, it could opt to expand rural projects like this demonstration farm in Gusau.

benefitted the middle and lower economic classes.

The drop in oil earnings – from $25 billion in 1980 to about $6 billion this year – has fundamentally altered Nigeria's economic prospects. At the same time, the interest payments on the country's foreign debt have multiplied from $1 billion to $6 billion in less than a decade. Total national debt now stands at $27 billion.

With revenues plummeting and costs rising, the government tried a succession of money-saving measures and reforms, culminating in a strict "structural adjustment program" that began in July, 1986. Among its main features are:
• The elimination of the licenses that were required from anyone wanting to import goods into the country, a measure officials say has halted rampant corruption in the issuing of the licenses;
• The scrapping of price controls on most items;
• The abolition of commodity boards that controlled produce prices, a common move to provide production incentives for farmers, which hits hard at consumers, particularly in urban areas;
• A restructuring of the "investment environment" to provide incentives and remove bureaucratic obstacles for investors;

• Implementation of a series of "privatization" measures, including the selling of government or quasi-government enterprises; and
• A wholesale restructuring of the civil service system.

Nigerian officials say the program, with its attendant hardships, has been accepted more readily by the people than an externally mandated plan would have been. But both the government and its critics are worried about the impact of the restructuring.

Per capita incomes have been cut in half since the 1986 program took effect. At the same time, there is an ever-increasing population competing for the shrinking pool of services such as education and health care. Nobody knows exactly how large the population is. Although there has not been a census since 1963, estimates are in the 100 million range—which means that one out of every four sub-Saharan Africans is a Nigerian.

But this month a senior Nigerian official said privately that his government has begun to wonder whether that estimate has any relation to reality. He pointed out that in the last elections, more than 77 million people registered to vote. Since young people of nonvoting age are thought to comprise more than half the country's population, and since registered voters are, in

most countries, a small proportion of those eligible to vote, the true population figure may be substantially larger than has been thought. There is hope that a census planned for 1991 will provide realistic figures.

To cope with the 2.7% annual population growth, the government has adopted a policy requiring women to limit their number of children to four. While not legally enforceable – and controversial because it doesn't apply to men who have more than one wife – the policy puts on record the government's concern about population pressures.

There is also, government officials say, a strong concern for the effect of economic restructuring on the poorest of the poor. They say that not being subject to an internationally imposed plan gives Nigeria the option to expand programs, especially in rural areas, that will minimize the pain of structural adjustment.

Among the government's plans for relief and growth is an ambitious effort to make the country self-sufficient in wheat in a single season. Although its project to turn Nigeria's six northernmost states into a "wheat belt" have been threatened by recent floods, officials are still predicting a successful harvest.

Increasingly, however, Nigerian officials are pressing their case that some form of debt relief is essential if Nigeria is to maintain a functioning economy and continue its moves to civilian rule. The government is proceeding with a step by step process towards two-party national elections in 1992, but senior officials are warning creditors that more belt-tightening could lead to public protests and disrupt the schedule.

Many economists fear that, even with restructuring, the debt service burden will continue to stifle both the economic growth and the job creation that are essential to fiscal recovery.

The World Bank, a leading champion of the free market economic measures Nigeria has introduced, has been supporting Nigeria's arguments internationally, calling the reform efforts "courageous." Last summer the Bank's representative in Lagos, the Nigerian capital, told *The Wash-*

ington Post that if commercial creditors don't listen to Nigeria's pleas, they could risk losing all their money. "With $6 billion in revenues from oil, Nigeria doesn't have to care about anybody else," Tariq Husain said. "It doesn't have to pay these debts."

The Bank advocates debt restructuring that will allow the economies of poor countries to grow enough to eventually repay their debts.

With World Bank backing, Nigeria reached an agreement on September 23 with international creditors to reschedule $5.2 billion of the country's debt to commercial banks over the next 20 years.

The accord also allows Nigeria's bank creditors three main options for "debt conversion" – a process by which a creditor exchanges debt for some form of equity in the debtor country. Without such a provision, debtor nations must repay their loans in international currencies such as U.S. dollars. In Nigeria's case, just to pay the annual interest on its foreign debt would take its entire $6 billion foreign exchange earnings from oil sales. In this case, Nigeria will offer the banks Nigerian currency, Nigerian investment bonds, or other forms of equity within Nigeria.

Although the agreement was good news for the government, it still must contend with creditors who think the government's restructuring hasn't gone far enough. And it must cope with domestic critics, who say the price at home has been too high.

Article 14

AFRICA NEWS
August 8, 1988

The Right to Choose

Many of the refugees whose status will be discussed next week at an international conference in Washington, D.C. have never seen their home country. And the government of that country – the east African nation of Rwanda – would be happier if they never did.

Twenty-five years ago, Rwanda, was embroiled in a bloody civil war between its two main ethnic communities, the once-dominant Tutsis and the minority Hutu. The Tutsis were defeated, and over the next two years, thousands fled to surrounding countries, leaving some 865,000 Tutsis in Rwanda today.

Most of those who left have never returned. Many have reared children and grandchildren and raised livestock in rural refugee settlements, while others – particularly the 2,000 or so who live in Kenya – have become fully integrated into urban society.

The memory of civil conflict is still fresh in Rwanda, and President Juvenal Habyarimana has, of late, been stressing his desire to keep his country on an even keel despite the pressures of overpopulation, a depressed economy and continuing ethnic divisions. "The peace and unity among Rwandans . . . are our petrol, gold and diamonds," Habyarimana said in a June speech opening the congress of the National Revolutionary Movement for Democracy.

Though Rwanda is "a country at peace"—and the crisis that precipitated the flight of so many Tutsis is over—the government has made it clear that it does not want the refugees back. Habyarimana said so on a visit to Uganda in February, and has repeated himself since. So, even though the government's official policy is to consider applications for repatriation on a case-by-case basis, "it takes forever," according to Roger Winter of the U.S. Committee for Refugees. Only about a half-dozen Rwandans are repatriated that way each year. "It's really more of a paper possibility than a real one," Winter says.

In fact, Rwanda is trying to move more of its nationals onto foreign soil: the government has held discussions with representatives of several countries, including Gabon and Uganda, aimed at finding new land for its burgeoning population.

Rwanda, which is about the size of New Hampshire, has one of the fastest-growing populations in the world. There are currently 5.75 million people in Rwanda, and the growth rate stands at 3.8%, nearly seven times that of the United States. And that figure is rising. About 225 Rwandans live on each square mile; even compared to other African nations, that is a high population density. In Niger, for instance, only 13 people occupy a square mile. Closer to Rwanda, in Uganda, the population density is 161 per square mile.

Habyarimana says Rwanda has enough trouble taking care of the

Most of the Rwandan refugees living in Uganda are cattle herders.

D.A. Bertoni/UNHCR

people within its borders and cannot afford to take back the nearly 125,000 refugees who live in Uganda, Tanzania and Kenya. "Everyone knows," the president told the party congress, "that Rwanda bears [the] heavy burden of an ever-growing population, and this growth makes land for cultivation scarce. Rwanda does not have enough natural wealth to help her create jobs and it has insufficient means to provide education for its children. So it cannot pretend to satisfy the needs [of the refugees.]"

But the refugees don't necessarily want to return. What those who are agitating for a change in government policy want is the *right* to return.

"Every human being is entitled to a nationality," writes George Rubagumya in the June issue of *Impuruza*, a newsletter for Rwandan refugees. Rubagumya, one of the conveners of next week's conference, is a lawyer in Texas. He believes that unless the stateless refugees – who now carry documents from the United Nations High Commissioner for Refugees or no documents at all – can claim their Rwandan heritage, they have no real protection in their host countries.

"This is so because individuals are protected from oppression by foreign governments by their country of nationality, and if you have none ... for

all practical purposes, you don't exist."

Rubagumya sets forth a series of demands on behalf of the refugees, and the question of freedom of choice is central to them. "If Rwanda is now at peace," he says, the government must state that any Rwandan "who fled or whose parents fled Rwanda and who wants to return to Rwanda is free to do so."

But, Roger Winter says, "the overwhelming majority of people who are in exile, while every one of them will say that they want the right to return to Rwanda, will not make that choice when offered the option."

In the early part of this decade, when Milton Obote took power for the second time in Uganda, many Rwandan Tutsis—plus some Ugandan nationals—were expelled to Rwanda. After Obote was removed from office in July 1985, almost all of those who had been expelled returned to Uganda.

"It is true," says Winter, "that the Rwanda government encouraged a few who didn't want to [go] back, but the majority went back because they had interests there. These were people who had become established in Uganda."

Ernest Chipman, the UN High Commissioner for Refugees head of desk for Kenya, Malawi, Tanzania, Uganda and Zambia, agrees that the refugees are fairly well off where they are. When then-President Julius K. Nyerere of Tanzania offered the 35,000 Rwandan refugees in his country citizenship in the early 1980s, Chipman was serving as the UNHCR's deputy representative to the east African nation.

"We encouraged the Rwandans to take citizenship," Chipman recalls. "Their children had been born on Tanzanian soil; the opportunity was there; they were settled and self-reliant. And the prospects of any other solution looked dim." About 15,000 refugees have taken the Tanzanians up on their offer, leaving 20,000 who have not yet done so.

Now, the UNHCR is hoping the other countries where Rwandan refugees live will grant them citizenship. Chipman calls this "the best durable solution."

The issue has become a hot one among the refugees themselves. "Some people have expressed fear that [the international refugee conference] shall ask the governments which are host to refugees to grant them mass citizenship without consideration for [the refugees] wishes," George Rubagumya says. He denies that the conference has such intentions.

But that sort of blanket solution to the problem is just what the Rwandan government appears to be looking for. "They are hoping they are going to be rescued by Uganda" (where 84,000 refugees live), according to Roger Winter. And, he says, "the current government in Uganda is as well disposed toward these refugees as any regime you will ever get."

But ironically, Winter says, it is the Habyarimana government that is putting roadblocks in the way of a Ugandan offer to nationalize the refugees. "By essentially saying, 'We can't let these people come back,'" the Rwanda government incites anti-refugee feelings in Uganda. "You get elements within the Uganda government who are cooperating with [President Yoweri] Museveni, but who would still have a problem with offering nationality to a lot of refugees. They say, 'Why should we take care of these people when their own government won't have anything to do with them?'"

So far, the Rwandan officials haven't shown any signs of being flexible enough to work with neighboring countries on a solution. "They hope [the problem] will go away," Winter says.

But it probably won't, partly because there seem to be some underlying issues the government is reluctant to discuss. Land distribution is one of them.

"One-seventh of the land [in Rwanda] is set aside for national parks that primarily serve Belgian and German hunters," Winter says, and that has been a sticking point for some refugees, who wonder why animal preserves take precedence over farmland.

Winter believes that by telling people that all the land has already been allocated, the government has boxed itself into a corner. "There are many in Rwanda for whom the passions related to the [Tutsis versus Hutu conflict] are very fresh." So if the government were to say that the refugees could come back en masse, "they can't guarantee that that wouldn't precipitate violence, because it would imply to the population at large that land would be taken away from them to accommodate the new arrivals."

In fact, Winter says, "it wouldn't take that much land to accommodate the refugees, so long as they were prepared to do without mass grazing."

A great majority of Rwandan refugees, such as this family, live in Uganda.

D. A. Bertoni/UNHCR

Every human being is entitled to a nationality.

What Winter and others concerned with the fate of Rwandan refugees believe is that Rwanda cannot afford to let these people return because of the social costs. The government is anxious to exclude all of the refugees, partly because their absence has eased ethnic tensions in Rwanda, and partly because they fear potential political agitators in the group.

So, though aid and refugee workers think Rwanda could safely offer repatriation to people who aren't likely to take it, the Habyarimana government seems unwilling to take the risk. ∎

Article 15

AFRICA NEWS
October 3, 1988

Resolution Condemns Violence

A congressional inquiry into the August massacres of thousands of people in Burundi has heard testimony that apparent attempts to reform an inequitable system may have played an unintended role in the tragedy. University of Florida Professor Rene Lemarchand told two House Foreign Affairs subcommittees that the reforms, designed to give more power to a largely disenfranchised ethnic group, had "set the stage for a violent confrontation."

Lemarchand testified September 22 before a joint session of the Africa subcommittee and the subcommittee on Human Rights and International Organizations. The two groups were meeting to consider a resolution, sponsored by Rep. Ted Weiss (D-NY), "concerning the United States response to the atrocities" in Burundi.

Lemarchand agreed with other witnesses that the world will probably never know exactly what led to the slaughter of 2,000 to 3,000 members of the minority Tutsi ethnic group, which effectively rules Burundi, by people from the majority Hutu group. But, the political science professor said, "by adopting a more 'liberal' stance on the Hutu-Tutsi problem than his predecessor," President Pierre Buyoya "created ... hopes (among Hutu) and apprehensions (among Tutsi)." Between 5,000 and 10,000 Hutus were killed in Tutsi retaliation attacks, and another 60,000 fled to already bulging Rwanda and other neighboring countries.

Deputy Assistant Secretary of State for African Affairs Kenneth L. Brown told the hearing that it was "sadly ironic that these tragic events should have taken place under President Buyoya" – who overthrew President Jean-Baptiste Bagaza in a bloodless coup last year – "because his government has committed itself to policy reform and ethnic reconciliation." Brown noted that Bagaza's "campaign of persecution against organized religion, particularly the Catholic Church," which included the closure of church schools, the expulsion of foreign missionaries and the imprisonment of dissenters, was "widely viewed as aimed at undercutting the Hutu majority." At the time of Buyoya's coup, Brown said, the human rights situation was "of such concern to the U.S. government that our diplomatic and aid relationship with the Bagaza regime was under review. ... Buyoya's coup d'etat dramatically altered the human rights situation in Burundi."

But, Lemarchand says, "what seems beyond question ... is that

Buyoya's call for 'liberalization'" in Hutu-Tutsi relations "had little

---

The House resolution calls on Buyoya to greatly increase recent efforts towards national reconciliation – or else.

---

impact on the attitudes and practices of local officials, most of whom stuck to a rigidly discriminatory posture."

"The crucial point," he says, is that support from the president "did raise the expectations of the Hutu." Lemarchand says the Hutu were bitterly disappointed to discover that "in spite of official statements to the contrary, nothing would alter the harsh realities of Tutsi supremacy."

The initial massacre, perpetrated by Hutu against Tutsi in mid-August, may have been the result of this disillusionment boiling over. Or, as other observers have suggested, the Hutu might have responded to threats from the Tutsi and simply lashed out in anticipation of an attack. Whatever the cause, the Hutu community paid dearly when the all-Tutsi Burundi army was sent in to

"stabilize" the situation. According to refugees now living in tents on the Rwanda-Burundi border, the army was primarily responsible for the brutal anti-Hutu backlash. "The Burundi government has admitted (and regretted) that in its efforts to restore order, uncontrolled elements of the army attacked innocent civilians," Kenneth Brown says, "but the government denies such acts were intended or ordered by it or the military."

The House resolution on the affair, which was approved by the Foreign Affairs Committee on September 27 and is scheduled to be voted on in the full House this week, condemns the violence and calls on the Buyoya government to "greatly increase its recent efforts towards national reconciliation" – or else. The resolution urges the president and secretary of state to review U.S.-Burundi relations "with a view towards the immediate suspension of United States assistance" if the Buyoya government hasn't met certain conditions within six months.

First, Burundi must cooperate with "credible international organizations" in conducting an impartial inquiry into the massacre. The government must also bring to

Dana Downie/Catholic Relief Services

Thousands of Burundians have fled to refugee settlements in Rwanda.

justice those responsible for atrocities, make "substantial progress" in promoting the safe return of refugees, and give foreign journalists and humanitarian aid workers access to the site of the violence.

The resolution also suggests that U.S. officials vote against future World Bank aid for Burundi unless the government has made "substantial progress" in ensuring the maintenance of discipline among military and civilian authorities and has

shown that it is working seriously toward "reversing historical patterns of discrimination against the majority Hutu."

A State Department spokesperson called the resolution "mild," but said that although things appear to be calm in Burundi, "the fundamental differences between the Hutu and Tutsi haven't changed and are unlikely to in six months to a year." She fears that the threat to cut off aid will result in an all-out government campaign for "premature repatriation" of

refugees, who may go back to Burundi before their safety can be assured.

U.S. aid to Burundi amounts to only $7.5 million this year, but the central African nation recently became the largest per capita recipient of World Bank low interest loans. The Bank has pledged $170 million to Burundi this year in the form of grants, concessional loans and funds from the special structural adjustment facility that has been set up to help countries in dire need. ∎

Article 16

Africa Recovery,
December 1988.

SITUATION IN SOUTH CRITICAL

Sudan reeling from disasters

By Paul Heath Hoeffel

The international donor community is in the midst of an emergency mobilization in response to the urgent November appeal by the UN Secretary-General on behalf of Sudan Prime Minister Sadiq El Mahdi to provide $71 mn in emergency humanitarian assistance to his nation. Sudan is reeling from the cumulative impact of a brutal civil war in the south and widespread disruption in the capital and northern regions caused by torrential rains in August.

These conditions have produced shocking famine conditions in the south where only small quantities of external food aid have arrived since a World Food Programme convoy was attacked in September by rebel forces in their effective campaign to cut off food supplies to government-held towns. WFP spokesman Paul Mitchell describes the situation in southern Sudan as "desperate", and certainly the worst in Africa at this time.

In late October WFP was finally able to resume airlifts of some 1,600 tons of maize from Entebbe to the besieged provincial

capital of Juba. Airlifts to Aweil organized by ICRC, USAID and UNICEF were also ready to resume pending assurances of safe passage from both government and rebel authorities.

Serious malnutrition and homelessness affect an estimated 2.5 million Sudanese around the country. Widespread instability, in part caused by a constantly shifting population of displaced people in several areas, has produced a logistical tie up that is difficult to co-ordinate even with massive amounts of external assistance.

The government appeal is aimed at the immediate problem of the estimated 1.5 million displaced persons in such diverse areas as northern Darfur and northern Kordofan, the Central Provinces, Upper Nile, Bahr el-Ghazal, Equatoria and the capital area of Khartoum. Khartoum alone, which along with the northern areas was inundated by floods, has a displaced population of 950,000.

Even areas of the country that have been

spared from drought, floods and war and benefitted from the best rains in forty years now face the threat of locust depredation that

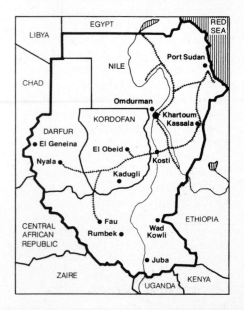

could wipe out the increases in cereal production.

August's rains, which flooded 80 per cent of the capital, destroyed some 200,000 houses and shelters especially in the shanty towns surrounding the city. The standing water did not recede in some areas until late September, paralyzing relief efforts for nearly two months.

The floods, which coincided with one of Sudan's worst economic crises, wiped out job opportunities for many displaced persons as well as their investments in housing and pushed the prices of food, drinking water, basic utensils, clothing and building materials to new highs. The Ministry of Health reports a steady rise in the rates of diarrhoeal diseases, malaria, respiratory infections, and undernutrition.

In the south, disruption caused by five years of continuous warfare between the Sudan People's Liberation Army (SPLA) and government forces has led to horrifying famine conditions affecting over 450,000 people. Reliable reports put the number of dead from starvation in several southern towns at between 10 and 100 persons a day during October.

Thousands of families have fled to the hinterlands to seek food and safety in the towns protected by the government. The principle towns of the south, including Fau, Aweil, Malakal and Torit, are now host to thousands of rural people living in spontaneous settlements and relief camps at the edge of the towns.

The conflict has also intensified in areas along the borders between the northern and southern regions. Thousands of displaced people have fled northward from Bahr el-Ghazal traveling by foot, truck or train. Some have fled eastwards to Ethiopia.

Displaced a priority

The UN appeal was prepared in close collaboration between government officials and a UN interagency mission in Sudan. A Joint Working Group on the displaced, chaired by the commissioner of the Ministry of Social Welfare, Zakat and Displaced (MSWZD) and composed of representatives from NGOs, UN agencies including WFP, UNICEF, UNDP, FAO, UNHCR and WHO, and the donor community as well as key government ministries, played a key role in the elaboration of the appeal.

The urgent humanitarian needs of displaced persons are the immediate priority, according to Charles La Munière, head of the UN Office for African Emergen-

Each day an estimated 200 families flee to northern Sudan from hunger and civil war in the south. The displaced persons make the trip by train, lorry and often on foot.

cies who worked on the appeal's timetable and operational framework in Khartoum.

"We are focusing first on the reception and settlement of people emerging from the conflict zones—people who are starved and sick and have nothing," explains La Munière. "The next step deals with the detailed preparation of settlement schemes aimed at reducing the stress on the national socio-economic infrastructure caused by the displaced population and refugees."

A second appeal in early 1989 will cover the rehabilitation needs of the displaced, including resettlement and the improvement of living conditions in Khartoum.

The cost of the additional food in 1989 is estimated at $16.6 mn and the cost of transportation, handling and distribution to displaced and refugee populations is likely to cost a further $12.2 mn.

For its part, the government has declared a policy of providing for the basic needs of the displaced, using reception centres at interregional boundaries to prevent unchecked migration to the north. It also hopes to keep

people as close as possible to their original homes, where it will try to resettle them in a "participatory and voluntary fashion".

There is a tendency for people to move on from the remote transitional areas, with people making their way to the cities of Nyala, El Obeid and Kosti. As these cities become crowded by the displaced, the job market has become saturated and the deteriorating situation is forcing further migration northward, ultimately to the settlements in the capital, in search of jobs and food.

Little relief in south

The immediate goals of the present relief efforts include the resumption of the food convoys entering the area from neighbouring Uganda and Northern Kordofan and increasing the number of barge trains to cities along the Nile. "Under the best of circumstances," says WFP spokesman Paul Mitchell, "we will be able to get supplies to only 250,000 of the 450,000 people who need help in the south."

Given the probable continuation of the

war, efforts are also being made to increase food security in and around Aweil and Fau so that food can trickle into the adjacent rural areas and help reduce local deficits and thereby decrease migration.

The government has proposed the establishment of an operations base at Babanusa which is in the centre of the transitional zone between the northern edge of Bahr el-Ghazal and southern Darfur and southern Kordofan. As a key railway center, Babanusa is a pivotal town for the migration of displaced persons from several affected areas and already possesses the infrastructure for relief activities.

To maximize relief assistance, local authorities and NGOs including OXFAM, SCF-UK and MSF-B are planning similar small-scale settlements, so-called "paired

---

NGOs Play Key Role in Flood Relief

Four local NGOs assumed major responsibility for relief activities during Sudan's recent flood emergency. The Sudan Council of Churches, the Sudanese Red Cross, the Islamic African Relief Agency and Sudan Aid provided medical and food aid, shelter and water to flood victims, with assistance from international NGOs.

Abdul Mohammed of the Sudan Council of Churches describes the experience as one which ushers in a new chapter in the relationship between local and international NGOs—one in which "local NGOs are no longer reduced to being spectators at their own country's emergency."

Sudanese NGOs, which have been given new confidence and a measure of respectability from their flood relief work, are hoping to institutionalize this relationship. They have recently formed a national NGO consortium.

---

village schemes", attached to the infrastructure of nearby towns so that improved water

systems, schools and clinics will benefit both the settlements and the towns.

Article 17

INTERNATIONAL AGRICULTURAL DEVELOPMENT
MARCH/APRIL 1988

Some of the "famine prevention" projects started in Ethiopia during the 1984/85 drought are leading to improved crop yields. Martin Whiteside takes a look at an imaginative project in Eritrean province

HEADING OFF THE PROSPECT OF FAMINE

Osman Ali Idris is a semi-nomadic peasant farmer from the Rora Habab plateau in Eritrea. He scratches a living from his sloping, stony fields in which he grows wheat and barley. He used to have a reasonable herd of livestock which, through occasional sales, provided him with the cash necessary to buy clothes, sugar and coffee.

This dramatically changed in the 1984 drought when he lost two thirds of his

animals. Now he doesn't even have a pair of oxen to plough his fields, let alone a surplus to sell.

Although Osman's small herd is gradually growing again, there are other worrying signs. "The trees are dying", he says, "and more and more soil is being washed away by the rainwater running off the bare hillsides."

Despite the environmental problems and the poor rains again this year, Osman's eyes light up when he starts describing what he

and his neighbouring farmers are doing to rehabilitate their devastated land.

"From January to April", he says, "we work in groups of 10 farmers, working in turn on each of our farms, building terraces across our fields to stop the soil being washed away. In May and June we plant trees on the bare slopes above our fields. The project has shown us how to do these things."

The Rora Habab plateau is a hilly area 2,500 metres high, covering 280 square kilometres. It is home for about 12,000 Eritreans—semi-nomadic farmers and their families.

Environmental change is not new to the area; tree cover has been declining for at least 100 years. However, the rate of tree loss increased during the drought in the early 1970s and has reached horrific levels since the 1984/85 drought. There are whole hillsides of dead and dying trees.

Just as worrying is that the ground between the trees is bare of all vegetation, with the result that more and more soil is washed away with each rainstorm. Drought may be the primary cause of tree loss and soil erosion, but overgrazing and tree cutting have also contributed. Water running of these bare upper slopes is causing further problems lower down the hillside where the few pockets of flatter arable land is affected by serious gully and sheet erosion.

The Rora Habab Project grew out of the desperate days of the last drought when famine stalked the plateau. Many families were kept alive by food provided by the Eritrean Relief Association (ERA). Determined to move on from relief to development and famine prevention, ERA and the Eritrean People's Liberation Front (EPLF) who form the local administration, started a comprehensive development project involving reafforestation, agriculture, water development, health, education and community development. Funds were provided by Norwegian Church Aid, ICCO (Netherlands) and Britain's Christian Aid.

Terraces improve yields

Terracing fields to reduce soil erosion proved a priority for many farmers. The farmers were taught to build stone terraces on the contour. After only two years, the terraces have begun to prove their worth. Soil is being trapped on the upper sides and yields in the terraced fields have almost doubled.

Further improvements are planned with locally made ox-drawn scoops used to level the soil between the terrace walls. With improved yields clearly visible, farmers are increasingly enthusiastic about terracing.

One farmer explained: "We see these terraces improving our yields. The yield we used to get from a piece of land which took two oxen five days to plough, we now get

Terraced fields in Ethiopia yield twice as much grain—and even in poor rains they still get a harvest Cr: M. Whiteside

from a piece that takes three days to plough"! (The local unit of land area is the amount two oxen can plough in a day). However the labour involved, 100 person days per hectare, is enormous; so despite the farmers' enthusiasm it will be several years before even the majority of fields are protected.

...Whilst trees protect the soil

Protecting the steeper, non-arable slopes from deforestation and erosion is proving difficult. So far the project has concentrated on rehabilitating small patches of land with bench terraces and planting them with fast-growing exotic trees. On a limited scale, this has been successful with good survival and growth rates despite the poor rain. Local farmers have learnt about planting and caring for trees for the first time.

"We have learnt trees can be planted as well as cut down" said a farmer.

The technique they use is very labour-intensive, taking up to 1,000 person days per hectare. Local labour resources can only replant a few hectares per year, while hundreds of existing hectares of trees are being lost every year. Clearly the existing

trees must be protected and forest loss halted.

Long term protection, however, threatens short term livelihoods.

The farming community has implemented strict controls on cutting live trees and is very aware of the dangers of deforestation. The controversial issue is grazing control.

Some farmers, having seen their herds halved in the recent drought, do not believe that their reduced herds can be damaging their environment. Others like Osman have watched the goats eating young trees, and have seen their sheep digging grass roots out of the ground in the dry season to get a little nourishment. "But what can we do?", he says, "animals are our livelihood."

Course

At a course for farmers run by the project, the subject of restricted grazing is hotly debated. "We must have grazing control, although it will be very painful", one says. "In the highlands of Eritrea they traditionally practised rotational grazing, which was good", adds another.

Ironically the project is in danger of exacerbating the pressure on grazing.

Traditionally the farmers and their families migrate from the plateau during the dry season in search of water and grazing. Communities living on the plateau experienced desperate water shortages with a bucket of water taking up to six hours to collect.

The project is in the process of building five much needed dams, but there is a real danger that the dams will enable livestock to remain on the plateau during the dry season, with devastating effect on the environment.

Improved schools, health services and community services are also incentives for families to stay throughout the year. Luckily it is not too late to redesign the capacities of some of the dams for human consumption only and negotiate with villagers how the water will be used. It is likely that in future some of the family will remain on the plateau while others travel with the livestock during the dry season.

"Many years"

It will take many years of hard work to break the famine cycle in Eritrea and in Ethiopia as a whole Meanwhile emergency food will be needed in low rainfall years to prevent widespread famine. While it is important that this relief rapidly reaches those in most need, it is essential that these short-term relief efforts do not divert attention from this vital longer-term famine prevention work.

Peace is also needed. The war between

The soil has gone, washed away. Only bare rocks remain Cr: M. Whiteside

the EPLF, fighting for Eritrean Independence, and the Ethiopian Government hits the headlines when food convoys are attacked. But war is a constant barrier to long-term development. With peace, projects like Rora Habab could be successful on a wider scale throughout Eritrea and northern Ethiopia. Then there would be faster progress towards breaking the famine cycle.

Martin Whiteside is an agriculturalist with the aid agency Christian Aid, P.O Box 100, London SE1 7RT

Article 18

The Christian Science Monitor,
October 6, 1988.

Kenya woos outside cash to stoke new jobs

By Julie Whipple
Special to The Christian Science Monitor

Nairobi, Kenya

Kenya is facing the challenge of creating 6 million new jobs in the next 12 years.

As shantytowns spread out around the urban areas and crime rates begin to climb, finding jobs for people has become an issue of security and national stability.

Traditionally, the agricultural sector has provided the bulk of the nation's employment, but only 17 percent of the land in Kenya is arable, so more and more people are turning to the cities in search of a livelihood. Although estimates vary widely, some observers say unemployment could be as high as 40 percent by the year 2000. Government concern about this "unemployment time bomb" and the increase in crime is at the heart of recent efforts to promote industrial growth.

Even at the official growth rate of 65,000 new slots a year, the country will be doing well if it adds just 1 million jobs in that time. Meanwhile, Kenya's population is growing at more than 4 percent a year – the fastest in the world.

Wanted: foreign investors

Key to Kenya's ability to create jobs and grow as an industrialized nation is retaining current foreign investment, and attracting more. Like many other third-world countries short of funds, Kenyan officials say, the nation is eager for offshore companies to open businesses here.

To this end, Kenya has established foreign investment protection rules that guarantee repatriation of capital and dividends and protect investors against nationalization of companies without due cause and compensation.

The country's boast of political stability, substantial cheap labor, and – in comparison with many of its neighbors – a fairly well-developed economy and industrial base – is considered by the government to be a very attractive package.

The government also offers incentives, including various cost rebates for export manufacturing, since these activities generate much-needed foreign exchange for the country. Recently, the government went even further and now allows companies to write off foreign-exchange losses from offshore loans.

Despite these efforts, Kenya hasn't had any significant new investment in the last seven years, and a number of foreign companies have recently sold their holdings to local enterprises.

One major disincentive is the fact that corporate profits produced by operations of multinational companies still cannot generally be repatriated, says one financial consultant, who asked not to be named. The government, despite repeated urgings from investors, shows little sign of changing its position.

According to Dan McCarthy, managing director of General Motors Kenya, one of the reasons is that, although Kenya's investment incentives are good, they still don't measure up to global standards. In Kenya, says Mr. McCarthy, "we must re-

'If the government says one thing but the reality is different, the businessman will go someplace else.'

FILE PHOTO/R. NORMAN MATHENY – STAFF

Vehicle assembler in Mombasa: many small firms have sprung up to supply GM

alize that we're competing with places like Korea, Mexico, Mauritius."

In these nations, "duty-free zones" have minimized production costs and government interference in manufacturing, and investors have little trouble obtaining their profits. In return, these countries get a transfer of technology and skills, hard currency in the form of rent and salaries, and lots of employment. On the small Indian Ocean island of Mauritius, 80,000 jobs were recently created in the free zone when the government turned actively to investment promotion.

Kenya has been talking about setting up a duty-free zone of its own for years, but so far little progress has been made. As a result, companies that are preparing to shift to new locations because of rising costs or other problems are paying little attention to Kenya. The technical manager of a Nike factory in South Korea says Indonesia is the most likely next stop for their operations. Another investor says north Africa is a place to watch for future export manufacturing activity.

Among multinational companies that recently sold majority shares to local private investors are Firestone Tire and Rubber, Eveready Batteries, and American Life Insurance Company. While the operations these companies started have by no means folded, the withdrawal of their offshore shareholders is a signal to potential investors that business conditions in Kenya might be less favorable than they are cracked up to be.

"Investors want transparency and consistency," says a Western diplomat who asked not to be named. "If the government says one thing but the reality is different, the businessman will go someplace else – it's not worth the risk."

General Motors, on the other hand, is staying – for now. During the nearly 12 years GM has been in Kenya, its presence has been the catalyst for the birth of 11 new industries and eight expansions.

Elmard Ouma Syongoh, an interior fittings manufacturer, says he began his own business in 1985, "specifically to service GM." Starting with three employees, he now has 12 on his staff, eight of whom were unemployed when they joined him. Today, 85 percent of his business is dedicated to GM.

GM's factory manager, Patrick Ndiema, was for years in charge of developing such local suppliers and says he has observed a great improvement in the level of competence among local producers as a result of GM's insistence on quality. As for the future of foreign investments like GM's, he only shrugs, saying, "We can act as an example, but investment promotion is a matter for the government. Whether they can implement it is something we'll have to wait and see."

Red tape and other troubles

Apart from the stiff competition, Kenya has some problems of its own to solve before investors are likely to start pouring in. The director of one large manufacturing company who asked not to be named said that although Kenya's policies "look good on paper," they are not always practiced. This, he said, is because of bureaucratic delays and even breaches of agreement. In the early '80s, for example, all export compensation payments were suddenly suspended for nearly a year. Currently, dividend remittances for most foreign companies are about two years behind.

Another problem has been the confusion surrounding Kenya's "indigenization" policies, which seek to ensure that indigenous Kenyans control the economy. Although the government insists that investors will remain free to control their businesses, conflicting messages abound in statements by politicians as well as amid several divestments that have occurred over the last few years.

Article 19

AFRICA REPORT
September-October 1988

Harvests Under Fire

CAROL B. THOMPSON

Carol B. Thompson, associate professor at the University of Southern California, has written extensively on SADCC, including a book in press, Southern Africa: Harvests Under Fire.

In southern Africa, crops are burning—set on fire by forces sponsored by apartheid South Africa. The most immediate threat to the region's agriculture, these wars pose serious security questions for the regional economic group, the Southern African Development Coordination Conference (SADCC, comprised of Angola, Botswana, Lesotho, Malawi, Mozambique, Swaziland, Tanzania, Zambia, and Zimbabwe). Secondary, but longer term challenges to southern Africa's agricultural development are American government attempts to influence SADCC agricultural policy.

The Mozambique National Resistance (known as Renamo or MNR) regularly burns peasants' fields and attacks food caravans the Mozambican government sends to assist the villagers: One-third of the 14 million population are "seriously affected" by the war and cannot grow their own food. In Angola, Unita plants Claymore mines (made in Louisiana) in the foot paths leading to peasants' fields, resulting in the highest amputee rate in the world.

At the July SADCC Council of Ministers meeting in Maputo, the opening statement by Mozambique's Minister of Transport, Armando Guebuza, desig-

> **Even the agricultural sector in the frontline states has fallen victim to South African destabilization and the political exigencies of Western governments. In its efforts to ensure regional food security, SADCC has found its agricultural policies under intense scrutiny, and the advice being offered may not be in the best interests of the region's farmers.**

nated security as integral to the success of SADCC's projects. For example, opening the Chicualuala railway to Maputo—over which Zimbabwean fruit and sugar can be shipped—will cost an estimated $20 million in initial security allocations to protect the line from Renamo.

Several donors (e.g. United Kingdom, Italy, and Scandinavia) have responded with non-lethal military aid. The U.S., however, refuses any such aid and instead increases financing for Unita's war against the Angolan government. Further, the U.S. often excludes Angola from its aid to SADCC, causing Executive Secretary Simba Makoni to reply: "SADCC is representative of all the nations. . . It is not a separate entity which can design programs that may include some nations and not others."

In this context, U.S. agricultural aid could appear to be a benign alternative. But SADCC emphasizes that aid to the region cannot ignore apartheid aggression. As one official in London stated, providing funds for projects without addressing South Africa's continued destabilization of the region is like "mopping up water while the tap is still running."

Further, the U.S. Agency for International Development (U.S.AID), as a major donor to the SADCC administrative unit on agriculture in Zimbabwe, agricultural research in Botswana, and a multimillion dollar project in agriculture at the University of Zimbabwe, brings its own interests to the region—not always compatible with SADCC's goals.

Master Farmers

American agriculture is perhaps the most efficient in the world in terms of yield per acre, but quite inefficient in cost per input. Historically, yield increases have been achieved by consolidation of land in large holdings to make high levels of mechanization cost-effective, utilizing high-yielding hybrids, sustained by fertilizers and pesticides. This formula increases grain availability, but not accessibility as small farmers are pushed off the land. More food is produced, but the policy can create an entire sub-class of marginal people—with no land or jobs. In the U.S., for example, from 1985-87, a farm went out of business every four to seven minutes, most of which were family farms.

To increase food production in Africa, U.S. AID has first encouraged making new inputs and information available to the master farmers, those who can benefit most readily from the inputs. In fact, however, master farmers are only more productive if they have tracts large enough to afford the expensive inputs, to make them cost-efficient.

A study of peasant agriculture in Chokwe, Mozambique, gives one example: "One of the effects of both government and donor policy in Chokwe is that the large private farmers are succeeding in acquiring the technical assistance and marketing resources available while the large number of family farmers are being left out." Many studies of African agriculture, however, have shown that peasants can grow food crops quite efficiently on very small plots; intensive labor inputs make up for what is lost in the small size of plots and in the lack of high technology.

Rarely, if ever, does U.S. AID cite land reform—redistribution of land to the poor who will grow food first—as a means to increase production. SADCC, in contrast, has gone on record that land reform is important to increased production. Southern Africa does not have the foreign exchange to purchase or distribute widely high technology inputs to farmers. What it does have is adequate and skilled labor, and peasants with land have shown that they are receptive to innovations that can be sustained after the field representative leaves or the outside funds dry up.

Specialization of Production

A second component of U.S. AID policy counsels each country to produce what it is most efficient in producing. For example, Botswana should forget about maize production; the "maize belt" across Zambia, Malawi, and Zimbabwe will take care of its needs. The policy is attractive and could provide Botswana with more maize for less—in good years. However, when drought hits, does Botswana still receive a percentage of Zimbabwean maize, forcing Zimbabwe to import maize?

In fact, the Botswana government did not have long to wait to be proven correct in its hesitancy to depend totally on neighbors. In late 1987, Zimbabwe stopped all maize exports because the drought that year had reduced grain reserves, which were retained for Zimbabwean domestic consumption.

Sadcc emphasizes that aid to the region cannot ignore apartheid aggression.

SADCC, therefore, accepts the logic of comparative advantage only for certain items. To follow comparative advantage to its logical conclusion could mean that Zimbabwe would produce most items, or in the case of a free South Africa, it would dominate regional grain sales. SADCC, therefore, encourages each member to produce grain as a strategic need. For

example, Botswana will grow more sorghum/millet (drought resistant) than maize, but will not forego maize production totally. Cost-benefit analysis will be tempered by political considerations of strategic food needs.

Hybrid Research

Promotion of hybrids by U.S. AID ignores the social equity problems which have emerged in "Green Revolution" nations in Asia. While hybrids greatly increased yields in Asian rice and wheat, they also greatly consolidated land under larger landowners who could afford the fertilizers and pesticides and buy access to irrigation. In short, the hybrids promoted the policy of creating master farmers. Now, while countries like India produce record amounts of grain, they also have larger absolute numbers of hungry.

SADCC officials speak highly of developing hybrids, but do not see them as a panacea. Instead, there is much interest in developing "stable producers" which will increase yields but not be as vulnerable to variations in inputs as the hybrids. The "Green Revolution" as defined by SADCC is a combination of new hybrids

Maize at Glendry farm, Zimbabwe: "SADCC encourages each member to produce grain as a strategic need"

and stable producers in traditional food crops such as sorghum and millet.

Triangular Trade

SADCC strongly supports triangular food exchanges: For example, Zimbabwe buys wheat from the U.S. and pays for it with exports of maize to Mozambique, which becomes American food aid to Mozambique. These arrangements reward surplus grain producers by assisting in their marketing, and deficit countries receive grains from neighbors more quickly and at lower transport costs.

In 1985, the U.S. Department of Agriculture (USDA) resisted such deals, insisting that Mozambique receive surplus American maize. When told that Mozambicans prefer white to American yellow maize, which they feed to animals, the USDA replied that Mozambicans would acquire a taste for yellow, thus providing a future market for the U.S.

After nine months of deliberations, the U.S. finally agreed to ship 7,000 tons of Zimbabwean maize to Mozambique. However, the U.S. remains resistant to triangular exchange (only 2,700 tons in 1987 and none so far in 1988), although the U.S. began shipping maize (22,000 tons) from Kenya to Mozambique. This caused a U.S.AID consultant to report: "Quite a bit of political pressure was exerted from time to time. . . cost and timeliness alone were certainly not the only criteria involved in the eventual selection of Kenya over Zimbabwe."

Privatization

The U.S. also admonishes SADCC governments to turn both distribution and production over to the private sector. Agreeing that state enterprises have often been inefficient, overcrowded with under-employed people, and sometimes corrupt, several governments have moved to tighten budgets and clarify channels of responsibility. However, most SADCC members do not agree that privatization is the best remedy.

State intervention occurred in the first place because private enterprise would enter only a few sectors with substantial profit margins. Providing transport to

The Logic of Aid?

Since the severe Sahelian drought in the early 1970s, analysts have advocated creating regional food reserves—yet few regions have been able to overcome political sensitivities concerning multilateral control over food reserves.

In 1973, the United States refused the Club of Rome's offer to purchase a few tons of U.S. grain surplus to be put under international control—it was feared that the reserves would distort international market prices or be used as political leverage against the U.S. The only region to succeed in establishing a multilateral reserve is ASEAN (Association of South East Asian Nations), which has regional rice reserves.

Since the long drought in southern Africa (1982-84, to 1988 for some countries), SADCC members have been coordinating requests for international food aid and have created national early warning systems throughout the region to anticipate future harvest failures. Recently, SADCC has proceeded with plans for regional food reserves, based on regular surplus production in Zimbabwe and Malawi. The grain would be bought from the surplus producer and put in storage under regional control; SADCC's eight years of cooperation provide a practical base of experience for decisions about allocations of the regional reserve to needy members.

Because of the high cost of setting up such a scheme, however, SADCC needs initial donor assistance. Gradually, over three to five years, SADCC members themselves will assume responsibility for the cost. The European Economic Community (EEC) especially, but also U.S.AID and Australia, have shown interest in helping with the initial expenses, and plans were advancing to establish the reserves, until the EEC set two conditionalities.

First, because Zimbabwe would be the major contributor of surplus grain, its pricing mechanism must be reformed; Zimbabwean maize prices are "too high" relative to the international grain market price. But this international price is for yellow maize no.2, and Zimbabwe produces white maize, used mainly within its own region. An agricultural economist from Michigan State University working at the University of Zimbabwe said that the price of yellow maize no.2 has no relevance whatsoever to Zimbabwe's production or market: "I think yellow maize no.2 becomes the international market price indicator because its price can be found in the books [on the desks of grain merchants]." Further, he pointed out that the price is the result of dumping maize on the international market, so of course Zimbabwean prices are "too high."

Second, the EEC insists that as a donor, it has the right to help make decisions about the purchase and allocation of the grain reserves. SADCC finds this demand a simple attempt at control. The head of the SADCC Food and Agricultural Administrative and Technical Unit in Zimbabwe, John Dhliwayo, replied: "We cannot allow foreigners to administer our food aid program. . . major food donors are creating employment for their own people besides using food aid as a weapon to influence policies of [beneficiary] governments."

With these two major disagreements under discussion, little progress has been made over the last several months in establishing a regional grain reserve. The early warning systems predict substantial surpluses in Zimbabwe and Tanzania in the 1988-89 growing season, but a regional deficit of 1.1 million tons. A regional reserve would reward the surplus producers by purchasing their grain and making it more readily available to the deficit neighbors.

—C.B.T.

small peasants in remote areas of Tanzania, for example, is not profitable. In fact, in the 1970s, it was the World Bank which encouraged the Tanzanian government to set up the state monopoly, National Milling, to rationalize prices and transport. Now the World Bank and U.S. AID want it fully privatized.

Moreover, SADCC has noticed that the U.S. does not follow its own advice, for in 1987, direct farm subsidies reached $70 million per *day*—and they were not to marginal farmers in need of a little more for survival. As reported in 1986, one Texas farm owned by International Paper Company and the crown prince of

Liechtenstein received $2.2 million in subsidies from American taxpayers.

When questioned about such extensive state intervention in farming, the U.S. replies that agriculture is a strategic industry. SADCC agrees and will maintain government intervention, in spite of criticism from aid agencies. SADCC explains as follows: "It is now recognized that in developing countries the inefficiency of commodity, factor, and capital markets reduces considerably the ability of the free market economic system to carry out its functions. Consequently, government intervention in the economy

through development planning has now come to be accepted as an essential and pivotal means of steering and accelerating *balanced* economic growth in developing countries."

The SADCC definition of food security emphasizes equity and distribution in both production and consumption, in order to provide employment as well as food on the table. SADCC will continue the serious debates about appropriate farming systems for food security, resisting inappropriate advice on southern African agriculture—whether technical or political.   ⭕

Article 20

AFRICA NEWS
April 4, 1988

Polls Menace Pretoria's Neighbors

Gaborone—The slaughter of four sleeping people in an early-morning March 28 raid on the Botswanan capital followed a familiar pattern: when right-wing pressures heat up at home, Pretoria dispatches commandos to kill some of its neighbors.

The latest raid came the day before white voters in the conservative stronghold of Randfontein went to the polls for a politically sensitive South African election. There were four violent incidents on election day itself: unknown assassins murdered Dulcie September, the African National Congress (ANC) representative in Paris; a small bomb exploded near the South African embassy in that city, causing slight damage; shots were fired from a passing car at the South African consulate in Marseilles; and the South African

Defense Force (SADF) claimed to have killed four "ANC terrorists" who had allegedly crossed into South Africa from Zimbabwe.

"I was awakened by gunshots and screams, and right away I knew the Boers were there," said one eyewitness to the Gaborone raid. Another said the automatic rifle fire – which shattered the peace in Gaborone's Phirig suburb an hour after midnight – went on for some time, subsided for a few minutes, and "then, as they were leaving the house, there were explosions inside."

Despite these shows of force, Conservative candidate Corne Mulder won the seat left vacant by the death of his father, Cornelius (Connie) Mulder. The

elder Mulder, a former information Minister, led the right-wing defection from the ruling National Party after he was disgraced in a foreign influence-buying scandal in the late 1970s. It was the third Conservative victory in a month - the two by-elections on March 3 were preceed by the February 24 crackdown on 17 anti-apartheid organizations (see *AN* , March 7).

The Conservative Party's vote share was increased, and leader Andries Treurnicht said the results "confirmed a dramatic rejection of the policy of so-called reform of the Nationalist Party." Treurnicht added, "The future is ours."

Similarly, in the run-up to last

South African President P.W. Botha reviews a military parade.

May's whites-only general election, Pretoria took credit for killing five Zambian civilians it claimed were "ANC terrorists" in a commando raid on the Victoria Falls resort town of Livingstone.

On May 19, 1986, the crucial day of South African cabinet meetings with the British Commonwealth's Eminent Persons Group (EPG), Pretoria killed four civilians in coordinated air and ground attacks on the capitals of Zimbawe, Zambia and Botswana. These raids forestalled the EPG effort to encourage Pretoria-ANC negotiations and temporarily molified right-wing critics who charged the government with softness for even considering such talks.

In addition, The past year has seen a steady rise in surreptitious violence against South Africa's neighbors. there have been more than a dozen unclaimed terror attacks against ANC members, other South African exiles, or people living in proximity to

them in countries surroundng South Africa.

The SADF has officially admitted killing 146 people in raids on Botswana, Lesotho, Mozambique, Swaziland, Zambia and Zimbabwe since 1981, according to a recap of the violence in the *ohannesburg Star* newspaper. But these account for only a small fraction of the raids Pretoria is suspected of perpetrating. And the *Star's* figures do not include the deaths – now numbering several hundred thousand according to a Unicef study – caused directly or indirectly by South African-sponsored rebels in Mozambique and Angola.

Even by past standards, the Gaborone raid was gruesome. "Everything inside was blackened and charred," said a witness who viewed what remained of the house soon after dawn on Monday. "There was a thick layer of soot and ash: burned paper, burned possessions and maybe burned flesh." All windows and

doors were smashed and only singed scraps of paper, some kitchen utensils and a few other household items survived.

After shooting their sleeping victims and riddling the house with bullets, the raiders doused the bodies and the house with gasoline and set everything ablaze, Foreign Minister Gaositwe Chiepe said. "How can anybody admit they have done this sort of thing, killing people and then burning the remains?"

This ugly scene bore little resemblence to South African Defense Minister Magnus Malan's description of the attack. He likened it to "a surgeon's incision against the ANC, with minimum force to achieve maximum advantage." The burning of the house and the bodies is seen here as an attempt to make identification of civilian victims difficult.

The SADF claimed it attacked the Botswana house based on "intelligence gathered" when "three terrorists were shot dead" by South African soldiers near the Botswana border on March 25.

The Botswana incursion brought condemnations from inside and outside South Africa, including a declaration by Anglican Archbishop Desmond Tutu that SADF men were becoming known as the "bully boys on the subcontinent."

The U.S. State Department srongly condemned the raid, but coupled its statement with an acknowledgement of Pretoria's claim that South Africa faces a real threat from its neighbors. "We are in touch with all parties to the violence in South and southern Africa to urge them to break the cycle of action and retaliation across borders," the U.S. said.

In a protest message to Pretoria, Botswana's Dr. Chiepe demanded compensation and an apology. She said South Africa had violated an understanding that it would ask Botswana to investigate charges terrorists moving through this country before taking action of its own.

ANC President Oliver Tambo, flanked by representatives of the UN and Organization of African Unity, at a funeral for victims of an earlier South African raid. Afrapix

But Chiepe acknowledged that South Africa is not likely to heed protests from a militarily weak desert nation of just over one million people. She said Botswana's last, slender hope for peace lies in tough pressure from the world community for an end to South African "aggression and destabilizaion."

While Botswana cannot afford to impose sanctions, as it is a landlocked country economically dependent on South Africa, Chiepe emphasized that "We don't discourage anyone else from doing that."

- Steve Askin
with reports from Botswana's
weekly *Mmegi Wa Dikgang*
newspaper

Renamo/Pretoria Links Cited

Paulo Filipe Barbosa de Oliveira, who has returned to Mozambique after six years in the exiled leadership of the right-wing anti-government Mozambique National Resistance (Renamo), has talked to reporters about what he describes as factional in-fighting and ongoing South African support for the organization.

At a two-and-a-half hour press conference March 23 in Maputo, the Mozambican capital, Oliveira said that as recently as January of this year, a South African Air Force DC-3 was used to ferry a top Renamo official into Mozambique. Evo Fernandes, a former general secretary of Renamo whom Oliveira called an "*eminence grise*" of the movement, was flown secretly into Mozambique from South Africa. He said the same plane later brought Fernandes back out of Mozambique, accompanied by the Renamo foreign relations secretary, Artur Januario da Fonseca.

Oliveira, a Portuguese citizen, said he served as Renamo representative for Western Europe based in Lisbon from mid-1984 to mid-1987. Earlier, he had directed the group's radio station in South Africa, the Voice of Free Africa. Oliveira apparently lost his post for being affiliated with what he called the "Washington-Paris axis," the faction of Renamo's leadership favoring looser ties with South Africa and stronger links to right-wing supporters in France and the U.S.

Pretoria, along with elements in West Germany, now exerts "a great deal of control" over Renamo, he said. He described a Renamo base in the Phalaborwa region of South Africa's eastern Transvaal Province, which he visited in 1983, and said there "is every indication" it continues to operate. "It certainly still has telephone and communications equipment," he added. Sophisticated gear, including an encoding/decoding

fascimile machine, for communicating between Phalaborwa and Lisbon was installed in his office in June of 1987, he said. Brigadier Cornelius (Charles) van Niekerk, who has been chief liaison with Renamo for the South African Defense Force, came to Lisbon to oversee the installation, Oliveira told reporters. Previous communication with Phalaborwa had been via telephone.

Oliveira also offered a new twist to the still-unsolved mystery surrounding the plane crash in South Africa on October 19, 1986, in which Mozambican President Samora Machel and 34 others died. In a tantalizing but inconclusive reference to the fatal crash, Oliveira said news that the presidential plane had gone down was passed from South Africa to Renamo's Lisbon office hours before Mozambique was informed. A call from Phalaborwa "confirmed the death of President Samora Machel and told me to be on standby, for it might be necessary for us to claim the action," he said.

AFRICA NEWS
December 21, 1987

Article 21

South African Connections

Harare - A convicted spy, released from Pretoria Central prison, has arrived here offering an insider's view of South Africa's covert war against Mozambique and other neighboring states.

Thirty-year-old Zimbabwean Patricia Hanekom was one of three young whites arrested in December 1983 for giving secret South African military documents to the outlawed African National Congress (ANC). The documents contained information on South African operations against Mozambique and Zimbabwe and were passed to the targeted governments by the ANC.

Also detained were Hanekom's husband Derek and South African Defense Force (SADF) Corporal Roland Hunter – who obtained the documents while working for a SADF covert operations unit. Derek Hanekom completed his sentence last year, but Hunter has two more years to serve.

The three could have been sentenced to death for high treason, but were allowed to plead guilty to lesser charges – including possession of a tape recording of exiled ANC President Oliver Tambo with intent to disseminate it – because South African authorities did not want to let defense lawyers examine files confiscated on the Hanekoms' farm near Johannesburg.

Until the arrests, Hunter was personal assistant to the SADF's Col. Cornelius (Charles) van Niekerk, who headed a covert operation to harass the Mozambican government. According to Hanekom, van Niekerk continued as South Africa's liaison to the Mozambique National Resistance (Renamo) even after South Africa signed the March 1984 Nkomati

Accord barring further aid to the group (see *AN* November 4, 1985).

Interviewed here after she was freed on November 20 and deported to Zimbabwe, Hanekom gave a detailed account of Hunter's work with SADF's clandestine operations.

She says Hunter, assigned to the anti-Mozambique *Operation Mila*, worked alongside units responsible for similar operations against Zimbabwe, Lesotho and Angola. All four covert schemes were run by the Directorate of Special Tasks under SADF's chief of staff intelligence. Though South Africa openly supports Unita rebels in Angola and has sent its own invasion forces into that country, the Pretoria government has repeatedly denied charges that it aids armed rebels in Zimbabwe, Lesotho and Mozambique.

Hunter was a reluctant draftee who contemplated leaving South Africa to avoid serving in apartheid's army but remained in the country when his father's friends in the military found him a non-combatant post. Assigned to guard a SADF building, he met van Niekerk, who took a liking to the young man and offered him a "more interesting job."

Hunter soon found himself at the center of a covert operation designed to meet all Renamo's needs, from clothing the group's leaders to secretly supplying them with weapons to promoting assassination of dissidents within the movement. Hanekom cites as an example the killing of one top Renamo leader, former Portuguese secret police officer Orlando Cristina. "A decision was taken by the operation to eliminate him," she says, amidst factional disputes within Renamo.

On several occasions, Hanekom

says, Hunter helped load new AK47 machine guns onto helicopters delivering monthly shipments of supplies to Renamo. A warehouse at SADF's Voortrekkerhoogte base in Pretoria contained thousands of the guns, with identifying marks removed. Some or all of them were manufactured in Czechoslovakia and obtained by South Africa through an unknown third party.

They were apparently supplied to Renamo to make it appear that the rebel group relies on weapons captured from the Mozambique army, which uses AK47s. Similarly altered guns have been recovered by the Zimbabwe army from anti-government forces here.

The helicopters Hunter loaded also carried seeds, fertilizer, propaganda leaflets, even pencils – from which the words "made in South Africa" had been removed – for use in a Renamo program to "win hearts and minds" in Mozambique.

Hanekom says Hunter was also responsible for daily delivery of *Operation Mila's* "Voice of Free Africa" tapes to their transmitter. Ostensibly beamed by Renamo from inside Mozambique, the tapes were actually broadcast from Johannesburg facilities of the South African Broadcasting Corporation, according to Hanekom, who says South African officials also ran a similar broadcast operation, "Radio Truth," directed against Zimbabwe.

Hunter visited three Renamo bases inside South Africa and was responsible for delivering monthly salary payments of 500-750 Rand (U.S. $250-$375) – more than ten times the average monthly wage of a worker in Maputo – to top officials of the group. On one occasion, when

Renamo President Afonso Dhlakama was preparing to lead a delegation to West Germany in 1983, Hunter was given 5,000 Rand to take them on a clothes shopping spree in Pretoria.

Though the cost of the *Operation Mila* program is not known, the size of van Niekerk's petty cash account – Hanekom says he was authorized to spend up to Rand 250,000 (U.S. $125,000) without approval from higher authorities – suggests that it was generously funded.

Drawn into the South African anti-apartheid movement while studying at the University of Cape Town in the late 1970s, Hanekom says she and the men arrested with her felt a "moral obligation" to pass information about South Africa's activities to the intended victims so they "would be able to defend their interests better."

She said she was a loyal Zimbabwean whose term in prison strengthened her "dedication to the struggle in South Africa." Like ANC leader Nelson Mandela and other political prisoners held for their work with the banned organization, Hanekom and her confederates rejected a South African offer of early release in exchange for rejecting violent resistance to the apartheid system.

As Patricia Hanekom settled into newfound freedom after serving her term for helping the ANC, another white woman was sentenced by Zimbabwe's High Court to 25 years in jail for spying for South Africa.

Odile Eone Harington was convicted of giving South African forces information that would help them pinpoint and kill ANC members on future raids into Zimbabwe.

Harington's defense was that she committed no crime – because South Africa is not an enemy of Zimbabwe and because she spied on the ANC, not the Zimbabwe government.

The 27-year-old former fine arts student posed as a refugee from apartheid when she came to Zimbabwe in October 1986. But confronted with letters to South African security agents intercepted by Zimbabwe police, she admitted in court that she was sent to infiltrate the ANC.

The letters contained ANC names, addresses, car registration numbers

BULLETIN BOARD

• The award-winning 1988 Church World Service Global Calendar and Greetings Cards are now available. The calendar features photographs, diagrams and short stories covering topics such as international trade from a poor nation's perspective, world pollution and the four major world religions. To place an order, contact Church World Service, P.O. Box 968, Elkhardt, IN 46515-0968. Calendars are $12 each; cards are $4 for a set of ten (prices include postage).

• The Smithsonian Institution will offer a 10-session course entitled "South Africa Today: Life in a Divided Society" from January 25 to April 4, 1988. Allan Boesak, Cyril Ramaphosa, Njabulo Ndebele, Jakes Gerwel and other scholars and personalities will speak on the ways South Africans are affected by their complex and disturbing society. For more information, contact Diana Parker at the Office of Folklife Programs, Smithsonian Institution, Washington, D.C. 20560. Telephone: (202) 287-3258.

• Operation Crossroads Africa, Inc. has launched the James H. Robinson Internships in International Development for Minority Candidates. Supported by a Ford Foundation grant, the program will provide paid 9- to 12-month internships with development organizations in Africa and the Caribbean and is open to U.S. citizens of black, Hispanic, Asian or Native American background. Fluency in French, Swahili and/or Portuguese is desirable, and experience outside the U.S. and its territories is preferred.

Crossroads is also seeking high school and college students to participate in community development projects in rural African and Caribbean villages during the summer of 1988.

For information on both programs, contact Dolores Vialet, Operation Crossroads Africa, Inc., 150 Fifth Ave., New York, N.Y. 10011. Telephone: (800) 422-3742; (212) 242-8550.

• Oxfam America has an opening for a West Africa Field Representative. Requirements include practical and academic understanding of west Africa, three-plus years rural development experience in the region and fluent French. To apply, send cover letter and resume by December 28 to Recruitment Committee-WAFR, Oxfam America, 115 Broadway, Boston, MA 02116.

• The Michigan Coalition for Human Rights, an interfaith, multi-racial network of activists for peace issues, is selling notecards and posters featuring a photograph of Archbishop Desmond Tutu and Winnie Mandela to raise funds for its 1988 South Africa programs. For more information, call or write Tom Fentin, MCHR Director, 4800 Woodward Ave., Detroit, MI 48201. Telephone: (313) 832-4400.

• Georgia-based *Seeds* magazine is currently recruiting for a Publisher/Executive Director to oversee production, fundraising, finances and circulation and to represent the organization. Management and communications skills are required, along with an understanding of hunger issues. Send resume by February 1, 1988 to Seeds, 222 East Lake Dr., Decatur, GA 30030.

• Bikes Not Bombs/Africa has issued a plea for funds to supply and ship new and reconditioned mountain bicycles to Mozambique. According to the organization, bikes are the cheapest, most reliable and most practical means of bringing humanitarian relief materials to remote areas of the southeast African country.

Bicycles will be shipped through Africare and the American Jewish World Service to Mozambique's Ministry of Health. Contact Bikes Not Bombs/Africa, P.O. Box 56538, Washington, D.C. 20011. Telephone: (301) 589-1810.

• The American Museum of Natural History will host the ninth annual Kwanzaa Celebration from December 27-30. Kwanzaa is an Afro-American holiday observed to commemorate the richness of African culture and its survival in the worldwide African diaspora. For more information, contact Erin McGrath, Office of Public Affairs, American Museum of Natural History, Central Park West at 79th St., New York, N.Y. 10024-5129. Telephone: (212) 769-5762.

and details on where people slept in one ANC residence. Harington said South Africa needed the information to find out where to go "to see the house or attack it."

Despite Harington's obvious inexperience as a spy, the threat of South African infiltration is taken seriously here. In May of last year, South African forces conducted raids into Zimbabwe, Botswana and Zambia, killing 17 people and destroying an ANC office in Harare. At the time, President P.W. Botha warned that South African troops would strike again "when the occasion demands."

South Africa is also believed to be responsible for three explosions in Harare residential neighborhoods

since Harington came here – the latest of which took place in October – including a rocket-grenade attack on a suburban house she identified as an ANC office. In the past 20 months, ANC offices in Zimbabwe have been bombed five times.

Harington said she acted from loyalty to South Africa and hostility toward the ANC. The ANC often attacks "innocent people," she charged, while "when South Africa launches attacks in neighboring states, at least it knows exactly who it is attacking and kills specifically people who endanger it."

During the trial, Harington charged that Zimbabwe security police beat her on the feet until she bled, re-

peatedly dunked her head in water while questioning her, held her in solitary confinement and, on one occasion, spat on her after forcing her to strip naked. She said the torture stopped when she was transferred from police custody to Harare's Chikurubi prison.

A prosecutor claimed the torture charges were exaggerated, but did not deny that Harington may have been mistreated. The judge considered the police brutality in sentencing but said the leniency he might have accorded Harington because of her treatment while in custody was limited by her "unrepentant" stance and the need to deter other spies.

–Steve Askin

Article 22

AFRICA NEWS
November 14, 1988

MOZAMBIQUE

Experimenting with Capitalism

MAPUTO, MOZAMBIQUE – Dramatic changes are taking place in Mozambique's war-scarred economy.

One year ago, the Mozambican government controlled the prices of virtually all goods except fresh produce, and the local currency, the Metical, was almost worthless. Today, most price controls are gone and the Metical has been devalued by 1500%. In addition, Western donors have responded to the reforms with new programs of support for private firms like Mabor General, the Mozambique affiliate of U.S.-based General Tire. Commodity import programs supported by the World Bank, Sweden, the U.S. and the European Economic Community let firms like Mabor use Metical earnings to import raw materials that can normally only be purchased with hard currency.

Economic "liberalization" helped Mabor earn a profit last year, the first since the factory opened in 1979. The company's new success is part of an unlikely business turnaround that is now beginning in Mozambique.

In addition to helping existing businesses, free market-oriented reforms have set in motion, if not a wave of investment, a significant ripple of new foreign investment. They also expanded the domestic private sector, because the government returned at least 30 state-run companies to private control, chiefly firms the state found itself compelled to take over when the former Portuguese owners abandoned them at independence.

Mozambique hasn't foresaken Marxism, emphasizes Central Bank governor Enease Comiche, but it does welcome private firms wherever "we

feel we don't have the capacity to manage."

Foreign skills are needed because industry still suffers from the fact that the Portuguese colonialists who ruled the country until 1975 generally refused to train Mozambicans for key jobs.

In the first years of independence, "almost all the landowners, managers, top- and middle-level executives of agricultural, industrial and service enterprises left the country," said a recent United Nations Industrial Development Organization (Unido) study. "The factories were in effect handed over to their Mozambican workers who did not have the technical competence for the task." As Unido noted, "there were also cases of deliberate destruction of machinery by those who were leaving the country."

Cotton mill workers in Maputo, Mozambique.

Africa News

"Mozambique doesn't suffer from a dozen years of Marxist rule," agreed a senior Western business executive in Maputo. "It suffers from 400 years of Portuguese rule."

Despite this crippling legacy, Mozambique's GDP grew in the late 1970s and early 1980s and began a dramatic downturn only with the acceleration of violence by the South African-backed Mozambique National Resistance (Renamo), starting around 1982. A Unicef study estimates that this destabilization campaign cost Mozambique $5.5 billion in physical damage and lost production in 1980-85.

> "There's almost nothing that Mozambique is not prepared to do to get a foreign investor."

Because of these factors, many Mozambicans emphasize that economic destabilization, not any failure of socialist strategies, forced their country to seek more private sector involvement.

Whatever the motives, Western diplomats like U.S. Ambassador

Melissa Wells praise the reforms in glowing terms. Mozambique is "dismantling the machinery of central economic control" and "there's almost nothing that they're not prepared to do to get a foreign investor," Wells says.

The main changes came after adoption of Mozambique's Economic Rehabilitation Program (PRE) in January 1987. But their roots are much older, says Canadian Ambassador Roger Bull. He traces the trend to a broader political shift that began in the months preceding the fourth Frelimo Congress, which took place in 1983, and at which the late President Samora Machel "made a decision to evolve toward better relations with the West and seek rapprochement with the U.S."

Though the PRE brought new financial support from Western governments and multilateral financial institutions, Mozambican officials have consistently emphasized that they were not "pressured" into launching the program.

"We didn't need the World Bank to tell us that it was wrong to heavily subsidize certain sectors of our economy," says Sergio Vieira, a former Bank of Mozambique governor who now heads the Center of African Studies at Maputo's Eduardo

Mondlane University. Frelimo, Vieira says, always favored a mixed economy but was forced into over-rapid public sector expansion by the post-independence Portuguese flight.

In principle, the government welcomed private economic initiatives even before the PRE, agrees Mozambican Chamber of Commerce President Americo Magaia. In practice, however, "all the privileges were directed to state companies" until last year.

Though the PRE has pleased capitalists and Western governments, the key test is its impact on ordinary Mozambicans. And the PRE has brought visible changes, especially evident in the flood of clothing, housewares and other consumer goods that price decontrol brought to previously empty shops.

PRE has also achieved some success in macro-economic terms. Before the program began, Mozambique had the world's fastest-shrinking economy, according to World Bank data. This trend was reversed in 1987, as Mozambique's GDP rose 4% and its industrial output rose 18%. And food production is on the rise. First quarter 1988 increases included: marketed agricultural production up 5%, fisheries up 11%, agro-industries up 37%.

Yet reforms here – like similar economic adjustments elsewhere in Africa – have squeezed the urban poor. Prices for food, housing and other essentials have skyrocketed, and wages have not kept pace. It now costs almost twice the minimum wage just to buy essential foods for a family of five, according to Mozambique's health ministry.

There was a "big reduction in consumption as a result of the rehabilitation program," says Angelo Dias, who runs a small factory in Maputo for U.S.-based Johnson & Johnson. Before, he says, even poor people had pockets full of unspent money, because there was almost nothing to buy. Today, "you have everything on the market, but at high prices. Things that were formerly very cheap, like rent and electricity, are now expensive, so people have no money."

Though the government retained

"Mozambique doesn't suffer from a dozen years of Marxist rule. It suffers from 400 years of Portuguese rule."
— a Western business executive

subsidies on a few basic commodities, some delegates to a July conference of the ruling Frelimo party complained that price decontrol went too far, too fast. One delegate even warned that workers who were fired as a result of the PRE – which mandated cuts in the state payroll and gave businesses the right to lay off employees for economic reasons – might be recruited into Renamo.

Consumer price hikes hurt the urban working class minority, concedes Bank Governor Comiche. But he insists that the hikes were essential. They allow the peasant majority to receive prices for their crops that are high enough to make them "feel motivated to increase their production and sell their products," Comiche says.

Foreign Investment

Despite the encouragement that Mozambique now offers to foreign investors, only a handful are actually prepared to risk their money in a nation so disrupted by war.

"Tell an American businessman you're going to Mozambique, and he looks at you like you're out of your head," California businessman Marshall Wais candidly admits while chatting at poolside over a cup of fresh-brewed coffee at Maputo's Polana Hotel.

But Wais, whose San Francisco-based Marwais Steel hopes to take over a state-run foundry near Maputo, believes he can turn a profit while helping to revive the economy of a famine-ridden nation suffering from a vicious campaign of anti-civilian violence.

Wais is not alone. British investor Tiny Rowland, known for his skill at scouting out profitable opportunities in risky African environments, was the first to see the prospects for profit here. His Lonrho Corporation now runs a gold mine near the Zimbabwe border and operates former state-owned farms in four Mozambican provinces. A U.S. firm, Edlow Resources, recently began prospecting for titanium on a mineral-rich northern coastal plain long avoided by would-be investors because of war.

The biggest potential investment involves South Africa's Anglo American Corporation, which is considering a $200 million plan to produce fertilizer from Mozambique's vast offshore natural gas fields.

Foreign investors willing to revive run-down state farms can rent the land for a few dollars per acre. Industrial investors get equally generous terms. And Mozambique has one of Africa's most flexible policies on repatriation of earnings, allowing some new investors to export from the country up to 80% of hard currency profits.

Western donors are using aid to encourage further investment. Lonrho's $3 million investment in Mozambican agriculture was matched with $6 million from the World Bank and European Investment Bank, and the U.S. government is paying half the cost of a Marwais feasibility study. The World Bank has pledged $115 million a year in low interest loans – many for private sector support – more than Mozambique earns annually from all exports combined.

But even the bravest investor probably wouldn't march into a war zone because of economic incentives alone. To encourage mining, agriculture and other non-urban enterprises, the government gives companies a free hand to set up what amount to semi-private militias. The government supplies troops and guns, while the investor feeds the troops, pays for shoes and uniforms, and may provide officers for training and leadership.

Investors "calculate security as part of the cost" of investment in Mozambique, says an economic consultant to the government.

Despite these measures, full recovery requires peace, says Carlo Esposti, Maputo representative of Anglo American. An Italian who is a long-time resident of Mozambique, Esposti says Renamo is made up of criminals, not genuine political dissidents. If the Western powers really want to help Mozambique recover, Esposti insists, they must augment their economic aid with the military support Mozambique needs to "eliminate" Renamo. ∎

Article 23

AFRICA NEWS
August 22, 1988

SOUTH AFRICA

"We Are Stronger"

In the largest South African labor action this year, 31,000 striking metalworkers tested their strength against one of the country's most conservative industries and came up with what the union is hailing as a victory.

Labor analysts say the concessions won by the National Union of Metalworkers of South Africa (Numsa) will significantly increase the union's strength and future bargaining power. "Numsa is a very experienced, sophisticated organization," says Eddie Koch, labor reporter for the Johannesburg *Weekly Mail*. "Members were willing to sacrifice their wage demands for the long term goal of a stronger union."

The strike, which began the first week in August, pitted metalworkers against Seifsa, the employer federation for the metal industry representing 6,000 members. Seifsa has been among the leaders of a "get tough" policy during the past year by both employers and the government, which had prompted labor analysts to question how workers would fare in a confrontation.

The metalworkers' strike suggests that creative tactics can still produce employee gains.

In the end, Numsa agreed to Seifsa's "final" minimum wage offer of R3.02 ($1.50) an hour, a $0.22 per hour increase. The union had demanded R3.21.

But Numsa won concessions it regarded as important enough to overshadow the wage issue. Most important is Seifsa's agreement to allow "stop orders" – what U.S. unions call dues check-off – a system in which the employer automatically deducts union dues from a member's pay check. The practice saves unions substantial administrative costs as well as guarantees a stable cash flow.

In addition, Seifsa pledged to alter its collective bargaining system, in effect recognizing Numsa as the main metalworkers' union, in place of CMBU, the Confederation of Mining and Building Unions, a grouping of nine small, white-dominated unions. In the past, Seifsa negotiated principally with CMBU, arguing that it represented the majority of unions in the industry. Numsa officials say the change represents a significant victory for "nonracialism" and for the attempt to eliminate racial discrimination among labor organizations.

Another concession the union regards as important is Seifsa's agreement to grant May 1 and June 16 as holidays. Those dates will be swapped for two previously recognized holidays, bringing the metal industry into line with a South African trend. For several years, workers have successfully pressed for holidays on the first of May – international labor day – and June 16 – the anniversary of the 1976 Soweto rebellion.

Seifsa also agreed to press its member companies to reinstate any workers dismissed during the strike, which it conceded was a legal job action. And the employee group gave

Timothy Smith

Metalworkers say their growing union will be able to represent them more effectively.

several smaller benefits, including bonus days, for specified numbers of shifts worked and back-dating of the pay increase to July 1.

In a statement announcing its call for members to return to work, the Numsa joint strike committees declared that the strike had damaged Seifsa's ability to keep its membership united against labor actions. Analysts say one of the union's most creative tactics was its offer to exempt from the strike any companies that agreed to a wage offer higher than Seifsa's. As a result, nearly a hundred firms broke ranks and held separate talks with union representatives. The union says that because of the separate bargaining, several firms are now paying over $2.00 an hour.

Another union strategy was to begin the strike at companies that were the most solidly organized, allowing the job action to spread as it gained strength. In the past, some unions have called national strikes, only to see them unravel at the weak points.

Numsa, which represents autoworkers as well as metalworkers, says its success will encourage the union's growth. Union leaders say they hope to add 40,000 new members by the end of the year, bringing total membership to 200,000. ∎

Article 24

U.S.NEWS & WORLD REPORT
July 20, 1987

The Horatio Algers of South Africa

Under apartheid, whites control the purse as well as the power. But a few black businessmen are finding ways to beat the system

Johannesburg

∎ This month, for the first time ever, the Johannesburg Stock Exchange will sell shares in a black-controlled company. Lebowa Bakeries, Ltd., which markets 200,000 loaves of bread a day in black sections of South Africa, is trying to raise money so it can build more bakeries. Its stock sale is a modest issue—2.15 million shares at 30 cents a share—and it's not likely to make a millionaire out of its chairman, Pothinus Mokgokong, or any of its 600 other black shareholders. What is important, says Mokgokong, who also doubles as the academic head of Transvaal's all-black University of the North, is that blacks finally are claiming a stake in the stock market. "Not all black South Africans," he smiles, "are socialists."

Indeed, some of the most unusual capitalists in the world regard South Africa as their home. They are the shrewd, daring and lucky blacks who have managed to succeed in business in a country where economic power is concentrated in white hands through a network of laws and customs specifically designed to keep it out of black hands. In almost all cases, they did it by beating the system and overcoming circumstances that would make a Horatio Alger hero look like a boy born with a silver spoon.

These South Africans have little in common with well-to-do blacks who developed their fortunes through cozy relationships with the white central government. Many black local officials appointed by the government have feathered their families' nests through political favors in return for a license granted, a contract awarded or a job provided. But a handful of businessmen who owe nothing to the country's white National Party government have managed to accumulate wealth through sheer drive and persistence.

Bones to riches

Perhaps no black businessman has driven harder and accomplished more than Ephraim Tshabalala, now 80, who sits in his grubby, unpretentious office in Johannesburg and harks back nearly a half-century to his first days as an entrepreneur. Actually, he was just a janitor in that era, at a white-owned slaughterhouse, and each night after sweeping the floors, he toted a sack full of bones and scraps to his black township, where meat-hungry families awaited his arrival. "People didn't want to eat cows' heads," he recalls, "so I told them they were from sheep in German Southwest Africa. When they complained that the meat was tough, I told them it was because the sheep had been a long time in cold storage. My wife made up packets of pepper and chili powder. We told the people that chewing the powder would make the meat tender. It also meant they couldn't taste what they were eating."

The shillings that Tshabalala accumulated for his cows' heads and offal allowed him to set up a butcher's market—with much better meat—and that business permitted him to expand into other trades. He bought movie houses and opened them to blacks. He purchased what had been a white-owned service station in Soweto, the sprawling black township outside Johannesburg, and, with help from Shell Oil, expanded it into a facility that sells 4 million gallons of gasoline a month. He now ranks as South Africa's No. 1 individual gasoline retailer.

In many South African enterprises, however, it's virtually impossible for Tshabalala or any other black to succeed. There are no black-owned mining companies, largely because of old laws that prevented black people from owning mineral rights. There are no black-owned food-producing firms, largely because of laws prohibiting blacks from owning land outside their tribal areas. Blacks own none of the nationwide retail chains, because the Group Areas Act prevents them from owning stores on prime city or suburban sites. Some of America's wealthiest blacks made their fortunes owning insurance companies that catered to blacks, but there are no black-owned insurance companies in South Africa. This means that all black policies and pension savings are channeled into insurance companies owned by whites.

Nor do blacks own any capital-intensive concerns in such areas as heavy engineering, large construction or mechanical engineering. Because blacks can't own land outside their tribal areas, they have nothing to offer banks as collateral for the big loans required for such businesses. The only "black" bank —the African Bank—probably controls no more than 1 percent of South Africa's total banking assets.

Hassles and commutes

The apartheid tradition is a major impediment for blacks even in businesses in which they are allowed to operate. After starting work for the Arthur Andersen accounting firm, Juneas Lekgetha discovered that white clients did not like the idea of being audited by a black accountant. So he and some of his black colleagues set up their own firm in 1982 in an office in Johannesburg's central business district. "We had to open there for the image it gave," he says. "But we were regularly hassled by the police because we were renting in a white area." Lekgetha's new firm—Ebony Management Services—works mostly for black businesses and is thriving, but residence laws restrict it in its ability to attract qualified black employes from areas other than Johannesburg. Lekgetha himself is forced to live in the black township of Vosloorus; his Mercedes moves fast, but he still has a daily round trip of nearly 70 miles to and from his office.

For others, though, the residence laws create pockets of opportunity. The black townships are where the mass markets exist. It's in Soweto, the biggest of them all, that Tshabalala built his string of butcher shops, supermarkets, cinemas and gas stations. Apartheid laws prevented blacks from opening stores in centers of white cities. But the other side of the coin is that white businessmen, long excluded from the black townships, have had no real experience with black customers. Perceptibly, black consumers are switching their purchasing power to black neighborhood traders. And that opens the door—just a crack so far—for a few black entrepreneurs to succeed despite apartheid.

Some cash in on bad situations. The liquor-distribution business that's operated by Zoli Kunene and his brothers sprang out of the 1976 Soweto uprising. Until then, liquor outlets in black townships were monopolies run by regional boards appointed by the government to manage local black affairs. Those beer halls were the first targets in the riots, with dozens burned by militants who saw them as a means of repression. As a result, the authorities were forced to place liquor distribution in private, black hands, like those of the Kunene brothers, who now enjoy several million dollars in sales per year.

Their business is one of the largest customers of South African Breweries, the white-owned malt-beer monopoly.

The appeal of soccer

A keen eye for a market always helps, and Kaizer Motaung developed his in the United States. As a young man, he spent six years as a professional soccer player for the now defunct Atlanta Chiefs. When he returned to his South African homeland in 1969, he took over his old team in Soweto and began using American promotion techniques to make it a crowd puller. He renamed the club the Kaizer Chiefs —with the logo of an American Indian decked in feathers—and convinced white executives at Premier Milling that its sponsorship of the team would help sell maize meal to the black market. The Chiefs now rank as the country's leading soccer team. Although Motaung professes to be apolitical, he delights in pointing to soccer's ability to break the barriers of apartheid. He notes that professional soccer teams are multiracial and have both black and white coaches. Yet he has only once met a white Sports Minister. That was "many years ago," and he sees no reason to meet the current government's Sports Minister. In this, Motaung is like other independent black businessmen to whom the existing government is irrelevant.

South Africa's self-made black businessmen seldom display the trappings of position common to their white counterparts. Zoli Kunene keeps a set of golf clubs, but they're placed close to a desk made of cheap steel that sits in an ill-lit office at the back of his store. His walls are decorated with a calendar from a local garage sporting pictures of vintage cars. Ephraim Tshabalala works out of a dingy office and retains his rural tribal ties. He attributes his four score years of life not to the saunas and health farms that are popular with white business executives but to a monthly 2-gallon dose of a tribal emetic. These black men have found it prudent—and rewarding—to stay close to home. ∎

by Jim Jones

Article 25

Africa RECOVERY
December 1988

Zambia's autonomous adjustment

Zambia's break with the IMF last year dramatized the difficulties of structural adjustment. In this special survey, **Tony Hodges** dissects Zambia's economic crisis, its tragic human costs, the failed IMF programme and the home-grown Interim National Development Plan that replaced it.

LUSAKA—The Government of President Kenneth Kaunda, which dented the credibility of the International Monetary Fund's structural adjustment strategy for Africa by jettisoning an IMF-backed adjustment programme in May 1987, is preparing to draw a balance sheet of the home-grown Interim National Development Plan which replaced it.

The interim plan, which expires in December, has been buoyed by an unusually good maize harvest and by a welcome revival in the price of copper, on which Zambia relies for almost all its foreign exchange earnings, after years of rock-bottom prices.

But not much progress has yet been made in reversing the long and painful economic decline wrought by the prolonged copper slump. There are fears here that a renewed surplus in the world copper market will soon undo the export gains of the past few months, plunging Zambia into a new chapter of crisis—at a time when donor assistance has diminished in anger at the break with the IMF and a huge rise in arrears since the accompanying imposition of a ceiling on debt service payments.

Stark plight

Almost no other African country has found adjustment to unfavourable external shocks so massive a task and so difficult to accomplish, economically, socially and politically, as this southern African nation which achieved independence in 1964 as a virtual hostage to the fortunes of the world copper market.

Zambia's plight, put in historical perspective, is stark. From British colonial times, its economy was geared to copper production for export to the industrialized countries of the North, and copper still accounts today for roughly 90 per cent of exports, leaving Zambia overwhelmingly dependent on a single, volatile and, in recent years, generally depressed commodity market.

Unable to adapt easily to the deterioration in its terms of trade, Zambia resorted to heavy borrowing, becoming one of the most heavily indebted countries in all of Africa. It is now caught in a debt trap, on top of its chronic dependence on copper.

Worse still, Zambia's commercially exploitable copper deposits are expected to run out in 15 to 20 years' time. So the country faces the daunting long term challenge of developing new sources of foreign exchange to replace copper earnings, while reducing its traditionally heavy dependence on imports.

There are huge, under-utilized tracts of potential farmland, so agriculture seems to be the sector with the best hope of filling the void left by copper. But it is a measure of the scale of the tasks ahead that agriculture's share of gross domestic product (only 11.7 per cent in 1987) would have to more than double to make up for the eventual demise of mining (15.3 per cent).

This is in a country where agriculture was accorded little importance in the colonial era and which only in rare years (1988 is one of them) has achieved food self-sufficiency. And it is in one of Africa's most urbanized societies: World Bank figures show that 48 per cent of Zambians were living in cities by 1986.

Making matters even more difficult is the shadow of South Africa, whose destabilization policies threaten the whole region and in particular Zambia's transport links with external markets, though Zambia's direct dependence on South African ports and railways is currently being diminished by major rehabilitation works on the Beira Corridor through Mozambique and the Tazara railway to the port at Dar es Salaam.

Origins of the crisis

The turning point in Zambia's post-colonial fortunes came in 1973-75. The quadrupling of oil prices and the beginning of the long slump in copper prices plunged Zambia into a crisis from which it has never recovered.

The commodity terms of trade fell more than 77 per cent between 1973 and 1984. Meanwhile, inadequate investment (itself partly a consequence of the foreign exchange squeeze) and rising production costs (due to declining yields and ore quality) resulted in the volume of copper exports declining by more than a third between 1972 and 1986.

Together, these adverse trends resulted in Zambia's total merchandise exports declining by half between their 1974 peak ($1,396 mn) and 1986 ($689 mn), a fall which in real terms was of course even steeper.

One repercussion was an acute contraction in imports in a country with minimal capacity to substitute locally produced goods due to the weakness of domestic production linkages. A recent study[1] of Zambia's economic plight published by Canada's North-South Institute shows that the "immense and pervasive shortage of foreign exchange" resulted in imports falling in real terms by 30 per cent between 1975 and 1980 and then by an "astounding two thirds" in 1981-85.

The Zambian economy was consequently beset by shortages, resulting in supply bottlenecks and low capacity utilization in domestic industries, negative real per capita growth, high inflation and the spread of black markets.

Zambia became steadily poorer, regressing in World Bank nomenclature from a "lower middle income" country to "low income" status. Per capita GDP fell in real terms by an annual average of 2.7 per cent during the 1970s and by over 3 per cent a year in the 1980s. Between 1977 and 1987, real per capita income fell by a full 26 per cent. Meanwhile, the rate of fixed investment fell from 18.2 per cent in 1980 to 10.7 per cent in 1987.

One other consequence of the slump in copper prices was the conversion of the copper mining industry from a mainstay of the Government budget (providing up to half of government income until 1971) into a loss-making burden, requiring large subsidies to stay afloat.

Deprived of copper receipts, the Government resorted to deficit financing—paid for by printing money—in a desperate attempt to maintain consumption and investment levels. And, as debt servicing obligations built up, the budget deficit came under even further strain.

In addition, while raising real prices for food producers, in an attempt to encourage higher agricultural production (a bid largely vitiated by the inefficiency of the

marketing system), the Government tried to shield urban consumers from the rising cost of living by subsidizing retail prices for basic foodstuffs, especially the staple maize meal, and this placed even further stress on government finances, contributing further to the growth in money supply and thus to inflationary pressures.

Crushed by debt

Large scale borrowing, largely on commercial terms, and later the accumulation of huge arrears on external payments landed Zambia with a daunting external debt, which by the end of 1987 totalled $6.51 bn according to the IMF. This was equivalent to no less than 915.5 per cent of the country's exports, the fifth worst debt/exports ratio in Sub-Saharan Africa—after Mozambique, Sudan, Guinea-Bissau and Somalia.

A comparison with Brazil, the world's biggest debtor in absolute terms, is instructive: Brazil's debt/exports ratio (437.5 per cent in 1986) is less than half Zambia's.

To make matters worse, most of Zambia's debt was contracted on relatively hard terms and much of it is not reschedulable because it is owed to the multilateral institutions which enjoy "privileged creditor" status in the international financial system.

In fact, Zambia, by virtue of its long history of borrowing from the IMF, dating back to 1972, has more debt outstanding owed to the Fund than any other country in Sub-Saharan Africa—a total of $957 mn as of the end of 1987.

If it was meeting all its debt service obligations, these would devour well over half the foreign exchange earned from exports of

goods and services. In practice, most debt service, interest payments included, has not been paid, either because it has been rescheduled (at commercial interest rates) or been added to arrears, resulting in continuous growth of the stock of debt.

Interlinked with the slump in copper export earnings and the colossal debt build-up has been a decline in capital inflows. The virtual collapse in loan disbursements by creditors (from $284 mn in 1980 to a mere $31 mn in 1986) is not surprising, given Zambia's low credit rating. But, even during the IMF-backed adjustment programme, official loan disbursements ($202 mn in 1986) were much lower (at current prices, let alone in real terms) than they had been at the start of the decade ($346.5 mn in 1980), though there was a considerable increase in grants (to $292 mn in 1986).

Since the break with the IMF and the unilateral imposition of a ceiling on debt servicing in May 1987, many bilateral donors have sharply reduced their assistance, and both the IMF and the World Bank have declared Zambia ineligible for further borrowing because of its arrears on past loans.

In IMF hands

Until May 1987, Zambia had been a Fund "patient" for longer than almost anywhere else in the world, with a first stand-by credit negotiated in 1973 and then successive Fund facilities for eleven years from 1976.

Short term measures were taken under the first IMF programmes, on the assumption that the downturn in copper prices was only temporary. More drastic measures, involving a strong dose of economic liberalization,

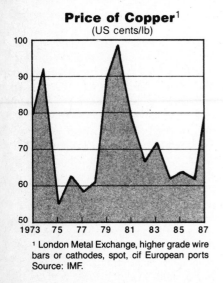

Price of Copper[1]
(US cents/lb)

¹ London Metal Exchange, higher grade wire bars or cathodes, spot, cif European ports
Source: IMF.

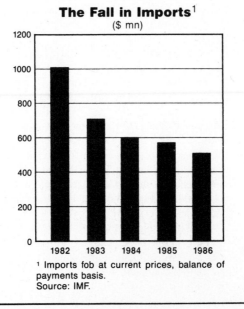

The Fall in Imports[1]
($ mn)

¹ Imports fob at current prices, balance of payments basis.
Source: IMF.

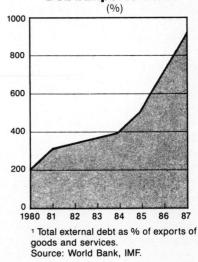

Debt/Exports Ratio[1]
(%)

¹ Total external debt as % of exports of goods and services.
Source: World Bank, IMF.

began from about 1982 and accelerated in October 1985 with the introduction of a foreign exchange auction system designed to allow market forces to determine the exchange rate and the allocation of foreign exchange.

One key objective was to bring about a substantial devaluation of the kwacha, designed to restore profitability to the copper mining industry (by raising the local currency value of copper earnings), to diminish the propensity to import, and to encourage non-traditional exports—the latter also benefitting from an earlier incentive, introduced in 1982, permitting exporters of such goods to retain 50 per cent of their foreign exchange earnings.

To reduce the budget deficit, the Government intended to phase out consumer subsidies, notably for maize meal, which accounted for 15 per cent of total government expenditure, and to introduce a wage freeze for civil servants and measures to enhance revenue collection.

Interest rates, which under Government controls had been consistently negative in real terms for many years, were liberalized in September 1985, on the assumption that this would encourage savings and improve resource allocation.

Last but not least, steps were taken from the end of 1982 to begin lifting controls on prices, which had originally been introduced to protect low income groups but which had in practice given rise to acute shortages and the spread of black market trading, in addition to causing severe liquidity problems for many firms.

The most striking development was the rapid devaluation of the kwacha. Its value fell by 55 per cent in the first auction, to K5 to the dollar. By the end of April 1987 the rate had reached K21 to the dollar, less than 11 per cent of its value before the auction system began.

One reason for this steep devaluation, which seemed destined to continue relentlessly until President Kaunda's reimposition of a fixed exchange rate in May 1987, was a continuing extreme shortage of foreign exchange, due to record low export earnings in 1986 and the failure of donors to provide adequate support. The current account deficit widened by 48 per cent in 1986.

Meanwhile structural rigidities (the extreme weakness of backward and forward linkages in the economy) virtually barred progress in import substitution. Indeed, it was inconceivable to imagine the devaluation reducing demand for imports, given the huge

The nutritional status of children in poorer families had deteriorated alarmingly because of the economic crisis.

contraction in the volume of imports that had already resulted from the foreign exchange crisis and the devastating impact this had had on both production and consumption.

Stagflation
The downward spiral in the value of the kwacha caused a huge increase in import prices in local currency terms, which fed through into accelerated inflation, generating social discontent and undermining political support for the whole adjustment programme.

It proved impossible for the Government to pursue sufficiently deflationary fiscal and monetary policies to offset the inflationary pressures set off by the auction system. In fact, the devaluation itself, by swelling the kwacha cost of debt servicing, exacerbated the budget deficit, which in 1986 reached 30 per cent of GDP. In consequence, the growth of money supply speeded up from 23 per cent in 1985 to 93 per cent in 1986, fuelling the inflationary process.

Consumer price inflation, as measured by the low income index for Lusaka, rose from 20 per cent in 1984 to 37.4 per cent in 1985 and 51.6 per cent in 1986.

Zambia was actually in the grips of stagflation. The production bottlenecks in the economy, due in large measure to the prolonged shortage of foreign exchange and the need for extensive rehabilitation, were still holding back growth. Thus, though the country did return to positive real growth in 1985 and 1986, this was so modest (1.6 per cent and 0.6 per cent respectively compared to annual population growth of around 3.5 per cent) that per capita GDP continued to decline.

Given the short period during which the auction system operated, non-traditional exporters had little time to take advantage of the beneficial exchange rate.

The devaluation did restore profitability to the copper industry and the auction system worked well for large manufacturing firms in the private sector, which obtained improved access to foreign exchange and thereby boosted capacity utilization. However, smaller indigenous businesses and state owned companies did badly at the auctions, because they could not raise the funds to bid competitively against the multinational companies.

Both small businesses and farmers were hit by the escalating cost of imported inputs and prohibitive bank borrowing rates, which rose to 25-30 per cent during the period of interest rate liberalization. In addition, farmers faced the removal of fertilizer subsidies.

Though these increases in farmers' costs were largely offset by rises in agricultural producer prices, agricultural performance remained generally disappointing, partly due to poor rainfall, especially in 1986/87, but also because of inefficient systems for input provision and marketing, as well as the deterioration in the country's transport infrastructure.

In the end, the IMF-backed adjustment programme proved politically unsustainable. Public support was alienated by the unchecked erosion in living standards as inflation soared. When the Government tried to double the price of maize "breakfast meal", a key staple, in December 1986, in an attempt to reduce the subsidy burden, riots swept through Zambia's major cities. Fifteen people were killed.

Going it alone

The price rise was immediately cancelled, and though the adjustment programme staggered on for another four months it was evidently dying. It was formally buried by President Kaunda on May Day 1987.

Dr. Kaunda announced the ending of the foreign exchange auctions, the revaluation of the kwacha (to K8 per dollar), the reimposition of controls on prices and interest rates, and a debt service ceiling set at 10 per cent of net foreign exchange earnings—net, that is, of essential foreign payments by the copper industry, by Zambia Airways and for imports of oil and fertilizer.

A New Economic Recovery Programme (NERP) was launched, beginning with the Interim National Development Plan (INDP), unveiled in July 1987. "The philosophy behind the plan was that it must take into account local economic reality, not just theory," says Lennard Nkhata, Permanent Secretary at the Ministry of Finance. "We wanted to ensure that economic policies worked in a Zambian environment."

One of the plan's declared objectives has

Carolyn Watson/UNICEF

Unloading food. There have been frequent and prolonged shortages of basic necessities, such as maize meal, sugar and cooking oil.

been to release resources for development by compressing non-essential and luxury imports and limiting debt service payments. In this way, the economy was to be "reactivated" by increasing capacity utilization in enterprises producing basic necessities, intermediate goods or products for export. Foreign exchange was thus to be used as a "strategic resource", allocated by a body known as the Foreign Exchange Management Committee (FEMAC), which meets every two weeks.

Steps were also to be taken to diversify exports, harder though this would be at the higher value of the kwacha, and to promote greater use of local raw materials, thereby saving foreign exchange.

"FEMAC has adhered to the principle of giving priority to essential items such as spare parts for rehabilitation of industry and raw materials not available in this country," Dr. Nkhata stressed. "Non-essentials, like

concentrate for Coca-Cola, which can be replaced by soft drinks made from local fruits, have not been allocated foreign exchange."

By fixing the exchange rate, reestablishing price controls and reducing interest rates (to between 15 and 20 per cent), the Government aimed to bring inflation under control. On the sensitive issue of consumer subsidies, the Government pledged to reduce subsidies gradually and focus them on the needy.

Initially, 21 items came under statutory price control, while all prices were subject to monitoring by the Prices and Incomes Commission. But the list of controlled items was reduced to twelve in the 1988 budget, when the Minister of Finance, Gibson Chigaga, acknowledged that "subsidies are now absorbing a disproportionate amount of our limited resources." Bread prices were liberalized in June 1988, reducing the number of price controlled items to eleven, but the Government has so far retained the socially, politically and fiscally critical subsidies on maize meal.

A preliminary balance sheet

At a press conference on 1 June, President Kaunda lauded the preliminary results of the Government's break with the IMF, claiming that the INDP had "confounded even our greatest critics." Key sectors of the economy were doing better than under the auction system, because they were being allocated more foreign exchange.

However, a sober analysis of the first nine months of the INDP, published by the National Commission for Development Planning in June, said that it was "clear" that the INDP "has not fully succeeded in tackling the problems of inflation, Government budget deficit, scarcity of essential commodities and the worsening levels of unemployment."

In the manufacturing sector, a significant increase in foreign exchange availability through FEMAC (from $110 mn during the 17 months of the auction period to $165 mn during the first nine months of the INDP) has improved supplies of vital inputs and allowed a number of firms to embark on rehabilitation programmes.

Overall capacity utilization is believed to have risen slightly, and the manufacturing sector is estimated to have grown by 2.3 per cent in 1987, but even in the best of circumstances it would take some time for the rehabilitation investments to be completed and thereby remove the supply bottlenecks that have been a major cause of shortages and inflation.

In the next year to January 1988, the low income consumer price index rose by 54 per cent, and to date there is little sign of inflation abating. This is partly because the inflationary spiral set off during the auction period has its own dynamic which is very difficult to rein in, at a time of high unit production costs and extensive shortages caused by the still relatively low level of capacity utilization and the large scale smuggling of goods to neighbouring countries.

Price monitoring, backed up by limited price controls, can do little to dampen inflation in such circumstances. Rather, administrative controls have spawned a flourishing parallel market economy, whose sky-high prices may not even be reflected in the official inflation statistics.

They have also provided tempting incentives to smuggle abroad, notably to Zaire, a substantial proportion of the goods that should be supplying the local market—maize meal being a prime example, because of the huge mark-up it obtains in Zaire compared with the low fixed price it sells for officially in Zambia. In March, the Minister of Commerce and Industry, Jameson Kalaluka, told Members of Parliament that about one third of domestically milled maize was being smuggled into Zaire.

Big profits are also made from smuggling such essential commodities as cook-

The INDP has "confounded even our greatest critics."
— President Kenneth Kaunda

John Isaac/UN

Zambia: Economic Indicators

	1983	1984	1985	1986	1987
GDP at current market prices (K mn)	4,181	4,931	7,072	12,954	18,080
Real GDP growth (%)	-2.0	-0.4	1.6	0.6	-0.2
Inflation (%)[1]	19.7	20.0	37.4	51.6	43.0
Employment[2] ('000)	...	364.2	360.5	360.5	356.6
Fixed investment/GDP (%)	14.7	12.6	10.3	10.7	10.7
Domestic credit (% change)	15.0	20.7	83.6	33.4	...
Money supply (% change)	11.1	17.2	23.3	93.3	60[3]
Agricultural production (1979-81=100)	102.8	105.7	114.8	122.2	122.5
Food production per head (1979-81=100)	93.2	90.9	96.9	99.8	94.4
Copper production[4] ('000 tons)	551.0	525.8	463.4	471.0	473.1
Manufacturing production (1973=100)	94.5	94.9	103.0	105.9	109.6[5]
Exports fob ($ mn)	923	893	797	689	907[6]
Imports fob ($ mn)	711	612	571	517	626[6]
Current account balance ($ mn)	-271	-153	-204	-302	-150[6]
Total external debt ($ bn)	3.78	3.86	4.42	5.30	6.51[7]
Average exchange rate (kwacha per $)	1.25	1.79	2.71	7.30	8.89[8]

[1] Low income index, Lusaka. [2] Formal sector. [3] Preliminary estimate. [4] ZCCM financial years beginning 1 April in year indicated. [5] July 1987. [6] National figures in kwacha, converted at average annual exchange rate; previous years from IMF (balance of payments basis). [7] IMF figure; previous years from World Bank. [8] Under foreign exchange auction system, exchange rate had reached K22 to the dollar by early May 1987; since then the rate has been fixed at K8 to the dollar.

Sources: IMF, World Bank, FAO, Central Statistical Office, National Commission for Development Planning, ZCCM.

ing oil, detergent, sugar, fertilizer, fuel and lubricants.

The Government has reacted by staging repeated joint military/police sweeps on city markets and by utilizing the Emergency Powers Act to seize the businesses of traders, many of them Asians, alleged to be black marketeering (the Act not requiring recourse to a court trial).

On the demand side, meanwhile, the high Government budget deficit and the related fast rate of money supply growth have continued to add to the inflationary pressures, though the Government can point to some success in both these areas. The budget deficit fell from 30 per cent of GDP in 1986 to 14 per cent in 1987, due to improved revenue collection and the ceiling on external debt service payments, and money supply growth decelerated from 93 per cent in 1986 to just under 60 per cent in 1987.

Fortuitous factors

The target growth rate set by the INDP (2.2 per cent a year) was higher than Zambia has achieved at any time since 1981, though still well below the rate of population growth. In reality, however, economic performance can be influenced enormously by exogenous factors beyond the planners' control.

Last year, which included the final months of the IMF Programme as well as the beginning of the INDP, saw GDP fall in real terms by 0.2 per cent, a very poor outturn partly attributable to drought. The maize harvest fell by 13.5 per cent.

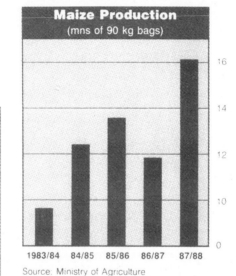

Maize Production
(mns of 90 kg bags)

Source: Ministry of Agriculture

In 1988, by contrast, the 2.2 per cent GDP growth target should easily be met, if only because the weather was more clement and the world copper market has been stronger.

The 1987/88 maize harvest was expected to bring in a record 16.14 mn bags (of 90 kg), more than a third higher than in the previous year and probably just enough—for the first time in several years—to cover domestic consumption needs and rebuild stocks.

While Zambia, as an oil importer, has gained from the slump in oil prices, it has also been earning increased foreign exchange since the recovery in copper prices in the last quarter of 1987, which was caused by worldwide supply bottlenecks and low world stocks.

Zambian copper sold for 1,208 pounds sterling per ton during the first nine months of the INDP, over a third higher than the 900 pounds assumption built into the plan when it was drafted. Prices have remained at high levels since then, though this may well continue only temporarily.

The increase in copper prices has fortuitously offset the adverse impact of the revaluation of the kwacha on the finances of the jointly state-private owned Zambia Consolidated Copper Mines (ZCCM), which runs the industry. The company boosted its pre-tax profits from K211 mn ($26 mn) in 1986/87 to K644 mn ($77 mn) in 1987/88.

Meanwhile, the decline in the volume of copper exports was arrested in 1986 and major rationalization measures and investments have been made by ZCCM with the aim of boosting efficiency and production. So far, there has not been more than a marginal rise in production, from 463,400 tons in ZCCM's 1985/86 financial year to 473,100 tons in 1987/88, because ZCCM has not been receiving as much foreign exchange as it needs to keep its investment programme on track and obtain adequate supplies of spare parts.

Informed observers say that if this continues, ZCCM may be unable to achieve its goal of raising output to 490,000 tons in 1987/88 and 562,000 tons by 1990/91.

Danger signs

While the current rise in copper prices helps Zambia's balance of payments, long term prospects for copper prices are not good. Demand is expected to be kept in check by sluggish world economic growth while supply is expanded by the reopening of marginal, closed mines, in response to the rise in prices. The International Wrought Copper Council predicts a substantial world copper surplus in the second half of 1988, ending the four years

Women pounding maize. This year Zambia has had a bumper maize crop, achieving self-sufficiency for the first time in several years.

of deficit that brought about the price rise.

A renewed slide in export earnings would cause acute balance of payments difficulties at a time when, in the absence of a rapprochement with the IMF and the World Bank (see box) and moves to repair relations with creditors (now owed about $1 bn in arrears), Zambia is unlikely to attract increased donor funding.

The Fund and the Bank halted all assistance in 1987, as a result of Zambia's mounting arrears on past loans and its renunciation of the policies advocated by the Washington institutions. In addition, several bilateral donors, notably the UK, have sharply re-duced their support, though this has been off-set, at least in part, by increased assistance from a number of more tolerant donors, includng Japan and Italy.

What is not clear is the extent to which the decline in capital inflows has been made up for by the ceiling on debt servicing, which reduced actual debt service payments to just $30 mn in the ninth months from July 1987 to March 1988, compared with $267.5 mn, including $143.9 mn to the IMF alone, in all of 1986.

The balance of payments situation remains precarious. In June the Bank of Zambia announced that there was insufficient foreign exchange available to cover the full $27.8 mn already allocated to importers that month by FEMAC. In this fragile context, preparations are being made for the country's next five year plan, due for launching when the interim plan period is over at the end of the year. The timing is propitious—shortly after the October elections which could set the stage for changes in the ministerial team and, at the end of the INDP, new policy initiatives for the next stage of Zambia's epic struggle for economic revival. ■

1. Zambia: Adjusting to Poverty, *by Roger Young (The North-South Institute, Ottawa 1988).*

AFRICA NEWS
December 7, 1987

Article 26

Art on the Frontlines

Behind a chain-link fence topped with barbed wire, five musicians dressed in South African army uniforms straddle a facsimile of a Casspir armoured truck. They launch into the rhythmic strains of *mbaqanga* music as a group of teenaged South Africans dance and sing on the stage in front of them. At the Mitzi I. Newhouse Theater in New York's Lincoln Center, a show that hard-line anti-apartheid activists might have picketed in previous years—even though they would have agreed with its politics—is being performed.

Sarafina!, the new play by Mbogeni Ngema, is not just another song and dance. Before the dramatic action proceeds too far, the characters are harassed by the army. One is detained, another assaulted. As the play unfolds, the children tell, in words and song, of their encounters with the South African power structure. One describes an assault on his father by army police dogs ("What would you do if your father came home with no pants and blood dripping down his legs?" he asks); another recounts a brutal rape.

The play's dramatic center is the story of Victoria Mxenge, a prominent Natal human rights attorney, defender of political prisoners and supporter of the anti-apartheid United Democatic Front, who was murdered on August 1, 1985 in the presence of her three children.

In the hands of Ngema, the marriage of art and resistance seems natural. But it is only in the last few months that some arguments about the role of culture in South Africa have begun to be resolved.

The movement to culturally isolate South Africa began in 1965, when the American Committee on Africa (ACOA) launched its "We Say No to Apartheid" campaign. Sixty-five prominent artists pledged to eschew "personal or professional association with the representatives of South Africa." Singer Harry Belafonte and tennis star Arthur Ashe evolved the concept into an all-out boycott of South Africa by artists and athletes three years later.

Since then, entertainers have often used their profession to take public stands against South Africa's racial policies. The latest efforts can be seen in movie theaters (*Cry Freedom*), in record stores (*Sun City*), on Broadway (*Sarafina!*) and in an exhibition at the United Nations ("Art Against Apartheid").

But controversy has swirled around many of the projects, mainly due to a lack of agreement on the circumstances under which the United Nations-implemented cultural boycott should be invoked.

Policy has mostly emanated from the UN Centre Against Apartheid, the exiled leaders of the African National Congress (ANC) and other liberation groups. Until this year, artists inside South Africa have felt excluded from the dialogue to such an extent that Joseph Shabalala – the creative force behind the Zulu vocal group Ladysmith Black Mambazo – commented that before he recorded with Paul Simon on the *Graceland* album, he had never even heard of the cultural boycott.

But the increasingly political nature of South African art has forced it out of the confines of a rigidly-imposed boycott. Consideration of new boycott guidelines – ones that encourage anti-apartheid art – was on the agenda of last week's international conference in Arusha, Tanzania, called by the ANC. The topic will also be one focus of an international gathering of 100 grass-roots cultural workers in Amsterdam December 12-20.

The cultural boycott is seen as a crucial part of the anti-apartheid movement, a complement to economic sanctions and bans on academic and sporting exchanges. Supporters argue that it increases the isolation of South Africans, denying them, in the words of one exile, "the feeling that they are accepted members of western culture and moral traditions."

Western artists performing in South Africa – particularly those, such as Frank Sinatra, who have appeared at Sun City – are seen by opponents of apartheid as legitimizing the white minority government.

Sun City – made famous by Little Steven Van Zandt's Artists Against Apartheid recording – is in the Bophuthatswana "homeland," an area granted nominal independence by Pretoria. Bophuthatswana's nationhood remains unrecognized outside South Africa, and anti-

---

People need to be reminded of how narrow the locus is of what artists are allowed to say.

---

apartheid activists say artists who play there tacitly endorse Pretoria's policies.

Supporters of a strict boycott also pledge to target South African performers who venture to the west, denying them access to worldwide fame and riches.

Critics of the total boycott believe the policy creates a double apartheid,

Ladysmith Black Mambazo

because artists who oppose government policies – including blacks – are discouraged from taking their work out of the country.

Hunter College professor Larry Short defended that position at a Howard University workshop last month. "It seems ironic," Short said, "to punish musicians and artists who have never supported apartheid and who, in their work, are performing an important part of the struggle for a new South Africa. It is doubly ironic if a black South African musician is boycotted merely because [he or she] is from South Africa."

In the beginning, it was relatively easy to decide who should be boycotted. When the play *Ipi-Tombi* came to New York it was quickly identified as a production backed by Pretoria, one that promoted the government's "homeland" policy. And when stars such as Liza Minnelli, Linda Ronstadt, Tina Turner, Tim Reid, Goldie Hawn, Liberace and many others performed in South Africa, their names soon appeared on the UN Centre Against Apartheid's "Register of Entertainers, Actors and Others Who Have Performed in Apartheid South Africa."

But the issue has become less clear in recent years. When the multi-racial pop band Juluka was picketed in London in 1982 and 1983, anti-apartheid activists said the group was

an "unfortunate casualty" of the boycott. Juluka, as well as Paul Simon, who was denounced for recording portions of *Graceland* in Johannesburg, technically violated the wording of the UN resolution requesting a boycott of "all cultural, academic, sporting and other exchanges with South Africa" and appealing to "writers, artists, musicians and other personalities to boycott South Africa."

Johnny Clegg, who co-founded Juluka with Sipho Mchunu, had been – and continues to be – an outspoken opponent of apartheid.

"I understood where the boycott was coming from," Clegg says. "Even when I was actually arguing against the boycott, I never, ever undermined [it]; I always pointed out its benefits. But I was always arguing for what is happening now – a redefinition of the boycott so that progressive music, progressive art and people involved in trying to break down barriers in South Africa were given an international platform."

Defining progressive art, though, is not always easy. Jennifer Davis, executive director of the American Committee on Africa, argues that even "progressive" shows can have ramifications that twist the intended purpose. Productions such as *Sarafina!*, she warns, may lead Westerners to believe that Pretoria has embarked on significant reforms. "People need to be reminded," she says, "that South Africa still holds the reins and of how narrow the locus is of what [artists] are allowed to say."

The redefinition of the boycott, she believes, "has a potential for a great deal of liberal fuzziness," with artists performing in the west without disclaimers about the state of affairs at home. Culture, she says "needs to be connected to a liberation struggle."

Indeed, the government does permit much opposition art, if only – as most activists believe – to promote the belief that freedom of expression is permitted in South Africa. "The regime will use any means to boost its own image," says Saths Cooper, president of the South African/ Azanian Student Movement.

Activists also worry that South Africa frequently disguises government-backed productions. A recent film, *Shaka Zulu*, produced by the South African Broadcasting Corporation, played on U.S. television with little controversy. It was billed as the joint production of a Los Angeles-based distributor and the "Zulu nation." The UN Centre Against Apartheid charges that the 10-part series was historically inaccurate and "generally designed to further South African government policies regarding the black population."

Most recently, the government has allowed the showing of Richard Attenborough's *Cry Freedom*, a film depicting the life and death of black consciousness movement leader Steve Biko, as seen through the eyes of newspaper editor Donald Woods. According to Director of Publications Braam Coetzee, that the film passed the censors un-cut "is an indication of the committee's objectivity." Yet 40,000 items—about half of which are political in nature—remain prohibited. And the same panel that approved *Cry Freedom* also banned South African Youth Congress stickers issued to celebrate the 70th birthday of ANC President Oliver Tambo.

E ven those who objected when Paul Simon recorded*Graceland* in South Africa credit the project with sparking the debate over redefinition of the cultural boycott. The record made international stars of Ladysmith Black Mambazo and guitarist Ray Phiri, and the subsequent tour rejuvenated the careers of South African exiles Hugh Masekela and Miriam Makeba. The overall effect of bringing a proud, vibrant black South African culture to the rest of the world was seen by many activists and artists as beneficial to the movement, even if most of the lyrics were not political in nature.

Performers like Ladysmith Black Mambazo, Hunter's Larry Short argues, contribute politically because "they are helping people to survive in this enormously horrible situation."

"Culture is not like computers and refrigerators and guns," Short says. "It's much more complex."

But since Simon refused to apologize directly for working in Johannesburg – a method many artists who performed in South Africa have used to get their names removed from boycott lists – the question of how to reshape the boycott to encourage the development of anti-apartheid culture remained.

Amidst much confusion, in which anti-apartheid leaders disagreed over whether or not Simon's name should be added to the artist register, the ANC's Tambo announced a major policy shift last May. "The genuine representatives" of the people "in all forms of human activity" should not be boycotted, he said, but should be "supported" and "encouraged."

Playwright Ngema believes it is crucial that the decision-making process regarding the new boycott include South African artists and says steps to ensure their participation have already been taken.

Likewise, the United Democratic Front (UDF) is changing its view of the cultural boycott. Days after Tambo's statement, the UDF said it would exempt performers if they were "supported by the democratic movement in South Africa, approved by overseas solidarity groups and contributed to the advancement of the national democratic struggle."

A spokesman for the UN Special Committee Against Apartheid says his organization intends to follow the lead of "the liberation movements."

It is also apparent that, in some

ways, anti-government activists are starting to take their cue from the artists. "The art we are seeing from the country, cultural performances like Ngema's," says Saths Cooper, "the praise songs and songs of liberation, are part of a new culture that is being developed. And it has a liberating influence not only inside the country, but is liberating people outside as well."

Ngema agrees. "Our struggle in South Africa is difficult because you are not only fighting the Pretoria regime, you are fighting America and Britain at the same time," he says. "It is the American government that gives the South African government so much support… and the British government. I hope that people [in the U.S.], after seeing the work South Africans bring over here, can begin to realize how much they are oppressing us themselves." ∎

Credits

GENERAL AFRICA

Page 162 Article 1. From *The World & I,* September 1988, pp. 512-521. Reprinted with permission from *The World & I,* a publication of The Washington Times Corporation, copyright © 1988.

Page 169 Article 2. *West Africa* magazine, November 21-27, 1988, pp. 2176-2177.

Page 171 Article 3. *West Africa* magazine, September 19-25, 1988, pp. 1712-1714.

Page 173 Article 4. From *Africa News,* November 28, 1988, pp. 5-6, 8. Copyright © 1988 by Africa News Service.

Page 176 Article 5. *Africa Report,* September/October 1988, pp. 13-14. Copyright © 1988 by The African-American Institute. Reprinted by permission of *Africa Report.*

Page 178 Article 6. From *Africa News,* November 30, 1987, pp. 1-4. Copyright © 1987 by Africa News Service.

Page 182 Article 7. *West Africa* magazine, November 7-13, 1988, pp. 2072-2073.

Page 184 Article 8. Courtesy of *The UNESCO Courier,* March 1988, pp. 27-29.

WEST AFRICA

Page 185 Article 9. From *Africa News,* July 11, 1988, pp. 1-3. Copyright © 1988 by Africa News Service.

Page 188 Article 10. *West Africa* magazine, September 5-11, 1988, pp. 1608-1609.

Page 191 Article 11. This article is reprinted from *International Agricultural Development* magazine, of Reading, UK, March/April 1988, pp. 8-10.

Page 194 Article 12. From *The New York Times,* November 11, 1988, p. A3. Copyright © 1988 by The New York Times Company. Reprinted by permission.

Page 196 Article 13. From *Africa News,* October 31, 1988, pp. 1-2, 4. Copyright © 1988 by Africa News Service.

CENTRAL AFRICA

Page 198 Article 14. From *Africa News,* August 8, 1988, pp. 6-7. Copyright © 1988 by Africa News Service.

Page 200 Article 15. From *Africa News,* October 3, 1988, pp. 7-8. Copyright © 1988 by Africa News Service.

EAST AFRICA

Page 202 Article 16. *Africa Recovery,* December 1988, pp. 3-4. Reproduced courtesy of Africa Recovery, a publication of the United Nations, New York.

Page 204 Article 17. This article is reprinted from *International Agricultural Development* magazine of Reading, UK, March/April 1988, pp. 13-14.

Page 206 Article 18. From *The Christian Science Monitor,* October 6, 1988, p. 12. Copyright © 1988 by Julie Whipple.

SOUTH AFRICA

Page 209 Article 19. *Africa Report,* September-October 1988, pp. 35-37. Copyright © 1988 by The African-American Institute. Reprinted by permission of Africa Report.

Page 212 Article 20. From *Africa News,* April 4, 1988, pp. 1-3. Reprinted by permission of Steve Askin and Africa News Service.

Page 215 Article 21. From *Africa News,* December 21, 1987, pp. 8-9. Reprinted by permission of Steve Askin and Africa News Service.

Page 217 Article 22. From *Africa News,* November 14, 1988, pp. 5-6. Copyright © 1988 by Africa News Service.

Page 220 Article 23. From *Africa News,* August 22, 1988, p. 9. Copyright © 1988 by Africa News Service.

Page 221 Article 24. From *U.S. News & World Report,* July 20, 1987, pp. 41-42. Copyright, July 20, 1987, U.S. News & World Report.

Page 223 Article 25. From *Africa Recovery,* December 1988, pp. 6-7, 9-11, 13. Reproduced courtesy of Africa Recovery, a publication of the United Nations, New York.

Page 229 Article 26. From *Africa News,* December 7, 1987, pp. 1-3. Copyright © 1987 by Africa News Service.

Glossary of Terms and Abbreviations

Acquired Immune Deficiency Syndrome (AIDS)   A disease of immune-system dysfunction assumed to be caused by the human immunodeficiency virus (HIV), which allows opportunistic infections to take over the body.

African Development Bank   Founded in 1963 under the auspices of the United Nations Economic Commission on Africa, the bank, located in Côte d'Ivoire, makes loans to African countries, although other nations can apply.

African National Congress (ANC)   Founded in 1912, and now banned, the group's goal was to work for equal rights for blacks in South Africa through nonviolent action. "Spear of the Nation," the ANC wing dedicated to armed struggle, was organized after the Sharpeville massacre in 1960.

African Party for the Independence of Guinea-Bissau and Cape Verde (PAICG)   An independence movement that fought during the 1960s and 1970s for the liberation of present-day Guinea-Bissau and Cape Verde from Portuguese rule. The two territories were ruled separately by a united PAIGC until a 1981 coup in Guinea-Bissau caused the party to split along national lines. In 1981 the Cape Verdean PAIGC formally renounced its Guinea links and became the PAICV.

African Socialism   A term applied to a variety of ideas (including those of Nkrumah and Senghor) about communal and shared production in Africa's past and present. The concept of African socialism was especially popular in the early 1960s. Adherence to it has not meant the governments have excluded private-capitalist ventures.

Afrikaners   South Africans of Dutch descent who speak Afrikaans and are often referred to as Boers (Afrikaans for "farmers").

Amnesty International   A London-based human-rights organization whose members "adopt" political prisoners or prisoners of conscience in many nations of the world. The organization generates political pressure and puts out a well-publicized annual report of human-rights conditions in each country of the world.

Aouzou Strip   A barren strip of land between Libya and Chad contested by both countries.

Apartheid   Literally, "separateness," the South African policy of segregating the races socially, legally, and politically.

Arusha Declaration   A document issued in 1967 by Tanzanian President Julius Nyerere, committing the country to socialism based on peasant farming, democracy under one party, and self-reliance.

Assimilado   The Portuguese term for Africans who became "assimilated" to Western ways. Assimilados enjoyed equal rights under Portuguese law.

Azanian People's Organization (AZAPO)   Founded in 1978 at the time of the Black Consciousness Movement and revitalized in the 1980s, a movement that works to develop chapters and bring together black organizations in a national forum.

Bantu   A major linguistic classification for many Central, Southern, and East African languages. Also, a derogatory term for Africans, used by the South African government.

Bantustans   Areas, or "homelands," to which black South Africans are assigned "citizenship" as part of the policy of apartheid.

Basarawa   Peoples of Botswana who have historically been hunters and gatherers.

Berber   The collective term for the indigenous languages and people of North Africa.

Bicameral   A government made up of two legislative branches.

Black Consciousness Movement   A South African student movement founded by Steve Biko and others in the 1970s to promote pride and empowerment of blacks.

Boers   The Dutch word for farmers of Dutch-German-French descent who settled in South Africa after 1652. See also *Afrikaner*.

Brotherhoods   Islamic organizations based on specific religious beliefs and practices. In many areas, brotherhood leaders and their spiritual followers gained political influence.

Cabinda   A small, oil-rich portion of Angola separated from the main body of that country by the coastal strip of Zaire.

Caisse de Stabilization   A marketing board that stabilizes the uncertain returns to producers of cash crops by offering them less than market prices in good harvest years while assuring them of a steady income in bad years. Funds from these boards are used to develop infrastructure, to promote social welfare, or to maintain a particular regime in power.

Caliphate   The office or dominion of a caliph, the spiritual head of Islam.

Cassava   A tropical plant with a fleshy, edible rootstock; one of the staples of the African diet. Also known as manioc.

Chimurenga   A Shona term meaning "fighting in which everyone joins," used to refer to Zimbabwe's fight for independence.

Coloured   The South African classification for a person of mixed racial descent.

Committee for the Struggle Against Drought in the Sahel (CILSS)   A grouping of eight West African countries to fight the effects of drought in the region.

Commonwealth of Nations   An association of nations and dependencies loosely joined by the common tie of having been part of the British Empire.

Congress of South African Trade Unions (COSATU)   Established in 1985 to form a coalition of trade unions to press for workers' rights and an end to apartheid.

Copperbelt   A section of Zambia with a high concentration of copper-mining concessions.

Creole   A person or language of mixed African and European descent.

Dergue From the Amheric word for "committee," the ruling body of Ethiopia after the revolution in 1974.

East African Community (EAC) Established in 1967, this organization grew out of the East African Common Services Organization begun under British rule. The EAC included Kenya, Tanzania, and Uganda in a customs union and involved common currency and development of infrastructure. It was disbanded in 1977, and the final division of assets was completed in 1983.

Economic Commission for Africa (ECA) Founded in 1958 by the Economic and Social Committee of the United Nations to aid African development through regional centers, field agents, and the encouragement of regional efforts, food self-sufficiency, transport, and communications development.

Economic Community of Central African States (CEEAC, also known as ECCA) An organization of all of the Central African states, as well as Rwanda and Burundi, whose goal is to promote economic and social cooperation among its members.

Economic Community of West Africa (CEAO) An organization of French-speaking countries formed to promote trade and regional economic cooperation.

Economic Community of West African States (ECOWAS) Established in 1975 by the Treaty of Lagos, the organization includes all of the West African states except Western Sahara. The organization's goals are to promote trade, cooperation, and self-reliance among its members.

Enclave Industry An industry run by a foreign company that uses imported technology and machinery and exports the product to industrialized countries; often described as a "state within a state."

Eritrean Peoples' Liberation Front (EPLF) The major group fighting the Ethiopian government for independence of Eritrea.

European Economic Community (EEC, or Common Market) Established in 1958, the EEC seeks to establish a common agricultural policy between its members as well as uniform trade and travel restrictions among members. A common currency is planned for 1992.

European Communities (EC) The umbrella organization encompassing the European Economic Community, the European Coal and Steel Company, and the European Atomic Energy Community.

Evolués A term used in colonial Zaire (Congo) to refer to Western-educated Congolese.

Food and Agricultural Organization of the United Nations (FAO) Established in 1945 to oversee good nutrition and agricultural development.

Franc Zone This organization includes members of the West African Monetary Union and the monetary organizations of Central Africa that have currencies linked to the French franc. Reserves are managed by the French Treasury and guaranteed by the French franc.

Freedom Charter Established in 1955, this charter proclaimed equal rights for all South Africans and has been a foundation for almost all groups in the resistance against apartheid during the last 4 decades.

Free French Conference A 1944 conference of French-speaking territories, which proposed a union of all the territories in which Africans would be represented and their development furthered.

French Equatorial Africa (FEA) The French colonial federation that included present-day People's Republic of the Congo, Central African Republic, Chad, and Gabon.

French West Africa The administrative division of the former French colonial empire that included the current independent countries of Senegal, Côte d'Ivoire, Guinea, Mali, Niger, Burkina Faso, Benin, and Mauritania.

Front for the Liberation of Mozambique (FRELIMO) Liberation forces established in 1963 to free Mozambique from Portuguese rule; after 1975 the dominant party in independent Mozambique.

Frontline States A caucus supported by the Organization of African Unity (consisting of Tanzania, Zambia, Mozambique, Botswana, and Angola) whose goal is to achieve black majority rule in all of Southern Africa.

Green Revolution Use of Western technology and agricultural practices to increase food production and agricultural yields.

Griots Professional bards of West Africa, some of whom tell history and are accompanied by the playing of the kora or harp-lute.

Gross Domestic Product (GDP) The value of production attributable to the factors of production in a given country regardless of their ownership. GDP equals GNP minus the product of a country's residents originating in the rest of the world.

Gross National Product (GNP) The sum of the values of all goods and services produced by a country's residents at home and abroad in any given year, less income earned by foreign residents and remitted abroad.

Guerrilla A member of a small force of irregular soldiers. Generally, guerrilla forces are made up of volunteers who make surprise raids against the incumbent military or political force.

Harmattan In West Africa, the dry wind that blows from the Sahara Desert in January and February.

Homelands See *Bantustans*.

Horn of Africa A section of northeastern Africa including the countries of Djibouti, Ethiopia, Somalia, and Sudan.

Hut Tax Instituted by the colonial governments in Africa, this measure required families to pay taxes on each building in the village.

International Monetary Fund (IMF) Established in 1945 to promote international monetary cooperation.

Irredentism An effort to unite certain people and territory in one state with another, on the grounds that they belong together.

Islam A religious faith started in Arabia during the seventh century A.D. by the Prophet Muhammad and spread in Africa through African Muslim leaders, migrations, and holy wars.

Jihad "Holy war" waged as a religious duty on behalf of Islam to rid the world of disbelief and error.

Koran Writings accepted by Muslims as the word of God, as revealed to the Prophet Mohammed.

Lagos Plan of Action Adopted by the Organization of African Unity in 1980, this agreement calls for self-reliance, regional economic cooperation, and the creation of a pan-African economic community and common market by the year 2000.

League of Nations Established at the Paris Peace Conference in 1919, this forerunner of the modern-day United Nations had 52 member nations at its peak (the United States never joined the organization) and mediated in international affairs. The league was dissolved in 1945 after the creation of the United Nations.

Least Developed Countries (LDCs) A term used to refer to the poorest countries of the world, including many African countries.

Maghrib An Arabic term, meaning "land of the setting sun," that is often used to refer to the former French colonies of Morocco, Algeria, and Tunisia.

Mahdi The expected messiah of Islamic tradition; or a Muslim leader who plays a messianic role.

Malinke (Mandinka, or Mandinga) One of the major groups of people speaking Mande languages. The original homeland of the Malinke was Mali, but the people are now found in Mali, Guinea-Bissau, The Gambia, and other areas where they are sometimes called Mandingoes. Some trading groups are called Dyoula.

Marabout A Muslim saint or holy man, often the leader of a religious brotherhood.

Marxist-Leninism Sometimes called "scientific socialism," this doctrine derived from the ideas of Karl Marx as modified by Vladimir Lenin; it is the ideology of the Communist Party of the Soviet Union and has been modified in many ways by other persons and groups who still use the term. In Africa, some political parties or movements have claimed to be Marxist-Leninist but have often followed policies that conflict in practice with the ideology; these governments have usually not stressed Marx's philosophy of class struggle.

Mfecane The movement of people in the nineteenth century in the eastern areas of present-day South Africa to the west and north as the result of wars led by the Zulus.

Mozambique National Resistance (MNR, also known as Renamo) A South-African-backed rebel movement which attacks civilians in attempting to overthrow the government of Mozambique.

Muslim A follower of the Islamic faith.

Naam A traditional work cooperative in Burkina Faso.

National Youth Service Service to the state required of youth after completing education, a common practice in many African countries.

National Union for the Total Independence of Angola (UNITA) One of three groups that fought the Portuguese during the colonial period in Angola, now backed by South Africa and the United States and fighting the independent government of Angola.

Nkomati Accords An agreement signed in 1984 between South Africa and Mozambique, pledging that both sides would no longer support opponents of the other.

Non-Aligned Movement (NAM) A group of nations that have chosen not to be politically or militarily associated with either the West or the communist bloc.

Non-Governmental Organization (NGO) A private voluntary organization or agency working in relief and development programs.

Organization for the Development of the Senegal River (OMVS) A regional grouping of countries bordering the Senegal River that sponsors joint research and projects.

Organization of African Unity (OAU) An association of all of the independent states of Africa (except South Africa) whose goal is to promote unity and solidarity among African nations.

Organization of Petroleum Exporting Countries (OPEC) Established in 1960, this association of some of the world's major oil-producing countries seeks to coordinate the petroleum policies of its members.

Pan Africanist Congress (PAC) A liberation organization of black South Africans which broke away from the ANC in the 1950s.

Parastatals Agencies for production or public service that are established by law and that are, in some measure, government organized and controlled. Private enterprise may be involved, and the management of the parastatal may be in private hands.

Pastoralist A person, usually a nomad, who raises livestock for a living.

Polisario Front Originally a liberation group in Western Sahara seeking independence from Spanish rule. Today, it is battling Morocco, which claims control over the Western Sahara (see *SADR*).

Popular Movement for the Liberation of Angola (MPLA) A Marxist liberation movement in Angola during the resistance to Portuguese rule; now the governing party in Angola.

Rinderpest A cattle disease that periodically decimates herds in savanna regions.

Saharawi Arab Democratic Republic (SADR) The Polisario Front name for Western Sahara, declared in 1976 in the struggle for independence from Morocco.

Sahel In West Africa, the borderlands between savanna and desert.

Sanctions Coercive measures, usually economic, adopted by nations acting together against a nation violating international law.

Savanna   Tropical or subtropical grassland with scattered trees and undergrowth.

Senegambia   A confederation of Senegal and The Gambia signed into agreement in December 1981 and inaugurated on February 1, 1982, to be ruled by a Cabinet of five Senegalese and four Gambians.

Sharia   The Islamic code of law.

Sharpeville Massacre   The 1960 pass demonstration in South Africa in which 60 people were killed when police fired into the crowd; it became a rallying point for many anti-apartheid forces.

Shengo   The Ethiopian Parliament.

Sorghum   A tropical grain that is a traditional staple in the savanna regions.

Southern African Development Coordination Conference (SADCC)   An organization of nine African states (Angola, Zambia, Malawi, Mozambique, Zimbabwe, Lesotho, Botswana, Swaziland, and Tanzania) whose goal is to free themselves from dependence on South Africa and to cooperate on projects of economic development.

South West African People's Organization (SWAPO)   Angola-based freedom fighters who have been waging guerrilla warfare against the presence of South Africa in Namibia since the 1960s. The United Nations and the Organization of African Unity have recognized SWAPO as the only authentic representative of the Namibian people.

Structural Adjustment Program (SAP)   Economic reforms encouraged by the International Monetary Fund which include devaluation of currency, cutting government subsidies on commodities, and reducing government expenditures.

Swahili   A widespread *lingua franca* in East Africa; an African-based Afro-Arab language and culture.

Tsetse Fly   An insect that transmits sleeping sickness to cattle and humans. It is usually found in the scrub-tree and forest regions of Central Africa.

Ujamaa   In Swahili, "familyhood." Government-sponsored cooperative villages in Tanzania.

Unicameral   A political structure with a single legislative branch.

Unilateral Declaration of Independence (UDI)   A declaration of white minority settlers in Rhodesia, claiming independence from the United Kingdom in 1965.

United Democratic Front (UDF)   A multiracial, black-led group in South Africa that gained prominence during the 1983 campaign to defeat the government's Constitution, which has given only limited political rights to Asians and Coloureds. UDF activities were banned by the South African government in 1988.

United Nations (UN)   An international organization established on June 26, 1945, through official approval of the charter by delegates of 50 nations at a conference in San Francisco, California. The charter went into effect on October 24, 1945.

United Nations Development Program (UNDP)   Established to create local organizations for increasing wealth through better use of human and natural resources.

United Nations Educational, Scientific, and Cultural Organization (UNESCO)   Established on November 4, 1946 to promote international collaboration in education, science, and culture.

United Nations High Commission for Refugees (UNHCR)   Established in 1951 to provide international protection for people with refugee status.

United Nations Resolution 435   Voted in 1978, this resolution calls for internationally supervised elections and independence for South African-ruled Namibia.

Villagization   A policy whereby a government relocates rural dwellers to create newer, more concentrated communities.

World Bank   A closely integrated group of international institutions providing financial and technical assistance to developing countries.

World Health Organization (WHO)   Established by the United Nations in 1948, this organization promotes the highest possible state of health in countries throughout the world.

Bibliography

RESOURCE CENTERS

African Studies Centers provide special services for schools, libraries, and community groups. Contact the center nearest you for further information about resources available:

African Studies Center
Boston University
270 Bay State Road
Boston, MA 02215

African Studies Program
Indiana University
Woodburn Hall 221
Bloomington, IN 47405

African Studies Educational Resource Center
100 International Center
Michigan State University
East Lansing, MI 49923

African Studies Program
630 Dartmouth
Northwestern University
Evanston, IL 60201

Africa Project
Lou Henry Hoover Room 223
Stanford University
Stanford, CA 94305

African Studies Center
University of California
Los Angeles, CA 90024

Center for African Studies
470 Grinter Hall
University of Florida
Gainesville, FL 32611

African Studies Program
University of Illinois
1208 W. California, Room 101
Urbana, IL 61801

African Studies Program
1450 Van Hise Hall
University of Wisconsin
Madison, WI 53706

Council on African Studies
Yale University
New Haven, CT 06520

Foreign Area Studies
The American University
5010 Wisconsin Avenue, N.W.
Washington, DC 20016

African Studies Program
Center for Strategic and International Studies
Georgetown University
1800 K Street, N.W.
Washington, DC 20006

REFERENCE WORKS, BIBLIOGRAPHIES, AND OTHER SOURCES

Africa South of the Sahara 1989 (updated yearly) (London: Europa Publications, Ltd., 1988).

Africa on Film and Videotape 1960–1961, A Compendium of Reviews (East Lansing: Michigan State University, 1982).

Africa Today, An Atlas of Reproductible Pages, rev. ed. (Wellesley: World Eagle, 1987).

Scarecrow Press, Metuchen, NJ, publishes *The African Historical Dictionaries*, a series edited by Jon Woronoff. There are more than 40 dictionaries, each under a specialist editor. They are short works with introductory essays and are useful guides for the beginner, especially for countries on which little has been published in English.

Colin Legum, ed., *Africa Contemporary Record* (New York: Africana) (annual). Contains information on each country for the reporting year.

Africa Research Bulletin (Political Series), Africa Research Ltd., Exeter, Devon, England (monthly). Political updates on current issues and events in Africa.

Chris Cook and David Killingray, *African Political Facts Since 1945* (New York: Facts on File, 1983). Chronology of events; chapters on heads of state, ministers, parliaments, parties, armies, trade unions, population, biographies.

MAGAZINES AND PERIODICALS

African Arts
University of California
Los Angeles, CA
Beautifully illustrated articles review Africa's artistic heritage and current creative efforts.

African Concord
5–15 Cromer Street
London, WCIH 8LS, England

Africa News
P.O. Box 3851
Durham, NC 27702
A weekly with short articles that are impartially written and full of information.

Africa Now
212 Fifth Avenue, Suite 1409
New York, NY 10010
A monthly publication that gives current coverage and includes sections on art, culture, and business, as well as a special series of interviews.

Africa Recovery
DPI, Room S-1061
United Nations
New York, NY 10017

Africa Report
African American Institute
833 UN Plaza
New York, NY 10017
This bimonthly periodical has an update section, but most of each issue is devoted to broad-based articles by authorities giving background on key issues, developments in particular countries, and United States policy.

Africa Today
Graduate School of International Studies
Denver, CO 80208

The Economist
P.O. Box 2700
Woburn, MA
A weekly that gives attention to African issues.

Newswatch
62 Oregun Rd.
P. M. B. 21499
Ikeja, Nigeria

UNESCO Courier
UNESCO, Place de Fontenox
75700 Paris, France
This periodical includes short and clear articles on Africa, often by African authors, within the framework of the topic to which the monthly issues are devoted.

The Weekly Review
Agip House
P.O. Box 42271
Nairobi, Kenya

West Africa
Holborn Viaduct
London, EC1A Z FD, England
This weekly is the best source for West Africa including countries as far south as Angola and Namibia. Continent-wide issues are also discussed.

NOVELS AND AUTOBIOGRAPHICAL WRITINGS

Chinua Achebe, *Things Fall Apart* (Portsmouth: Heinemann, 1965).
This is the story of the life and values of residents of a traditional Igbo village in the nineteenth century and of its first contacts with the West.

_____, *No Longer at Ease* (Portsmouth: Heinemann, 1963).
The grandson of the major character of *Things Fall Apart* lives an entirely different life in the modern city of Lagos and faces new problems, while remaining committed to some of the traditional ways.

Okot p'Bitek, *Song of Lawino* (Portsmouth: Heinemann, 1983).
A traditional Ugandan wife comments on the practices of her Western-educated husband and reveals her own lifestyle and values.

Buchi Emecheta, *The Joys of Motherhood* (New York: G. Braziller, 1979).
The story of a Nigerian woman who overcomes great obstacles to raise a large family and then finds that the meaning of motherhood has changed.

Nadine Gordimer, *July's People* (New York: Viking, 1981).
This is a troubling and believable scenario of future revolutionary times in South Africa.

_____, *A Soldier's Embrace* (New York: Viking, 1982).
These short stories cover a range of situations where apartheid affects peoples' relations with each other. Films made from some of these stories are available at the University of Illinois Film Library, Urbana-Champaign, IL and Boston University Film Library, Boston, MA.

Cheik Amadou Kane, *Ambiguous Adventure* (Portsmouth: Heinemann, 1972).
This autobiographical novel of a young man coming of age in Senegal, in a Muslim society, and, later, in a French school, illuminates changes that have taken place in Africa and raises many questions.

Alex LaGuma, *Time of the Butcherbird* (Portsmouth: Heinemann, 1979).
The people of a long-standing black community in South Africa's countryside are to be removed to a Bantustan.

Camara Laye, *The Dark Child* (Farrar Straus and Giroux, 1954).
This autobiographical novel gives a loving and nostalgic picture of a Malinke family of Guinea.

Winnie Mandela, *Part of My Soul Went With Him* (New York: W. W. Norton, 1985).
Details the personal and political saga of the wife of jailed ANC leader Nelson Mandela, an activist in her own right.

Ousmane Sembene, *God's Bits of Wood* (Portsmouth: Heinemann, 1970).
The railroad workers' strike of 1947 provides the setting for a novel about the changing consciousness and life of African men and women in Senegal.

Joyce Sikakane, *A Window on Soweto* (London: International Defense and Aid Fund, 1977).

Wole Soyinka, *Ake: The Years of Childhood* (New York: Random House, 1983).
Soyinka's account of his first eleven years is full of the sights, tastes, smells, sounds, and personal encounters of a headmaster's home and a busy Yoruba town.

Ngugi wa Thiong'o, *A Grain of Wheat* (Portsmouth: Heinemann, 1968).
A story of how the Mau-Mau Movement and the coming of independence affected several individuals after independence as well as during the struggle that preceded it.

INTRODUCTORY BOOKS

A. E. Afigbo, E. A. Ayandele, R. J. Gavin, J. D. Omer-Cooper, and R. Palmer, *The Making of Modern Africa,* vol. II, *The Twentieth Century,* 2nd ed. (London: Longman, 1986).

An introductory political history of Africa in the twentieth century.

Gwendolen Carter and Patrick O'Meara, eds., *African Independence: The First Twenty-Five Years* (Bloomington: Indiana University Press, 1985).

Collected essays surrounding issues such as political structures, military rule, and economics.

Basil Davidson, *The African Genius* (Boston: Little, Brown, 1979). Also published as *The Africans.*

Davidson discusses the complex political, social, and economic systems of traditional African societies, translating scholarly works into a popular mode without distorting complex material.

_____, *Let Freedom Come* (Boston: Little, Brown, 1978).

A lively and interesting history of Africa in the twentieth century.

John Fage and Roland Oliver, *Cambridge History of Africa,* 6 vols. (New York: Cambridge University Press, 1975). Comprehensive descriptions of regional histories.

Bill Freund, *The Making of Contemporary Africa: The Development of African Society Since 1800* (Bloomington: Indiana University Press, 1983).

Recent African history from an economic-history point of view, with emphasis on forces of production.

Adrian Hastings, *A History of African Christianity, 1950–1975* (Cambridge: Cambridge University Press, 1979).

A good introduction to the impact of Christianity on Africa in recent years.

Goren Hyden, *No Shortcut to Progress: African Development Management in Perspective* (Berkeley: University of California, 1983).

An assessment of development in relation to obstacles, prospects, and progress.

John Mbiti, *African Religions and Philosophy* (Portsmouth: Heinemann, 1982).

This work by a Ugandan scholar is the standard introduction to the rich variety of religious beliefs and rituals of African peoples.

Phyllis Martin and Patrick O'Meara, eds., *Africa,* 2nd ed. (Boomington: Indiana University Press, 1986).

This collection of essays covers history, culture, politics, and the economy.

J. H. Kwabena Nketia, *The Music of Africa* (New York: Norton, 1974).

The author, a Ghanian by birth, is Africa's best-known ethnomusicologist.

Chris Searle, *We're Building the New School: Diary of a Teacher in Mozambique* (London: Zed Press, 1981; distributed in the United States by Laurence Hill & Co., Westport).

A lively book that shows that the lives of students and teachers in the nation of Mozambique are both exciting and difficult.

Timothy Shaw and Adebayo Adedeji, *Economic Crisis in Africa: African Perspectives on Development Problems and Potentials* (Boulder: L. Rienner, 1985).

J. B. Webster, A. A. Boahen, and M. Tidy, *The Revolutionary Years: West Africa Since 1800* (London: Longman, 1980).

An interesting, enjoyable, and competent introductory history to the West African region.

Frank Willett, *African Art* (New York: Oxford University Press, 1971).

A work to read for both reference and pleasure, by one of the authorities on Nigeria's early art.

COUNTRY AND REGIONAL STUDIES

Tony Avirgan and Martha Honey, *War in Uganda: The Legacy of Idi Amin* (Westport: Laurence Hill & Co., 1982).

John E. Bardill and James H. Cobbe, *Lesotho: Dilemmas of Dependence in Southern Africa* (Boulder: Westview Press, 1985).

Gerald Bender, *Angola Under the Portuguese: The Myth and the Reality* (Berkeley, University of California Press, 1978).

William Bigelow, *Strangers in Their Own Country* (a curriculum on South Africa), 2nd ed. (Trenton: Africa World Press, 1989).

Allan R. Booth, *Swaziland: Tradition and Change in a Southern African Kingdom* (Boulder: Westview Press, 1984).

Marcia M. Burdette, *Zambia: Between Two Worlds* (Boulder: Westview Press, 1988).

Gwendolen Carter, *Continuity and Change in South Africa* (Gainesville: African Studies Association and Center for African Studies, University of Florida, 1985).

Christopher Clapham, *Transformation and Continuity in Revolutionary Ethiopia* (Cambridge: Cambridge University Press, 1988).

Maureen Covell, *Madagascar: Politics, Economy, and Society* (London and New York: F. Pinter, 1987).

Toyin Falola and Julius Ihonvbere, *The Rise and Fall of Nigeria's Second Republic, 1979–1984* (London: Zed Press, 1985).

Robert Fatton, *The Making of a Liberal Democracy: Senegal's Passive Revolution, 1975–85* (Boulder: L. Rienner, 1987).

Foreign Area Studies (Washington, DC: Government Printing Office). Includes country study handbooks with chapters on history, politics, culture, and economics, with maps, charts, and bibliographies. There are more than 20 in the series, with new ones added and revised periodically.

Marcus Franda, *The Seychelles: Unquiet Islands* (Boulder: Westview Press, 1982).

Sheldon Gellar, *Senegal: An African Nation Between Islam and the West* (Boulder: Westview Press, 1982).

Joseph Hanlon, *Mozambique: The Revolution Under Fire* (London: Zed Press, 1984).

Tony Hodges, *Western Sahara: The Roots of a Desert War* (Westport: Laurence Hill & Co., 1983).

P. M. Holt and M. W. Daly, *A History of Sudan: From the Coming of Islam to the Present Day* (Boulder: Westview Press, 1979).

Allan and Barbara Isaacman, *Mozambique from Colonialism to Revolution, 1900–1982* (Boulder: Westview Press, 1983).

Richard Joseph, *Democracy and Prebendel Politics in Nigeria: The Rise and Fall of the Second Republic* (Cambridge: Cambridge University Press, 1987).

Michael P. Kelley, *A State in Disarray: Conditions of Chad's Survival* (Boulder: Westview Press, 1986).

David D. Laitin and Said S. Samatar, *Somalia: Nation in Search of a State* (Boulder: Westview Press, 1987).

J. Gus Liebenow, *Liberia: Quest for Democracy* (Bloomington: Indiana University Press, 1987).

Tom Lodge, *Black Politics in South Africa Since 1945* (New York: Longman, 1983).

David Martin and Phyllis Johnson, *The Struggle for Zimbabwe: The Chimurenga War* (Boston: Faber & Faber, 1981).

Norman N. Miller, *Kenya: The Quest for Prosperity* (Boulder: Westview Press, 1984).

Malyn Newitt, *The Comoro Islands: Sturggle Against Depencency in the Indian Ocean* (Boulder: Westview Press, 1984).

Julius Nyerere, *Ujamaa: Essays on Socialism* (Dar es Salaam: Oxford University Press, 1968).

Thomas O'Toole, *The Central African Republic: The Continent's Hidden Heart* (Boulder: Westview Press, 1986).

Jack Parson, *Botswana: Liberal Democracy and the Labor Resource in Southern Africa* (Boulder: Westview Press, 1984).

Deborah Pellow and Naomi Chazan, *Ghana: Coping with Uncertainty* (Boulder: Westview Press, 1986).

Bereket Habte Selassie, *Conflict and Intervention in the Horn of Africa* (New York: Monthly Review Press, 1980).

Study Commission on U.S. Policy Toward Southern Africa, *South Africa: Time Running Out* (Berkeley and Los Angeles: University of California Press, 1981).

Rachid Tlemcani, *State and Revolution in Algeria* (Boulder: Westview Press, 1987).

Michael Wolfers and Jane Bergerol, *Angola in the Frontline* (London: Zed Press, 1983).

Rodger Yeager, *Tanzania: An African Experiment* (Boulder: Westview Press, 1983).

Westview Press specializes in country studies and has many additional ones forthcoming.

Sources for Statistical Reports

U.S. State Department, *Background Notes* (1986–1988).

C.I.A. *World Factbook* (1988).

World Bank, *World Development Report* (1988).

UN *Population and Vital Statistics Report* (January 1989).

World Statistics in Brief (1988).

Statistical Yearbook (1988).

The Statesman's Yearbook (1988).

Population Reference Bureau, *World Population Data Sheet* (1988).

World Almanac (1989).

Demographic Yearbook (1988).

Index